Intercultural Communication

Second Edition

Intercultural Communication

Globalization and Social Justice

Second Edition

Kathryn Sorrells
California State University, Northridge

Los Angeles | London | New Delhi
Singapore | Washington DC

Los Angeles | London | New Delhi
Singapore | Washington DC

FOR INFORMATION:

SAGE Publications, Inc.
2455 Teller Road
Thousand Oaks, California 91320
E-mail: order@sagepub.com

SAGE Publications Ltd.
1 Oliver's Yard
55 City Road
London EC1Y 1SP
United Kingdom

SAGE Publications India Pvt. Ltd.
B 1/I 1 Mohan Cooperative Industrial Area
Mathura Road, New Delhi 110 044
India

SAGE Publications Asia-Pacific Pte. Ltd.
3 Church Street
#10-04 Samsung Hub
Singapore 049483

Printed in the United States of America

ISBN 978-1-4522-9275-5

Acquisitions Editor: Matthew Byrnie
Associate Editor: Natalie Konopinski
Editorial Assistant: Janae Masnovi
eLearning Editor: Gabrielle Piccininni
Production Editor: Laura Barrett
Copy Editor: Janet Ford
Typesetter: C&M Digitals (P) Ltd.
Proofreader: Jeff Bryant
Indexer: Sylvia Coates
Cover Designer: Leonardo March
Marketing Manager: Ashlee Blunk

This book is printed on acid-free paper.

SUSTAINABLE FORESTRY INITIATIVE
Certified Chain of Custody
Promoting Sustainable Forestry
www.sfiprogram.org
SFI-01268

SFI label applies to text stock

15 16 17 18 19 10 9 8 7 6 5 4 3 2 1

Brief Contents

Detailed Contents

3 Globalizing Body Politics: Embodied Verbal and Nonverbal Communication 52

4 (Dis)Placing Culture and Cultural Space: Locations of Nonverbal and Verbal Communication 76

5 Privileging Relationships: Intercultural Communication in Interpersonal Contexts 100

6 Crossing Borders: Migration and Intercultural Adaptation 126

7 Jamming Media and Popular Culture: Analyzing Messages About Diverse Cultures 151

8 The Culture of Capitalism and the Business of Intercultural Communication 177

9 Negotiating Intercultural Conflict and Social Justice: Strategies for Intercultural Relations   201

10 Engaging Intercultural Communication for Social Justice: Challenges and Possibilities for Global Citizenship   229

Preface

PURPOSE OF THE TEXT

I wrote *Intercultural Communication: Globalization and Social Justice* with the goal of creating a new kind of introductory text for the undergraduate intercultural communication course that would provide students with critical and social justice perspectives on the dynamics of globalization that have brought so many people and cultures into contact and conversation. I want to help students understand and grapple with the interconnected and complex nature of intercultural communication in the world today. Students in my intercultural communication courses are clearly affected in direct and indirect ways on a daily basis by the forces of globalization. Their lives, livelihoods, and lifestyles are influenced in both challenging and beneficial ways by the forces of globalization—through rapid advances in communication and transportation technologies as well as changes in economic and political policies locally and globally. Globalization has catapulted people from different cultures into shared physical and virtual spaces in homes, in relationships, in schools, in neighborhoods, in the workplace, and in political alliances in unprecedented ways.

CULTURE IS DYNAMIC AND MULTIFACETED

Central to this text is the idea that our understanding of culture must be dynamic and multifaceted to address the fast-paced, complex, and often contradictory influences that shape intercultural communication today. The advantage of this approach is that it reflects a world that students will recognize as their own: a world in which notions of culture are fluid, not static. Therefore, this text aims to move beyond the basic distinctions between international and domestic U.S. communication issues to also highlight the many connections between local and global issues. To help students better understand the challenges and complexities of intercultural communication in the global context, I have also drawn attention to histories of intercultural conflict and the role power plays on macro- and micro-levels in intercultural relations. Thus, my aim in writing was to produce a text as vibrant, multifaceted, conflicting, and creative as intercultural communication itself!

Intercultural Communication: Globalization and Social Justice is built around these key concepts:

- A globalization framework
- A critical, social justice approach

- An emphasis on connections between the local/global and micro-, meso-, and macro-levels

- An emphasis on *intercultural praxis*

A Globalization Framework

Globalization provides a ubiquitous and complex context for studying intercultural communication. The context of globalization is characterized by an increasingly dynamic, mobile world and an intensification of interaction and exchange among people, cultures, and cultural forms; a rapidly growing global interdependence leading to shared interests and resources as well as greater intercultural tensions and conflicts; a magnification of inequities both within and across nations and cultural groups with significant impact on intercultural communication; and a historical legacy of colonization, Western domination, and U.S. hegemony that continues to shape intercultural relations today. Studying intercultural communication in the context of globalization allows us to highlight the following:

- Definitions of culture that address cultural continuity, contestation, and commodification

- Intercultural dimensions of economic, political, and cultural globalization

- Role of power and the impact of asymmetrical power relations on intercultural communication

- Rapid movement of people, cultures, verbal and nonverbal languages, and rhetoric through interpersonal and mediated communication

- Multifaceted, hybrid, and negotiated cultural identities

- Resignification of identity categories such as race, culture, gender, and sexuality today

- Changing nature of intercultural relationships and intercultural alliances

- Culture of capitalism and the commodification of culture

- Intercultural conflict through a multidimensional framework

- Dynamic intercultural alliances and movements for social justice

A Critical Social Justice Approach

This text takes a critical social justice approach that provides a framework to create a more equitable and socially just world through communication. In the context of globalization, finding solutions to local and global challenges inevitably requires intercultural communication. Today, some of the most innovative answers to difficult social, political, and economic problems develop through intercultural alliances. And, regrettably, some of the most egregious injustices—exploitation of workers in homes, fields, and factories and violence perpetrated through racial profiling, ethnic cleansing and religious fervor—are performed within intercultural contexts and are enabled by intercultural communication.

Today, we face many intercultural challenges—for example, wealth disparity in the United States and globally and the percentage of people in the world living under the poverty line have become steadily worse in the new millennium. It is my hope that this text will not only help students develop a deeper understanding of the opportunities and challenges of intercultural communication today but also empower students to use their knowledge and skills to confront discrimination and challenge inequities.

Over the past five year, I have had the honor and privilege of working directly with Reverend James M. Lawson Jr., a close associate of Dr. Martin Luther King Jr. and leading architect of the civil rights movement, on the Civil Discourse & Social Change Initiative at California State University, Northridge (CSUN). Reverend Lawson's deep regard for all humanity, his appreciation of cultural differences, and his unwavering respect for the power of intercultural alliances stem from and are informed by his years of work in India in the 1950s, his leadership in the civil rights movement, his efforts to dismantle racism and sexism, and his efforts to gain living wages for workers and equal rights for lesbian, gay, bisexual, and transgender (LGBT) communities. We all have the opportunity to use the knowledge, attitudes, and skills gained by studying and practicing intercultural communication to build relationships, imagine possibilities, and develop alliances to create a more equitable and socially just world.

Local/Global Connection and Multilevel Framework of Analysis

Life in the globalized 21st century is characterized by a complex web of linkages between the local and the global as well as the past and present. People—and their languages, identities, cultural practices, and ideas—are based in particular geographic locations, but they are also simultaneously connected—whether through communications technology (e.g., phone, e-mail, social media), interpersonal networks (e.g., friends, family), and memories with different locations around the globe. Studying intercultural communication in the context of globalization requires us to pay attention to continuities and fragmentations of global communities over time and place.

For example, globalization links the distant towns of Villachuato, Mexico, and Marshalltown, Iowa, through global flows of capital, goods, and labor. A meatpacking plant in Marshalltown employs many Mexican workers, who return regularly to Villachuato for annual religious events, weddings, and funerals. Like many towns across the United States and Mexico, the lives of people from Villachuato and Marshalltown are intertwined and interdependent in the global context. Intercultural connections do not necessarily require travel to forge links across the globe. For example, diasporic Indian communities in the United States and around the world enjoy watching Hindi films and keeping up on the latest popular culture from India. Much more than entertainment, these experiences of cultural consumption educate younger generations born outside of India about their culture, serve as cultural bridges across time and place, and play a role in developing their bicultural identities. Of course, global intercultural links are not solely positive. The roots of many intercultural conflicts happening today can be linked to historic transgressions and involve communities that are interconnected around the globe.

In this text, key concepts in intercultural communication—identity construction; the use of verbal and nonverbal communication; the creation and re-creation of cultural spaces;

interpersonal relationships; as well as migration, adaptation, and intercultural conflict—are addressed in ways that underscore the connections and disjuncture between the local and the global and the relationships between the past and the present. A multilevel framework that focuses attention on three interrelated levels—(1) the micro (individual level), (2) the meso (intermediate, group-based level), and (3) the macro (broad economic–political level)—is introduced and applied to various case studies throughout the text to examine the complexities of intercultural communication in the context of globalization.

Intercultural Praxis

This text engages students in a process of critical, reflective thinking and acting—what I call intercultural praxis—that enables them to navigate the complex, contradictory, and challenging intercultural spaces they inhabit interpersonally, communally, and globally. At all moments in our day—when we interact with friends, coworkers, teachers, bosses, and strangers; when we consume pop culture and other entertainment; when we hear and read news and information from the media outlets; and in our daily routines and travel—we have the opportunity to engage in intercultural praxis. The purpose of engaging in intercultural praxis is to raise our awareness, increase our critical analysis, and develop our socially responsible action in regard to intercultural interactions in the context of globalization.

Through six interrelated points of entry—(1) inquiry, (2) framing, (3) positioning, (4) dialogue, (5) reflection, and (6) action—intercultural praxis uses our multifaceted identity positions and shifting access to privilege and power to develop our consciousness, imagine alternatives, and build alliances in our struggles for social responsibility and social justice. The focus on intercultural praxis is intertwined with the content of the text from initial discussions of culture in the global context to explorations of our identities and finally in our roles as global citizens.

ORGANIZATION OF THE TEXT

This book offers an innovative approach to address the rapid, complex, and often contradictory forces that propel and constrain intercultural communication in the context of globalization.

A fundamental goal of the book is to understand and analyze intercultural communication on three interlocking and interrelated levels: (1) the micro, individual level; (2) the meso, cultural group level; and (3) the macro, geopolitical level. I think of it as breathing in and breathing out. As we breathe in, we focus our attention on individual levels of communication and then, breathing out, we expand to the broader levels of cultural group and macro-level intercultural communication issues. This metaphor helps my students understand the movement between levels from chapter to chapter as well as the connections that are made throughout the text between the past and the present. My goal is to encourage and support a way of thinking and being in the world that accounts for multiple frames of reference—like zooming in and zooming out on a Google map—across place and time.

Given that certain topics—language use, nonverbal communication, and cultural identity, for example—are so central to and interconnected with all facets of intercultural communication, these areas are addressed throughout the text in all chapters rather than isolated within stand-alone chapters. The organization of this text, therefore, highlights the many interconnections that define intercultural communication while also offering complete coverage of all topics commonly addressed in an introductory intercultural communication text.

NEW TO THE SECOND EDITION

The second edition augments and updates keys features and themes of the first edition. My goal then and now is to contextualize, historicize, and politicize our understanding and practice of intercultural communication. To accomplish this, the subject of each chapter is presented as a whole highlighting broad systemic views of the content as well as in-depth treatment of interrelated concepts and issues. Case studies, new and expanded in the second edition, illuminate critical concepts, address current events, and illustrate how intercultural communication is a site of negotiation and contestation. Extended examples and case studies are also used to demonstrate methods of analysis central to intercultural praxis.

In the second edition, content on interpersonal relationships in the workplace is addressed in Chapter Five in conjunction with friendship and romantic relationships. This re-organization allows for more extended treatment of the commodification of culture in Chapter Eight. The new edition also attends in greater depth to the centrality of new media for intercultural communication in the global context as well as the increasing impact of religious fundamentalism throughout the world. The theme of social justice and our roles as students and practitioners of intercultural communication in imagining, creating, and enacting a more social just world is introduced earlier in the text and threaded throughout.

New in the second edition:

- Chapter objectives

- Additional case studies

- Updated statistics

- Extended examples addressing current events

- Expanded treatment of new media

CONTINUING PEDAGOGICAL FEATURES OF THE TEXT

A number of special features appear in each chapter of this text to encourage reflection and to move theory into practice for teachers and students of intercultural communication. Highly popular in the first edition, additional textboxes both revised and new appear in the second edition.

Engaging Textbox Features Highlight the Challenges and Rewards of Intercultural Communication

- **Communicative Dimensions Boxes** allow students to explore vivid examples of intercultural communication in action to see how different facets of communication—language use, nonverbal communication, rhetoric, and symbolic representation—play out in the global intercultural context.

- **Cultural Identity Boxes** help students understand how communication and culture shape and reflect identity and in turn how identity plays a role in communicating within and across cultures.

- **Intercultural Praxis Boxes** emphasize ways of developing our awareness and using our power and positionality to enable more equitable and socially just relationships across different cultures by engaging in dialogue, reflecting, and taking informed action.

ANCILLARY MATERIAL

In addition to the text, a full array of ancillary website materials for instructors is available at **study.sagepub.com/sorrells2e**. The password-protected site contains a test bank, PowerPoint presentations, sample syllabi, lecture notes, course projects, in-class activities, video links, and web resources. These ancillaries further support the goals of critical reflection, engaged learning, and informed action for social change presented in *Intercultural Communication: Globalization and Social Justice*.

Acknowledgments

$\mathbf{A}$ book like this, while written by one person, could not have been imagined or completed without the critical and creative contributions of many. In writing the second edition, I have received invaluable feedback, suggestions, and insights from students and colleagues who I work with daily, from those who teach and engage in intercultural research across the United States as well as from those using the book in Japan, Mexico, China, India, and Europe. I am honored and grateful for these meaningful conversations, connections, and opportunities to engage with others in making a difference in the world. Sachi Sekimoto, my former undergraduate and graduate student and now Associate Professor, provided invaluable research and editorial assistance and developed the discussion questions and activities at the end of the chapters for both the first and second editions. Our work together as co-editors of the book *Globalizing Intercultural Communication: A Reader* provided opportunities for lengthy and lively discussions as well as careful reading of compelling and innovative research in the field of intercultural communication, which enriched and strengthened the conceptual and theoretical foundations of the second edition. I want to thank Julie Chekroun and Hengameh Rabizadeh, also former graduate students, for their meticulous edited and research assistance for the text. Thanks also to Mandy Paris and Robert Loy for their assistance with the ancillary material. A second edition is inevitably an extension and elaboration of a vision and groundwork developed in the first edition; thus, I continue to feel tremendous gratitude for my colleagues Sheena Malhotra and Bill Kelly for their careful reading and rereading of each chapter of the first edition. Sheena's insightful comments and encouragement, her examples that illustrate subtlety and ambiguity, and her feedback from using chapters in her classes all enhance the first and second editions tremendously. Over the years, I have benefited greatly from hours of conversation with Gordon Nakagawa, Breny Mendoza, Lara Medina, and Reverend James M. Lawson Jr. who, each in their own way, have had a hand in guiding the critical theoretical approach of the book. I also want to acknowledge both of my parents, Daniel Jackson Sorrells and Eleanor Kathryn Sorrells, whose love for learning and cultures continues to inspire me. Their memory is inextricably bound to this book as they both passed away during the research and writing of the first edition.

The team at SAGE deserves many thanks for all their support, patience, and sustained effort. Matthew Byrnie, believing in the importance of the project, brought the first edition to fruition and enthusiastically embraced the second edition. The expert and patient assistance of Natalie Konopinski gently yet firmly moved this project forward. Janae Masnovi's helpful and timely assistance put all the final pieces together to complete the project. I want to thank Janet Ford for her careful editing of the book. Finally, I am grateful to the production editor, Laura Barrett, and marketing manager, Ashley Blunk, for bringing the second edition of the book into the world!

The book was much improved by the encouragement, insights, critical comments, and suggestions offered by the reviewers. I would like to thank Andy O. Alali (California State University, Bakersfield), Nilanjana Bardhan (Southern Illinois University, Carbondale), Devika Chawla (Ohio University), Daniel Chornet Roses (Saint Louis University, Madrid Campus), Robbin D. Crabtree (Loyola Marymount University), Melissa L. Curtin (Southern Illinois University, Carbondale), Alexa Dare (The University of Montana), Sara DeTurk (University of Texas at San Antonio), Jane Elvins (University of Colorado, Boulder), Gloria J. Galanes (Missouri State University), Rebecca S. Imes (Carroll College), Peter Oehlkers (Salem State College), Ruma Sen (Ramapo College of New Jersey), and Curtis L. VanGeison (St. Charles Community College).

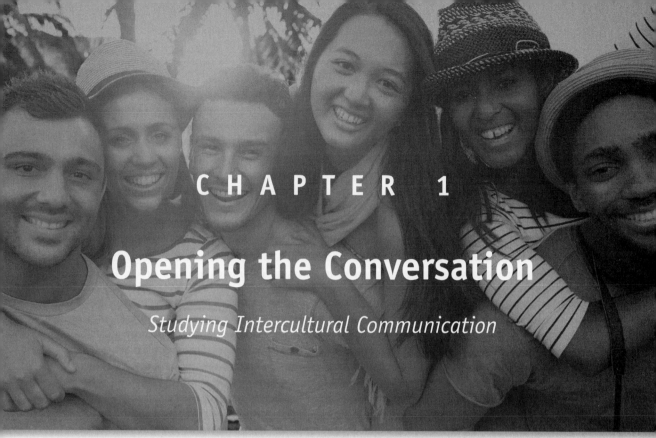

CHAPTER 1

Opening the Conversation

Studying Intercultural Communication

What creates positive intercultural interactions?

Learning Objectives

1. Identify the opportunities and challenges of intercultural communication in the context of globalization.

2. Describe three definitions of culture that influence intercultural communication in the global context.

3. Explain how our social location and standpoint shape how we see, experience, and understand the world differently.

4. Describe the goals and six points of entry into intercultural praxis.

We, the people of the world—over 7 billion of us from different cultures—find our lives, our livelihoods, and our lifestyles increasingly interconnected and interdependent due to the forces of globalization. Since the early 1990s, changes in economic and political policies, governance, and institutions have combined with advances in communication and transportation technology to dramatically accelerate interaction and interrelationship among people from different cultures around the globe. Deeply rooted in European colonization and Western imperialism, the forces of this current wave of globalization have catapulted people from different cultures into shared physical and virtual spaces in homes, in relationships, in schools, in neighborhoods, in the workplace, and in political alliance and activism in unprecedented ways.

Today, advances in communication technology allow some of us to connect with the world on wireless devices sitting in the backyard or in our favorite café. While almost 40% of the world's people wake up each morning assured of instant communication with others around the globe (ITU World Telecommunication, 2014), about 50% of the world's population live below the internationally defined poverty line, starting their day without the basic necessities of food, clean water, and shelter (Global Issues, 2013). Through the Internet, satellite technology, and cell phones, many of the world's people have access to both mass media and personal accounts of events and experiences as they unfold around the globe. However, in this time of instant messages and global communication, about 775 million or one out of five young people and adults worldwide do not have the skills to read (UNESCO Institute for Statistics, 2013). Today, advances in transportation technology bring families, friends, migrants, tourists, businesspeople, and strangers closer together more rapidly than ever before in the history of human interaction. Yet, some have the privilege to enjoy intercultural experiences through leisure, recreation, and tourism, while other people travel far from home and engage with others who are different from themselves out of economic necessity and basic survival.

People from different cultural backgrounds have been interacting with each other for many millennia. What makes intercultural communication in our current times different from other periods in history? The amount and intensity of intercultural interactions; the degree of intercultural interdependence; the patterns of movement of people, goods, and capital; and the conditions that shape and constrain our intercultural interactions distinguish our current context—the context of globalization—from other periods in history. Consider the following:

- About 232 million people live outside their country of origin (United Nations, 2013).

- U.S. cultural products and corporations—films, TV programs, music, and the iconic Barbie doll, as well as McDonalds, Walmart, Starbucks, and Disney—saturate the world's markets, transmitting cultural values, norms, and the "American" way of life as they dominate the global economy (Crothers, 2013).

- In the fallout and slow recovery from the 2008 economic crisis, the great backlash against globalization has arrived. Anti-immigrant, protectionist, and populist policies, often fueled by xenophobia and racism, are ushering in new forms of nationalism around the world (Roubini, 2014).

- WeChat or *Wēixìn* (微信), a text and voice messaging communication service developed in China by Tencent, connects nearly 400,000,000 users worldwide. With growing popularity outside of China, WeChat has approximately 100 million users in India, Indonesia, and Malaysia as well as Argentina, Brazil, Italy, and Mexico (Lim, 2014).

- The United States is projected to become a majority-minority nation for the first time in 2043. While the non-Hispanic White population will remain the largest single group, no group will make up a majority. Minorities, now 37% of the U.S. population, are projected to comprise 57% of the population in 2060 (U.S. Census Bureau, 2012).

- "The world," [Miami] Heat forward Shane Battier said, "is getting smaller every day." The National Basketball Association final series between the Miami Heat and the San Antonio Spurs aired in 215 countries. Commentary on the games appeared in 47 languages and social media attracted attention globally. Nine players on the 2014 NBA Championship team, the San Antonio Spurs, are international players (Reynolds, 2014).

- The gap between the wealthy and the poor is increasing within countries and around the world. The wealth of the world is divided in two with approximately 50% of the wealth attributed to the top 1%. Eighty-five of the richest people in the world have the combined wealth of 3.5 billion of the poorest people (Oxfam, 2014).

- In many instances, ethnic tension and open conflict between ethnic groups has intensified in the global context. For example, while ethnic and religious differences certainly play a role in conflicts in Israel, Iraq, Afghanistan, Syria, Ukraine, Chechnya, Sudan, Burma, and China to name only a few, economic and political issues with deep historical dimensions are at the root of the conflicts (Cordell & Wolff, 2013).

Clearly, cultural interaction is occurring, and intercultural communication matters. The goal of this book is to position the study and practice of intercultural communication within the context of globalization, which then enables us to understand and grapple with the dynamic, creative, conflictive, and often inequitable nature of intercultural relations in the world. This book provides theories, conceptual maps, and practical tools to guide us in asking questions, making sense, and taking action in regard to the intercultural opportunities, misunderstandings, and conflicts that emerge today in the context of globalization. Throughout the book, intercultural communication is explored within this broader political, economic, and cultural context of globalization, which allows us to foreground the important roles that history, power, and global institutions—political, economic, and media institutions—currently play in intercultural communication.

This first chapter is called "Opening the Conversation" because the relationship between you, the readers, and me, the author, is a special kind of interaction. I start the conversation by introducing various definitions of culture that provide different ways to understand intercultural communication today. Then, some of the opportunities and challenges of studying intercultural communication are addressed by introducing positionality, standpoint theory, and ethnocentrism. This chapter ends with a discussion of intercultural praxis. As we "open the conversation," I invite you to engage with me in an ongoing process of learning, reflecting, and critiquing what I have to say about intercultural communication and how it applies to your everyday experiences.

DEFINITIONS OF CULTURE

Culture is a concept that we use often, yet we have a great deal of trouble defining. In the 1950s, anthropologists Clyde Kluckhohn and Arthur Kroeber (1952) identified over 150 definitions of culture. Culture is central to the way we view, experience, and engage with all aspects of our lives and the world around us. Thus, even our definitions of culture are shaped by the historical, political, social, and cultural contexts in which we live. Historically, the word *culture* was closely linked in its use and meaning to processes of colonization. In the 19th century, European anthropologists wrote detailed descriptions of the ways of life of "others," generally characterizing non-European societies as less civilized, barbaric, "primitive," and as lacking "culture." These colonial accounts treated European culture as the norm and constructed Europe as superior by using the alleged lack of "culture" of non-European societies as justification for colonization. By the beginning of World War I, nine-tenths of the world had been colonized by European powers—a history of imperialism that continues to structure and impact intercultural communication today (Young, 2001).

With this assumption of the superiority of European culture, the categorization system that stratified groups of people was based on having "culture" or not, which, in turn, translated within European societies as "high" culture and "low" culture. Those in the elite class, or ruling class, who had power, were educated at prestigious schools, and were patrons of the arts, such as literature, opera, and ballet, embodied **high culture**. Those in the working class who enjoyed activities, such as popular theater, folk art, and "street" activities—and later movies and television—embodied **low culture**. We see remnants of these definitions of culture operating today. The notion of culture continues to be used in some situations to stratify groups based on the kinds of activities people engage in, thereby reinforcing beliefs about superior and inferior cultures. Over the past 50 years, struggles within academia and society in general have legitimized the practices and activities of common everyday people, leading to the use of the term **popular culture** to reference much of what was previously considered low culture. However, in advertising, in media representations, and in everyday actions and speech, we still see the use of high and low cultural symbols not only to signify class differences, but also to reinforce a cultural hierarchy. The growing and overwhelming appeal and consumption of U.S. culture around the world, which coincides with the superpower status of the United States, can be understood, at least partially, as a desire to be in proximity as well as have contact with the United States, and therefore to exhibit the signs of being "cultured."

Anthropologic Definition: Culture as a Site of Shared Meaning

The traditional academic field of intercultural communication has been deeply impacted by anthropology. In fact, many of the scholars like Edward T. Hall (1959), who is considered the originator of the field of intercultural communication, were trained as anthropologists. In the 1950s, Edward T. Hall, along with others at the Foreign Service Institute, developed training programs on culture and communication for diplomats going abroad on assignment. Hall's applied approach, focusing on the micro-level of human interaction with particular attention to nonverbal communication and tacit or out-of-awareness levels of information exchange, established the foundation for the field of intercultural communication (Rogers, Hart, & Miike, 2002).

Clifford Geertz, another highly influential anthropologist, emphasized the pivotal role symbols play in understanding culture. According to Geertz, culture is a web of symbols that people use to create meaning and order in their lives. Concerned about the colonial and Western origins of anthropology, he highlighted the challenges of understanding and representing cultures accurately. Anthropologists engage in interpretive practices that, for Geertz, are best accomplished in conversation with people from within the culture. In his widely cited book, *Interpretation of Culture*, Geertz (1973) said culture "denotes an historically transmitted pattern of meaning embodied in symbols, a system of inherited conceptions expressed in symbolic forms by means of which men communicate, perpetuate and develop their knowledge about and attitudes towards life" (p. 89).

Culture, then, from an anthropological perspective, is **a system of shared meanings** that are passed from generation to generation through symbols that allow human beings (not only men!) to communicate, maintain, and develop an approach and understanding of life. In other words, culture allows us to make sense of, express, and give meaning to our lives. Let's look more closely at the various elements of this definition.

At the core of this definition is the notion of symbols and symbol systems. **Symbols** stand for or represent other things. Words, images, people, ideas, and actions can all be symbols that represent other things. For example, the word *cat* is a set of symbols (the alphabet) that combine to represent both the idea of a cat and the actual cat. A handshake—whether firm or soft, simple or complex—a raised eyebrow, a hand gesturing "ok," a veil, a tie, or "bling" are all symbolic actions or things that carry meaning. An image or an object like the U.S. flag, the twin towers, a T-shirt that reads "Keep Calm and Party On," a cell phone, or graffiti are also symbols that stand for ideas, beliefs, and actions. How do we know what these and other symbols represent or what they mean? Are the meanings of symbols somehow inherent in the things themselves, or are meanings assigned to symbols by the people who use them? While the meaning of symbols may seem natural or inherent for those who use them, the anthropological definition that was previously offered indicates that it is the act of assigning similar meanings to symbols and the sharing of these assigned meanings that, at least partially, constitute culture.

The definition by Geertz (1973) also suggests that culture is a system. It is a system that is expressed through symbols that allow groups of people to communicate and to develop knowledge and understanding about life. When we say culture is a system, we mean that the elements of culture interrelate to form a whole. The shared symbols that convey or express meaning within a culture acquire meaning through their interrelation to each other and together create a system of meanings. Consider this example: As you read the brief scenario that follows, pay attention to what you are thinking and feeling.

Imagine a young man who is in his mid- to late 20s who works at a job making about $70,000 a year. OK, what do you think and how do you feel about this man? Now, you find out that he is single. Have your thoughts or feelings changed? For you, and for the majority of students like you in the United States, the picture of this man and his life is looking pretty good. Generally, both female and male students from various cultural backgrounds in the classroom think and feel positively about him. Now you find out that he lives at home with his parents and siblings. Have your thoughts or feelings about him changed? Without fail, when this scenario is used in the classroom, an audible sigh of disappointment comes from students when they learn that he lives with his parents. What's going on here? How does this information contradict or challenge the system of meaning in the dominant U.S. culture that was being created up to that point? The image of this young man, who was looking so good, suddenly plummets from desirable to highly suspect and, well, according to some students, "weird," "strange," and "not normal." The dominant U.S. culture is a system of shared meanings that places high value and regard on individualism, independence, consumerism, and capitalism, which are symbolically represented through the interrelated elements of income, age, sex/gender, and in this case, living arrangements. Students in the classroom who ascribe to the dominant cultural value system ask questions like the following: Why would he want to live at home if he has all that money? Is he a momma's boy? What's his problem? Does he have low self-esteem? Others, operating from similar assumptions, suggest that he might be living at home in order to save money to buy a house of his own. In other words, he may be sacrificing his independence temporarily to achieve his ultimate (and of course, preferable) goal of living independently.

After the disappointment, disbelief, and concern for this poor fellow has settled down, I often hear alternative interpretations from students who come from different cultural backgrounds or who straddle multiple cultural systems of meaning-making. The students suggest that "he lives at home to take care of his parents," or that "he likes living with his family," or "maybe that's just the way it's done in that culture." These students' interpretations represent a different system of meaning-making that values a more collectivistic than individualistic orientation and a more interdependent than independent approach to life. The students who do speak up with these alternative interpretations may feel a bit ambivalent about stating their interpretation because they realize they are in the minority; yet, they have no problem making sense of the scenario. In other words, the scenario is not viewed as contradictory or inconsistent; rather, it makes sense. My purpose in giving this example at this point is to demonstrate the ways in which culture operates as a system of shared meanings. The example also illustrates how we—human beings—generally assume that the way we make sense of things and the way we give meaning to symbols is the "right," "correct," and often "superior" way. One of the goals in this book is to challenge these ethnocentric attitudes and to develop the ability to understand cultures from within their own frames of reference rather than interpreting and negatively evaluating other cultures from one's own cultural position.

In summary, a central aspect of the anthropological definition of culture is that the patterns of meaning embodied in symbols that are inherited and passed along through generations are assumed to be shared. In fact, it is shared meaning that constitutes culture as a unit of examination in this definition of culture. The cultural studies definition of culture from a critical perspective offers another way to understand the complex notion of culture (see Photo 1.1).

© iStockphoto.com/visual7

© iStockphoto.com/skynesher

© iStockphoto.com/mseidelch

© iStockphoto.com/shelma1

© iStockphoto.com/ Stephen Krow

© iStockphoto.com/AnderAguirre

Photo 1.1 Are the meanings associated with these images shared or contested within cultures and across cultures?

Cultural Studies Definition: Culture as a Site of Contested Meaning

While traditional anthropological definitions focus on culture as a system of shared meanings, cultural studies perspectives, informed by Marxist theories of class struggle and exploitation, view **culture as a site of contestation** where meanings are constantly negotiated (Grossberg, Nelson, & Treichler, 1992). Cultural studies is a transdisciplinary field of study that emerged in the post–World War II era in England as a challenge to the positivist approaches to the study of culture, which purported to approach culture "objectively." The goals of Richard Hoggart, who founded the Birmingham Centre for Contemporary Cultural Studies, and others who followed, such as Stuart Hall, are to develop subjective approaches to the study of culture in everyday life, to examine the broader historical and political context within which cultural practices are situated, and to attend to relations of power in understanding culture. Simon During (1999) suggested that as England's working class became more affluent and fragmented in the 1950s, as mass-mediated culture began to dominate over local, community cultures, and as the logic that separated culture from politics was challenged, the old notion of culture as a shared way of life was no longer descriptive or functional.

Through a cultural studies lens, then, the notion of culture shifts from an expression of local communal lives to a view of culture as an apparatus of power within a larger system of domination. A cultural studies perspective reveals how culture operates as a form of **hegemony,** or domination through consent, as defined by Antonio Gramsci, an Italian Marxist theorist. Hegemony is dominance without the need for force or explicit forms of coercion. In other words, hegemony operates when the goals, ideas, and interests of the ruling group or class are so thoroughly normalized, institutionalized, and accepted that people consent to their own domination, subordination, and exploitation. Developments in cultural studies from the 1980s forward focus on the potential individuals and groups have to challenge, resist, and transform meanings in their subjective, everyday lives. John Fiske (1992) stated, "The social order constrains and oppresses people, but at the same time offers them resources to fight against those constraints" (p. 157), suggesting that individuals and groups are both consumers and producers of cultural meanings and not passive recipients of meanings manufactured by cultural industries. From a cultural studies perspective, meanings are not necessarily shared, stable, or determined; rather, meanings are constantly produced, challenged, and negotiated.

Consider, for example, the images of nondominant groups in the United States, such as African American; Latino/Latina; Asian American; American Indian; Arab American; or lesbian, gay, bisexual, and transgender (LGBT) people. Nondominant groups are often underrepresented and represented stereotypically in the mass media leading to struggles to affirm positive identities and efforts to claim and reclaim a position of respect in society. When any of us—from dominant or nondominant groups—speak or act outside the "norm" established by society or what is seen as "normal" within our cultural group, we likely experience tension, admonition, or in more extreme cases, shunning. As we engage with media representations and confront expected norms, we challenge and negotiate shared and accepted meanings within culture and society. Meanings associated with being an African American, a White man, or Latino/Latina are not shared by all in the society; rather, these meanings are continuously asserted, challenged, negotiated, and rearticulated. From a cultural studies perspective, meanings are continually produced, hybridized, and reproduced in an ongoing struggle of power (Hall, 1997a). Culture, then, is the "actual, grounded terrain" of everyday practices—watching TV, consuming and wearing clothes, eating fast food or dining out, listening to music or radio talk shows—and representations—movies, songs, videos, advertisements, magazines, and "news"—where meanings are contested.

While older definitions of culture where a set of things or activities signify high or low culture still circulate, the cultural studies notion of culture focuses on the struggles over meanings that are part of our everyday lives. Undoubtedly, the logic of understanding culture as a contested site or zone where meanings are negotiated appeals to and makes sense for people who experience themselves as marginalized from or marginalized within the centers of power, whether this is based on race, class, gender, ethnicity, sexuality, or nationality. Similarly, the logic of understanding culture as a system of shared meanings appeals to and makes sense for people at the centers of power or in a dominant role, whether this position is based on race, class, gender, ethnicity, sexuality, or nationality. This, itself, illustrates the struggle over the meaning of the notion of culture.

Nevertheless, it is important to note that we all participate in and are constrained by oppressive social forces. We all, at some points in our lives and to varying degrees, also challenge and struggle with dominant or preferred meanings. From a cultural studies perspective, culture is a site of analysis—in other words, something we need to attend to and critique. Culture is also a site of intervention, where we can work toward greater equity and justice in our lives and in the world in the ongoing struggle of domination and resistance.

The initial aim of the transdisciplinary field of cultural studies to critique social inequalities and work toward social change remains today; however, the academic field of cultural studies as it has traveled from England to Latin America, Australia, the United States, and other places has taken on different forms and emphases. In the mid-1980s, communication scholar Larry Grossberg (1986) identified the emerging and significant impact cultural studies began to have in the United States, particularly in the communication discipline. Today, as we explore intercultural communication within the context of globalization, a cultural studies approach offers tools to analyze power relations, to understand the historical and political context of our intercultural relations, and to see how we can act or intervene critically and creatively in our everyday lives.

Globalization Definition: Culture as a Resource

Influenced by cultural studies, contemporary anthropologist Arjun Appadurai (1996) suggested in his book *Modernity at Large: Cultural Dimensions of Globalization* that we need to move away from thinking of culture as a thing, a substance, or an object that is shared. The concept of culture as a coherent, stable entity privileges certain forms of sharing and agreement and neglects the realities of inequality, difference, and those who are marginalized. He argued that the adjective *cultural* is more descriptive and useful than the noun *culture.* Consequently, focusing on the cultural dimensions of an object, issue, practice, or ideology is to recognize differences, contrasts, and comparisons. Culture, in the context of globalization, is not something that individuals or groups possess, but rather a way of referring to dimensions of situated and embodied difference that express and mobilize group identities (Appadurai, 1996).

George Yúdice (2003) suggested that culture in the age of globalization has come to be understood as a **resource.** Culture plays a greater role today than ever before because of the ways it is linked to community, national, international, and transnational economies and politics. In the first decades of the 21st century, culture is now seen as a resource for economic and political exploitation, agency, and power to be used or instrumentalized for a wide range of purposes and ends. For example, in the context of globalization, culture, in the form of symbolic goods, such as TV shows, movies, music, and tourism, is increasingly a resource for economic growth in global trade. Mass culture industries in the United States are a major contributor to the gross national product (GNP) and function globally as purveyors of U.S. cultural power (Crothers, 2013). Culture is also targeted for exploitation by capital in the media, consumerism, and tourism. Consider how products are modified and marketed to different cultural groups; how African American urban culture has been appropriated, exploited, commodified, and yet it operates as a potentially oppositional site; or how tourism in many parts of the world uses the resource of culture to attract foreign capital for development. While the commodification of culture—the turning of culture, cultural practices, and cultural space into products for sale—is not new, the extent to which culture is "managed" as a resource for its capital-generating potential and as a "critical sphere for investment" by global institutions like the World Bank (WB) is new (Yúdice, 2003, p. 13).

Culture, in the context of globalization, is conceptualized, experienced, exploited, and mobilized as a resource. In addition to being invested in and distributed as a resource for economic development and capital accumulation, culture is used as a resource to address and solve social problems, such as illiteracy, addiction, crime, and conflict. Culture is also used today discursively, socially, and politically as a resource for collective and individual empowerment, agency, and resistance. Groups of people in proximity to each other or vastly distant due to migration organize collective identities that serve as "homes" of familiarity; spaces of belonging; and as sites for the formation of resistance, agency, and political empowerment. Consider how over twenty years, the Indigenous Front of Binational Organizations (FIOB), an organization of indigenous Mixteco and Zapoteco immigrants from Oaxaca, Mexico, has become a transnational network where indigenous people re-claim indigenous forms of knowledge and cultural practices to resist discrimination, reframe colonization, and re-invent their cultural identities (Mercado, 2016). Or, consider how hip hop culture—transplanted and refashioned around the globe—uses music, dance, style, and knowledge to give voice to the silenced, challenge discrimination, and create platforms for activism that support cultural empowerment. Today, in the context of globalization "the understanding and practice of culture is quite complex, located at the intersection of economic and social justice agendas" (Yúdice, 2003, p. 17).

As you can see from our previous discussion, there are various and different definitions of culture. The concept of culture, itself, is *contested*. This means that there is no one agreed on definition, that the different meanings of culture can be understood as being in competition with each other for usage, and that there are material and symbolic consequences or implications attached to the use of one or another of the definitions. The definitions presented here—(1) culture as shared meaning, (2) culture as contested meaning, and (3) culture as resource—all offer important and useful ways of understanding culture in the context of globalization. Throughout the book, all three definitions are used to help us make sense of the complex and contradictory intercultural communication issues and experiences we live and struggle with today.

Communicative Dimensions
Communication and Culture

What is the relationship between communication and culture? The three different approaches to culture illustrate different assumptions about communication.

According to the *anthropological definition* of culture as a shared system of meaning, communication is a process of transmitting and sharing information among a group of people. In this case, communication enables culture to be co-constructed and mutually shared by members of a group.

In the *cultural studies definition,* culture is a contested site of meaning. According to this view, communication is a process through which individuals and groups negotiate and struggle over the "agreed on" and "appropriate" meanings assigned to reality. Through verbal and nonverbal communication as well as the use of rhetoric, some views are privileged and normalized while other perspectives are marginalized or silenced. Thus, communication is a process of negotiation, a struggle for power and visibility rather than a mutual construction and sharing of meaning.

Finally, in the *globalization definition,* culture is viewed as a resource. In this case, communication can be viewed as a productive process that enables change. We usually associate the word *productive* with positive qualities. However, "productive" here simply means that communication is a generative process. People leverage culture to build collective identities and exploit or mobilize for personal, economic, or political gain. Communication is a process of using cultural resources.

STUDYING INTERCULTURAL COMMUNICATION

In recent years, when I ask students to speak about their culture, many find it a highly challenging exercise. For students who come from the dominant culture, the response is often "I don't really have a culture." For those students from nondominant groups, responses that point to their ethnic, racial, or religious group identification come more readily; however, their replies are often accompanied by some uneasiness. Typically, people whose culture differs from the dominant group have a stronger sense of their culture and develop a clearer awareness of their cultural identity earlier in life than those in the dominant group.

Cultural identity is defined as our situated sense of self that is shaped by our cultural experiences and social locations. Our identities develop through our relationships with others—our families, our friends, and those we see as outside our group. Our cultural identities are constructed from the languages we speak, the stories we tell, as well as the norms, behaviors, rituals, and nonverbal communication we enact. Histories passed along from within our cultural group in addition to representations of our group by others also shape our cultural identities. Our cultural identities serve to bond us with others giving us a sense of belonging; cultural identities also provide a buffer protecting us from others we or our group see as different from ourselves; and cultural identities can also function as bridges connecting us to others who are viewed as different. Our cultural identities intersect with and are impacted by our other social identities, including our ethnic, racial, gender, class, age, religious, and national identities. In the context of globalization, our identities are not fixed; rather, our identities are complex, multifaceted, and fluid.

What definitions of culture do you think are operating in the minds of my students when asked to speak about their culture? How might their cultural identities—consciously or unconsciously—affect their understanding of culture? What accounts for the different responses among students from dominant and nondominant cultures? We can see how the anthropological definition of culture as shared meaning and culture as something that groups possess is presumed in the students' responses. Students who identify with U.S. dominant culture are encouraged to see themselves as "individuals," which often underlies their claim that they "have no culture." Since their culture is pervasive and "normal" in the United States, European American or White students don't recognize the language, stories, values, norms, practices, and shared views on history as belonging to a culture. While students in nondominant groups see themselves as having culture or a cultural identity based on the ways in which they are different from the dominant group, dominant group members see the difference of nondominant groups and label it "culture," and their own seeming lack of "difference" as not having culture. While the dominant culture is also infused with "difference," it is not as evident because the cultural patterns of the dominant group are the norm.

Additionally, we can see how those from the dominant culture understand culture as a resource, which others have, but which they, rather nostalgically, are lacking. Interestingly and importantly, the fact that people from the dominant group do not see their culture as a resource is highly problematic. When members of the dominant group do not recognize their culture as a resource, their knowledge and access to cultural privilege and White privilege are erased and invisibilized by and for the dominant group (Frankenberg, 1993; Nakayama & Martin, 1999). We can also see the cultural studies definition of culture as contested meaning manifested in the differences between these students' responses.

To a great extent, culture or cultural dimensions of human interaction are unconsciously acquired and embodied through interaction and engagement with others from one's own culture. When one's culture differs from the dominant group (e.g., people who are Jewish, Muslim, or Buddhist in a predominantly Christian society, or people who identify as African American, Asian American, Latino/Latina, Arab American, or Native American within the predominantly White or European American culture) then he or she is regularly, perhaps even on a daily basis, reminded of the differences between his or her own cultural values, norms, history, and possibly language and those of the dominant group. In effect, people from nondominant groups learn to "commute" between cultures, switching verbal and nonverbal cultural codes as well as values and ways of viewing the world as they move between two cultures. If you are from a nondominant group, the ways in which the dominant culture is different from your own are evident.

This phenomenon is certainly not unique to the United States. People of Algerian or Vietnamese background who are French, people who are Korean or Korean–Japanese in Japan, or people of Indian ancestry who have lived, perhaps for generations, in Africa, the Caribbean, or South Pacific Islands are likely to experience a heightened sense of culture and cultural identification because their differences from the dominant group are seen as significant, are pointed out, and are part of their lived experience. Cultural identities serve as a place of belonging with others who are similar and a buffer from those who perceive you and are perceived as different.

On the other hand, people from the dominant cultural group in a society are often unaware that the norms, values, practices, and institutions of the society are, in fact, deeply shaped by and infused with a particular cultural orientation and that these patterns of shared meaning have been normalized as "just the way things are" or "the way things should be." So, to return to our earlier question, what accounts for the differences in responses of my students when asked about their culture?

Positionality

The differences in responses can be understood to some extent based on differences in students' **positionality**. Positionality refers to one's social location or position within an intersecting web of socially constructed hierarchical categories, such as race, class, gender, sexual orientation, religion, nationality, and physical abilities, to name a few. Different experiences, understanding, and knowledge of oneself and the world are gained, accessed, and produced based on one's positionality. Positionality is a relational concept. In other words, when we consider positionality, we are thinking about how we are positioned in relation to others within these intersecting social categories and how we are positioned in terms of power. The socially constructed categories of race, gender, class, sexuality, nationality, religion, and ableness are hierarchical systems that often connote and confer material and symbolic power. At this point, consider how your positionality—your positions of power in relation to the categories of race, gender, class, nationality, and so on—impacts your experiences, understanding, and knowledge about yourself and the world around you. How does your positionality impact your intercultural communication interactions?

Standpoint Theory

The idea of positionality is closely related to **standpoint theory** (Collins, 1986; Harding, 1991; Hartsock, 1983) as proposed by feminist theorists. A standpoint is a place from which to view and make sense of the world around us. Our standpoint influences what we see and what we cannot, do not, or choose not to see. Feminist standpoint theory claims that the social groups to which we belong shape what we know and how we communicate (Wood, 2005). The theory is derived from the Marxist position that economically oppressed classes can access knowledge unavailable to the socially privileged and can generate distinctive accounts, particularly knowledge about social relations. For example, German philosopher G. W. F. Hegel, writing in the early 19th century, suggested that while society in general may acknowledge the existence of slavery, the perception, experience, and knowledge of slavery is quite different for slaves as compared to masters. One's position within social relations of power produces different standpoints from which to view, experience, act, and construct knowledge about the world.

All standpoints are necessarily partial and limited, yet feminist theorists argue that people from oppressed or subordinated groups must understand both their own perspective and the perspective of those in power in order to survive. Therefore, the standpoint of marginalized people or groups, those with less power, is unique and should be privileged as it allows for a fuller and more comprehensive view. Patricia Hill Collins's (1986) notion of "outsiders within" points to the possibility of dual vision of marginalized people and groups, which in her case was that of a Black woman in predominantly White institutions. On the other hand, people in the dominant group, whether due to gender, class, race, religion, nationality, or sexual orientation, do not need to understand the viewpoint of subordinated groups and often have a vested interest in not understanding the positions of subordinated others in order to maintain their own dominance. As put forth by feminist theorists, standpoint theory is centrally concerned with the relationship between power and knowledge and sees the vantage point of those who are subordinated as a position of insight from which to challenge and oppose systems of oppression.

Standpoint theory offers a powerful lens through which to make sense of, address, and act on issues and challenges in intercultural communication. It enables us to understand the following:

- We may see, experience, and understand the world quite differently based on our different standpoints and positionalities.

- Knowledge about ourselves and others is situated and partial.

- Knowledge is always and inevitably connected to power.

- Oppositional standpoints can form, challenging and contesting the status quo.

Ethnocentrism

The application of standpoint theory and an understanding of the various positionalities we occupy may also assist us in avoiding the negative effects of ethnocentrism. Ethnocentrism is derived from two Greek words: (1) *ethno,* meaning group or nation, and (2) *kentron,* meaning center, referring to a view that places one's group at the center of the world. As first conceptualized by William Sumner (1906), **ethnocentrism** is the idea that one's own group's way of thinking, being, and acting in the world is superior to others. Some scholars argue that ethnocentrism has been a central feature in all cultures throughout history and has served as a mechanism of cultural cohesion and preservation (Gudykunst & Kim, 1997); yet, the globalized context in which we live today makes ethnocentrism and ethnocentric approaches extremely problematic. The assumption that one's own group is superior to others leads to negative evaluations of others and can result in dehumanization, legitimization of prejudices, discrimination, conflict, and violence. Both historically and today, ethnocentrism has combined with power—material, institutional, and symbolic—to justify colonization, imperialism, oppression, war, and ethnic cleaning.

One of the dangers of ethnocentrism is that it can blind individuals, groups, and even nations to the benefits of broader points of view and perceptions. Ethnocentrism is often marked by an intensely inward-looking and often nearsighted view of the world. On an interpersonal level, if you think your group's way of doing things, seeing things, and believing about things is the right way and the better way, you are likely to judge others negatively and respond arrogantly and dismissively to those who are different from you. These attitudes and actions will likely end any effective intercultural communication and deprive you of the benefits of other ways of seeing and acting in the world. If you are in a position of greater power in relation to the other person, you may feel as if it doesn't matter and you don't really need that person's perspective. From this, we can see how ethnocentrism combines with power to increase the likelihood of a more insular, myopic perspective.

On a global scale, ethnocentrism can affect perceptions of one's own group and can lead to ignorance, misunderstandings, resentment, and potentially violence. In late December 2001, the *International Herald Tribune* reported the results of a poll of 275 global opinion leaders from 24 countries. "Asked if many or most people would consider US policies to be 'a major cause' of the September 11 attacks, 58 percent of the non-US respondents said they did, compared to just 18 percent of Americans" (*Global Poll,* 2001). According to the report, findings from the poll indicate "that much of the world views the attacks as a symptom of increasingly bitter polarization between haves and have-nots." In response to the question of how there can be such a difference in perception between what Americans think about themselves and what non-Americans think about Americans, authors Ziauddin Sardar and Meryl Wyn Davies (2002) suggested the following:

> Most Americans are simply not aware of the impact of their culture and their government's policies on the rest of the world. But, more important, a vast majority simply do not believe that America has done, or can do, anything wrong. (p. 9)

Being a student of intercultural communication at this point in history presents unique opportunities and challenges. The increasing diversity of cultures in educational settings, workplaces, entertainment venues, and communities provides an impetus and resource for gaining knowledge and alternative perspectives about cultures that are different from one's own. The accelerated interconnectedness and interdependence of economics, politics, media, and culture around the globe also can motivate people to learn from and about others. Yet, for those positioned in the United States, rhetoric proclaiming the United States as the greatest and most powerful nation on Earth can combine with an unwillingness to critically examine the role of the United States in global economic and political instability and injustice. This can result in highly problematic, disturbing, and destructive forms of ethnocentrism that harm and inhibit intercultural communication and global intercultural relations. Ethnocentrism can lead to one-sided perceptions as well as extremely arrogant and misinformed views that are quite disparate from the perceptions of other cultural and national positions, and dangerously limit knowledge of the bigger global picture in which our intercultural communication and interactions take place.

Positionality, standpoint, and ethnocentric views are closely tied to our cultural identities. Our identities, based on socially constructed categories of difference (i.e., middle class, White male, American citizen), also position us in relation to others. Our positionality gives us a particular standpoint (i.e. "in American society, anyone can become successful if they work hard") and ethnocentric views may emerge (i.e., "American culture is more advanced and civilized than other cultures") if we have a limited understanding of others' positionalities and standpoints. When cultural identity is understood as a situated sense of self, we see how our positionality is not neutral, our standpoint is never universal, and our ethnocentric views are always problematic.

The study and practice of intercultural communication inevitably challenge our assumptions and views of the world. In fact, one of the main benefits of intercultural communication is the way in which it broadens and deepens our understanding of the world we live in by challenging our taken-for-granted beliefs and views and by providing alternative ways to live fully and respectfully as human beings. Ethnocentrism may provide temporary protection from views, experiences, and realities that threaten one's own, but it has no long-term benefits for effective or successful intercultural communication in the context of globalization.

INTERCULTURAL PRAXIS IN THE CONTEXT OF GLOBALIZATION

One of my goals in this book is to introduce and develop a process of critical reflective thinking and acting—what I call **intercultural praxis**—that enables us to navigate the complex and challenging intercultural spaces we inhabit interpersonally, communally, and globally. I hope that by reading this book you not only learn "about" intercultural communication, but also practice a way of being, thinking, analyzing, reflecting, and acting in the world in regard to cultural differences. Differences based on race, ethnicity, gender, class, religion, and nationality are real. Differences manifest in language, dress, behaviors, attitudes, values, histories, and worldviews. When people from diverse backgrounds come together, differences exist. Yet, the challenge in intercultural communication is not only about cultural differences; differences that are always and inevitably situated within relations of power. Thus, a central intention of the intercultural praxis model is to understand and address the intersection of cultural differences and hierarchies of power in intercultural interactions.

All moments in your day—when you are interacting with friends, coworkers, teachers, bosses, and strangers; when you are consuming pop culture in the form of music, clothes, your favorite TV shows, movies, and other entertainment; when you hear and read news and information from the media and other outlets; and in your routines of what and where you eat, where you live, how and where you travel around—are all opportunities to engage in intercultural praxis. To begin to understand intercultural praxis, I offer six interrelated points of entry into the process: (1) inquiry, (2) framing, (3) positioning, (4) dialogue, (5) reflection, and (6) action.

The purpose of engaging in intercultural praxis is to raise our awareness, increase our critical analysis, and develop our socially responsible action in regard to our intercultural interactions in the context of globalization. The intercultural praxis model provides a blueprint for joining our knowledge and skills as intercultural communicators with our ability to act in the world to create greater equity and social justice. Education scholars Maurianne Adams, Lee Anne Bell, and Pat Griffin (2007) defined **social justice** as both a goal and process in their book *Teaching for Diversity and Social Justice*: "The goal of social justice is full and equal participation of all groups in a society that is mutually shaped to meet their needs" (p. 1). Social justice includes a vision of the equitable distribution of resources where social actors experience agency with and responsibility for others. The process of reaching the goal of social justice should be "democratic and participatory, inclusive and affirming of human agency and human capacities for working collaboratively to create change" (Adams et al., p. 3).

The six points or ports of entry in the intercultural praxis model direct us toward ways of thinking, reflecting, and acting in relation to our intercultural experiences, allowing us to attend to the complex, relational, interconnected, and often ambiguous nature of our experiences. All six ports of entry into intercultural praxis are interconnected and inter-related. As we foreground each one individually, keep the others in your mind and consider how they inform the foregrounded port of entry. The six points of entry into intercultural praxis are introduced here and developed in greater depth through subsequent chapters (see Figure 1.1).

Inquiry

Inquiry, as a port of entry for intercultural praxis, refers to a desire and willingness to know, to ask, to find out, and to learn. Curious inquiry about those who are different from ourselves leads us to engagement with others. While it may sound simple, inquiry also requires that we are willing to take risks, allow our own way of viewing and being in the world to be challenged and perhaps changed, and that we are willing to suspend judgments about others in order to see and interpret others and the world from different points of view. A Vietnamese American student, Quynyh Tran, recounted an intercultural experience she had before enrolling in one of my intercultural classes. When being introduced in a business setting to a man she did not know, she extended her hand to shake his. He responded that it was against his culture and religion to shake hands. She remembers feel-ing rather put off and offended by his response, deciding without saying anything that she was not interested in talking or working with him!

Reflecting on this incident in class, she realized that she missed an incredible opportu-nity to learn more about someone who was different from herself. She realized that if she could have let go of her judgments about those who were different and had not reacted to the man's statement as "weird, strange, or unfriendly," she may have been able to learn something and expand her knowledge of the world. She regretted not stepping through one of the doors of entry into intercultural praxis. Yet, by entering into reflection, she learned from this experience that inquiry, curiosity, a willingness to suspend judgment, and a desire to learn from others can be tremendously rewarding and informing. She could also see that what she reacted to as "weird" and "strange" was framed by her culture and positionality.

Framing

I propose **framing** to suggest a range of different perspective-taking options that we can learn to make available to ourselves and need to be aware of in intercultural praxis. First, the concept and action of "framing" connotes that frames always and inevitably limit our per-spectives and our views on ourselves, others, and the world around us. We see things through individual, cultural, national, and regional frames or lenses that necessarily include some things and exclude others. As we engage in intercultural praxis, it is critical that we become aware of the frames of reference from which we view and experience the world.

Figure 1.1 Intercultural Praxis Model

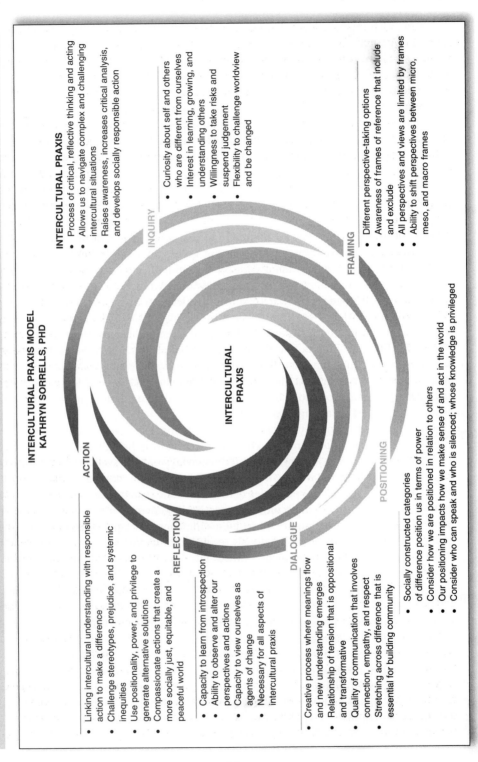

**INTERCULTURAL PRAXIS MODEL
KATHRYN SORRELLS, PHD**

INTERCULTURAL PRAXIS

INTERCULTURAL PRAXIS
- Process of critical, reflective thinking and acting
- Allows us to navigate complex and challenging intercultural situations
- Raises awareness, increases critical analysis, and develops socially responsible action

INQUIRY
- Curiosity about self and others who are different from ourselves
- Interest in learning, growing, and understanding others
- Willingness to take risks and suspend judgement
- Flexibility to challenge worldview and be changed

FRAMING
- Different perspective-taking options
- Awareness of frames of reference that include and exclude
- All perspectives and views are limited by frames
- Ability to shift perspectives between micro, meso, and macro frames

POSITIONING
- Socially constructed categories of difference position us in terms of power
- Consider how we are positioned in relation to others
- Our positioning impacts how we make sense of and act in the world
- Consider who can speak and who is silenced; whose knowledge is privileged

DIALOGUE
- Creative process where meanings flow and new understanding emerges
- Relationship of tension that is oppositional and transformative
- Quality of communication that involves connection, empathy, and respect
- Stretching across difference that is essential for building community

REFLECTION
- Capacity to learn from introspection
- Ability to observe and alter our perspectives and actions
- Capacity to view ourselves as agents of change
- Necessary for all aspects of intercultural praxis

ACTION
- Linking intercultural understanding with responsible action to make a difference
- Challenge stereotypes, prejudice, and systemic inequities
- Use positionality, power, and privilege to generate alternative solutions
- Compassionate actions that create a more socially just, equitable, and peaceful world

Source: © Kathryn Sorrells

Design: Jessica Arana (www.jessicaarana.com)

Secondly, "framing" means that we are aware of both the local and global contexts that shape intercultural interactions. Sometimes it is very important to narrow the frame, to zoom in, and focus on the particular and very situated aspects of an interaction, event, or exchange. Take, for example, a conflict between two people from different cultures. It's important to look at the micro-level differences in communication styles, how nonverbal communication may be used differently, the ways in which the two people may perceive their identities differently based on cultural belonging, and the ways in which the two may have learned to enact conflict differently based on their enculturation. However, in order to fully understand the particular intercultural interaction or misunderstanding, it is also necessary to back up to view the incident, event, or interaction from a broader frame. As we zoom out, we may see a history of conflict and misunderstanding between the two groups that the individuals represent; we may observe historical and/or current patterns of inequities between the two groups that position them differently; and we may also be able to map out broader geopolitical, global relations of power that can shed light on the particular and situated intercultural interaction, misunderstanding, or conflict. As we zoom in and foreground the micro-level of intercultural communication, we need to keep the wider background frame in mind as it provides the context in which meaning about the particular is made. Similarly, as we zoom out and look at larger macro-level dimensions, we need to keep in mind the particular local and situated lived experience of people in their everyday lives. "Framing" as a port of entry into intercultural praxis means we are aware of our frames of reference. It also means we develop our capacity to flexibly and consciously shift our perspective from the particular, situated dimensions of intercultural communication to the broader global dimensions, and from the global dimensions to the particular while maintaining our awareness of both.

Positioning

Where are you positioned as you read this sentence? Your first response may be to say you are lounging in a chair at home, in a café, in the break room at work, or in the library. If you "zoomed out" utilizing the framing strategy in the previous discussion, you may also respond by stating your location in a part of a neighborhood, city, state, nation, or region of the world. **Positioning** as a point of entry into intercultural praxis invites us to consider how our geographic positioning is related to social and political positions. As you read these sentences, where are you positioned socioculturally? The globe we inhabit is stratified by socially constructed hierarchical categories based on culture, race, class, gender, nationality, religion, age, and physical abilities among others. Like the lines of longitude and latitude that divide, map, and position us geographically on the earth, these hierarchical categories position us socially, politically, and materially in relation to each other and in relation to power.

Understanding how and where we are positioned in the world—the locations from which we speak, listen, act, think, and make sense of the world—allows us to acknowledge that we, as human beings, are positioned differently with both material and symbolic consequences. It is also important to note that your positionality may shift and change based on where you are and with whom you are communicating. For example, it could vary over the course of a day, from occupying a relatively powerful position at home as the oldest son in a family to having to occupy a less powerful positionality in your part-time job as a personal assistant. Sometimes the shift may be even more drastic, as in the case of some-one who is a doctor and part of a dominant group in her home culture and then shifts class and power positions when she is forced to migrate to the United States for political reasons. She finds herself not only part of a minority group, but also positioned very differently when her medical degree is not recognized, forcing her into more manual work and part-time student positionalities.

Positioning, as a way to enter into intercultural praxis, also directs us to interrogate who can speak and who is silenced; whose language is spoken and whose language is trivialized or denied; whose actions have the power to shape and impact others, and whose actions are dismissed, unreported, and marginalized. Positioning combines with other ports of entry, such as inquiry and framing encouraging us to question whose knowledge is privi-leged, authorized, and agreed on as true and whose knowledge is deemed unworthy, "primitive," or unnecessary. Positioning ourselves, others, and our knowledge of both self and others allow us to see the relationship between power and what we think of as "knowl-edge." Our knowledge of the world—whether knowledge of meridians of longitude and latitude or hierarchical categories of race, class, and gender—is socially and historically constructed and produced in relation to power.

Intercultural Praxis
Negotiating Differences

To begin using the Intercultural Praxis model as a tool for navigating the complexities of cultural differences and power differences in intercultural situations, read the following statements and consider your response to each. On a continuum, do you strongly agree with the statement, disagree, or is your response somewhere in between?

1. Hard work is all it takes for me to succeed in school, work, and life.
2. Big cities are generally not safe and people are not as friendly there.
3. In the United States, women are treated fairly and as equals to men.
4. The police are viewed with suspicion in my neighborhood.
5. Going to college/university is my primary responsibility.
6. Gay marriage is legalized in many states, so homophobia is increasingly a problem of the past.
7. Religious freedom is what makes the United States a great country.
8. I have to work twice as hard to prove I am as capable and competent as others.
9. For the most part, I can go pretty much anywhere in my city, town, or region without feeling afraid for my safety.
10. Interracial and intercultural relationships cause problems. People should stay with their own kind.

11. I am one of the only ones in my family who has the opportunity to go to college/university.

12. Since the United States has a Black president, the country has basically moved beyond racism.

13. I can get financial support from my family to pay for college/university, if necessary.

Now that you have read the statements, consider the following:

- How do your cultural frames inform your responses?
- How are your responses related to your positionality?
- How do cultural frames and positionality intersect to shape your responses?
- Share these statements with a friend, partner, or coworker and then dialogue about how your responses may be similar or different.
- Reflect and dialogue with the other person about how our differences in terms of power and positionality impact our standpoints.
- Reflect on the assumptions and judgments you may have about people who would make each of these statements.
- How is dialogue with people who are different in terms of culture and positionality a step toward creating a more equitable and just world?

Dialogue

While we have all heard of **dialogue** and likely assume that we engage in it regularly, it's useful to consider the derivation of the word to deepen our understanding of dialogue as an entry port into intercultural praxis. A common mistake is to think "dia" means two and dialogue, then, is conversation between two people. However, the word *dialogue* is derived from the Greek word *dialogos*. *Dia* means "through," "between," or "across," and *logos* refers to "word" or "the meaning of the word" as well as "speech" or "thought." Physicist and philosopher David Bohm (1996) wrote the following:

> The picture or the image that this derivation suggests is of a *stream of meaning* among and through us and between us. This will make possible a flow of meaning in the whole group, out of which may emerge a new understanding. It's something new, which may not have been in the starting point at all. It's something creative. (p. 6)

Anthropologist Vincent Crapanzano (1990) suggested that "dialogue" necessarily entails both an oppositional as well as a transformative dimension. Given the differences in power and positionality in intercultural interactions, engagement in dialogue is necessarily a relationship of tension that "is conceived as a crossing, a reaching across, a sharing if not a common ground of understanding. . . " (p. 277).

According to philosopher Martin Buber, dialogue is essential for building community and goes far beyond an exchange of messages. For Buber, dialogue requires a particular quality of communication that involves a connection among participants who are potentially changed by each other. Buber refers to such relationships as I–Thou, where one relates and experiences another as a person. This relationship is quite different from an I–It relationship where people are regarded as objects and experienced as a means to a goal. Dialogue occurs only when there is regard for both self and other and where either/ or thinking is challenged allowing for the possibility of shared ground, new meaning, and mutual understanding.

Dialogue offers a critical point of entry into intercultural praxis. Cognizant of differences in cultural frames and positionalities as well as the tensions that emerge from these differences, the process of dialogue invites us to stretch ourselves—to reach across—to imagine, experience, and creatively engage with points of view, ways of thinking and being, and beliefs different from our own while accepting that we may not fully understand or come to a common agreement or position.

Reflection

While cultures around the world differ in the degree to which they value reflection and the ways in which they practice **reflection,** the capacity to learn from introspection, to observe oneself in relation to others, and to alter one's perspectives and actions based on reflection is a capacity shared by all humans. Many cultures, including the dominant culture of the United States, place a high value on doing activities and accomplishing tasks, which often leaves little space and time for reflection. However, reflection is a key feature of intercultural praxis. Consider how reflection is central to the other points of entry into intercultural praxis already addressed. To engage in curious inquiry, one must be able to reflect on oneself as a subject—a thinking, learning, creative, and capable subject. The practices of framing and positioning require that one consciously observe oneself and critically analyze ones relationships and interrelationships with others. Similarly, reflection is necessary to initiate, maintain, and sustain dialogue across the new and often difficult terrain of intercultural praxis.

Brazilian educator and activist Paulo Freire (1998) noted in his book *Pedagogy of Freedom* that critical praxis "involves a dynamic and dialectic movement between 'doing' and 'reflecting on doing'" (p. 43). Reflection is what informs our actions. Reflection that incorporates critical analyses of micro- and macro-levels of intercultural issues, which considers multiple cultural frames of reference, and that recognizes our own and others' positioning enables us to act in the world in meaningful, effective, and responsible ways.

Action

Influenced by the work of Paulo Freire (1973/2000), the concept of intercultural praxis refers to an ongoing process of thinking, reflecting, and acting. Intercultural praxis is not only about deepening our understanding of ourselves, others, and the world in which we live. Rather, intercultural praxis means we join our increased understanding with responsible **action** to make a difference in the world—to create a more socially just, equitable, and peaceful world.

Each one of us takes multiple and varied actions individually and collectively that have intercultural communication dimensions and implications every single day of our lives. We take action when we decide to get an education, to go to class or not, and when we select classes or a field of study. Our actions in an educational context are influenced by cultural, gendered, national, and class-based assumptions, biases, or constraints. We take action when we go to work and when we speak out or don't about inequity, discrimination, and misuses of power. Watching or reading the news is an action that affords opportunities to understand how cultural and national interests shape, limit, and bias the news we receive. Our consumption of products, food, and entertainment are all actions. When we know who has labored to make the goods we consume and under what conditions, we confront ourselves and others with the choices we make through our actions. We take action when we make decisions about whom we develop friendships and long-term relationships with and when we choose not to be involved. When we feel strongly enough about an issue, we are moved to organize and take action.

What informs our choices and actions? What are the implications of our actions? In the context of globalization, our choices and actions are always enabled, shaped, and constrained by history; relations of power; and material conditions that are inextricably linked to intercultural dimensions of culture, race, class, religion, sexual orientation, language, and nationality. Intercultural praxis, offers us a process of critical, reflective thinking and acting that enables us to navigate the complex and challenging intercultural spaces, we inhabit interpersonally, communally, and globally. Intercultural praxis can manifest in a range of forms, such as simple or complex communication competency skills, complicit actions, and oppositional tactics, as well as through creative, improvisational, and transformational interventions.

SUMMARY

As we "open the conversation," it is evident that there is a critical need for skillful and informed intercultural communicators in the current context of globalization. To assist us in making sense of intercultural communication in the rapidly changing, increasingly interdependent, and inequitable world we inhabit, I introduced various definitions of culture: (1) culture as shared meaning, (2) culture as contested meaning, and (3) culture as resource. Each definition provides different and necessary ways of understanding culture in our complex age. Studying intercultural communication in the context of globalization offers opportunities and challenges. To guide our approach and to increase our awareness, the basic concepts of positionality, standpoint theory, and ethnocentrism were introduced. Because we want to become more effective as intercultural communicators, thinkers, and actors in the global context, intercultural praxis—a set of skills, processes, and practices for critical, reflective thinking and acting—was outlined to navigate the complex, contradictory, and challenging intercultural spaces we inhabit. In the next chapter, we explore the historical, political, and economic factors and forces that have contributed to globalization and discuss various dimensions of intercultural communication in the context of globalization.

KEY TERMS

high culture
low culture
popular culture
culture as shared meaning
symbols
culture as contested meaning
hegemony
culture as a resource
cultural identity
positionality

standpoint theory
ethnocentrism
intercultural praxis
social justice
inquiry
framing
positioning
dialogue
reflection
action

DISCUSSION QUESTIONS AND ACTIVITIES

Discussion Questions

1. In the anthropologic definition, culture is defined as a site of shared meaning. How is this definition useful in understanding culture? In what ways does globalization complicate our understanding of culture as a site of shared meaning?

2. What is your positionality and how does it shape your standpoint? Why are these concepts important in studying intercultural communication?

3. How does hegemony—defined as domination through consent—function to produce and maintain relations of power in society? What are the examples of hegemonic forces that influence your life? Where do those hegemonic forces come from?

4. Do you think there are universal human values? If so, what are they? Is the belief in universal human values inherently ethnocentric?

5. The chapter defines Intercultural Praxis as a process of critical, reflective thinking and acting shaped by six ports of entry. In what ways is this approach different from learning a predetermined set of rules and norms for intercultural communication? Why does Intercultural Praxis emphasize the self-reflexive process of thinking and acting rather than following established rules of communication?

Activities

1. Exploring the Cultural Dimensions That Shape You
   a. Write a brief paragraph exploring the cultural dimensions that shape you using the definitions of culture discussed in this chapter. How do you understand your culture as a system of shared meanings? As a site of contestation? As a resource?

(For example, as an American, I value independence and individualism, which are cultural values that I share with many others from the United States. As a woman, I feel like I am constantly negotiating representations of what it means to be a woman. My gender culture is a site of contestation. Women, in this society, are often turned into objects like resources that can be exploited, packaged, and sold. Yet, I am proud to be a woman and experience this cultural dimension of myself as an empowering resource. As a White American, I know my experiences are different from other racial groups. I am learning how I am different from others and not just how they are different from me as a member of the dominant group. The privileges I have from being White are resources, even or especially when I can't see these invisible advantages.)

b. Share your paragraph responses with your classmates, and discuss the similarities and differences among your cultural dimensions.

c. Discuss the usefulness and limitations of each definition of culture.

2. Positioning Yourself and Your Cultural Dimensions

a. Using your responses to the first activity, develop your ideas on how you are positioned in relation to others in terms of race, class, gender, ethnicity, sexuality, nationality, religion, and ableness.

b. Discuss how your positionality influences your standpoint on the world around you and how you engage in intercultural communication.

3. Intercultural Praxis—Group Activity

In a group of four to five students, consider and discuss the following:

a. Inquiry: What do you already know about each other? What stereotypes, preconceptions, and assumptions might you have about students in your class or those in your group? What would you like to know about the cultural background of those in your group? What skills and experience do you bring to the process of inquiry?

b. Framing: In what ways does your cultural background frame the way you see and experience others in your group? What frames of reference are useful in understanding the members of your group? What can you see if you "zoom in" and look at the micro-level in terms of the cultural dimensions of your group? What can you see if you "zoom out" and look at the macro-level in terms of the cultural dimensions of your group?

c. Positioning: How are you positioned sociohistorically in relation to others in your group? How does your positionality change in different contexts and frames of reference?

d. Dialogue: With whom do you frequently engage in dialogue? How can you expand the circle of people with whom you engage in dialogue? What qualities are required to engage effectively in dialogue? How do relationships of power shape the process of dialogue?

e. Reflection: As you reflect on your inquiry, framing, positioning, and dialogue, what have you learned about yourself, your group, and intercultural praxis?

f. Action: How and when can you engage in intercultural praxis? How can you use what you have learned in this chapter to effect change for a more equitable and just world? What are the consequences and implications of lack of action?

g. Finally, discuss the challenges of engaging in intercultural praxis. Keep your dialogue and reflections from this group activity in mind as you read the following chapters.

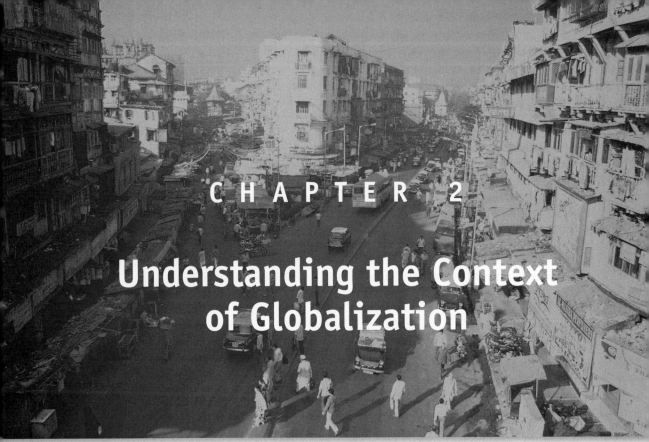

CHAPTER 2

Understanding the Context of Globalization

© iStockphoto.com/ISnap

How do you imagine life in Mumbai (Bombay), India, as different from or similar to your life?

Learning Objectives

1. Describe the complex and contradictory influences of globalization on intercultural communication.

2. Explain the important role history plays in shaping intercultural communication today.

3. Explain how relationships of power impact intercultural communication in our everyday lives.

4. Identify the intercultural dimensions of economic, political and cultural globalization.

26

Scenario One: In the hallway of a university in Southern California, three students—Hamza, an international student from Morocco; Cathy, who came to the United States four years ago from France; and Immaculee from Rwanda, who immigrated 17 years ago—spend the 15-minute break during their intercultural communication class speaking with each other in French, relishing in the comfort that speaking a language of "home" offers and forming an intercultural relationship, however temporary and transitory. Why would they all speak French?

Scenario Two: The Trans-Pacific Partnership, the latest giant free-trade deal currently in the making between the United States and Australia, Canada, Chile, Brunei, Japan, Malaysia, Mexico, New Zealand, Peru, Singapore, Vietnam, and likely Korea accounts for some of the United States' largest and fastest growing trade partners. These countries combined are responsible for 40% of the world's GDP and 26% of the world's trade. The size, scope and level of secrecy of the agreement distinguish it from other agreements. A range of controversial issues has stalled approval of the agreement in the United States and other countries (DePillis, 2013). What might be the concerns of these trade partners? Which large country in the Pacific region is not part of the partnership and why?

Scenario Three: Which movie star is wealthier than Tom Cruise, Tyler Perry, or Johnny Depp? Many automatically think of a U.S. star; yet, the answer is Shah Rukh Khan, one of India's most famous and awarded actors whose popularity extends way beyond the borders of India (Kim, 2014). Mumbai's (Bombay) film industry, Bollywood, is the largest in the world and is now a global phenomenon, producing more than 1,200 films viewed around the world. Simran Chopra (2012) of BusinessofCinema.com writes about superstar SRK, "Not just national, but his charisma traverses across the imaginary lines of divisions drawn up globally. His magnetism draws his fans across the seven seas. They watch him, they pray for him, they worship him." Outside of Indian American communities, why are so few in the United States aware of this superstar?

Scenario Four: Occupy Wall Street (OWS), a people-powered protest movement started on September 17, 2011, in Zuccotti Park in New York City's Wall Street financial district, brought people from diverse backgrounds together in over 100 cities across the United States and 1,500 cities around the world to challenge economic inequity and wealth distribution. "We are the 99%," the OWS slogan, highlights income and wealth disparities between the wealthiest 1% and the rest of the population. OWS, drawing inspiration from uprisings in Egypt and Tunisia, struggles against multinational corporations and elites who are writing the rules for an increasingly uneven global economy and corroding democratic processes (Occupy Wall Street, 2014).

Scenario Five: Filipina American Grace Ebron recalls, "I arrive at the Rome Airport, thrilled at the notion of living in Italy. As I step out of the customs hall, I immediately see my boyfriend, waiting to meet me. His parents, whom I've never met, are with him and as I turn to them with my perfectly-rehearsed Italian greeting, they appear very confused. 'No- no' they stammer, a perplexed expression on their faces. They turn to Massimo: 'But where is your girlfriend—the American? Why did she send the maid?'" (Ebron, 2002).

What themes are interwoven through the fabric of all of these scenarios? Without erasing the obvious and more subtle differences between the situations, what common factors and forces shape the world that these scenarios describe? Hamza, Cathy, and Immaculee made personal journeys from different parts of the globe to the United States and find themselves relating to each other through a common language and connected to each other through a history of colonization. Through worldwide distribution of Hindi films, numerous websites, and social media, fans from around the world can stay up to date on Shah Rukh Khan's latest public appearances and movies. Rapid communication and transportation technologies as well as free-trade policies favorable to corporations link businesses across the Pacific creating a new "trans-Pacific" economic region. The exclusion of China from the partnership suggests the political dimensions of "free-trade" agreements. The Occupy Wall Street movement catalyzed national and international debate and discussion shedding light on the magnified economic inequities of globalization. While highlighting growing tensions between the "haves" and "have nots," the movement also strengthened intercultural alliances across groups challenging the increasing control of corporations and global financial institutions, such as the **World Trade Organization (WTO),** over their lives and cultures. Grace Ebron, excited to reconnect with her Italian boyfriend, benefits from her global mobility, and yet is confronted with stereotypes and racialized assumptions due to colonial histories and the migration of Filipina laborers to Italy as part of a development policy based on the export of labor.

All the scenarios illustrate the dynamic movement, confluence, and interconnection of peoples, cultures, markets, and relationships of power that are rooted in history, and yet are redefined and rearticulated in our current global age. Through advances in technology—both communication technology and transportation technology—and open markets, people from around the globe with different cultural, racial, national, economic, and linguistic backgrounds are coming into contact with each other; consuming each others' cultural foods, products, and identities; developing relationships and struggling through conflicts; building alliances and activist networks; and laboring with and for each other more frequently, more intensely, and with greater impact today than ever before. In the workplace and the home, through entertainment and the Internet, in politics and the military, and through travel for leisure, work, pleasure, and survival, intercultural communication and interactions have become common, everyday experiences.

This chapter begins with an introduction of the central roles that history and power play in intercultural communication and explores the broader context of globalization within which intercultural communication occurs today. To grasp the complexity of globalization, we examine the facets of economic globalization, political globalization, and cultural globalization. Each facet is treated separately here to highlight the ways intercultural communication is integral to globalization. Yet, these three facets of globalization are inextricably intertwined; thus, the interrelationship among economic, political, and cultural issues is also addressed.

THE ROLE OF HISTORY IN INTERCULTURAL COMMUNICATION

Certainly, as we know from a study of history, for several millennia people have traveled and moved great distances exchanging cultural goods, ideas, and practices and experiencing significant intercultural contact. While both the Islamic and Mongol empires had broad reaches, Held, McGrew, Goldblatt, and Perraton (1999) noted in their book *Global Transformations: Politics, Economics and Culture* that the European conquest starting in the 16th century transformed global migration patterns in ways that continue to impact us today. During the European colonial era, people moved from Europe, Spain, Portugal, and England primarily, but also from France, Holland, Belgium, and Germany to the Americas, Oceania, Africa, and Asia for the purpose of conquest, economic expansion, and religious conversion. Settlers from these countries then followed, reinforcing the flow from Europe to the outlying colonies. Between the 1600s and the 1850s, 9 to 12 million people were forcibly removed from Africa and transported to the colonies—primarily in the Americas—to serve as enslaved laborers during the transatlantic slave trade. In the 19th century, Indians (from the sub-continent of India) subjected to colonial British rule were relocated as laborers—often as indentured servants—to British colonies in Africa and Oceania. The process of colonization, which was based on the extraction of wealth through the exploitation of natural and human resources, established Europe as the economic and political center of the world and the colonies as the periphery (Young, 2001).

Later in the 19th century, after the British and Spanish colonies in the Americas had gained independence from colonial rule, a mass migration occurred with the expulsion of working class and poor people from the economically stretched and famine-torn centers of Europe to the United States, Canada, and the Southern Cone, including Argentina, Chile, Brazil, Uruguay, and others. Movements of indentured laborers from Asia—primarily China, Japan, and the Philippines—to European colonies and former colonies—mainly the United States and Canada—swelled the number of migrants to over 40 million during the 25 years before World War I (WWI).

WWI brought the unprecedented closure of national borders and the implementation of the first systematic immigration legislation and border controls in modern times. The ethnically motivated violence of World War II (WWII). led to the movement of Jews out of Europe to Israel, the United States, and Latin America. In the wake of unprecedented devastation of human lives, economies, and natural habitats experienced across Europe, Russia, and Japan as a result of WWII, the first institutions of global political and economic governance—the United Nations, the **World Bank (WB),** and the **International Monetary Fund (IMF)**—were established.

Since the 1960s with the rebuilding of European economic power and the rise of the United States as an economic and political center, we see a shift in migratory patterns. While earlier periods saw the movement of peoples from the center of empires to the peripheries, increasingly people from the former colonies or peripheries are migrating toward the centers of former colonial power. In search of jobs and in response to demands for labor, migrants are moving from Turkey and North Africa to Germany and France, respectively, and from more distant former colonies in Southeast Asia and East and West Africa to England, France, Germany, Italy, and the Scandinavian countries. The transatlantic migration from Europe to the United States at the turn of the 20th century is matched today by the numbers of immigrants from Latin America and Asia to the United States.

We also see flows of people to the oil-rich countries of the Middle East from Africa and Asia and new patterns of regional migration within Latin America, Africa, and East Asia. In the last two decades, the numbers of people seeking asylum, refugees fleeing internally strife-stricken countries in the developing world, and those who have been displaced for a variety of political and economic reasons in Africa, the Middle East, and Latin America have risen exponentially and trends indicate the number of displaced people will continue to grow (United Nations High Commissioner for Refugees, 2012). Today, South-South migration, or migration of people from countries in the Global South to other countries in the south, is as common as South-North migration. Asians and Latin Americans constitute the largest groups living outside their countries of origin in the global diaspora (United Nations Population Division, 2013).

Intercultural Praxis
Historicizing the Field of Intercultural Communication

When engaging in intercultural praxis, framing is a process by which you zoom in and out using your analytical lens to understand a situation from micro-, meso-, and macro perspectives. While always partial and incomplete, the frame of reference we use can radically change the nature of "history" that we accept as true. The origin of the field traces back to several key anthropologists, most notably Edward T. Hall, who in the 1950s worked for the Foreign Service Institute training U.S. diplomats to communicate effectively in foreign countries. This "genesis" of the field is significant because growing U.S. hegemony after World War II and during the Cold War shaped the political context and motivation for the field.

The late awakening in the United States to the significance of global cultures points to its privileged positionality in the world as the emergent superpower. While the United States may have come to terms with the importance of cultural diplomacy in the post-WWII period, groups of people who were colonized by the West—indigenous peoples of the Americas, Africa, and Asia—had already been made aware of the significance of "cultural differences" marked by unequal colonial relations of power. Contextualizing the origin reveals how the development of the field was deeply intertwined with the cultural, social, economic, and political environment in the United States at that time (Sorrells & Sekimoto, 2016).

As noted earlier, people have engaged in intercultural contact for many millennia, yet the European conquest starting in the 16th century transformed global migration patterns in ways that continue to impact intercultural relations today. The brief historical overview of world migrations since the colonial period reminds us that movements of people and therefore intercultural interactions are directly related to economic and political forces. It also suggests that intercultural misunderstanding and conflict occurring today among individuals, groups, or nations may be rooted deeply in histories of dispute, discrimination, and de-humanization. Additionally, the brief overview points to how networks of connection and global relationships of power experienced today are a continuation of worldwide intercultural contact and interaction over the past 500 years. Therefore, in order to understand the dynamics of intercultural communication today, we must place them within a broad historical context. The process of colonization by Europe of much of the world, which included the exploitation of natural resources and human labor, established Europe and later the United States as the economic and political centers of the world. The colonial process initiated the division between "the West and the Rest" that we experience today. Figures 2.1 and 2.2 reflect the colonization and global expansion of the West that propelled the development of capitalism, which required then, and continues to require today, the expansion of markets and trade and the incorporation of labor from the former colonies, or what have been referred to as the Third World or developing countries (Dussel, 1995; Wallerstein, 2011) also.

The terms *First World*, *Second World*, and *Third World* are relics of the Cold War period and explain concepts initially used to describe the relationship between the United States and other countries. The **First World** referred to countries friendly to the United States that were identified as capitalist and democratic. The **Second World** referred to countries perceived as hostile and ideologically incompatible with the United States, the former Soviet bloc countries, Cuba, China, and their allies, which were identified as communist. The **Third World** referred to countries that were seen as neutral or nonaligned with either the First World (capitalism) or the Second World (communism). While the relationship between the First World and Third World was ostensibly positive, the history of the last half of the 20th century

Figure 2.1   Colonized World in 1800

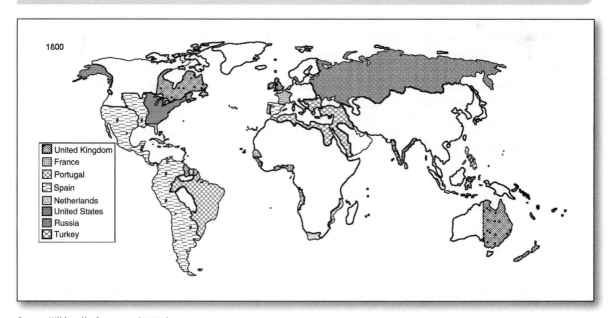

Source: Wikimedia Commons (2008a)

Figure 2.2 Colonial Powers 1914

1914

United Kingdom
France
Portugal
Spain
Netherlands
Belgium
United States
Russia
Italy
Germany
Turkey

Source: Wikimedia Commons (2008b)

reveals the so-called "Third World" as sites of anticolonial struggles and battlegrounds between the First and Second Worlds. Since the fall of the Soviet Union and the end of the Cold War, the meaning of First and Third Worlds is less clearly defined and more closely associated with levels of economic development. The terms ***developing country*** and ***developed country***, more commonly used today, are based on a nation's wealth (gross national product [GNP]), political and economic stability, and other factors. The terms ***Global South*** and ***Global North,*** also in usage today, highlight the socioeconomic and political division between wealthy, developed nations (former centers of colonial power) in the Northern Hemisphere, and poorer developing nations (formerly colonized countries) in the Southern Hemisphere. As is evident, the labels, products of historical moments, are flawed and limited in their accuracy and represent a particular standpoint. As this book unfolds, significant historical periods that have shaped and continue to shape our world today, such as European colonization and the period immediately following WWII, are discussed in greater depth.

THE ROLE OF POWER IN INTERCULTURAL COMMUNICATION

Let's return to the scenarios again. While intercultural interactions can be engaging, delightful, informing, and even transformative, they are also often challenging, stressful, contentious, and conflicting. What else can we say about these scenarios? What other themes or threads are evident? Are Hamza, Cathy, and Immaculee positioned equally in terms of power? Are their claims of "French-ness" the same? Are they likely to experience similar or different receptions from people in the United States based on race, nation of origin, gender, class, religion, and post–9/11 attitudes? Are the countries in the proposed Trans-Pacific Partnership positioned equally in terms of political and economic power? Are international business relations influenced by these inequities? Well, sure, most of us would answer. Therefore, it is important to consider the impact on intercultural relations when the people communicating come from different and inequitable positions of power.

Have you heard of Shah Rukh Khan? If you said, "no," you are not alone among people from the United States. Khan, or "King Khan" as he is affectionately known, is one of the biggest movie stars in cinematic history and enjoys worldwide renown. So, how, in this global age with highly advanced mass communication technology, is it that so few Americans outside the Indian American community know about this superstar? While Bollywood (the film industry in India is primarily centered in Mumbai and is often referred to as "Bollywood," a melding of the city's colonial name, Bombay, with Hollywood) produces over 1,200 feature films per year, roughly three times more than Hollywood, and reaches a larger audience worldwide, U.S. films continue to dominate the U.S. market. Why do you think that is?

Initially dismissed by mainstream media, Occupy Wall Street had garnered tremendous mainstream and social media attention by late September 2011, accelerating the spread of the protest movement across the United States and the world. While CNN, the *New York Times,* and other major media outlets reported that OWS wanted to increase regulations and taxes on millionaires, the vast majority of OSW organizers were calling for the end to capitalism (Bray, 2013). What explains this vast difference between what was reported in mainstream media and what was demanded? Whose interests are served by mainstream media and whose voices are less likely to be heard?

In our study of intercultural communication in the context of globalization, we must consider how global movements of people, products, cultural forms, and cultural representations are shaped and controlled by relationships of power. What and who is controlling these positions and practices of power, and how have these power relationships been established? For example, it is important for us to ask and investigate who are the media giants who shape the content and the distribution of news, information, and popular culture? Who is the 1% who has amassed such wealth? How does this inequity influence political and economic policies and decisions that impact the 99%? How are people-driven movements, such as Occupy Wall Street, the Arab Spring sweeping the Middle East, the DREAM Act movement organizing undocumented students, and the Zapatista movement for indigenous rights in Chiapas, Mexico, among many others building power bases, independently and together, to challenge global capitalism, imagine alternatives, and bring about social change? In later chapters, we delve into how differences in power among individuals, groups, nations, and global regions have come about historically and what trends we see for the future.

> ### Intercultural Praxis
> ### Communication and Power
>
> Intercultural praxis is a kind of exercise—both mental and embodied—to investigate and transform unequal relations of power embedded in our culture. Power can be conceptualized as a constraining and enabling force that regulates our culture and communication. Power may be physical (i.e., violence and coercion) or ideological (i.e., persuasion and representation). The concept of power implies that the world as we know it is not neutral or natural. Rather, the world as we know and understand it is constructed and regulated by people throughout history. Thus, intercultural communication both produces and reflects relations of power.
>
> The six ports of entry into intercultural praxis allow us to investigate the way our culture and communication are regulated and constrained by physical and ideological power. You may inquire who produces knowledge and regulates social relations, examine your position of privilege or disadvantage in relation to other cultural groups, and understand how your frame of reference is shaped by relations of power. At the same time, intercultural praxis is about using our power to enable more equitable and socially just relationships across different cultures by engaging in dialogue, reflecting, and taking informed, socially responsible action.

INTERCULTURAL COMMUNICATION IN THE CONTEXT OF GLOBALIZATION

As illustrated in the five scenarios, the context of globalization within which intercultural communication occurs is characterized by the following:

- An increasingly dynamic, mobile world facilitated by communication and transportation technologies, accompanied by an intensification of interaction and exchange among people, cultures, and cultural forms across geographic, cultural, and national boundaries

- A rapidly growing global interdependence socially, economically, politically, and environmentally, which leads to shared interests, needs, and resources together with greater tensions, contestations, and conflicts

- A magnification of inequities based on flows of capital, labor, and access to education and technology, as well as the increasing power of multinational corporations and global financial institutions

- A historical legacy of colonization, Western domination, and U.S. hegemony that continues to shape intercultural relations today

These characteristics of globalization point to the centrality of intercultural communication as a fundamental force shaping our current age. In face-to-face interactions, our differences across cultures in values, norms, verbal and nonverbal communication, as well as communication styles often lead to misunderstanding and misperceptions. Our assumptions and attitudes based on differences in physical appearance—socially constructed as racial, gender, class, and religious systems—frequently condition our responses and shape who we communicate with, build friendships and alliances with, in addition to who we avoid, exclude, and engage in conflict with. The increased exposure today through interpersonal and mediated communication to people who differ from ourselves deeply impacts how we make sense of, constitute, and negotiate our own identities as well as the identities of others. Additionally, histories of conflict among groups, structural inequities that are rooted in the past and exacerbated today, along with ideological differences frequently frame and inform our intercultural interactions.

Globalization refers to the complex web of forces and factors that have brought people, cultures, cultural products, and markets, as well as beliefs and practices, into increasingly greater proximity to and interrelationship with one another within inequitable relations of power. The word *globalization* is used here to address both the processes that contribute to and the conditions of living in a world where advances in technology have brought the world's people spatially and temporally closer together; where economic and political forces of advanced capitalism and neoliberalism have increased flows of products, services, and labor across national boundaries; and where cultural, economic, and political ideologies "travel" not only through overt public campaigns, but through mass media, consumer products, and global institutions, such as the WB, the IMF, and the WTO.

I recognize that globalization is an extremely complex concept and perhaps the ideas and vocabulary used here are new to you. For that reason, in the following pages, I start out by "deconstructing" the main forces and factors that contribute to globalization while addressing the consequences of globalization for people's lived experiences and for intercultural communication. As the book progresses, we explore together the multiple and layered meanings of the word and how globalization is understood differently by people and groups with different interests, positionalities, and standpoints.

While the term *globalization* came into common usage in the 1990s, the various factors or forces that constitute globalization have been in play for a much longer time. For the purpose of making sense of this rather unwieldy and highly contested concept, we examine three interrelated facets of globalization: (1) economic globalization, (2) political globalization, and (3) cultural globalization. Throughout the three sections that follow, the intercultural communication dimensions are highlighted and the interconnection among the three facets is noted.

INTERCULTURAL DIMENSIONS OF ECONOMIC GLOBALIZATION

In the Trans-Pacific Partnership scenario described at the beginning of the chapter, what intercultural challenges and benefits can you imagine when multicultural and multinational teams from Chile, Australia, and Malaysia engage in business,? Why have U.S. corporations established export production centers, or **maquiladoras,** in Mexico on the United States and Mexico border? When Korean corporations employ Guatemalan women as laborers and Korean women and men as managers, what intercultural communication issues arise? How do cultural differences in values, norms, and assumptions play out when Filipinas leave their homes and country out of economic necessity to work in the homes of middle- and upper-class families in Italy, Greece, or Japan as introduced in Scenario Five?

Global Business and Global Markets

Economic globalization—characterized by a growth in multinational corporations; an intensification of international trade and international flows of capital; and internationally interconnected webs of production, distribution, and consumption—has increased intercultural interaction and exchange exponentially. To get a sense of how you are situated within this web of economic globalization, think about your daily activities, the products and services you consume, and your future dreams. Your smartphone, for example, that wakes you every morning and connects you instantly to your world is constructed from components from around the world, likely containing raw materials mined in African and assembled in China under exploitative working conditions. Take a look at the labels on your clothes or shoes. Where does the raw material come from, where were the products made, and under what conditions? How far did the gasoline used to fuel your mode of transportation travel to reach you? How have your job prospects and wages changed since your parents' generation? When you dial customer service or answer a telemarketing call, what country does the person live in who is talking to you? Will you live and work in your country of origin? With whom will you work, and how will cultural differences impact your workplace?

By considering these questions, you begin to see how economic globalization has magnified the need for intercultural awareness, understanding, and training at all levels of business. Cultural differences in values, norms, and behaviors play a significant role in team building, decision making, job satisfaction, marketing and advertising, as well as many other aspects of doing business in the context of economic globalization. Some intercultural misunderstandings are rather humorous and others disturbing; however, they point to the difficulties of "translating" business practices, products, and markets across cultures. Take, for example, this popular Pepsi slogan: "Pepsi Brings You Back to Life." The slogan, translated into Chinese, reads, "Pepsi Brings Your Ancestors Back From the Grave." Umbro, a sports manufacturer firm from the United Kingdom had to withdraw its new trainers (sneakers) called the Zyklon. Receiving complaints from many individuals and organizations, the company realized zyklon was the name of the gas used by the Nazis to murder millions of Jews in concentration camps. The Chevy Nova, introduced into the Spanish market, didn't sell very well. In Spanish "No va" literally means "it doesn't go," which isn't very encouraging when buying a car.

As amusing and horrifying as intercultural mistakes can be, they are also often costly. Researcher and marketing expert at Sejong University in South Korea, Choe Yong-shik criticizes the use of "Konglish" in corporate slogans arguing that it damages the image of Korean companies. "The more they invest in marketing overseas, the worse their image may become," referring to the awkward use of Korean cultural values translated into English phrases (Kitae & Staines, 2005). Anticipating the intercultural challenge every multinational communicator must solve, former West German chancellor Willy Brandt stated, "If

I'm selling to you, I speak your language. If I'm buying, *dann müssen Sie Deutsch sprechen*" (as cited in Nurden, 1997, p. 39).

The examples direct our attention to the intercultural dimensions of economic global-ization. Languages are complex and nuanced repositories of culture. Languages, both verbal and nonverbal, convey meanings about the values, beliefs, and assumptions of a culture. Translation across cultures can lead to confusion, misunderstanding, and com-munication failures if the culture as a system of meaning, as discussed in Chapter 1, is not understood. The confluence and interplay of languages in the global context also leads to hybrid forms, such as *Konglish* and *Spanglish,* which challenge shared systems of mean-ings within cultures and introduce what may be viewed as "outside" and "undesirable" influences. The former West German chancellor's statement, "If I'm selling to you, I speak your language. If I'm buying, *then you must speak German,*" demonstrates how language and language use are intricately interwoven with relationships of power. The common reference to hybrid languages (*Konglish, Spanglish, Hinglish,* etc.) also points to the hege-mony of English as a global language, which, through the proliferation of the language, shapes perceptions, values, and perspectives globally.

As we have seen, advances in technology—both communication and transportation technology—have enabled the growth of multinational corporations, an increased global interconnection in the production of goods and services, and the distribution of products through global markets. What other forces combine with advances in technology to define economic globalization?

Free Trade and Economic Liberalization

Shifts in international economic policies since WWII and most markedly since the 1990s have dramatically increased the movement of capital (money), commodities (products), services, information, and labor (people) around the globe. A primary factor propelling these economic shifts is **economic liberalization**, also known as trade liberalization, or free trade. Broadly speaking, what this means to us today is that the movement of goods, labor, ser-vices, and capital is increasingly unrestricted by tariffs (taxes) and trade barriers. Historically, taxes and tariffs on foreign products and services were put in place by national governments to protect the jobs, prices, and industries of a nation-state. The countries we consider today as developed nations, or First World nations, used protectionist policies (taxation of foreign-made products and services) until they accumulated enough wealth to benefit from free trade. In fact, until the last 35 to 45 years, the United States opposed "free-trade" policies in an effort to protect U.S. jobs, products, and services (Stiglitz, 2002). What we see in the 1990s and 2000s, however, is the promotion and support of **free-trade agreements** by the United States and other First World nations, which liberalize trade by reducing trade tariffs and bar-riers transnationally while maintaining protection for some of their own industries. **Neolib-eralism** is an economic and political theory—a new kind of liberalism—promoting free trade, privatization of natural resources (water, natural gas, air) and institutions (education, health care, prisons, the military, and security), reliance on the individual and minimal gov-ernment intervention or support for social services. The use of the term "liberalism" is often confused with the term "liberal," which refers to people who support progressive reform. In fact, neoliberal policies and people who identify as "liberal" are most often at opposite ends of ideological spectrums in relation to political and economic policies.

As a result of neoliberalism, economic liberalization, and free trade along with advances in transportation and communication technologies, manufacturing sectors and more recently service sectors of the economy have moved offshore or outside the geographic boundaries of the corporate ownership's country of origin. In search of cheaper labor, few if any labor and environmental regulations, and tax breaks, U.S.-based multinational corporations, as well as corporations based in other First World nations, such as Europe, Australia, Canada, and Japan, have relocated their sites of production to Mexico, Central America, China, and countries in Asia. In addition, corporations in search of ways to expand their markets turn to populations in other countries. As a result, most all business transactions today have an intercultural component.

With the signing of the **North American Free Trade Agreement (NAFTA)** by Canada, Mexico, and the United States in January 1994, one of the boldest experiments in free trade or economic liberalization, which supports the free movement of goods, services, and capital without trade or tariff barriers, was put into play. Two decades after the experiment of NAFTA, first among many free-trade agreements, was initiated, the implications of its policies remain highly controversial and contested. As you can imagine, people with varying standpoints, positionalities, and interests have judged its success and/or failure differently. Communication about the free-trade agreement on corporate and governmental websites, in the news, in face-to-face interactions, and at protest sites differs greatly based on its impact on people's lives and livelihood. The Trans-Pacific Partnership, the proposed free-trade agreement among 11 Asian and Latin American countries and the United States, mentioned at the beginning of the chapter, is based on enlarging the scope of NAFTA. Proponents, primarily governments, the Chamber of Commerce, and multinational corporations insist on the necessity and success of free-trade agreements in raising standards of living, creating jobs, and stimulating the economy; opponents, including labor unions, workers and farmers, citizen watch groups, and environmentalists assert that NAFTA has caused massive job loss, economic instability, and displacement as well as increased involuntary migration and environmental degradation.

Clearly, economic globalization and the policies of free trade have dramatically accelerated the amount and intensity of intercultural communication. Individuals, families, institutions and businesses, as well as nations are increasingly interwoven into complex webs of intercultural relations. Using intercultural praxis, we can see how the economic context, the broader macro-frame, propels and shapes intercultural interactions among groups, visible through the meso-frame and among individuals, when we shift to the micro frame. It is also critical to underscore how different actors on the global stage—governments, multinational corporations, labor union representatives, farmers, and environmental and citizen rights groups—are positioned differently; thus, their experience, frame, and meaning-making about economic globalization is vastly different.

Global Financial Institutions and Popular Resistance

Occupy Wall Street (OWS) introduced in Scenario Four echoes the Alter-Globalization or Global Justice movement that came to the world's attention during the protests against the

WTO in Seattle, Washington, in November 1999, where over 40,000 people from around the globe, representing a wide variety of groups and interests, rallied together to challenge the decision-making power of the WTO. What is the WTO, and why would 40,000 people want to stop discussion of "free trade"? In 1995, the WTO was formed as a successor to the post–WWII General Agreement on Tariffs and Trade (GATT) as "the only international organization dealing with the global rules of trade between nations. Its main function is to ensure that trade flows as smoothly, predictably and freely as possible" (WTO, 2014). GATT (now the WTO), IMF, and the WB were set up immediately following WWII to maintain global economic stability and to address poverty through development. These three organizations are the primary institutions governing economic globalization.

Economic globalization, spearheaded by free-trade agreements that are often mandated by the IMF, financed by the WB, and negotiated and monitored by the WTO, certainly has led to increased intercultural business transactions and economic interdependence internationally. From a business perspective, individuals and companies must become effective in communicating interculturally in order to participate and compete in global markets. Multinational corporations are by nature composed of people from different national and cultural backgrounds who are accustomed to "doing business" differently, not to mention the range of languages, managerial styles, work ethics, negotiating styles, and marketing practices that are brought together in multinational and multicultural teams.

The integration of global markets within and across the First and Third Worlds offers some individuals and groups on both sides of the divide an opportunity to increase their wealth. However, economic globalization and the policies of neoliberalism have resulted in increased economic disparities between the wealthy and the poor not only globally, but within the United States and has magnified economic stratification based on race and gender (Lui, Robles, Leondar-Wright, Brewer, & Anderson, 2006; Stiglitz, 2012; also see Figure 2.3).

After this brief discussion, we see more clearly how economic globalization and neoliberalism intensify the need for intercultural communication as regions, groups, and nations are integrated—by choice or force—into global markets. Economic liberalization and free-trade agreements increase economic interdependence and propel migration around the world creating intercultural collaboration and conflict. We also see how economic globalization magnifies the gap between the wealthy and the poor exacerbating economic stratification in the United States based on race and gender. Accelerated economic integration, increased migration, and growing wealth disparities go hand in hand with political policies, political rhetoric, and political interests. As political and economic agendas coalesce and collide, people and cultures are deeply impacted. In the next section, the political dimensions of globalization are explored and the impact on intercultural communication is discussed.

INTERCULTURAL DIMENSIONS OF POLITICAL GLOBALIZATION

As we see an increase in economic interdependence and growing inequities in terms of control of wealth and resources, we also see a trend toward the interconnectedness of nation-state politics, the formation of bodies of global governance, as well as global movements resisting increasing inequities in political power. Political agendas of

Figure 2.3   Global Wealth Distribution by Population and Region

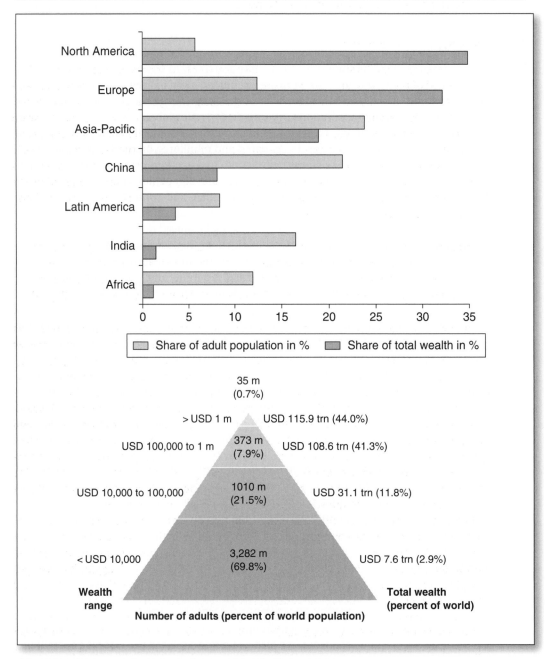

Source: Davies, Lluberas, & Shorrocks, *Credit Suisse Global Wealth Report 2014*

democratization, or at least, market-driven democratization, are closely linked to free-trade agreements and the agendas of the WTO, the WB, and the IMF. Thus, these global financial institutions also serve political purposes.

Democratization and Militarism

Since the fall of the Berlin Wall in 1989, the collapse of the former Soviet Union in 1990, and the end of the Cold War, there has been a widely held belief that democracy and capitalism go hand in hand to bring about both national and global prosperity and peace. Harvard political scientist Samuel Huntington (1993) documented a global trend toward democratization since WWII. While the concept and practice of democracy is contested, **democratization** in this case refers to the transition from an authoritarian to a democratic political system that ensures the universal right to vote. U.S. political economist Francis Fukuyama (1992) wrote what is considered a classic in democratization studies titled *The End of History and the Last Man,* which argues for the inevitable rise of *Western* liberal democracy in the post–Cold War era.

> What we may be witnessing is not just the end of the Cold War, or the passing of a particular period of post-war history, but the end of history as such: that is, the end point of mankind's ideological evolution and the universalization of Western liberal democracy as the final form of human government. (Fukuyama, 1992, p. 1)

In 1974, 39 of the world's 165 countries were democracies. By 1990, that number had risen to 76. By 2008, 121 of 193 countries or 62% were technically seen as democracies using popular sovereign elections as the sole criteria to define "democracy" (Biggs, 2008). While a correlation between free-market capitalism and democratic governance exists, research and experience also provide ample evidence that the two are in conflict with one another. True free-market capitalism inevitably results in inequitable distribution of wealth and resources, which is fundamentally undemocratic and tends to produce tension and unrest that destabilizes democracies (Biggs, 2008). The Occupy Wall Street movement that spread across the United States and to cities around the world brought to the world's attention the economic inequities between the very wealthy 1% and the rest of the 99%. The use of force and surveillance by the police and military to monitor and control social protest and activism calls into questions the very foundations of democracy.

In the context of globalization, advances in communication technologies, such as the Internet and social media sites, connect and mobilize protestors both within and across cultures. Occupy Wall Street was informed by popular resistance movements, such as the Arab Spring, a revolutionary wave of demonstrations and protests started in 2011. In Egypt, for example, "people-powered" nonviolent uprisings opposed the repressive authoritarian regime and demanded democratic reforms. Since the uprisings began, authoritarian regimes have been toppled in Tunisia, Egypt, Libya, and Yemen; civil wars have broken out in Syria and Bahrain; and unrest continues in Sudan, Gaza, Jordan, and elsewhere. As military and other totalitarian regimes assert and reassert power in these countries, the struggle for democracy continues. "People-powered" movements for social change represent a drive toward *Earth Democracy*, a

Flickr.com/South Bend Voice

Photo 2.1 People's Climate March 2014 in New York City

term coined by environmental social activist, Vandana Shiva (2012). **Earth Democracy** refers to democracy grounded in the needs of people and a sustainable, peaceful relationship with the planet as opposed to free-market democracy, which relies on wars against the Earth, natural resources, and against people. More than 400,000 people joined Vandana Shiva and other high-profile environmentalists in New York City for the People's Climate March in September 2014, a few days before the United Nations climate summit. People from diverse cultural, racial, class, and national backgrounds; from varied ideological positions; and from religious and scientific communities joined forces in major cities around the world to call for sustainable environmental policies and practices.

Ideological Wars

The attacks on 9/11 illustrate some of the shifting, contradictory, and contested political facets of globalization and the intercultural communication dimensions that have emerged. While it is not my intention to condone any form of violence for political or other purposes, it is useful to examine carefully the historical and political forces that led up to 9/11 and the dynamics that shape our post–9/11 world. In the 1980s, the United States was politically and militarily aligned with the founders of al-Qaeda (Arabic for the "base" or "foundation"), an organization composed of international independent cells who were credited with the 9/11 attacks. Called "freedom-fighters" by the United States for their resistance to the Soviet invasion and occupation of Afghanistan, al-Qaeda opposes U.S. military occupation of Arab nations (Cooley, 2002). From an international, geopolitical intercultural perspective, military force is increasingly used to address political conflicts and to maintain access to raw materials like oil, as demonstrated by the extended occupation of Afghanistan and Iraq in the name of the "War on Terror." The challenges of advancing Western-style democracy in the context of militarization and extended occupation played out in full force in Iraq. Even as various ethnic, religious, and secular factions drafted a constitution in 2005, the country wavered on the verge of civil war in 2007. In 2014, Iraq was again in crisis, plagued by religious and ethnic tensions, repression, violence, and genocide. ISIS (Islamic State in Iraq and Syria), also known as ISIL (Islamic State in Iraq and the Levant) and IS (Islamic State), is an offshoot of al-Qaeda Iraq, which was formed in 2006 from Iraqi military who were not allowed to serve under the new Iraq government when Saddam Hussein's military was disbanded. Later, in 2013, this group joined with a militant group from Syria.

Sebastian Gorka (2012), an asymmetrical warfare specialist and contributor to the book, *Fighting the Ideological War: Winning Strategies from Communism to Islamism*, argued that in the past ten years the U.S. military has been successful at diminishing the threat of al-Qaeda to inflict harm on the United States; yet, he claims that al-Qaeda's power really rests in the domain of ideological warfare. Syndicated columnist Charles Krauthammer states that the battle against ISIS is a "global ideological war" extending to many nations because of its roots in Islam, which is practiced by a billion people around the world. Krauthammer further argues that in identifying the threat, President Obama should use the word "Islamist" instead of the term "extremists" for the militant groups involved (Carruthers, 2014). President Obama, on the other hand, has focused primarily on diplomatic and military strategies to defeat Islamic insurgents and has called for the de-escalation and rejection of inflammatory anti-Islamic rhetoric. In an address to the United Nations in September 2014, President Obama called on the world to help defeat ISIS by embracing the peaceful teachings of Islam and rejecting the ideology of violence, destruction, and genocide. Directly addressing young Muslims, the President said, "You come from a great tradition that stands for education, not ignorance; innovation, not destruction; the dignity of life, not murder. Those who call you away from this path are betraying this tradition, not defending it . . ." (Jenkins, 2014).

Ideology is defined as a set of ideas and beliefs reflecting the needs and aspirations of individuals, groups, classes, or cultures that form the basis for political, economic, and other systems. Dominant ideologies include beliefs about gender, race, class, and religion as well as the economy, politics, and the environment. For example, dominant ideologies regarding neoliberal globalization characterize it as an opening of borders and an unfettered flow of people, goods, and ideas across national boundaries; yet, as evidenced by rising anti-immigrant rhetoric, claims that migrants threaten national unity, and calls for more restrictive immigration policies in Europe, Australia, the United States and elsewhere, "free" movement of people across borders is highly conditional and is directly related to political and economic power. The term, **ideological wars**, then, refers to clashes or conflicts between differing belief systems which are used to strategically advance certain interests.

Ideological wars frame issues in the public arena in ways that profoundly impact intercultural communication in people's everyday lives. Ideological battles often employ false dichotomies—requiring adherence to a belief in freedom versus adherence to Islam or immigrant rights versus national unity—to galvanize the public while obscuring the complexities and nuances of intercultural issues. Rhetoric that emerges from ideological wars often scapegoats one group—for example, Muslims or immigrants—for the challenges and ills of the world, or a society instilling and perpetuating prejudices and animosity as well as inciting violence among cultural groups.

Global Governance and Social Movements

One of the critical issues of globalization is the question of governance. Questions of governance on global, national, state, and local levels are closely linked to intercultural communication. Who is at the table, literally and figuratively, when decisions that affect people close by and in the far reaches of the world are made? Whose voices are represented, and whose interests are served? What standpoints and positionalities are silenced or dismissed? Whose language, political processes, and economic system dominate? Whose rules, behaviors, communication styles, values, and beliefs are privileged and normalized? Interestingly, in a time of increased "democratization," we see a magnification of the concentration of decision-making power in the hands of a few First World nations. As Stiglitz (2002) noted, most of the activity of the IMF and WB is in the developing world, while the control of the global financial institutions is in the hands of developed nations.

He argued that the current system run by the IMF, WB, and WTO is "one of taxation without representation" (p. 20). He also said it's a system that could be called:

> global governance without global government, one in which a few institutions—the World Bank, the IMF, the WTO—a few players—the finance, commerce, and trade ministries, closely linked to certain financial and commercial interests—dominate the scene, but in which many of those affected by their decisions are left almost voiceless. (p. 22)

Yet, individuals, groups, and organizations are coming together across national, ethnic, and cultural lines to form intercultural alliances that challenge the domination of global financial and political institutions and work together to create alternatives to racial, ethnic, and class discrimination and exploitation. Susan George (2004), author of *Another World Is Possible If . . .* , stated that people opposed to the policies and practices of the WTO, the IMF, and WB:

> refer to themselves collectively as the "social movement," the "citizens' movement," or the "global justice movement." In a pinch, if headline space is really at a premium, they'll settle for "alter-" or "counter-," as preferable to the inaccurate, even insulting, "anti-" globalization. The movement is not "anti," but internationalist and deeply engaged with the world as a whole and the fate of everyone who shares the planet. (p. ix)

In a speech delivered at Occupy Wall Street in October, 2011, award-winning journalist, author, and social critic Naomi Klein noted that while pundits on TV in the United States were baffled by the protests, citizen activists in Italy, Greece, Spain, Ireland and elsewhere welcomed U.S. participation in the global citizens' movement for social justice. Calling attention to the new normal of economic and ecological disasters, she states:

> We all know, or at least sense, that the world is upside down: We act as if there is no end to what is actually finite—fossil fuels and the atmospheric space to absorb their emissions. And we act as if there are strict and immovable limits to what is actually bountiful—the financial resources to build the kind of society we need.

> The task of our time is to turn this around: to challenge this false scarcity. To insist that we can afford to build a decent, inclusive society—while at the same time, respect the real limits to what the earth can take. (Klein, 2011)

Political globalization is complex and often contradictory. At this point, it is important to note that the forces of globalization have led to the spread of Western-style democracy, an increase in interethnic tension and violence as free-market economic policies combine with democratic processes of universal suffrage, an escalation in militarization as a form of conflict resolution and as a means for the imposition of democratic principles, and an increased concentration of power in the hands of international institutions of governance. While some argue that our current times are marked by an increased sense of alienation, powerlessness, and apathy toward political engagement, the wide range of participation in intercultural resistance movements, international labor organizations, and multicultural activism suggests otherwise.

INTERCULTURAL DIMENSIONS OF CULTURAL GLOBALIZATION

As people move around the globe—whether for tourism, work, or political asylum; in the military; in search of economic opportunity; or for survival—we carry our culture with us and make efforts, however elaborate or small, to re-create a sense of the familiar or a sense of "home." While the complex notion of culture cannot be reduced to objects that are tucked away in a suitcase or packed in a backpack, the things we take as we move, travel, or flee are significant in representing our culture, just as the languages we speak, the beliefs that we hold, and the practices we enact. In the following section, I introduce a few of the more salient aspects of **cultural globalization**, including migration and the formation of cultural connectivities, cultural flows within the context of unequal power relations, and the emergence of hybrid cultural forms and identities.

Migration and Cultural Connectivities

Due to the forces of globalization, people from different cultural backgrounds—ethnic/racial cultures, religious cultures, class cultures, national cultures, and regional cultures—find their lives, their livelihoods, and their lifestyles increasingly intertwined and overlapping. People from different backgrounds have been engaging with each other and experiencing intercultural contact for many millennia; however, the degree and intensity of interaction, the patterns and directions of movement, and the terms of engagement in the context of globalization are different than earlier eras of human interaction. All of this, as anthropologists Jonathan Xavier Inda and Renato Rosaldo (2001) claimed, points to "a world in motion. It is a world where cultural subjects and objects—that is, meaningful forms, such as capital, people, commodities, images, and ideas—have become unhinged from particular localities" (p. 11). They argued that culture, in the context of globalization, is **deterritorialized**, which means that cultural subjects (people) and cultural objects (film, food, traditions, and ideas) are uprooted from their "situatedness" in a particular physical, geographic location and **reterritorialized**, or relocated in new, multiple, and varied geographic spaces. Meanings of cultural forms, such as Hindi movies starring Shah Rukh Khan, or TV programs from the United States, such as *NCIS* or *Modern Family,* that are broadcast around the world take on different meanings in different locations. Similarly, a person's or group's sense of identity, who migrates from Iran to Israel to the United States, for example, is reinscribed in new and different cultural contexts, altering, fusing, and sometimes transforming that identity.

In previous times, when people moved voluntarily or forcibly to distant locations, they likely stayed there. While they may have had intermittent contact with home, they were unlikely to visit frequently or maintain regular communication as is possible today through the Internet, nor were they likely to consider several places in the world as "home." Today, due to advances in communication and transportation technology, we see the emergence of global

Kathryn Sorrells

Photo 2.2 What are the effects of the uneven distribution of cultural products globally?

circuits of cultural connection and community interconnection between multiple geographic locations crossing national and continental boundaries. Someone who migrates from Mexico, Central America, or Latin America to the United States may return regularly to work or visit. We also see the formation of economic and social networks or associations that operate internationally where communities of people from one location, for example, Mexico or South Korea, may unite to support each other in the new location and maintain ties and connections, sending financial support or **remittances** as a community to the city or regional community at home.

The reality of groups of people migrating to new locations and maintaining connections to "home" is not a new phenomenon. Take, for example, the notion of **diasporic communities**, groups of people who leave their homeland and who maintain a longing for—even if only in their imagination—a return to "home," such as the expulsion and dispersion of the Jews during the Babylonian Exile in 700 BCE, the African diaspora that forcibly uprooted and transplanted Africans to the Americas and the Caribbean during the period of British colonization, or the Armenian diaspora in the early part of the 20th century that resulted from the genocide of approximately 1.5 million Armenians. What is different today in the context of globalization is that communities are able to maintain transnational connections that are not only in the imagination, but where "home" can literally be in multiple places, where one's neighborhood may cross national boundaries, and where one's community is spread around the globe.

Cultural Flows and Unequal Power Relations

With Starbucks's 23,000 coffeehouses in 65 countries around the globe, McDonald's spread around the world, Coca-Cola ubiquitous in even the most remote areas, and Mickey Mouse the most internationally recognized figure, what are the implications for local and/or national cultures? Responses to global flows of culture and cultural products range from outraged efforts to protect local cultures to a full embrace of the "McDonaldization" of the world, yet what are the effects of the global flow of cultural products on local and national cultures? Is the flow of cultural products, such as music, films, food, and media evenly distributed with equitable, multidirectional movement? Most observers, even proponents of economic globalization, recognize an asymmetrical power relationship that magnifies inequities in the flow of culture and cultural forms. What are the implications of dramatically uneven distribution of culture and imbalanced diffusion of cultural products that are ideologically infused?

Some argue that globalization has brought about a homogenization, and specifically an **Americanization** of the world's cultures that need to be examined carefully not only from an economic point of view, but also from the perspective of U.S. dominance and cultural imperialism. **Cultural imperialism** is the domination of one culture over others through cultural forms, such as popular culture, media, and cultural products. Economic globalization has exacerbated an inequitable spread of U.S.-based corporations and cultural products that, while providing additional goods and services, also has led to the bankruptcy of local industries and has had a dramatic impact on local cultural values, traditions, norms, and practices. For example, in France, where the French language and cultural practices, such as finely prepared food and films are integrally linked to national cultural identity, there is active resistance to how U.S. popular culture, the English language and fast-food chains have invaded the physical and representational landscape of the country. Responding to a sense of loss of culture, political leaders pass laws intended to protect the distinctiveness of French culture (Crothers, 2013). In China, McDonald's is one of the most popular places to host children's birthday parties, which is particularly surprising since traditionally Chinese did not celebrate birthdays. Marketing that targets Chinese children, who are told they can make choices independent of their parents, also challenges and changes traditional cultural norms of parental authority. Grewal (2005) argued that in India, production and consumption of Barbie dressed in a sari (traditional Indian dress) advances notions of universal female subjectivity—what it means to be female in the world today—that is essentially bound to White American norms and values, and yet is "veiled" in Indian attire. The former prime minister of Canada Kim Campbell noted the following:

> For Americans, cultural industries are industries like any others. For Canadians, cultural industries are industries that, aside from their economic impact, create products that are fundamental to the survival of Canada as a society. The globalization of the world economy and communications has been a vehicle for the Americanization of the globe. For Canada and other countries, globalization has been a phenomenon within which their distinct, non-American cultures must struggle to survive. (Globalization 101.org, n.d.)

The "struggle to survive" for non-American cultures, and for many nondominant cultures within the United States, is an ongoing, daily contestation among local/national cultural industries, products, and identities and the overwhelming dominance of U.S. cultural products, cultural industries, and culturally produced identities in the world market today. The unequal diffusion of Western, specifically United States cultural products, identities, and ideologies and control of mass media can be seen as a form of cultural imperialism, where cultures outside the center of power (those outside the United States or those within who do not identify with the dominant mainstream culture) are saturated through market-driven globalization by American cultural ideals, and become, over time, increasingly "Americanized" and homogenized by and assimilated to American culture.

John Tomlinson (1999) argued that cultural imperialism in the context of globalization is a continuation of earlier forms of imperialism as evidenced in the colonization process of the 16th to 19th centuries and represents "an historical pattern of increasing global cultural hegemony" (p. 144). Cultural imperialism today can be understood as the domination of Western cultural forms—from music to architecture to food to clothing styles—Western norms and practices—from gender norms to dating practices to eating habits—and Western beliefs—from individualism to Western-style democracy to Western notions of "freedom" and human rights—around the globe.

As you can imagine, U.S. cultural imperialism, the Americanization of the world, and the notion that the cultures of the world are becoming homogenized—meaning that cultures, over time, will become the same—are hotly debated topics within the cultural dimensions of globalization. So, what do you think? How does this picture of the world mesh with your experience and understanding? Even those who fervently oppose the notion of homogenization recognize the tremendous impact U.S. popular culture and U.S. cultural industries have on cultures around the globe. However, they also suggest that the cultural imperialism approach is too one-sided, limiting, and simplistic. If the world's cultures are not becoming homogenized, and yet are deeply influenced by the distribution and dissemination of U.S./Western cultural products and ideologies, then what is going on?

Hybrid Cultural Forms and Identities

Without erasing the asymmetrical power relations and the dominance of U.S. and Western cultural forms, it is important to note the power, voice, and agency of those who are impacted by or are recipients of these dominant U.S. cultural products. Can we assume, for example, that similar meanings are derived from television shows, such as *The Big Bang Theory, House of Cards,* and *Breaking Bad,* when they are viewed by people in India, Costa Rica, and China, or in different cultural communities within the United States?

Inda and Rosaldo (2008) identified another important question to ask. Is the flow of culture and cultural products only from the West to the rest of the world, or is there movement in multiple directions? The international success of Indian superstar Shah Rukh Khan indicates that there are directions of flow and circuits of cultural influence impacting cultures around the world other than those originating from the United States. When we look closely at our lived experience in the context of globalization, we see that the overlap and intersection of cultures create **hybrid cultural forms**, or a mix that produces new and distinct forms, challenging the idea that there is only a unilateral dissemination of culture and cultural forms from the United States and Western cultures to the rest of the world.

Take, for example, reggaeton, a blend of rap and reggae with Latin influence and origins, which soared into popularity in the mid-2000s. After being nominated for a Latin Grammy in 2005, Daddy Yankee, the Puerto Rican reggaeton artist, said in an interview, "In the past year we didn't have a true genre that speaks for the Latino's. Right now we have that with the reggaeton" (Daddy Yankee Interview, n.d.). In his 2014 song "Palabras Con Sentido" (Spanish for "Words With Sense"), Daddy Yankee responded to criticism of reggaeton as social poison arguing that urban music saves lives and provides work. I am sure that you can think of other music forms that could be considered hybrid or fusion forms, such as jazz, rock, Raï—originating from Western Algeria with Arabic, French, and Spanish influence—or Kwaito, a fusion of U.S. house music and African rhythms popular in townships in South Africa.

Communication scholar Radha Hegde (2002) defined the creation of hybrid cultures and hybrid cultural forms as a type of resistance that nondominant groups employ out of fear of total assimilation and as a means of cultural maintenance in the midst of powerful dominant cultural forces. "Hybrid cultures, therefore, are not always a romantic return to the homeland; they are also cultures that develop and survive as forms of collective resistance" (p. 261). Throughout the book, we explore in greater detail how individuals, cultural groups, communities, and nations adapt to, resist, and negotiate their collective cultural identities, sense of cultural agency, and cultural productions within the context of U.S./Western cultural imperialism and the global forces of cultural homogenization.

SUMMARY

Do you have a clearer understanding of globalization at this point? As you can tell, it is an extremely complex phenomenon with multiple historical, cultural, political, and economic influences. In this chapter, globalization is defined as the complex web of forces and factors that have brought people, cultures, cultural products, and markets, as well as beliefs and practices into increasingly greater proximity to and interrelationship with one another. Globalization is characterized by an increasingly dynamic and mobile world that has led to an intensification of interaction and exchange among people, cultures, and cultural forms across geographic, cultural, and national boundaries. It has also resulted in a rapidly growing global interdependence, which translates into shared interests, needs, and resources, as well as greater tensions, contestations, and conflicts over resources. A magnification of inequities based on flows of capital, labor, and access to education and technology, as well as the increasing power of multinational corporations and global financial institutions, is a very real part of globalization. These forces and factors did not just develop independent of world history. Rather, globalization must be understood in relation to the **historical legacy of colonization**, Western domination, and U.S. hegemony that shapes intercultural relations today.

While it is somewhat artificial to divide globalization into economic, political, and cultural aspects, we can more easily highlight and understand the intercultural dimensions of globalization by this approach. As workplaces, communities, schools, and people's lives become more intricately interwoven in global webs, intercultural communication is increasingly present in all areas of our lives. To analyze, understand, and effectively act in intercultural situations, we need to be able to take broad macro-level perspectives as well as micro-level views. The purpose of this chapter was to introduce you to global dynamics that shape intercultural communication—the role of global governance systems like the WTO, IMF, and WB as well as the global resistant or "alter-globalization" movements; the processes of democratizing, militarization, and the ideological wars; as well as cultural imperialism and cultural hybridity—that influence who we interact with, frame our attitudes about and experiences of each other, and structure our intercultural interaction in relationships of power. Since intercultural communication is an embodied experience and most often an embodied experience of "difference," our next chapter focuses on understanding how and what our bodies communicate, how our bodies have been marked by difference historically, and how performances of the body communicate in the context of globalization.

KEY TERMS

World Trade Organization (WTO)
World Bank (WB)
International Monetary Fund (IMF)
First World
Second World
Third World
developing country/developed
   country
Global South/Global North
globalization
maquiladoras
economic globalization
economic liberalization
free-trade agreements
neoliberalism

North American Free Trade Agreement
   (NAFTA)
democratization
Earth Democracy
ideology
political globalization
cultural globalization
deterritorialized
reterritorialized
remittances
diasporic communities
Americanization
cultural imperialism
hybrid cultural forms
historical legacy of colonization

DISCUSSION QUESTIONS AND ACTIVITIES

Discussion Questions

1. Consider the scenarios at the beginning of the chapter. What themes are interwoven through all of the scenarios? Without erasing the obvious and more subtle differences between the situations, what common factors and forces shape the world that these scenarios describe? What intercultural communication issues are evident in the scenarios?

2. What is the relationship between colonialism and globalization? What are the similarities, and what are the differences? Using concrete examples, discuss how the legacy of colonialism impacts the process of globalization today.

3. How are economic, political, and cultural globalization interconnected? Using concrete examples from the chapter and/or your own observation/knowledge, discuss the relationships among economic, political, and cultural globalization.

4. Is globalization a process of Americanization and cultural homogenization? Or, does globalization produce hybrid culture forms and thus create cultural heterogeneity? What is your position on this debate? What does this debate tell us about the complex nature of globalization?

Activities

1. Historicizing Globalization—Group Activity

   a. The class is divided into three groups. The first group is assigned to research the history of economic globalization, the second group on political globalization, and the last group on cultural globalization.

   b. Each group should focus on three to five major historical events, time periods, key individuals, institutions, and so on, that shaped the course of globalization from economic, political, and cultural dimensions.

   c. Each group draws a historical timeline.

   d. Compare the three timelines, and examine how the three facets of globalization are interconnected with each other.

2. Spatializing Globalization—Group Activity

   a. In small groups, research the current global movement of people, circulation of information and products, political and economic partnership, international and regional conflicts, and so forth.

   b. Draw a map so that people can understand the dynamics of globalization visually.

   c. Once the global map is drawn to describe the macro picture of globalization, discuss the following questions:

      i. What are the patterns of movements you can see on the map?

      ii. What are the relationships of power you can read in the transnational movements of people and commodity shown on the map?

      iii. If you were to position yourself in the map of globalization, where would you find yourself geographically, economically, politically, and culturally?

      iv. How are the patterns of global movements reflected in the dynamics of intercultural communication at the interpersonal and local levels?

3. Research the IMF, WB, and WTO—Group Activity

   a. In small groups, conduct research on the three international organizations that are the powerful players of globalization.

   b. Report your findings to the class, and discuss how the roles and functions of international organizations shape the process of globalization today.

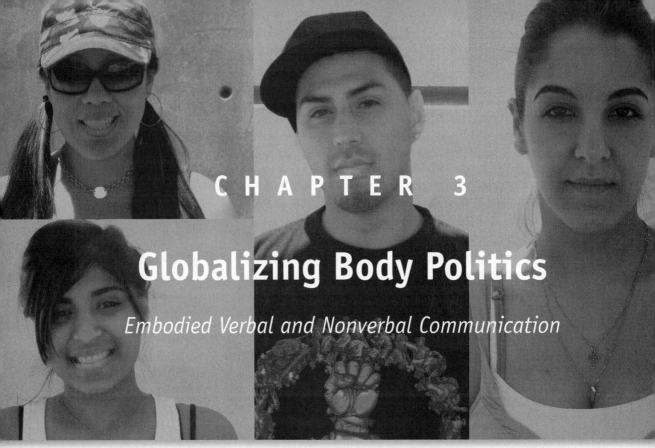

CHAPTER 3

Globalizing Body Politics

Embodied Verbal and Nonverbal Communication

Why are categories based on physical differences so important? What do differences communicate and why?

Learning Objectives

1. Describe how our physical bodies are sites where categories of social difference (race, gender, etc.) are marked and negotiated.

2. Explain how "race" is a social construct that was "invented" historically to serve economic and political ends.

3. Identify a process of "reading" body politics to reveal the social, economic, and political implications of the meanings we attach to "difference."

4. Explore how we, as intercultural communicators, can resist and transform socially constructed categories that maintain hierarchies of difference.

Intercultural communication is an embodied experience. Much of our knowledge and understanding, as well as many of our misconceptions, stereotypes, and prejudices about other cultures are exchanged through our physical bodies—in face-to-face interactions or through media images. Similarities and differences in language use, communication styles, and nonverbal communication, such as the use of space, gestures, eye contact, and clothes, are all conveyed and performed through our bodies. Both historically and today, categories used to distinguish "us" from "them" and to establish hierarchies of difference are often based on how our bodies appear to be similar to or different from others. Take a look at the photos at the beginning of the chapter. What comes to mind as you look at each picture? Did you consciously or unconsciously place each person into categories based on race, gender, or nationality? Why are these categories so important in our everyday lives and communication? What assumptions, relations of power, and histories of intercultural interaction underlie our processes of categorization?

From a very early age, we are taught implicitly and explicitly how to read, interpret, and assign meanings to our own and others' bodies based on our culturally informed codes. Skin color, hairstyles, facial features, and expressions, as well as gestures and clothing, all convey meanings within complex cultural systems of signification, shaping our thoughts, actions, and experiences. Our communication with others is inevitably mediated through our bodies. "Reading" and making sense of the body politics—in other words, how power is written and performed symbolically on and through the body—requires that we understand how socially constructed categories, such as race, gender, and culture have been encoded on our bodies historically, how these signification systems are linked to power, and how these categories are recoded in the context of global power structures (Butler, 1993; Foucault, 1978; Winant, 2001).

This chapter starts with our bodies as sites where categories of social difference are constructed. **Body politics,** as used here, refers to the practices and policies through which power is marked, regulated, and negotiated on and through the body. The concept of social construction and the semiotic approach to understanding difference provide a foundation for examining body politics. We look at how "difference" in terms of gender and race is marked and normalized on the body. We then examine the history of race, how racial hierarchies were "invented" and imposed on the body in the colonial context, and how these racial codes persist and have changed in the global context. Hip hop culture is introduced as a site where old racial regimes are contested and where alternative spaces for intercultural communication emerge in the context of globalization. Throughout, we point to the ways our everyday communication constructs, reinforces, and sometimes challenges categories of difference.

HIP HOP CULTURE

Yo! Whaz up? What does hip hop culture have to do with intercultural communication? Well, for one thing, hip hop culture is global. You can find hip hop culture around the world—from Japan to Israel, South Africa to Germany; from Chile to Iran, Honduras,

Australia, Pakistan, Senegal; and of course, from the urban to suburban and rural settings of the United States. It's a global phenomenon driven not only by corporate interests, commodification, and capitalism, but by unique values, norms, behaviors, and beliefs. Hip hop culture also has a complex language, nonverbal codes, and a history born of struggle, creative resistance, and contestation (Chang, 2005; Kitwana, 2003).

For those of you who are suspicious about calling hip hop a "culture," who think of hip hop as only a type of music and assume it is a passing "fad" or "phase" of youth culture; or perhaps you are so thoroughly disgusted by the violence, misogyny, and homophobia of some of the leading spokespeople and lyricists of hip hop, just hang on. Indeed, the intercultural space of hip hop culture is sometimes messy, sometimes oppressive and exploitative, and sometimes violent, just like the broader global culture, nations, cities, and neighborhoods we all live in. A key entry point into intercultural praxis is the ability to suspend judgment, be curious, and learn from what is different from our own culture, standpoint, or cultural viewpoint that challenges our position, life experience, or point of view. For some of you, this process is relatively easy because you already identify with and experience yourself as part of hip hop culture. For others, you may be curious and have some exposure to artists or various aspects of the culture. Yet, for others, it will be tremendously difficult to go beyond the stereotypes that you have formed and the assumptions and judgments you hold about hip hop culture. These positions regarding hip hop culture are not so different from attitudes people hold about national, racial, ethnic, and religious cultures. For now, engage in intercultural praxis. Stay open to thinking about the past, present, and future in ways that may challenge your assumed or received knowledge. We're going to "break it down" here—social constructs and the semiotic approach to difference—and get back to hip hop a little bit later.

CONSTRUCTING SOCIAL WORLDS THROUGH COMMUNICATION

A **social construct**, or a **social construction**, is an idea or phenomenon that has been "created," "invented" or "constructed" by people in a particular society or culture through communication. Social constructs exist only because people agree to act like and think like they exist and agree to follow certain conventions and rules associated with the construct (Berger & Luckman, 1966; Searle, 1995). For example, languages are social constructs. Languages are developed by the people who use them and carry meaning because the people who use them agree to the meanings and follow certain rules of the language. Money is another fairly easy example to understand. Think of a note or coin of any national currency—a yen, a peso, a deutschmark (which has been replaced by the euro), a dollar, a pound, or a yuan. The value and meaning of the currency is not in the note itself, but rather is constructed by people through their conventional social usage within an economic system that places value on the note as currency. Peter L. Berger and Thomas Luckmann (1966) introduced their sociological theory of knowledge in their book *The Social Construction of Reality.* The core idea of their theory is that human beings participate in the creation of our own realities. Our knowledge about ourselves, the world, and everyday reality is created through communication about our ongoing, dynamic social interactions. In other words, knowledge about the world does not exist "out there" in the external world waiting to be found or discovered. Rather, knowledge about ourselves and the world around us is created or constructed through our social interaction and communication with others.

Semiotic Approach to Difference

In the late 1800s, Swiss linguist Ferdinand de Saussure introduced an approach to understanding how things—objects, words, ideas, and actions—come to mean what they do. Saussure contributed the groundwork for the field of study called **semiotics**, or the study of the use of signs in cultures, which provides a useful way to understand how meaning is socially constructed. **Signs**—a stoplight, clothes, or more complicated social phenomenon, such as race—are composed of a signifier and signified. The body, things, actions, images, or words are understood as **signifiers** and what they represent—the idea or concept—as the **signified.** Saussure noted several key features about signs. First, the relationship between the signifier and signified is arbitrary. In a stoplight, for example, the fact that the red light means "stop" and the green light means "go" is arbitrary, right? These meanings have been assigned, fixed, and normalized by convention and use. Signs do not have permanent or essential meanings. Second, signs belong to systems, and their meaning comes from their relationship to other signs within the system. The red and green lights are part of a traffic control system, and their meaning—go or stop—is derived from their relationship to each other. Third, the meaning of signs is created through the marking of difference. What signifies or has meaning is the *difference* between green and red (Saussure, 1960). Cultural studies scholar Stuart Hall (1997a) summarized, "Meaning does not inhere *in* things, in the world. It is constructed, produced. It is a result of a signifying practice—a practice that produces meaning, that *makes thing mean*" (p. 24).

Therefore, in order to understand social constructs like race and gender, we have to examine how difference is marked and how meaning is associated with differences through communication within the racial signification system and the gender/sex system. To do this, we need to examine the historical construction of race and gender as signs as well as how the two systems intersect; study how different meanings have been associated with racial and gender categories through communication over time and place; and explore how preferred meanings regarding race and gender have been constructed, negotiated, contested, and changed. It is also imperative to look at how the preferred meanings of social constructs are linked to power; how groups who benefit from a preferred meaning and hegemony work hard to maintain these meanings; and how people and groups who are negatively impacted may work even harder to resist, challenge, and change the social construction of our realities (Barthes, 1972; Foucault, 1975; Hall, 1997a). One of the implications of analyzing signs and making apparent the social construction of reality is that if our perceived reality is created through social interaction and communication, we, as human beings, are powerful agents who can alter and change our worlds. Let's take a look at the body politics of gender and racial differences.

MARKING DIFFERENCE THROUGH COMMUNICATION

Gender Difference

Among other things, physical differences in human bodies are used to construct two mutually exclusive gender categories: (1) women and (2) men. A conversation with parents or grandparents, a quick review of films from 50 years ago, or engagement with different cultural groups informs us that what it means to be a woman or a man has changed throughout history and is different across cultural, racial, religious, and class groups. Sociologists Judith Lorber and Susan Farrell (1991) noted that biological differences are not what distinguish the categories of feminine and masculine. Rather, gender differences are constructed through communication and imposed on our bodies. The normative **social construction of gender** refers to the use of physical differences in human bodies to construct two mutually exclusive gender categories: (1) women/men and (2) femininity/masculinity.

Differences between masculinity and femininity are symbolically embodied, performed, and communicated within our specific cultural contexts through the way we walk; through our gestures, speech, touch, and eye contact patterns; through the way we use physical space and the gendered activities we participate in; through our hairstyles, clothing, the use of makeup or not; and through colors, smells, and adornments (Butler, 1990; Stewart, Cooper, & Stewart, 2003; Wood, 2005).

Within and across cultures, meanings are constructed and assigned through communication to these categories of difference—man/women, masculine/feminine—often as polar opposites or dichotomies of strong/weak, rational/emotional, and significant/insignificant. While the meanings have been "normalized" and "naturalized" historically, they have also been challenged, contested, and changed through communication over time. The notion of what it means to be a woman has changed and is challenged today in societies around the world as a result of women's and feminist social movements. The "reading" and "marking" of two gender categories based on physical differences is contested by **third gender** people and gender nonconforming people, who live across, between, or outside of the socially constructed two-gender system of categorization. Today, the field of transgender studies questions the normative links we make between the "sexually differentiated human body" and the gender norms to which bodies are expected to conform (Stryker & Whittle, 2006, p. 3). **Transgender** refers to people whose gender identities do not match their biological sex. This would be the case for a person born with a male body, but who identifies as female. Or someone born with a female body, but who identifies as male. The "trans" community is an umbrella term that includes a variety of identities, including *transvestites* or *cross-dressers* (someone changing their clothes and appearance at times to perform a sense of belonging to the other sex), *intersex people* (persons born with XXY or XYY chromosomes who may have nonnormative genitalia), and *transsexuals* (persons changing genitals to claim membership in the other sex) (Stryker & Whittle, 2006, p. 4). Others may express gender on a continuum, which means they embody a gender expression that disrupts the social norms and expectations associated with their biological sex, and are gender nonconforming. Misconception and stereotypes about transgender or gender nonconforming people abound today, including a common mistaken belief that transgender people have appeared recently on the human stage and only in modern or postmodern societies. Quite to the contrary, transgender and gender nonconforming people have existed historically and exist today in societies around the world, such as *hijras* in India and Pakistan, *fa'afafine* in Samoa, and two-spirits in indigenous North American cultures, to mention only a few.

"Normalized" meanings that construct the two-gender system and the differences between men and women reflect and embody relationships of power. Consider how the verbal and nonverbal communication of men and women—language use, who is speaking and who is silent, body positions, gestures, degrees of activity, and so on—in popular cultural forms, such as hip hop music videos, video games, and TV soap operas, constructs gender "difference." These gendered performances, where women generally embody subordinated power positions and men embody dominance, also structure and impact intercultural communication dynamics in the global context. Assumptions about feminine passivity, submissiveness, and subservience allow for and "normalize" the global exploitation of women in the workplace, sex trade, and "marriage" markets. When walking across a university campus in the United States, a Chinese woman who was a visiting scholar was stopped by a European American man. After chatting briefly, he said he wanted to marry an Asian woman because Asian women showed more respect toward men than American women. When she asked him what he meant by "respect," he responded, "You know, less assertive and more willing to do what you want."

Communication scholar Julia Wood (2005) noted that while biological differences between men and women exist, there are far more similarities between the two groups than there are differences. Why, then, do cultures around the world persist in marking and performing gender difference and constructing rigid divisions between the categories of men and women? Why are third-gender people so demonized and erased? What social, political, and economic purposes are served by constructing and performing differences between men and women and reinforcing a two-gender system? Lorber and Farrell (1991) stated the following:

> The reason for gender categories and the constant construction and reconstruction of differences between them is that gender is an integral part of any social group's structure of domination and subordination and division of labor in the family and the economy. (p. 2)

In societies where gender inequity exists (almost everywhere), women and their social, economic, and political roles are inevitably devalued. Gender inequity is closely related to patriarchal systems that normalize, elevate, and reward masculine perspectives, values, and behaviors. *Patriarchy* is a form of social organization where men are dominant and women are subordinated. Patriarchy is historical. Anthropological evidence suggests that hunter-gather societies were relatively egalitarian; however, as animals were domesticated, agriculture developed, and people settled approximately 5,000 to 6,000 years ago, male-dominated societies emerged, along with the attitudes, practices, and justifications of this social order. As people acquired the notion of private ownership of animals, tools, and crops, women and their progeny were increasingly regulated and controlled for the purpose of bloodline inheritance, labor, and reproductive capacities (Lerner, 1986). While this system has certainly altered in significant ways over thousands of years and across cultures, patriarchy as a structure that confers power and dominance to men is alive and well today. Who benefits from the gendered construction and performance of unequal power relations today? How does the body politics of rigidly constructing differences between men and women through communication exclude and erase third gender? The intercultural encounter between the Chinese scholar and the White American student that was just mentioned leads us to ask this question: How are the social categories of gender, sexuality, and race connected?

Racial Difference

Our bodies and the physical characteristics of our bodies, such as skin color, facial features, hair, and body type, have been used and are used today to separate people into categories that are customarily referred to as race or racial groups. Yet, the majority of scientists and social scientists today agree that race is a social construct (Cohen, 1998; Montagu, 1997). Evolutionary biologist Joseph L. Graves (2005) stated, "The traditional concept of race as a biological concept is a myth" (p. xxv). In other words, the categorization of people into groups based on physical characteristics has no biological basis; the association of physical, mental, emotional, or attitudinal qualities with these socially constructed groups also has no biological basis. Rather, science has been used to normalize, naturalize, and validate a system that was historically and socially constructed and that was and still is linked closely to power in today's global context. If you're thinking this is crazy and you know race exists because you can see it, you're not alone. Most college students in the United States, Graves (2005) reported, think that biological race exists.

There is no question that human differences are visible and physically embodied. Human beings differ in a wide variety of ways, including height, weight, eye color, and a preference for using the right or left hand, to mention only a few. Imagine if we grouped people into categories based on these physical differences and attributed innate characteristics to members of these groups. Tall people are smarter than short people. Brown-eyed people are more industrious than green-eyed people. Right-handers are better at sports than left-handers. It sounds absurd, right? Well, the concept of race as it operates today would sound equally absurd to us if it were not for the systematic construction of race and the reinforcement of racial hierarchies through laws, science, medicine, economics, education, literature, and forms of media for the past 500 years. While physical differences of all sorts do, of course, exist, it is the grouping or categorization of people based on these characteristics and the creation of racial hierarchies through the attribution of value-laden qualities (industrious, smart, athletic, lazy, violent, etc.) that is socially constructed through communication. Body politics examines how race and gender are socially constructed within historical, political, and economic contexts, resulting in social inequities that continue to impact us today in the context of globalization.

Intersectionality

Complex forms and degrees of exclusion and inclusion are created as race, gender, socioeconomic class, sexuality, and culture intersect. **Intersectionality**, introduced by feminist theorists (Collins, 1990; Crenshaw, 1989; Moraga, Anzaldúa, & Bambara, 1984), is an approach to understanding how socially constructed categories of difference—race, gender, class, and sexuality—operate in relationship to each other. These markers of difference do not function separately or independently in society, but rather interrelate and intersect with each other on multiple levels magnifying and complicating positions of disadvantage and privilege. Using the analytical tool of intersectionality, we see how systems of oppression—sexism, racism, classism, and discrimination based on sexuality—interlock to create distinct lived experiences and situated knowledge. For example, women may share some common experiences and similar understanding of the world based on their gender. Yet, the experience and knowledge of the world of women of color and White women likely differ in significant ways based on race. Differences in class and sexual orientation, in conjunction with race and gender, also shape experiences, identities, as well as degrees of discrimination and access. Thus, intersectionality is a means of analysis and empowerment aimed at addressing the intersection of multiple identities and the unique experiences, positionalities, and standpoints that are produced.

Cultural Identity
Intersection of Gender, Race, and Class

The intersection of race, class, gender, sexuality, and other socially constructed categories of difference shapes our cultural identities and impacts our access to employment, decent wages, and wealth. Sexism, racism, and classism, the historical legacy as well as current discriminatory practices and policies, result in continued economic disparities and social inequalities today. Consider the following facts:

- In 2013, among full-time, year-round workers, women were paid 78% of what men were paid.
- The gender pay gap impacts all women; yet, the intersection of race and gender means women of color experience the greatest shortfalls.
- Asian American women's earnings were 90% of White men's earnings.
- African American women's earnings were 64% of the amount White men earn.
- Latina and Hispanic women were paid only 54% of what White men were paid.
- A smaller gender pay gap (gap between women and men) among African Americans, Latinos/Hispanics and American Indians results only because men of color are paid substantially less than White men.
- The gender pay gap also increases with age. Women over 55 are paid significantly less than men of the same age.

These statistics clearly show how gender, race, class, and age intersect to shape people's social location, positionality, and experience in the United States today.

Source: American Association of University Women (2014).

THE SOCIAL CONSTRUCTION OF RACE: FROM COLONIZATION TO GLOBALIZATION

Race has been fundamental in global politics and culture for half a millennium. It continues to signify and structure social life not only experientially and locally, but national and globally. Race is present everywhere: it is evident in the distribution of resources and power, and in the desires and fears of individuals from Alberta to Zimbabwe. Race has shaped the modern economy and nation-state. It has permeated all available social identities, cultural forms, and systems of signification. Infinitely incarnated in institution and personality, etched on the human body, racial phenomena affect the thought, experience, and accomplishments of human individuals and collectives in many familiar ways, and in a host of unconscious patterns as well. (Winant, 2001, p. xv)

As with all social constructs, what "race" means and what it signifies have changed during different historic periods and across geographic areas of the world. Certainly groups of people throughout human existence have distinguished themselves from others based on a wide range of differences, including linguistic, regional, religious, and, in some cases, physical differences. Precursors also exist for the idea of a hierarchy of human beings that place one group in a position of superiority in relation to others as articulated by Plato's concept of the natural scale. Yet, the systematic categorization of people into a relatively small number of groups or "races" based on physical qualities and the ascription of qualities—intelligence, character, physical, as well as emotional and spiritual capacities—was not developed until the colonial era of the past 500 years (Todorov, 1984; Winant, 2001). How is it that into the 21st century a system of racial/cultural hierarchy still exists that assumes the natural or cultural superiority of people who are light-skinned or "White," and the inferiority or lack of

Photo 3.1 What is a diverse workforce? While people may appear "different," often everyone is expected to assimilate to dominant mainstream norms.

cultural development of people with darker skin? How is it that some nonverbal practices (e.g., giving a firm handshake, wearing a shirt and tie, and using direct eye contact) have come to signify "professionalism" and "the right way to do business" in the global workplace? As you read the following sections, consider how the body politics of race and racial superiority, rooted in colonization, are communicated and persist in the global era.

Inventing Race and Constructing the "Other"

Conquest, colonization, and the rise of capitalism were the terrain on which race, racial identities, and racial hierarchies were forged. As Europeans expanded their reach around the globe in the 15th to 19th centuries, intercultural contact on a scale previously unknown occurred. In these "encounters," any "differences" and most especially differences as they were marked or represented through the body were constructed as significant and were infused with meaning through a hierarchical racial system that justified and promoted domination and exploitation.

Undoubtedly, the physical bodies, as well as the cultural, linguistic, and nonverbal practices of people, were different, for example, when the indigenous peoples of the Americas came in contact with the Portuguese, Spanish, and British, and when Africans and Asians first came in contact with the Dutch, French, and Germans. However, the meanings that were given over time to these differences—in other words, what, how, and why these physical differences and communication practices came to signify what they did—are what we want to understand as we deconstruct race and racial hierarchies.

Just as the notion of "race" differs from place to place today—for example, a student is considered White in Costa Rica and a person of color in the United States—the process of inscribing the body with racial signification varied in different parts of the colonial world. The Spanish colonizers of the Americas, assisted by the Catholic Church, developed a highly complex hierarchical racial scale or system that linked "racial purity" with socioeconomic class—starting with the Spanish at the top and descending to Criollo, mestizo, castizo, mulatto, morisco, coyote, lobo, and so on. To maintain social order and control and to protect the economic and political interests and supremacy of the ruling Spanish "pure-blood" class, the signification system promoted "racial whitening" or *blanqueamiento*, a process by which racial mixing would produce lighter-skinned children and improve social status (Garcia Saiz, 1989). In North America, European Americans or Whites instituted the "one-drop" rule that legalized the racial signification system such that anyone with even one drop of non-White blood was not White (Lopez, 1996). In South Africa, a four-tiered "racial" system was constructed: Whites, Coloreds, Asians, and Blacks (Davis, 1991). While variation exists, what is the one aspect of the racial hierarchies that was consistent across continents and time?

Yes, the people primarily responsible for narrating the story, developing the discourse, and constructing the text about race—the colonizers, people of European descent—placed themselves at the top of the **racial hierarchy** and relegated the "Other," those designated as non-White, to lower and inferior positions in the hierarchy. The marking of difference establishes lines of inclusion within the group through the exclusion of others. Sociologist Howard Winant noted (2001) the following:

> "Othering" came not from national, but from supranational distinctions, nascent regional distinctions between Europe and the rest of the world, between "us" broadly conceived, and the non-Christian, "uncivilized," and soon enough non-white "others," whose subordination and subjugation was justified on numerous grounds—religious and philosophical as much as political and economic. (p. 22)

Constructing the "Other" is a process by which differences marked on or represented through the body are constructed as significant and are infused with meaning through a hierarchical racial system that justifies and promotes domination and exploitation. With variations across continents, these socially constructed racial systems were based on an advanced system of White supremacy. **White supremacy** is a historically based, institutionally perpetuated system of exploitation and oppression of continents, nations, and people of color by people and nations of European descent for the purpose of establishing and maintaining wealth, privilege, and power (Martinez, 1998).

In the 16th century, Las Casas, a Catholic priest from Spain, witnessing the atrocious treatment of indigenous peoples in the Americas at the hands of the colonizers initiated a serious debate regarding the native "Indians." The question of the day was as follows: Do Indians have souls? The discussion among the conquistadors, the Spanish Crown, and the Church represented a rigorous debate about whether Indians were humans or not. Could they be saved? Was it acceptable to work them to death and treat them like animals (Las Casas, 1542/1992; Todorov, 1984)? While the nature of this debate sounds archaic, we need to ask ourselves whose humanity—whose inclusion in the human species—is in question today?

Note that the **social construction of race** is not only a question of "difference," but the relationship between signs of difference in a system of power—body politics. The hierarchical relationship between the signs—bodies that are constructed as White or red, White or Black, civilized or uncivilized, Western or Other, for example—is where meaning is produced. Marking the body by "race" in the colonial era not only served to demarcate group membership—who was in the dominant group and who was "Other"—but also constructed a stratified labor system that justified and normalized the exploitation of laborers, which was integral to the development of capitalism during the colonial era (Macedo & Gounari, 2006; Winant, 2001). Racial differences came to mark and signify labor relations of owner/ slave. Slavery—the selling and purchasing of people as commodities—was the first global business on a grand scale, the prototype of multinational capitalism (Walvin, 1986).

The Power of Texts

By the end of the 1700s, Johann Friedrich Blumenbach, a German anatomist, physician, and anthropologist, extended Linnaeus's system of categorizing all living things by formulating a **hierarchy of difference**, a system of classification of people predicated on the socially constructed idea of superior and inferior races. Based on his analysis of human skulls, Blumenbach (1775/1969) divided the human species into five races as follows: (1) the Caucasians or White race (people of European descent) were placed at the top of the hierarchy; in the middle were (2) the Malay or the brown race (people of Malaysian descent), and (3) the Americans or the red race (people of the Americas); and at the bottom of the hierarchy were (4) the Mongolian or yellow race (people of Asian descent), and (5) the Ethiopian or Black race (people of African descent). The color-coded schema Blumenbach worked out reflected the White supremacist ideologies of his time and was instrumental in legitimizing, codifying, and promoting a system of domination. His "scientific" explanation resonated with popularly constructed beliefs and practices that justified and normalized inequitable social, political, and economic systems.

As European colonial explorers, priests, chroniclers, scientists, and anthropologists scrutinized, studied, labeled, named, and categorized the "Other," they created elaborate texts attesting to the inferiority of non-White groups while implicitly and explicitly inscribing their own White European superiority (Winant, 2001). The process that constructed the "Other" through religious, "scientific," scholarly, and popular texts, as well as through art, law, and philosophy, also created or constructed the colonizers (Said, 1978). As authors in control of the production of written texts in the colonial world, European colonizers and their descendants narrated, consolidated, and legitimized their versions of history, knowledge, and "truth." During the colonial era and well into the 20th century in many parts of the world, access to writing, reading, printing, publishing, and distributing texts or narratives was curtailed or severely limited for the majority of people who were not White. Considering who has control over the production of texts, whose version of history is authorized and preferred, and what perspectives, experiences, and stories are left out draws attention to **the power of texts** in constructing, maintaining, and legitimizing systems of inequity and domination. Control over and access to the production of "official" written texts structured, enforced, and reinforced inequitable relations of power. Yet, people from cultures and societies who were colonized did pass along their own histories and create versions of their stories in oral and written forms.

Communicative Dimensions
The Power of Texts

In *Exemplar of Liberty: Native America and the Evolution of Democracy*, Donald Grinde and Bruce Johansen (1991) illustrated how Native American societies, particularly the Iroquois, have influenced the development of American democracy, freedom, and political system since the late 18th century. The publication of their book resulted in heated debates among historians and scholars. Some welcomed this revision of history that shed light on the silenced histories of Native American people and their contribution to U.S. society. Others rejected the authors' thesis arguing that their use of "evidence" was inadequate.

The power of texts, evident in this controversy, is foundational to the way we understand history. The lives of people who are considered unimportant or periphery to the history of a nation are excluded from official historical records. Without documented records, critics who are invested in tracing American democracy to its European origin can easily dismiss alternative accounts.

The plight of Native Americans is not solely a tragedy of the past. Today, Native American tribes struggle and fight for economic independence and self-determination as the long history of contestation over federal control of their land, natural resources, and culture continues in the United States. On September 13, 2007, the General Assembly of the United Nations adopted the Declaration of Rights of Indigenous Peoples. A majority of member nation-states voted in favor of the Declaration, which delineates the right to indigenous self-determination, institutions, culture, and traditions as well as prohibits discrimination of approximately 370 million indigenous peoples around the world. The United States, along with Australia, Canada, and New Zealand were the only countries that voted against it. In 2010, President Obama reversed the decision of the previous administration becoming the last nation to endorse the Declaration.

While the Las Casas debate ended with the determination that the indigenous people of the Americas were, indeed, humans with souls, this "fact" was incorporated into the colonial project as a rationale to "civilize" and "save" them. Regardless of how indigenous peoples of the Americas were constructed, over 100 million died from genocide, exposure to disease,

Photo 3.2 Civil rights march on Washington, D.C., 1963

and the disruption of their sociocultural systems as a result of conquest (Smith, 2005). In *American Holocaust: Columbus and the Conquest of the New World,* David Stannard (1992) wrote, "The destruction of the Indians of the Americas was, far and away, the most massive act of genocide in the history of the world" (p. x). The devastating genocide of indigenous peoples of the Americas is one of many silenced histories. The phrase **silenced histories** refers to the hidden or absent accounts of history that are suppressed or omitted from official or mainstream versions of history. How can such conspicuous destruction, devastation, and genocide be hidden? Further, what is the impact of silenced histories on intercultural communication and sensitivity to various cultural experiences and perspectives today? Imagine, for example, if Germany celebrated its Holocaust with a "Hitler Day" as the United States does with Columbus Day? While the events of history cannot be reduced to stories, the way we receive and understand history is through stories codified into texts—or better stated, versions of stories that reveal and privilege certain perspectives while concealing others. Understanding how power operates to highlight and hide, reveal, and distort certain "truths" about history as well as current events is critical to intercultural communication. Lack of knowledge about the historical realities that have created current conditions of inequity perpetuates misunderstanding, stereotypes, and prejudices that fuel and reproduce social, economic, and political injustice.

RESIGNIFYING RACE IN THE CONTEXT OF GLOBALIZATION

Clearly, the social construction of race, racist ideology, and White supremacy has had a devastating and demoralizing impact on non-White people around the globe through genocide, exploitation, and sociocultural destruction.

Photo 3.3 Black Lives Matter, Ferguson, Missouri, 2014

Yet, powerful collective identities and social movements for liberation and justice emerged in the late 19th century and continue today to resist the systematic dehumanization, exploitation, and subordination of people of color through economic, political, and social means. The anti-colonial and anti-imperialist struggles of the peoples of Latin America since the 19th century, the anticolonial movements in Africa and Asia that culminated in independence from colonial rule in the middle part of the 20th century, the civil rights movement of the 1950s and 1960s in the United States, and the long-awaited dismantling of the apartheid system in South Africa in 1994 challenged the myth of race and the global ideology of White supremacy. Struggle and resistance to oppressive conditions forged collective race-based and nation-based identities for mobilization and empowerment. Anticolonial, national independence, and civil rights movements were monumental collective actions where colonized, oppressed, and disenfranchised people demanded the rights of democratic participation, self-governance, and self-determination around the globe (see Photo 3.2). These movements, coalescing in the post–WWII era, forced a major rupture in the world racial order (Winant, 2001). Race has been resignified in the context of globalization in complex, shifting, and contradictory ways (see Photo 3.3).

In the early 21st century, the notion of race as a biological concept has been scientifically debunked, yet race as it was constructed in the colonial era and marked on the body continues to have real consequences for people around the globe today. No biological or genetic difference exists between so-called "races" that determines intelligence, sexual appetite, reproduction, or athletic abilities. Yet, these common myths about race persist with weighty consequences (Graves, 2005). At the same time, claims circulate that we now live in a raceless or post-race society and have reached "the end of racism"; however, the body politics of stratification, discrimination, profiling, and exclusion based on racial categories persist in our society. Discourses of a color-blind society collide with representations of diversity that depict images of one person from each "racial" group. How can we make sense of these competing claims, discourses, and realities?

From Race to Culture: Constructing a Raceless, Color-Blind, Post-Race Society

David Theo Goldberg (2006) delineated two dominant ideologies that inform our understanding of race today. He argued that **racial naturalism**, or the claim that White people of European descent are "naturally" or biologically superior to non-White people, lingers today. However, in the post–WWII era, this ideology was challenged as a premodern relic from an earlier period and gave way in many parts of the world to racial historicism. **Racial historicism,** as a dominant ideology, shifts the focus from biological deficiencies to cultural ones, claiming the lack of "cultural development" or "progress" in non-White peoples and nations. In the worldwide pursuit of modernization, progress, and development, the rationale of racial historicism goes something like this: *Through education, the less advanced, less modern, and backward cultures are capable of developing civilizing behaviors, democratic values, and self-determination, which will, over time, allow them to be absorbed into society.*

Racial historicism insists on and constructs a "racelessness," "color-blind," or "post-race" society. How frequently we hear people say things like the following: I'm not racist. I don't see color. I'm color-blind. Racial historicism, where "race" is recoded as "culture," challenges the old racial signification system and at least on the surface, appears to go beyond race, leading to claims of "the end of racism." But, let's take a closer look. Read the italicized sentence (at the end of the previous paragraph) again. What are the underlying assumptions behind this statement? Who is the invisible narrator? Whose cultural (racial) standards are used to determine and judge this hierarchy of development? We know that the construction of "race" structured, justified, and normalized stratified and exploitative economic, social, and political conditions during the colonial era. What does the construction of "racelessness," and a "color-blind," "post-race" society do today?

Claims of a raceless, color-blind or post-race society erase or neutralize the centuries of historical injustice, exploitation, and asymmetrical relations of power that have produced current conditions of race-based inequity. The year 2013 was the 50th anniversary of the March on Washington for Jobs and Freedom, where Dr. Martin Luther King delivered his historic "I Have a Dream" speech in August of 1963. The work of challenging economic injustice and the racial economic divide that Dr. King devoted his life to remains unfinished. The average net worth of White families is more than six times higher than the average net worth of Black families, and 5.7 times greater than the average worth of Latino families. The Great Recession between 2007 and 2010 had an impact on all families in the United States. Yet, the average net worth of White families decreased by 6.7%, whereas Black families lost 27.1% of their average net worth, and Latino families lost 43%. As a result, Black and Latino families emerged from the Great Recession with much higher debt than White families. Authors of *The State of a Dream 2013: A Long Way From Home* state: "Our national history of racially discriminatory policies and practices created the racial wealth divide; current policy that ignores its existence perpetuates it and in some cases makes it worse" (Sullivan, Ali, de Alejo, Miller & Baena, 2013, p. 1).

The notion of racelessness also serves to mask the unmarked elevation of Whiteness—White norms and ways of thinking, knowing, being, and doing—as the standard for all (Goldberg, 2006). Whiteness is difficult to define because it is a default category, the category of the invisible narrator. Whiteness is a category that people who are White do not need to name given that it is the dominant norm. Part of the privilege of being White is the position to define, describe, and evaluate others based on a dominant White norm or standard that is invisibilized, a position of power that extends from the colonial era forward. Feminist sociologist Ruth Frankenberg (1993) outlined three interlocking dimensions of Whiteness: **Whiteness** is a location of structural advantage, a standpoint, and a set of core values, practices, and norms.

A location of structural advantage means that the systems in place within society—political, economic, and social systems that take on concrete forms in education, laws, law enforcement, medicine, employment, and many others—benefit or advantage people who are White. Of course, not all White people have equal advantage or privilege. Whiteness is mediated by class, gender, and sexuality among other things. Yet, the point is that the systems that are in place within U.S. society were constructed historically and continue to perpetuate advantage and privilege for the dominant White group today. Erasing or at least masking the existence of these privileges and advantages perpetuates the power conferred through locations of advantage.

The second dimension linked to locations of structural advantage that defines Whiteness is a particular standpoint from which to see the world and oneself. While great diversity exists within and across the group of people who are categorized as White, White people in the United States often espouse similar perspectives and are often blind to other perceptions. According to the Pew Research Center (2013), the U.S. public was sharply divided over the not guilty verdict in the 2013 trial in Florida of George Zimmerman for the fatal shooting of Black teen Trayvon Martin. Their research revealed that 49% of Whites were satisfied with the verdict, while 30% expressed dissatisfaction. This contrasts with an overwhelming 80 % of Blacks who were dissatisfied with the acquittal in the death of Martin and 5 % who were satisfied. Only 28 % of Whites said the case raised important issues about race and more than double that number, 60 % of Whites, said the issue of race was getting too much attention. How can we explain these differences in perspective? A standpoint informed by life experiences where the institutions in place—schools, police, courts, and media—treat you and those around you fairly, equitably, and justly constructs a very different standpoint from life experiences where these same institutions treat you and those around you unfairly, inequitably, and unjustly. The motto of the police "to protect and to serve" is understood and experienced quite differently for Whites than for Blacks (and other minorities) in the United States. Whiteness and the power it gives to the dominant group are maintained by not marking a particular standpoint that is linked to locations of structural advantage.

Intercultural Praxis
Positionality and Standpoint Theory

With the inauguration of President Obama in 2009, the first Black president of the United States, the media was saturated with post-racial sentiment. Electing a Black president was claimed as proof by some of the end of racism and the beginning of a "post-racial" society. Communication Studies scholar Mark Orbe (2011) conducted research with a diverse pool of over 300 participants from across the country to highlight different perceptions on the idea that Barack Obama's election has ushered in a post-racial era in the United States.

According to Orbe (2016), European American young people were most likely to describe President Obama's election as illustrative of a post-racial United States reflecting a dominant racial location where white privilege does not require critical attention to race. Underlying this perspective is the assumption that President Obama's election was the result of a color-blind approach to politics. On the other hand, African American participants resolutely refuted claims that President Obama's election was evidence of a post-racial United States. As standpoint theory indicates, this perception emerges from lived experiences informing a racial standpoint that is critical of hegemonic power. Incorporating intersectionality with standpoint theory, Orbe noted a third group, participants from diverse cultural backgrounds, who did not see President Obama's election as proof of a post-racial society, and yet did view his election as reflecting a society where racial differences are becoming less salient. Orbe's research provides insight into the complex ways in which inequitable relations of power inform perceptions and communication with others and how standpoint theory can increase intercultural awareness and understanding.

The third dimension of Whiteness outlined by Frankenberg is a set of core symbols, norms, and labels. Due to the location of structural advantage of Whites and White culture, many of these core values, behaviors, and symbols are hard to identify simply because they are seen and accepted as the norm—just the way things are. A strong adherence to individualism, an emphasis on doing and accomplishing tasks, and an orientation to thinking and to time that is linear are just a few of the core values associated with White American culture. These values are often seen by those who share and practice them as universal human values, as the "right way," or the "best way," and are used subtly as standards to measure other cultures. In this way, White American cultural norms are invisibly elevated to universal human norms and standards to which all should strive and by which all are judged. A position of structural advantage enables the dominant group, Whites in the United States, to label, generalize, and make claims about others while remaining in a position that is unnamed, individually unique, and outside of generalization and categorization. Delineating the concept of Whiteness is one step toward describing and disrupting a system that creates and sustains inequity. The three dimensions of Whiteness—(1) a location of structural advantage, (2) a standpoint, and (3) a set of core symbols and labels—interlock to invisibilize, mask, and normalize the maintenance and promotion of White American hegemony. The ways in which Whiteness and White hegemony function in the global context are discussed in depth in later chapters. It is critical to note that Whiteness can be practiced by non-White people and is not inevitably attached to White bodies. In a supposedly "raceless," "post-race" society, Whiteness is an ideological perspective or position to which people who are not White can and do ascribe. Whiteness is also an ideological perspective that people who are White can confront and attempt to change (Carrillo Rowe & Malhotra, 2006).

From Race to Class: Rearticulating Race in the Neoliberal Context

We often hear comments like this: "Race doesn't matter anymore. All that matters is money." In societies like the United States that are ideologically constructed as raceless, post-race, and color-blind, race is rearticulated in the neoliberal context in terms of class. In other words, it's all about the color of money! Yet Goldberg (2006) argued that there is an invisibilized process of Whitening that is required as people of color rise to the middle and upper classes. Membership in these classes is predicated on assimilation and allegiance to Whiteness. People of color who accept these conditions benefit from the privileges and advantages of Whiteness, often espouse standpoints that support Whiteness, and associate with values, practices, and norms of the dominant White culture. We might understand this as modern or postmodern "cultural whitening" based on accepting, performing, and supporting the dominant White culture. The "absorption" into society is complete as people of color achieve highly visible positions of power in the government, military, on the Supreme Court, and in multinational corporations, serving, in rather contradictory ways as icons for diversity in a raceless, post-race society.

Yet, class does not provide complete protection against racism, sexism, and other forms of exclusion, even in, or perhaps especially in a supposedly raceless, post-race society. Using intersectionality, we see how class status interlocks with gender, race, ethnicity as well as sexual orientation to create distinct lived experiences and situated knowledge. For example, while an individual may be advantaged by class status, he or she also may be targeted based on race, or ethnicity, or sexual orientation. Socioeconomic class assists, limits, and denies access to everything from basic human needs of food, water, safety, and housing to health care, education, and property ownership, to the ability to accumulate luxury items and wealth. But, class alone does not determine access.

In the context of globalization, resignifying "race" as "culture" allows for the invention of a raceless, post-race, and color-blind society that masks how race, as it is written on the body, persists as a marker for social, economic, and political stratification. It also invisibilizes Whiteness as the universal standard and norm. Rearticulating "race" as "class" in the global context hides the way that race and gender intersect with class and how the intersectionality of these social categories continues to structure the lives, material conditions, and access to opportunities of people around the world today. In an article titled "Of Race and Risk," Patricia J. Williams (2004) recounted her experience of buying a house. After talking with a mortgage broker on the phone, she was quoted a mortgage interest rate. When she received the forms, she saw that the racial category of White was marked and that the broker must have assumed, apparently based on her use of Received Standard English, that she was White. When she changed it to Black and returned the form, suddenly the bank wanted more money, more points, and a higher interest rate. In her negotiations to contest this outcome, the justification used by the bank was that she represented a financial "risk." Patricia Williams was made aware through this process that she, as a Black

Figure 3.1   How does race intersect with income to create disproportionate disadvantages?

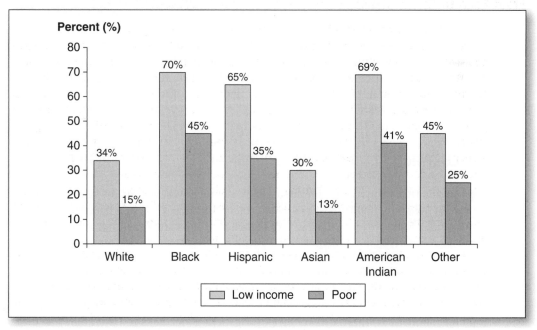

Source: Yang, M., Ekono, M. & Skinner, C. (2014)

Courtesy of Kathryn Sorrells

Photo 3.4 Hip hop culture offers an alternative to the existing racial order

woman, *is* the "risk," not because of her financial ability to follow through with the loan (that had not changed when she shifted from White to Black). Rather, she is the risk as her home ownership as a Black woman in the neighborhood diminishes the value of the property owned by White residents. Historically, when a Black person or family moves in, Whites flee and take funding and social resources with them. Race, in an ideologically constructed "raceless" society, is rearticulated as "financial risk," masking through economic language a body politics that perpetuates racism, and hiding a system that sustains Whiteness.

Intercultural interactions in the context of globalization are deeply embedded in the legacy of colonization, intersecting systems of oppression, and inequitable relations of power. Yet, struggles against racism and White supremacy also continue. While mass media representations draw attention to and exacerbate the violent, criminal, and destructive aspects of hip hop culture, many people around the world experience hip hop culture as offering possibilities for disrupting the hegemonic racial order and providing spaces for new forms of coalition building across racial lines. We turn now to the contested cultural space of hip hop culture.

HIP HOP CULTURE: ALTERNATIVE PERFORMANCES OF DIFFERENCE

Meet Darren Dickerson, who identifies as Black (not pictured); Sun Yu Young, who is Korean American (left); Jani (Janithri) Gunaesekera (second from left), whose parents immigrated to the United States from Sri Lanka; Izzy (Israel) Pereź (second from right), whose mother is Mexican American and father is Puerto Rican American; and Sheh (Venoosheh) Khaksar (right), who identifies as Iranian American. These folks were presented at the beginning of the chapter (see chapter opening photo). Each one of them acknowledges that the gender and racial codes marked, performed, and constructed on and through their bodies impact their lives every day. Each also identifies as being part of hip hop culture and experiences hip hop culture as an alternative to the existing racial order. Let's see what they had to say when asked this question: What does hip hop culture mean to you?

Darren Dickerson: I was born into hip hop culture. I am hip hop culture. Hip hop culture is speaking out and expressing what's real. The values of hip hop culture? Honesty, truth, respect, courage, and credibility. Hip hop culture comes out of a history of struggle, a history of having been denied and forgotten. It's fundamentally about the struggle—the struggle against powerful forces that have marginalized all sorts of people. But, at the end of the day, it's about keeping it real.

Sun Yu Young: Hip hop to me isn't just a genre of music. It truly is an entire culture in every sense of the word, with its own individual language, music, fashion, and most important, history. I don't just "listen" to hip hop—I feel like I really live it. I also don't consider myself just a casual listener. I'm pretty good about knowing about and enjoying an artist's or producer's entire body of work, not just the songs that are released on the radio. Sometimes I think that my life is like one huge soundtrack—hip hop culture has truly influenced every aspect of my life. I don't think I would be the same person I am today without it. It's helped me understand different viewpoints and cultures other than my own, and it's helped me come together with people of different cultures, solely based on the fact that we both are a part of hip hop culture. So, answering the question "what hip hop means to me," I guess can be summed up in a word: life.

Jani (Janithri) Gunaesekera: Since I am Sri Lankan, it is very hard for me to identify with a certain group. I want to say I can relate to the American side of me, but sometimes I feel it is limited. Then when I try to relate to my Sri Lankan side, I feel there is a big gap. When I was introduced to hip hop, I felt there was finally something that doesn't see me as a race or ethnicity. I felt like it took me in and gave me an identity that I could deal with . . . being different and not having a certain group to be part of was hard.

Izzy (Israel) Pereź: Hip hop culture is so many things—like all cultures it's pretty hard to define. Hip hop brings people together—some who normally wouldn't get along can share a common interest. It connects people from all over the globe. Because it's different every place, you can learn about different experiences from others—it's a collaboration and expression from all over the world. But, then there's the whole masculine side of hip hop with the "beefs" and rivalries. The whole point is to emasculate the other person, character assassination, "dis" and embarrass the other person. A lot of this is about setting the record straight about false accusations. It's also pretty homophobic. But, what so many people can relate to is that it's about constant struggle, the ability to rise up, and overcome. It creates solidarity between people and groups who can relate—the poor, immigrants, and other struggling people.

Sheh (Venoosheh) Khaksar: As an Iranian, it wasn't easy being different growing up in a small town in Washington—I call it Pleasantville. An Asian American girl and a few Hispanic students and I were the only ones who were not like the rest. When I first heard Tupac, I thought, yeah, he's saying something to me and about me. He's talking about things I feel and putting them into words—expressing them so well. He's talking about the experience of minorities. It may not be exactly what I experienced, but I can relate. Hip hop culture is about struggle and overcoming obstacles. Hip hop is the voice of a people—a voice that speaks in various ways.

As you can see from these statements, hip hop culture clearly offers an alternative to the old racial signification system. The folks here do not seem to buy into the myth of a race-less society. They see and experience race as it is written on their bodies every day. Yet, in the context of a racialized society, they experience hip hop as a cultural space where, as Darren says, people can speak out and "struggle against powerful forces that have marginalized all sorts of people." Darren and Sheh see hip hop as the voice of the people—people who have been forgotten, disenfranchised, and oppressed by interlocking systems of exclusion based on race, class, and gender. Izzy notes that hip hop culture is fundamentally about "the ability to rise up and overcome" the challenges and obstacles that people face. Hip hop culture is a site where meanings about race, class, gender, sexuality, love, hate, violence, history, the government, family, and many other things are challenged, negotiated, and transformed. Hip hop tells the stories of resistance and resilience—stories of how people live their lives and how they challenge and survive powerful forces that work to silence their voices and diminish their lives. In 1989, Public Enemy's Chuck D said, "Rap is the Black CNN," offering an alternative interpretation of current events as well as history. Jay Woodson (2006) from Z-Net noted that "hip hop articulated something so universal and revelatory that White kids wanted (to listen) in. Some even began to question the skin privilege into which they had been born."

Sun finds that hip hop culture is a place where racial hierarchies break down and connection and coalition across socially constructed lines of race are made possible to provide a source of learning and pleasure, as well as political and economic empowerment. Hip hop culture offers hope for coalition-building across historically divided and stratified groups. In rural Washington, Sheh discovered that hip hop spoke to and about her and offered her a place of connection and identification. Jani articulates the ways in which she is caught between various racial and ethnic identifications—American and Sri Lankan—not feeling like she fits in either. For her, hip hop culture is a site where colonial constructions of race and racial hierarchies are contested and new body politics based on inclusion rather than exclusion are created. Jani states, "Hip hop did something to me that made me feel like it was okay to be different and that no matter what race I was I could be part of that world." Darren argues, "That's why so many people around the world connect with it—it's about creating a new system, an alternative system." Bakari Kitwana (2005), former editor of *The Source* and author of several books, agrees that hip hop culture has the potential to challenge and disrupt the old racial politics. As a powerful tool for social, economic, and political change, hip hop is doing just that. He stated the following:

> As young people worldwide gravitate to hip-hop and adapt it to their local needs, responding to the crises of our time, they are becoming equipped with a culture that corporate and political elites can't control. It's a youth-centered culture that is self-motivating and only requires its participants to have a mouth, the ability to listen and frustration with business as usual. This cultural movement is currently making way for hip-hop's emerging political movement. Given the way the culture is being absorbed by young people around the globe, these movements may be the catalysts necessary to jump-start an international human rights movement in this generation, a movement with the potential to parallel if not surpass yesterday's civil rights successes. (pp. 10–11)

The goal here is not to uncritically valorize hip hop culture. As Izzy noted, hip hop culture is troubled by a hypermasculinity that often denigrates, objectifies, and violates women, sexual minorities, and men. Hip hop culture often idealizes and glamorizes violence, drugs, and rampant consumerism. Aspects of the culture play off of and reinforce centuries-old racial stereotypes, promoting deeply ingrained patterns of domination and subordination. In these ways, hip hop culture reflects, normalizes, and advances the racist, patriarchal, homophobic, and capitalist ideologies of our larger society. Tricia Rose (1994) stated that hip hop "brings together a tangle of some of the most complex, social, cultural, and political issues in contemporary American society" (p. 2). So the point here is not to gloss over the difficult, ugly, controversial, or contested nature of hip hop culture. After all, at the core, hip hop culture is about keeping it real. Intercultural communication in the context of globalization situates us in the midst of complex and messy tensions. We need to learn how to hold contradictions and address the muddled, chaotic, and difficult challenges that arise in the nexus of oppositional realities. For example, we need to see how hip hop culture is *both* a site of inclusion across racial and cultural groups *and* a site where exclusion based on gender and sexuality occurs. Hip hop is *both* a space of empowerment *and* a space where oppressive and exploitative conditions are enacted and performed. Taking a **both/and approach** guards against essentializing, stereotyping, and enacting closure and allows us to step into rather than away from the complex, confusing, and untidy terrain of intercultural communication today.

SUMMARY

Our goal in this chapter was to introduce the process and practice of "reading" body politics in the age of globalization. We began with the assumption that intercultural communication is an embodied experience. Since our engagement with others is through our bodies, we looked at how differences are marked on the body—how our bodies are signs that communicate—in the socially constructed systems of race, gender, and class that impact global and local intercultural interactions. We provided an overview of the historical construction of race to show how social constructs are linked to power—social, political, and economic power. Since social constructs are invented, used, and institutionalized by people through communication, they can and have changed over time, yet we note how the preferred meanings of deeply engrained signification systems that benefit those in power are difficult to disrupt and change. The social constructions of race and racial hierarchies through communication, which are linked historically to colonization, capitalism, and national/regional identities, have been resignified in the global context. In a supposedly raceless society, race is rearticulated as culture and class; however, in these barely masked forms, race as it intersects with class, gender, and culture continues to impact the lives of people around the globe today. As we take on the project of analyzing our intercultural encounters and understanding the global context of intercultural relations, the semiotic approach and the concept of intersectionality are useful tools for critical analysis. Voices and visions born out of hip hop culture suggest that alternative spaces exist that resist and transform the old, colonial regime of racial naturalism and the more recently constructed racial regime of a raceless society. Yet, hip hop culture also points to the complex and contradictory nature of intercultural communication today where sites that resist and contest hierarchies of difference can also reinscribe and reproduce racism, sexism, classism, and homophobia.

KEY TERMS

body politics

social construction of gender

third gender

transgender

social construct

social construction

semiotics

signs

signifiers

signified

patriarchy

racial hierarchy

constructing the "Other"

White supremacy

social construction of race

hierarchy of difference

the power of texts

silenced histories

racial naturalism

racial historicism

Whiteness

intersectionality

both/and approach

DISCUSSION QUESTIONS AND ACTIVITIES

Discussion Questions

1. What are some examples of "body politics" based on this chapter and your life experiences? How are race and gender used to negotiate social relations of power throughout history?

2. How is your body a site where your identity, in terms of race, gender, sexuality, and so on, is constructed and communicated? In what ways do you negotiate your identities through bodily expressions and performance?

3. Why is there a rigid binary gender system? Why are gender and sexual identities outside of normative heterosexuality demonized and/or erased from mainstream society?

4. How would you describe your intersectional identities? How does the notion of intersectionality help you understand your positionality and standpoint and that of others?

5. What does it mean when we say that race is a social construct? Aren't our skin color, hair texture, and facial features all biological? How is the discourse of biology used to justify racial stereotypes, prejudices, and inequalities?

6. Why is a color-blind ideology problematic? Why can't we ignore "color" and create a raceless society?

7. How does Whiteness function as a location of structural advantage? What is your relationship to Whiteness? How does Whiteness operate in different cultures and countries through the process of globalization?

Activities

1. "Reading" Body Politics

    a. Find visual images of the body (photographs, advertisements, paintings, movie posters, etc.).

    b. Address the following questions using the semiotic approach:

        i. In the particular visual image of the body, what signifiers can you identify? Pay close attention to gesture, eye contact, posture, clothing, physical type, size, colors, and so forth.

        ii. What do the signifiers mean? In other words, what is signified?

        iii. How are racial and gender differences constructed on and through the body?

        iv. How is "hierarchy of difference" constructed through the visual image?

2. Unpacking the Everyday Performance of Race and Gender—Group Activity

    a. Think about specific examples in which you perform your race and gender in everyday practices, consciously or unconsciously.

    b. Enact the performance in front of the class.

    c. Now think about specific examples in which you violate the expected norms of gender/race performances.

    d. Enact the performance in front of the class.

    e. After the performance from each group, discuss the following questions:

        i. How does it feel to enact your everyday performance of race and gender?

        ii. How does it feel to violate the norms of race/gender performance?

        iii. What happens when you violate the norms of gender/race performance?

        iv. How does the body communicate? How does the body set the context for intercultural encounter?

3. Unpacking Whiteness—Group Activity

    a. Whiteness is defined as "a location of structural advantage, a standpoint and a set of core values, practices and norms in which White ways of thinking, knowing, being and doing are normalized as the standard."

    b. Write down a scenario in which Whiteness may manifest in intercultural communication.

    c. Enact the scenario in front of the class.

    d. Address the following questions:

        i. How does Whiteness shape intercultural interactions?

        ii. Can people of color enact Whiteness?

        iii. Can we disengage from and challenge Whiteness?

CHAPTER 4

(Dis)Placing Culture and Cultural Space

Locations of Nonverbal and Verbal Communication

Hybrid cultural space in Shanghai, China

Learning Objectives

1. Describe the relationships among culture, place, cultural space, and identity in the context of globalization.

2. Explain how people use communicative practices to construct, maintain, negotiate, and hybridize cultural spaces.

3. Explain how cultures are simultaneously placed and displaced in the global context leading to segregated, contested, and hybrid cultural spaces.

4. Describe the practice of bifocal vision to highlight the linkages between "here" and "there," as well as the connections between present and past.

T ake a look around yourself. Notice the place where you are and the space that surrounds you. Perhaps you are in your dorm room, apartment, home, or office. How is this space "cultural" space? How is the use and organization of space, the objects or artifacts that fill the space, and the verbal and nonverbal language used in this space cultural? Is there a sense of gender, ethnic, racial, national, and/or religious identity communicated? Now consider the neighborhood you live in, where you shop, consume food and entertainment, and meet with friends. Can you identify cultural dimensions of these spaces? Don't forget that places and spaces you may see as "normal," "just the way things are," or even "lacking in culture"—a shopping mall or your school campus, for example—are, in fact, products of culture. While spaces of nondominant groups are often marked as "cultural," those unmarked spaces in the United States that are constructed and shaped by the dominant European American or White culture are also cultural. As you imagine moving in a broader circle from where you are to your neighborhood, then to your geographic region, to the nation, and then across national boundaries, do you experience a layering, intersection, or friction between different cultural spaces?

Expanding on the previous chapter, we now move outward from the body to explore and "read" the cultural and intercultural communication dimensions of place, space, and location. In this chapter, we examine how cultures are simultaneously placed and displaced, inevitably located in specific places, and yet dislocated from their sites of origin in the context of globalization. Since the early 1990s, the confluence of forces that shape the terrain of globalization has dramatically accelerated the displacement and replacement of people, cultures, and cultural spaces. Given this displacement and fragmentation of cultures, we investigate how human beings use communicative practices to construct, maintain, negotiate, reconstruct, and hybridize cultural spaces. Penetration, disruption, and mixing of cultural spaces have occurred on a worldwide scale since the European colonial era. Understanding globalization as a legacy of colonization allows us to recognize how cultural spaces experienced today—segregated, contested, and hybrid cultural spaces—sustain historically forged relations of unequal power. Yet, these cultural spaces are also sites where Western hegemony is negotiated, challenged, and changed. Building on the case study introduced in the previous chapter, hip hop culture is used to illustrate the cultural and intercultural dimensions of place, space, and location in the context of globalization.

PLACING CULTURE AND CULTURAL SPACE

Historically, notions of culture have been closely bound to place, geographic location, and the creation of collective and shared cultural spaces. The traditional anthropological definition of culture, as noted in Chapter 1, implies that cultures are bounded entities that are grounded in place, which allows for shared meanings to develop and be passed along. Based on this definition, a reciprocal relationship exists between culture and place. To understand place is to understand culture and vice versa. Introducing an anthology of essays by anthropologists called *Senses of Place,* philosopher Edward S. Casey (1996) argued the following:

> Given that culture manifestly exists, it must exist somewhere, and it exists more concretely and completely in places than in minds or signs. The very word *culture* meant "place tilled" in Middle English, and the same word goes back to Latin *colere,* "to inhabit, care for, till, worship." To be cultural, to have a culture, is to inhabit a place sufficiently intensely to cultivate it—to be responsible for it, to respond to it, to attend to it caringly. Where else but in particular places can culture take root? (pp. 33–34)

Cultural practices, norms, behaviors, and values, then, have historically been understood as emerging from and being defined by ongoing interactions among people who are situated in specific locations, and through shared interaction, construct cultural spaces. Yet today, culture and cultural spaces have been deterritorialized, removed from their original locations and reterritorialized or resituated in new locations through global flows of people, technology, finance, and ideas (Inda & Rosaldo, 2008). These global flows have created fragmented and disjointed cultural "scapes" and cultural spaces (Appadurai, 1996). What do we mean by cultural space?

Communicative Dimensions
Space and Cultural Differences

Na-young, an international student from South Korea, tells a story about space and cultural differences:

A few months after I moved to the United States, a professor of mine and her husband invited me to their house for dinner. They had just moved into this very nice, big house. When I arrived, they asked me if I wanted to see the house. First, they took me to their living room and kitchen, which was very nicely decorated. In the hallway, they had many pictures framed on the wall with their family and wedding photographs.

I enjoyed the tour very much until they took me to their master bedroom. Then it got really awkward for me. Looking at their king size bed, I was so confused and thought to myself 'why are they showing me their bedroom?' To me, a bedroom is a private space and it was really strange that my professor was showing her student her bedroom.

I have been in the United States for a couple of years now and I learned that it is a part of custom here to show your guests around the house—all the house! Some people use their living space to express their identity, lifestyle, and accomplishments.

Cultural Space

Building on Judith Martin and Thomas Nakayama's (2004) definition, **cultural space** is defined as the communicative practices that construct meanings in, through, and about particular places. Let's examine the concept of cultural space more closely. Can you identify some of the verbal and nonverbal communicative practices that define an academic cultural space? Do you use language in the classroom that may not easily translate in conversations with your family or friends outside of campus? The buildings on a campus, the exterior and interior spaces, and the kind and arrangement of furniture certainly all construct academic cultural space. Are there also nonverbal communication norms that are specific to the cultural space of a classroom? When you are in a club—a sports bar, a karaoke club, or a country western bar—or when you go to places of worship, such as a synagogue, church, mosque, or temple, there are particular architectural features, artifacts, uses of space, and language, as well as verbal and nonverbal practices that construct the cultural space of these particular places. These are all cultural spaces that are constructed through the communicative practices developed and lived by people in particular places. Communicative practices include the languages, accents, slang, dress, artifacts, architectural design, the behaviors and patterns of interaction, as well as the stories, the discourses, and histories. Places and the cultural spaces that are constructed in particular locations also give rise to collective and individual identities.

Place, Cultural Space, and Identity

In greater metropolitan Los Angeles, residents make broad identity distinctions based on place; for example, people talk about being from "the city" or from "over the hill" in "the Valley." As you can imagine, all sorts of stereotypes, assumptions, and judgments, as well as emotional attachments, feelings of belonging, and identification, underlie being from "the city" or "the Valley." In the Seattle, Washington, area, as in all places around the world, the neighborhood or area where you live—"where you come from," such as the Central District, Queen Anne Hill, Rainier Valley, Mercer Island, or Kent—communicates meaning about your identity, class status, power positions, and history. In small towns in the United States, people use the expression that "they (as opposed to "us") live on the wrong side of the tracks," the "bad" part of town, geographically placing or positioning the "Other" in terms of hierarchies of class and sometimes race or ethnicity. The way people who live in one place talk about and make meaning about their identity and their "home" or cultural space can be very different from how they are labeled, represented, and seen by others. For example, the South Side of Chicago, the South Bronx in New York, or South Los Angeles (formerly South Central Los Angeles) are represented in mainstream media as drug and crime infested, dangerous places. However, residents likely have very different versions of the story about the place called "home." Meanings about places, cultural spaces, and the collective identities that arise from them are constructed, negotiated, and circulated within a context of unequal relations of power. This example illustrates the difference between **avowed identity**, the way we see, label, and make meaning about ourselves, and **ascribed identity**, the way others may view, name, and describe us and our group.

Cultural Identity
Views on "Home" and Identity

Monica is Japanese American born and raised in Chicago, Illinois. Sayaka is an international student born and raised in Tokyo, Japan. They discuss their views on "home," and cultural identity:

Monica: "When I came to university in a small town, I had so many people ask me 'where are you from?' When I say 'I'm from Chicago,' they often respond, 'well, where are you really from?' It's frustrating when people do not believe that I belong here. This is the only country I know. My grandparents immigrated to the United States from Japan, but I see myself as an American."

Sayaka: "When people ask me where I am from, I'm proud to say, 'I'm from Japan.' It's complicated though when they start asking me all kinds of questions about Japan. I feel like I have to represent all people in Japan. There are so many kinds of people in Japan. It makes me feel like they see me only as Japanese and nothing else."

Monica's avowed identity is American, yet many people ascribe a Japanese or foreign identity to her, which causes tension. An unexamined assumption that "American" means "White" underlies the responses she gets. For Sayaka, congruence exists in terms of national culture between her avowed and ascribed identities, yet, in conversations, her cultural "difference" obscures her other identities and she is expected to speak for all Japanese people.

How do each of their identities and positionalities impact what they can say and what others expect to hear?

As noted in previous chapters, it is important to consider who has control and power over the texts (in this case, mass media texts) that are constructed. Like the texts that were written and circulated constructing and legitimizing the ideology of race in the colonial era, mass mediated texts disseminating stories about the South Bronx, South Los Angeles, and the South Side of Chicago are narrated by invisible sources who appear to come from neutral positions. Yet, just as locations, such as the South Bronx, South Los Angeles, or the South Side of Chicago are marked in terms of race, class, and culture, mainstream media texts derive from a position or location literally and figuratively and perpetuate certain interests and points of view. Places or locations marked by the intersection of race, class, gender, and culture as well other categories of difference correlate to **locations of enunciation**—sites or positions from which to speak. An individual's or group's location of enunciation can be a platform from which to voice a perspective and be heard. An individual's or group's location of enunciation can also be a site of silencing and erasure—a voiceless place. Differing locations of enunciation that are structured by asymmetrical relations of power impact our intercultural communication in interpersonal, community, national, and global interactions. In the global arena, race and gender combine with nationality and geopolitical regions (the West, the East, the North, or the South) to construct different locations of enunciation that enable and constrain the ability to speak and to be heard for groups and individuals. Territorial maps of difference that connect cultural spaces and identities to particular places are deeply rooted in historical and contemporary intercultural interactions, political contestation, and economic struggle. Consider your city, state, the nation, and the world. How are differences in terms of race and class mapped onto geographic locations? How do these mappings shape locations of enunciation? Now consider how cultural spaces are gendered and how gender impacts locations of enunciation.

Intercultural Praxis
Locations of Enunciation

In a suburb of St. Louis, Missouri, in August 2014, a Black teenager, Michael Brown, was fatally shot by a White police officer, Darren Wilson. Residents of Ferguson and supporters from around the country protested in the streets demanding the arrest of Wilson. The highly disputed circumstances of the shooting ignited longstanding racial tensions between the majority Black community and the majority White city government and police. Sixty-seven percent of residents of Ferguson are Black; 94% of the police force is White; yet, historically, Black residents account for the vast majority of arrests (Swaine, 2014). In the days immediately following the shooting, police dressed in riot gear fired tear gas and rubber bullets at protesters to disperse crowds. Demonstrators and civil rights activists decried the militarization of Ferguson evidenced by the use of armored vehicles, camouflage gear, and martial law tactics. In the months following the shooting, at least five police officers other than Wilson and a former officer in Ferguson were named in federal lawsuits alleging excessive use of force.

In September 2014, prosecutors convened a St. Louis grand jury to decide whether to charge Darren Wilson or not. However, before the grand jury decision, information in the form of autopsy and forensic reports as well as the testimony of unnamed Black witnesses was leaked to the public. Michael Brown's family, supporters, and civil rights leaders opposed the grand jury proceeding for the very reason that it shrouded the case in secrecy and allowed authorities too much control over the "facts" of the case and timing of releases. "The family wanted a jury trial that was transparent, not one done in secrecy, not something that they believe is an attempt to sweep their son's death under the rug," an attorney of the Brown family, Benjamin L. Crump, said (Kindly & Horowitz, 2014).

- How are the locations of enunciation different for the protesters, the Brown family and supporters, the police, and the grand jury?
- In what ways were the protesters and Black residents of Ferguson reclaiming a location of enunciation?
- How does the concept of the *power of the text* discussed in the previous chapter relate to the sources and timing of media texts in this case?
- How do racial/cultural frames and positionality shape perspectives on the shooting and the protests?
- What role do histories of inequity, disenfranchisement and silencing play in this situation?
- How can you use the intercultural praxis model to make sense of new information that has emerged since the shooting, the protests, and the grand jury decision?

As mentioned earlier, cultures and cultural spaces have been studied historically as if they were distinct entities bound to particular places and specific geographic locations. While place is central to the construction of cultural spaces and identities, Appadurai (1988) noted that "natives, confined to and by the places to which they belong, groups unsullied by contact with a larger world, have probably never existed" (p. 39). We know that precolonial societies traded with each other creating *regional patterns of intercultural exchange*. Armies of emperors, tribal leaders, and feudal lords fought in regional conflicts resulting in the collision, occupation, and overlap of cultural spaces. Colonization, beginning in the 15th century, linked regional circuits of intercultural exchange creating *worldwide interconnection*, which broadened the scope of displacement of people as well as the mixing and collision of cultural spaces. In other words, the dislocation, intersection, and contestation of cultural spaces we experience today are not entirely new. Yet, while globalization has historical antecedents, the deterritorialization, or uprooting of people and cultural forms, and the reterritorialization, or relocation of people and cultural products, as well as the fragmentation and fusion of cultures on a global scale are exponentially greater than in the past.

DISPLACING CULTURE AND CULTURAL SPACE

Culture has been displaced and unhinged from its geographic moorings in our highly dynamic, mobile, and globalized world. However, Xavier Inda and Renato Rosaldo (2008) noted that culture is not simply floating out there in some unidentifiable space; rather, culture is constantly and continually replaced in new environments and new places, however temporary, cyclical, or fleeting the replacement may be. I use the phrase **(dis)placing culture and cultural space** in the chapter title to capture the complex, contradictory, and contested nature of cultural space and the relationship between culture and place that has emerged in the context of globalization. As people and cultural products circulate globally, new cultural spaces are created, intersecting and colliding with existing cultural spaces, in locations often quite distant and geographically removed from their places of origin. Imagine walking the narrow Spanish colonial streets in "Old Town" San Juan, Puerto Rico, and stepping through the doorway of Tantra, a restaurant that serves a delicious fusion of Latin and Indian food to tourists and locals while a Puerto Rican woman belly dances. Picture weaving along the bumpy, rutted dirt roads on the outskirts of Bangalore, India, where glass and steel corporate call centers contrast with the bustling street vendors and pedestrians outside. Consider surfing the channels on the TV in Bangkok, Thailand. You can see a collage of "virtual" cultural spaces from the Korean hip hop scene, to the U.S. "reality-show" *Survivor*, to Thai soap operas. Visualize driving through Beijing where T.G.I. Friday's, McDonald's, KFC, and other fast-food chains dot the urban landscape, often occupying prime locations adjacent to historic sites symbolic of Chinese culture. These visual juxtapositions indicate the displacement of local cuisines and cultures. What examples of displaced and replaced cultural spaces can you identify in your neighborhood, town, or city?

Globalization is characterized by a **time–space compression** bringing seemingly disparate cultures into closer and closer proximity, intersection, and juxtaposition with each other (Harvey, 1990). Time and space are experienced as compressed due to increasingly rapid communication and transportation technologies. As time needed for people and messages to travel across distances is shortened physically through air travel and representationally through electronically mediated communication, time and space are experienced as condensed. Of course, the actual distance from New York to New Delhi has not changed. However, we experience time–space compression as people, media, money and ideas move more frequently and more rapidly today.

Photo 4.1 Past and present converge and collide as corporate interests brand historic sites

As cultural spaces are permeated, disrupted, transported, and relocated in new places around the globe, a continuous process of fragmentation, contestation, hybridization, and fusion of cultures and cultural spaces occurs. Yet, place and location still matter. Anthropologist Clifford Geertz (1996) stated the following:

> For it is still the case that no one lives in the world in general. Everybody, even the exiled, the drifting, the diasporic, or the perpetually moving, lives in some confined and limited stretch of it—"the world around here." The sense of interconnectedness imposed on us by the mass media, by rapid travel, and by long-distance communication obscures this more than a little. (p. 262)

Our goal, then, is to investigate "the world around here." By "here," I mean the localized and situated embodiments of culture and intercultural interactions in particular places that are inevitably influenced by globalizing forces.

Glocalization: Simultaneous Forces of Globalization and Localization

In the context of globalization, "the world around here" is infused with, shaped by, and connected to many different cultures that are both "here" and "there"—both present and distant in space and time. Sociologist Anthony Giddens (1994) explicates the "stretching" of social relations across distance as a way to deepen our understanding of connectivity in the context of globalization. For example, what you purchase, "here," where you are located, affects the livelihood of someone out "there," around the world. Women, seeking economic survival for themselves and their families, move around the world to care for other people's children. In this way, social relations are "stretched" across great distances as individuals and families relocate for economic and political reasons; as goods produced in one part of the world are consumed on the other side of the globe; and as cultural products and representations from one location disseminate globally constructing meanings, desires, and identities.

Given the intensifying levels of connectivity, we need to investigate how this particular "here" is linked to "there" and how this linkage of places not only reveals connections across distances, but also over time. We are interested in how present-day spatial connectivity also uncovers colonial histories and postcolonial realities. **Glocalization** refers to the dual and simultaneous forces of globalization and localization. First introduced in relation to Japanese business practices in the 1980s and later popularized by sociologist Roland Robertson (1992), the concept of glocalization allows us to think about how globalizing forces always operate in relationship to localizing forces. Given that globalization "happens" in specific locals, glocalization points to the intersection of the global and the local in particular places.

For example, on a street in a metropolitan area in the United States, you might find a Korean evangelical church next to an Iranian bakery and, across the street, a steak house next to a Thai boxing gym. It's likely that migrants from distant or not-so-distant places labor in the back and the people who frequent these sites are from many different cultural backgrounds. How is the juxtaposition of cultural spaces we experience "here," in this particular local intercultural context, related to and interconnected with places around the globe through historic and contemporary webs of connectivity? Contemporary multicultural spaces, "the world around here," are always layered with histories of intercultural interaction and contestation, as well as assimilation and integration of cultural communities and cultural spaces. In order to understand the intercultural dynamics occurring in cultural spaces around us, we need to dig beneath the surface to examine the histories of interaction that literally and figuratively shape and construct meanings about the ground on which we stand today. Thus, cultural spaces embody and materialize webs of connectivity across both space and time.

In this instance, the specific place designated as "here" where a Korean evangelical church, Iranian bakery, steak house, and Thai boxing gym create a multicultural space is in Los Angeles, California. This particular "here" was previously the homeland of indigenous American Indians, which was invaded and conquered by the Spanish at the beginning of the European colonial era in the 16th century. This location was inhabited by citizens of Mexico who were later displaced by the "Westward Movement" of White Americans (experienced as the "Eastern Invasion" by those who were there). In the past 100 years, this place—this particular "here"—has been "home" to Black Americans who moved to the area in the 1920s and 1930s. Fleeing Jim Crow segregation laws of the South, they experienced other types of spatial segregation in their new home. Following WWII, Japanese Americans, attempting to recover their dignity, economic losses, and "place" within U.S. society after their criminalization and detention in "internment camps" (the dominant U.S. phrase for "concentration camps") also made this place home.

This neighborhood in Los Angeles, California, with its layered, negotiated, and contested cultural spaces, reflects and embodies a complex history of intercultural relations. Today it is home to a small Japanese American community, a significant African American population, and a large Latino/Latina population. The growing presence of Latinos/Latinas in this neighborhood and across the United States can be understood as a result of the displacement of people, culture, and cultural space due to the forces of neoliberal globalization. The increasing Latino/Latina population is also interpreted by some in the United States as an "invasion" from the South. Yet, if we take a longer historical view, connecting the present to the past, we can also make sense of the changing populations and shifting cultural spaces as a return of people to their home—both a precolonial indigenous ancestral homeland and a Mexican homeland before U.S. annexation. This example illustrates how the patterns and flows of displacement and replacement of peoples and the creation of cultural spaces in the context of globalization are not random. An excavation of "the world around here," whether "here" is your neighborhood, the site of your university, or the central cross streets of your city, uncovers histories of overlapping and contested cultural spaces that link particular local places to global historical and contemporary events. A statement popularized by immigrant rights groups in Europe and the United States captures this dynamic: "We are here because you were there." Understanding and "reading" the intercultural dimensions of place, cultural space, and location today requires bifocal vision that attends to the linkages between past and present as well as between place-based dimensions of "here" and "there."

Let's take a look at hip hop culture to illustrate concepts and issues relating to the intercultural dynamics of place, space, and location discussed thus far in the chapter. Hip hop culture is only one of many case examples that could be used to explicate the complex relationships among culture, place, and power. Other music-based cultures with historic roots in particular locations and places, such as rave culture, jazz culture, or punk culture could be explored. Neighborhoods or cities that have distinct, hybrid, and contested spaces based on ethnicity, race, or class could be used. Your university or college could be analyzed to uncover the intercultural dimensions of cultural space. As you read the following section, notice how communication is used to construct hip hop cultural spaces, how hip hop cultural spaces that emerge out of particular places define locations of enunciation, and how hip hop youth represent themselves, avowing identities that challenge and contest the ways they have been represented. Also pay attention to how hip hop culture illustrates processes of deterritorialization/reterritorialization and glocalization. The case study illuminates intercultural communication dynamics and processes operating in cultures in the context of globalization. Segregated, contested, and hybrid cultural spaces are introduced through the case study and are addressed in greater depth after the case study.

CASE STUDY: HIP HOP CULTURE

South Bronx

Hip hop culture emerged out of the harsh burned-out, poverty-stricken, gang dominated urban spaces of the South Bronx. Grandmaster Flash and the Furious Five (1982) described the cultural space as a jungle, where lack of education and escalating inflation made him wonder "how I keep from going under." Black and Puerto Rican youth took what was available to them—their bodies, their cultural forms of expression, and their innovation—to reclaim their "place." The reclaimed place of hip hop culture is a literal geographic space, a cultural space of belonging and identification as well as a location of enunciation—a sociopolitical and economic site from which to speak. Through creative forms of cultural expression with deep ancestral ties, such as break dancing, graffiti, and rap music, the South Bronx was transformed into a site of pleasure and protest (Rose, 1994). The youth of the South Bronx used the streets, parks, subways, abandoned buildings, and trains as locations for creating, writing, and voicing their own "texts" about their struggles. Transplanted and resignified in urban contexts around the world today, the communicative practices of hip hop culture are rooted in transatlantic African diasporic colonial history. In "The Roots of Hip Hop" (1986), *RM HIP HOP MAGAZINE* stated the following:

> In the beginning there was Africa, and it is from Africa that all today's black American music—be it Jazz, R'n'B, Soul or Electro—is either directly or indirectly descended. The ancient African tribal rhythms and musical traditions survived the shock of the transportation of millions of Africans as slaves to the Americas, and after 300 years of slavery in the so called Land of the Free the sounds of Old Africa became the new sounds of black America. Rapping, the rhythmic use of spoken or semi-sung lyrics grew from its roots in the tribal chants and the plantation work songs to become an integral part of black resistance to an oppressive white society.

The South Bronx in the 1970s was an urban wasteland—"a Necropolis—a city of death" (Chang, 2005, p. 16). Like many urban centers in the United States, New York City was devastated by the loss of jobs as the forces of globalization geared up and manufacturing industries sought cheaper labor conditions outside the United States in a process called **deindustrialization**. New York City's officials mounted a tremendous revitalization program in the 1970s, but areas like the South Bronx, home to working-class and poor Blacks and immigrants, were left out of the plan and off the map. Joblessness, slum landlords, economic divestment, and depopulation from the displacement of over 170,000 residents due to the construction of the Cross-Bronx Expressway led to the rapid deterioration of the social and economic fabric of the South Bronx community. Out of these conditions, hip hop culture rose as a vibrant, expressive, and oppositional urban youth culture. Trisha Rose (1994) stated, "Hip hop is a cultural form that attempts to negotiate the experience of marginalization, brutally truncated opportunity, and oppression within the cultural imperatives of African American and Caribbean history, identity and community" (p. 21).

Back in the Day

From the beginning, the communicative practices of hip hop culture—break dancing, graffiti writing, DJing, and rapping—developed in relationship to particular places, an identification with and defense of territory, and an awareness of sociopolitical locations. Communication scholar Murray Foreman (2004) quoted Grandmaster Flash, one of the first hip hop DJs, as he identified the division of space and place during the early years of hip hop cultural formation:

> We had territories. It was like, Kool Herc had the west side. Bam had Bronx River. DJ Breakout had way uptown past Gun Hill. Myself, my area was like 138th Street, Cypress Avenue, up to Gun Hill, so that we had our territories and we all had to respect each other. (p. 202)

The original DJs: Kool Herc, Afrika Bambaataa, and Grandmaster Flash of the South Bronx and other Black and Puerto Rican youth who followed, used two turntables; a microphone; sound systems; and the soul, funk, and blues music of earlier times to create new sounds and styles that spoke to, about, and from the inner-city urban Black and Latino/Latina experience. This was their location of enunciation. They borrowed old beats from Africa and the Caribbean and reterritorialized them in the urban Bronx context in creative and inspiring ways, looping colonial histories of oppression with contemporary, postcolonial struggles for survival. Block parties reminiscent of those in Jamaica brought MCs forward who layered words on top of beats, rapping in ways that recalled African and Jamaican cultural communicative practices of toasting or playing the dozens, where rhyming slang is used to put down enemies or tease friends (George, 1998; Rose, 1994).

In the transition from gang affiliations to hip hop culture, gang communicative practices, such as "tagging"—the marking of either your own territory to signify authority and dominance or the marking of others' territory to provoke—morphed into graffiti "writing," where individual and group "writers" used the city—walls, buildings, buses, and trains—as their canvas. The initial writing of code names (Taki 183, Kase 2, Lady Pink, etc.) that literally inscribed the identities of individuals and graffiti crews on the urban landscape offered previously dispossessed and silenced youth notoriety and credibility. As the numbers and boldness of writers increased and the size and shapes of their work expanded to murals on subway trains, intense resistance from city officials mounted. The South Bronx youth's desire to "talk back," reclaim their space, and represent themselves was criminalized by city offices. The dominant powers spent millions of taxpayer dollars to reassert power, regain control, and take back the "public" space. As Rose (1994) noted, New York City in the mid-1970s was "a city at war to silence its already discarded youths" (p. 45).

Going Commercial

With the recording of "Rapper's Delight" in 1979, hip hop culture catapulted into the complex and contested terrain of commercialization and commodification. As hip hop commercialized and "went national" in the late 1980s, the regional place-based split or "beef" between the East and West Coasts gained prominence. Brian Cross (1993) argued that the rise of hip hop culture on the West Coast and specifically in Compton was "an attempt to figure Los Angeles on the map of hip hop" in a direct communicative "reply to the construction of the South Bronx/Queensbridge nexus in New York" (p. 37). The commercial success of rap has led to artist-owned businesses and independent labels providing employment and economic viability for many African Americans. The industry

Photo 4.2 Towering buildings and graffiti mark cultural spaces in New York

©iStockphoto.com/ Lisa-Blue

fosters entrepreneurial endeavors that have advantaged many dispossessed and marginalized people. Yet, hip hop is a highly contested cultural space. Mainstream middle- and upper-class Whites and Blacks decry the corrosive moral effects of hip hop culture. Yet, the vibrant lyrics of rap and the locations of enunciation pictured and voiced in music videos capture the attention of youth across the United States and the globe.

> In rap videos, young mostly male residents speak for themselves and for the community, they speak when and how they wish about subjects of their choosing. These local turf scenes are not isolated voices; they are voices from a variety of social margins that are in dialogue with one another. (Rose, 1994, p. 11)

Fascinated and lured by narratives of rebellion, oppositional identities, and locations on the margin, youth of all ethnic racial backgrounds and particularly White Americans are the primary consumers.

Global Hip Hop Culture

Today, hip hop cultural spaces are materializing around the globe. In urban, suburban, and rural settings in Europe, Africa, Latin America, and Asia, hip hop culture has been deterritorialized from the urban centers of the United States and reterritorialized in new locations creating hybrid cultural spaces that illustrate processes of glocalization. Distinctive communicative practices—particular styles of DJing, rapping, break dancing, and graffiti writing—originally constructed hip hop cultural spaces in the South Bronx, traveled to the urban centers of the U.S. Northeast, the West Coast, across the United States, and now around the globe. While the communicative practices of hip hop cultures around the world are clearly linked to the African diasporic colonial experience, they also rework the qualities of flow, layering, and rupture in their place-based specificity as global forces converge with local forces (Rose, 1994). From his research in Cuba, Brazil and South African, anthropologist Marc Perry (2012) argues that hip hop serves as a conduit for transnational Black cultural identification, where hip hop music, dance, and graffiti communicate Black political consciousness and counter-hegemonic resistance globally. Hip hop culture and styles developed across Europe provide spaces to address local issues of racism, concerns over police brutality, and other challenges faced by disenfranchised youth. In "Hip-Hop à la Française" in the New York Times, professor of African American Studies and French, Samir Meghelli (2013) stated:

> There are few cultural forms more American than hip-hop, and yet it has taken firm hold in France. Over the last three decades, France has grown to become the largest market in the world (behind only the United States) for the production and consumption of this genre. But French hip-hop is not a copy of its American precursor. On the contrary, it is a rich scene of French artists who rap in their national language (and local argot) and narrate their own unique socio-political realities.

Indigenous hip hop artists from Australia, Chile, New Zealand, Tanzania, and the United States claim that hip hop culture emerging in their communities blends traditional stories and aesthetics with contemporary beats and moves empowering First Nation youth to negotiated differences between tribal and non-tribal cultures (Verán, 2012). Sociologist Andy Bennett (2004) noted that:

> the commercial packaging of hip hop as a global commodity has facilitated its easy access by young people in many different parts of the world. Moreover, such appropriations have in each case involved a reworking of hip hop in ways that engage with local circumstances. In every respect then, hip hop is both a global and a local form. (p. 180)

The appropriation of cultural forms and practices originally improvised and created in Black and Puerto Rican inner-city ghettos is central to the global flow of hip hop culture today. The meaning of **appropriation** varies along a continuum from the idea of "borrowing" to "mishandling" to "stealing" and raises questions about authenticity, ownership, and relations of power. Is hip hop essentially a Black thing? Is it disrespectful, inauthentic, or a subtle continuation of colonial practices for White rappers like the Beastie Boys, Eminem, Mac Miller, and Yelawolf to borrow, mimic, use, and rework Black cultural practices? Sociologist Paul Gilroy (1993) argued that "the transnational structures which brought the black Atlantic world into being have themselves developed and now articulate its myriad forms into a system of global communications constituted by flows" (p. 80). In other words, Gilroy pointed out how the African diaspora is rooted in the development of Western capitalism. Today, hip hop circulates through a global communication system as a result of the networks of connectivity established during the colonial era. "Black" culture becomes global culture as hip hop is deterritorialized and reterritorialized around the globe, and the music and styles mesh with and call forth local responses (Bennett, 2004).

Hip hop cultural spaces, forms, and practices illustrate the complex and paradoxical nature of intercultural communication in the context of globalization. While enabling economic mobility and providing a platform for speaking—a visible and audible location of enunciation—mainstream rap narratives often promote stereotypes about communities of color and valorize danger, violence, misogyny, and homophobia. The commodification of hip hop culture—turning the culture into a product for sale and appropriating a message of rebellion and protest to sell everything from jeans to Jeeps—defuses and neutralizes the potentially resistive and counter-hegemonic message of hip hop. Tricia Rose (2008) argues that hip hop's "tragic trinity"—black gangstas, pimps, and hos—driven by corporate mass media and facilitated by mainstream White America, black youth and black industry moguls have nearly destroyed hip hop. The "hip hop wars," a battle framed by those who adamantly reject hip hop and those who uncritically defend it, mask critical factors—massive corporate consolidation, new media technologies, an increasing appetite for racially stereotypical entertainment, and a valorization of violence and misogyny—that create toxic conditions in hip hop and the broader mainstream culture (Rose, 2008).

Today, hip hop cultural spaces are places of belonging and identification, spaces of opposition and resistance, as well as spaces where ideologies of domination and exclusion are disseminated around the globe. Hip hop cultural spaces are locations of enunciation where the stories of the dispossessed and marginalized "Others" spin and spit alternative texts that can and do challenge, resist, and rewrite dominant narratives. Yet, the commodification of hip hop culture has manufactured "mainstream" or "commercial" hip hop, which produces texts that comply with and shore up dominant ideologies. Consuming and enjoying hip hop beats does not constitute socially responsible action; nor does this alone create social change. Creative and conscious participation in hip hop culture that challenges inequities and uplifts the community can and does create social change. The case study on hip hop culture points to the central role of power—economic, social, political, and discursive power—in the formation, maintenance, and disruption of cultural spaces. In the following section, segregated, contested, and hybrid cultural spaces are examined highlighting the way power circulates in each.

CULTURAL SPACE, POWER, AND COMMUNICATION

Throughout history and today, space has been used to establish, exert, and maintain power and control. Power is signified, constructed, and regulated through size, shape, access, containment, and segregation of space. In other words, the use of space communicates. Consider the largest metropolises in the world today—Tokyo, Japan; Jakarta, Indonesia; Delhi, India; Seoul, Korea; Manila, Philippines; Shanghai, China; Karachi, Pakistan; New York City, United States; and San Paulo, Brazil. How do you think power is symbolized through the use of space in these cities today? In the Middle Ages in Europe, churches were the tallest buildings and occupied central locations in cities signifying the importance of religious authority. In the Ottoman Empire, no building was built higher than the minarets of mosques. European colonizers erected churches on top of local religious sites from the Americas to India and Africa to materially and symbolically impose colonial rule. Massive, elaborate, and substantial buildings were constructed in Europe and the colonies during the period of nation-state building, signifying governmental power.

Today, the signs of power in metropolises around the world are the financial buildings—the towering, glitzy, eye-catching economic centers of transnational capitalism. Financial centers around the globe like the Twin Towers in New York City are symbols of wealth, prosperity, and participation in global, transnational flows of capital. In other words, they signify access to resources and communicate power. Like all signs, buildings that are erected with multinational and transnational capital acquire meaning within a signification system that includes its opposite, or the lack of access to wealth and power. Towering skyscrapers also signify unequal relations of economic and political power. As Edward T. Hall (1966) elaborated in his book *The Hidden Dimension*, the way cultures use space communicates. Let's take a look now at how power is exerted and negotiated through communication in the construction of segregated, contested, and hybrid cultural spaces.

Segregated Cultural Space

Around the world, spatial segregation exists today and has existed historically in cities and rural areas based on socioeconomic, racial, ethnic, political, and religious differences.

Ethnic, racial, religious, as well as sexual minority cultural groups may choose to live in communities in close proximity as a way to reinforce and maintain cultural spaces and to buffer themselves from real or perceived hostile forces around them. These cultural spaces—more appropriately understood as voluntary separation rather than segregation— often provide and reinforce a sense of belonging, identification, and empowerment. Yet, there are many historical and contemporary examples of **segregated cultural spaces**: the imposition and use of spatial segregation to maintain the hegemony of the dominant group and to restrict and control access of nondominant groups to power and resources. The word *ghetto,* used primarily today to refer to ethnic or racial neighborhoods of urban poverty, originally referred to an area in Venice, Italy, where Jews were segregated and required to live in the 1500s. The reservation system imposed on Native Americans, the Jim Crow laws that segregated Blacks, and the isolation of Japanese Americans during WWII are examples of forced segregation that maintained the hegemony of European Americans and limited access for nondominant groups in the United States.

On the long road from slavery to freedom that many still walk in the United States, African Americans have encountered tremendous obstacles, including various insidious forms of segregation. From the abolition of slavery in 1865 until the civil rights laws of the 1960s, more than 400 state laws, constitutional amendments, and city ordinances were passed by White lawmakers to legalize racial segregation and discrimination against Blacks (and other minorities in the western United States) in the majority of states in the United States. Jim Crow laws segregated Blacks and Whites, first and foremost, restricting contact between the two groups by imposing legal punishment for those who crossed the color line and secondly, restricting interracial marriage (Litwack, 1998). Visible signs marked the public spaces where Blacks were allowed. If Blacks entered spaces on trains or buses, in public buildings, hospitals, restaurants, theaters, or schools that were not designed for "coloreds" or crossed the line into the "Whites only" area, they were subjected to beating, arrest, and on occasion, death. Today, the use of the word *colored* to refer to people of color or non-White people is problematic and often experienced as derogatory because of the dehumanizing use of the term historically. Jim Crow laws maintained and managed a system of White supremacy constructed through colonization and slavery (Litwack, 1998).

Real estate covenants restricted where Blacks and people of color could live and "Whites-only" towns officially and unofficially segregated Blacks, forcing them into areas where economic resources from businesses to jobs and public services, such as schools and health care, were and continue to be substandard and scarce. Sociologist James Loewen (2006) argued that "Whites-only" towns, what are called "sundown towns," exist today. "Sundown towns," so named for their threats of violence aimed at Blacks after the sun sets, are places that have deliberately excluded Blacks for decades and that, today, increasingly exclude Latinos/Latinas. You might think that racial, ethnic, and cultural segregation is a phenomenon of the past in the United States. I often hear students say, "That's history. It's over now. Let's move on." Well, unfortunately, it isn't over. First, systemic inequities and injustices of the past continue to impact the present and the future. Second, while laws that blatantly led to segregation, such as the Jim Crow laws, have been abolished, other formal and informal practices support de facto (by practice) segregation today. As discussed in Chapter 3, in the context of neoliberal globalization, race is recoded as class. Given the legacy of colonization and the history of systemic discrimination, the contours of class segregation are closely linked to race. Rearticulating race as class obscures the racial, as well as gender, dimensions of class.

Six decades ago the Supreme Court ruled that segregated schools were inherently unequal and, thus, unconstitutional; yet, today, schools in the United States are more segregated than they were a few decades ago. Data from the U.S. Department of Education indicate that 80% of Latino and 74% of Black children attend schools where the majority of students are not white. Approximately 43% of Latino and 38% of Black students are in "intensely segregated schools," which means less than 10% of their classmates are white (Zalan, 2014). According to the Executive Summary of the UCLA Civil Rights Project (Orfield, Frankenberg, Ee, & Kuscera, 2014):

- Segregation is typically segregation by both race and poverty. Black and Latino students tend to be in schools with a substantial majority of poor children, but White and Asian students are typically in middle-class schools.

- Segregation is by far the most serious in the central cities of the largest metropolitan areas, but it is also severe in central cities of all sizes and suburbs of the largest metro areas, which are now half non-White. Latinos are significantly more segregated than Blacks in suburban America.

- The Supreme Court has fundamentally changed desegregation law, and many major court orders have been dropped. Statistical analysis shows that segregation increased substantially after the plans were terminated in many large districts.

- A half-century of research shows that many forms of unequal opportunity are linked to segregation. Further, research also finds that desegregated education has substantial benefits for educational and later life outcomes for students from all backgrounds. (p. 2)

Another vivid and compelling illustration is the devastation experienced by victims of Hurricane Katrina. While all people living in New Orleans and the Gulf area were impacted by the natural disaster, low-income, working-class neighborhoods were hit the hardest. Working-class and poor neighborhoods were the least protected from the storm and most vulnerable to the substandard relief efforts that followed. Historically, racial segregation imposed geographic color lines in New Orleans as it did in cities across the United States, and current class segregation maintains these divisions. The New Orleans parish with 67% Black residents was the hardest hit by the storm and floods. Representative Cynthia McKinney (2006) from Georgia reported the following:

Poverty cuts across ethnic divisions, but there is another side to this story . . . whites were evacuated before blacks while blacks were detained or turned back, as happened on the bridge to Gretna. The media stereotyped blacks as "looters" and whites as "takers" and fueled fears of blacks that led to the "invasion" of New Orleans, shockingly by hired mercenaries.

The plight of victims was exacerbated by long-standing and present-day systematic racism and neglect.

These examples illustrate how segregation of cultural spaces structure and reinforce different power positions within socioeconomic, political, and cultural hierarchies. Segregation, whether it is class, race, gender-based, or an intersection of all three, is a powerful means to control, limit, and contain nondominant groups. Spatial segregation is imposed and enforced by systems put in place by a dominant group—in the United States, European Americans or Whites, who maintain White supremacy. Formal and informal institutional systems that restrict access to places and spaces continue to limit the material, social, political, and economic potential of nondominant groups in the United States today. What other examples can you think of that suggest segregated cultural spaces are not relics of the past? As in the case of the forgotten and disenfranchised Black and Latino/Latina youth in the South Bronx, segregated cultural spaces that produce the exclusion of groups from resources—material, symbolic, political, and social resources—have been challenged in the past and are disputed today resulting in contested cultural spaces.

Contested Cultural Space

Chinese immigrants who came to the United States to work from the 1850s onward were forced to live in isolated ethnic enclaves known as Chinatowns in large cities, such as San Francisco and New York. In an article titled "The First Asian Americans" in the *Asian-Nation: The Landscape of Asian America*, C. N. Le (2006) stated the following:

> Because they were forbidden from owning land, intermarrying with Whites, owning homes, working in many occupations, getting an education, and living in certain parts of the city or entire cities, the Chinese basically had no other choice but to retreat into their own isolated communities as a matter of survival. These first Chinatowns at least allowed them to make a living among themselves.
>
> This is where the stereotypical image of Chinese restaurants and laundry shops, Japanese gardeners and produce stands, and Korean grocery stores began. The point is that these [occupations] did not begin out of any natural or instinctual desire on the part of Asian workers, but as a response to prejudice, exclusion, and institutional discrimination—a situation that still continues in many respects today.

After the devastating 1906 earthquake and fires in San Francisco, White city leaders and landlords wanted to relocate Chinatown, which was situated on prime real estate in the city center, to the outskirts of town claiming that it was an "eyesore and health hazard." A political battle ensued with the Chinese community leaders strongly protesting the forced displacement. Finally, they were able to convince the White civic leaders that Chinatown could be rebuilt in a "traditional Oriental" style to attract tourists and contribute to the city's revenue and appeal. We can see how Chinatown is a polysemic cultural space as well as a contested cultural space. A **polysemic cultural space** means that multiple meanings have been constructed about Chinatown over time. Chinatown was originally seen as a place to exclude and isolate Chinese immigrants by White city power brokers. It was seen and experienced as a refuge, a safe haven, and "home" by and for Chinese immigrants. Powerful White leaders denigrated Chinatown and its residents calling it an "eyesore and health hazard" with a masked goal of repossessing it as a desirable and valuable piece of property. Chinatown was redefined as a "cultural resource" by Chinese immigrant organizers for community empowerment and a product or commodity for sale. Chinese leaders of the dispute had to agree to represent themselves and their community in ways that would appeal to and be marketable to tourists from the dominant European American culture. In a way, Chinatown was appropriated by city power brokers, whether we understand that as borrowed or stolen, for the purpose of commodifying and selling it. The competition or dispute over various meanings and interests—economic, community, symbolic, political, and social meanings and interests— make Chinatown a contested cultural space. Anthropologists Setha Low and Denise Lawrence-Zúñiga (2003) define **contested cultural spaces** as geographic locations where conflicts engage actors defined by unequal control and access to resources in oppositional and confrontational strategies of resistance.

When we look carefully and critically at our neighborhoods, cities, state, nation, and the world, we can find many examples of contested cultural spaces. In places where different cultural group overlap—based on race, ethnicity, class, sexuality or religion—contestation or friction and disagreement over identity, ownership, and representation often fester. For example, when cultural groups with languages, norms and practices that differ from the group that is dominant settle in an area, arguments and conflicts over whose neighborhood it is, what languages should be used for public signage and how the area is changing as a result of newcomers manifest and magnify. Multiple, intersecting dimensions, rooted in the present and in the past, underlie contested cultural spaces.

In September 2014, one month after the shooting, Ferguson, Missouri, was burning. Protesters marched in the streets demanding justice in the violent and deadly clash between an unarmed African American youth and a White police officer. The police responded to the protests with militarized force. Citizens supporting Michael Brown and resisting police brutality carried signs, such as: Black Lives Matter; Don't Shoot, I am not a Threat; Hands Up, Don't Shoot; Truth is on the Side of the Oppressed; My Blackness is Not a Weapon, Don't Shoot. Those who supported and identified with Darren Wilson, the police officer, carried signs that said: Support our Police, Pray for Peace; We are Your Voice PO Wilson; It's About the Rule of Law; I Don't Support a Race, I Support the Truth. While an initial photo used by mainstream media showed Michael Brown smiling at his high school graduation in a cap and gown, the more commonly used image of him was in a red jersey throwing what could be construed as a gang sign—although friends said it was a peace sign.

Joshua LOTT/AFP/Getty Images

Photo 4.3 Community youth protest police violence in Ferguson, Missouri

Clearly, Ferguson, Missouri, is a contested cultural space. As in many similar incidents, the immediate physical and representational contestations are undergirded by multiple and intersecting racial, ideological, economic, and deeply historical dimensions. Cultural spaces are complex and multifaceted. Understanding Ferguson as a contested cultural space means we dig into the messy, violent, and disturbing terrain to excavate these deep layers. What is the history between the different racial groups in Ferguson? Between citizens and the police? What is the relationship among cultural spaces, race, and power? How do standpoint theory and positionality inform our understanding of this contested cultural space? How does the focus on the innocence or guilt of the police officer mask larger issues of structural inequity and violence? How does media attention on "looting" and "rioting" frame the uprising and protests? Using intercultural praxis, what other issues need excavating to understand contested cultural spaces like Ferguson?

Setha Low and Denise Lawrence-Zúñiga (2003) noted, "Spaces are contested precisely because they concretize the fundamental and recurring, but otherwise unexamined, ideological, and social frameworks that structure practice" (p. 18). Ferguson, Missouri, as a contested cultural space, concretizes and exposes the highly racialized terrain of the United States; the differential access to and identification with authority and power, as well as the criminalization of Black youth and the normalization of structural violence. Let's take a look at how hybrid cultural spaces are sites of negotiation, resistance, and change.

Hybrid Cultural Space

On the surface, the notion of hybrid cultural spaces appears fairly simple. Most people agree that there is a mixing or blending of cultures in the world today, and through intercultural overlap and intersection, hybrid cultural spaces are constructed. Yet, what is the nature of the blending and mixing? Is it simply an equal mix of two or more cultural ingredients—like food preparation—that creates hybridity and hybrid cultural spaces? The following three examples of hybrid cultural spaces help us understand the power dynamics that structure the terms and conditions of mixing in hybrid cultural spaces.

Imagine you are sitting in a McDonald's in Moscow, Russia. You might expect to find a situation similar to what you experience here in the United States—a fast, inexpensive, (fat) filling meal in a familiar and standardized space (each one is pretty much like the next one) where you sit down, eat your meal, and leave *or* take the drive-through option. You might assume you will have an experience of "American" culture in Russia. However, when Shannon Peters Talbot (as cited in Nederveen Pieterse, 2004, p. 50) conducted an ethnographic study of McDonald's in Moscow, Russia, she found something quite different. Moscowites came to McDonald's to enjoy the atmosphere, often hanging out for more than an hour. They pay more than one third of the average Russian daily wage for a meal and are drawn to this cultural space for its uniqueness and difference. Instead of "one size fits all" management practices that are generally applied in the United States, McDonald's in Moscow offers a variety of incentive options for employees (Nederveen Pieterse, 2004).

The proliferation of multinational entities around the globe suggests a corporatization and homogenization of cultural spaces. This McDonaldization of the world (think 23,000 Starbucks in 65 countries; 11,000 Walmart stores in 27 countries outside the United States; 35,000 McDonald's in 116 countries; etc.) is the result of unequal power relations, which manifests in an asymmetrical global flow of cultural products. Do we see the proliferation of Russian restaurants, coffee shops, and department stores in the United States or around the world? Undoubtedly, this is an example of cultural imperialism or the domination of one culture over others through cultural forms, such as pop culture, media, and cultural products. Without erasing the asymmetrical power relations and the dominance of U.S. and Western cultural forms, it is important to note the hybrid nature of the cultural space—the mixing of cultural influences, the altered way the space is used, and the new meanings that are produced about the space—in this reterritorialized McDonald's. Sociologist Jan Nederveen Pieterse (2004) used Talbot's ethnography in Moscow as an example of intercultural hybridization. McDonald's in Moscow is a hybrid cultural space. **Hybrid cultural space** is defined as the intersection of intercultural communication practices that construct meanings in, through, and about particular places within a context of relations of power. Digging under the surface appearance of blending and mixing reveals **hybrid cultural spaces as sites of intercultural negotiation.** Hybrid cultural spaces are innovative and creative spaces where people constantly adapt to, negotiate with, and improvise between multiple cultural frameworks.

Communication scholar Radha Hegde (2002) described the hybrid cultural space in an Asian Indian immigrant home:

> The aroma of Indian cooking replete with cinnamon, cardamom, saffron, and ginger rises in the air as friends arrive. The colors of Indian saris stand out, making a statement of embodied difference. The afternoon warms up with an array of appetizers—a tantalizing multicultural spectacle ranging from salsa and chutney to tahini! The conversation also spans a vast geographical and cultural terrain. (p. 259)

Hegde continued by describing the multiple and varied conversations that move from the delicious taste of samosas, reminders of home, to concerns over cholesterol and heart disease. Conversations about mothering in a bicultural world merge into a heated discussion over the stoning of a local Indian temple. Here is how she ended the scenario:

> Just then a new batch of samosas arrives from the kitchen, ready to be savored. There is a roar from the adjoining room. The football game gets intense. "American football is where the action is. What did you say, cricket? Can't take it anymore—just too drawn out." (p. 260)

Hegde argued that the hybrid cultural space described here is constructed by Asian Indian immigrants as a response to what Salome Rushdie (1991) called the triple dislocation: a disruption of historical roots, language, and social conventions. This triple dislocation penetrates to the very core of migrants' experiences of identity, social connections, and culture. The construction of hybrid cultural spaces, then, is an active and creative effort to maintain and sustain one's culture in the context of global displacement and replacement. Constructed in the context of differential power relations, hybrid cultural spaces are forms of resistance to full assimilation into the dominant culture. As noted in the case study about hip hop, hybrid cultural spaces are *both* highly innovative, improvisational, creative, *and* "also cultures that develop and survive as a form of collective resistance" (Hegde, 2002, p. 261). Hybridity—hybrid cultures, spaces, and identities—challenge stable, territorial, and static definitions of culture, cultural spaces, and cultural identities. Therefore, we can understand **hybrid cultural spaces as sites of resistance.**

In a third example, Chicana feminist scholar Gloria Anzaldúa (1987) described the fluid, contradictory, and creative experience of living in the hybrid cultural space she calls the "Borderlands/borderlands":

> . . . the Borderlands are physically present wherever two or more cultures edge each other, where people of different races occupy the same territory, where under, lower, middle and upper classes touch, where the space between two individuals shrinks with intimacy. I am a border woman. I grew up between two cultures, the Mexican (with a heavy Indian influence) and the Anglo (as a member of a colonized people in our own territory). I have been straddling that *tejas*-Mexican border, and others, all my life. It's not a comfortable territory to live in, this place of contradictions. Hatred, anger and exploitation are the prominent features of this landscape. However, there have been compensations for this *mestiza*, and certain joys. Living on borders and in margins, keeping intact one's shifting and multiple identity and integrity, is like trying to swim in a new element, an "alien" element. There is an exhilaration in being a participant in the further evolution of humankind, in being "worked" on. (p. 1 of unnumbered preface)

Amidst the pain, hardship, and alienation, Anzaldúa expressed "exhilaration" at living in, speaking from, and continually constructing hybrid cultural spaces—the Borderlands. In the ongoing confrontation with and negotiation of "hegemonic structures that constantly 'marginalize' the mixtures they create" (Tomlinson, 1999, p. 146), Anzaldúa experienced and constructed a location of enunciation, a position, and a cultural space (both a literal and figurative space) from which to speak and claim an oppositional identity. Nederveen Pieterse (2004) stated, " . . . it's important to note the ways in which hegemony is not merely reproduced but *reconfigured* in the process of hybridization" (p. 74). Therefore, we can understand **hybrid cultural spaces as sites of transformation.** We have explored segregated, contested, and hybrid cultural spaces through historical and contemporary examples. This discussion of cultural spaces and the excavation of underlying power dynamics provides a foundation for investigating the intercultural dynamics of border crossing, identity construction, and relationship building in later chapters.

SUMMARY

In this chapter, the cultural and intercultural communication dimensions of place, space, and location were investigated. I discussed the ways that human beings construct, negotiate, contest, and hybridize cultural spaces though communicative practices highlighting the role of power historically and today. The concept of glocalization was introduced to focus attention on how specific places are impacted by globalizing and localizing forces. I also proposed the notion of bifocal vision or the ability to attend to the linkages between "here" and "there" as well as the connections between the present and past to understand the complex, layered, and contested dimensions of places, cultural spaces, and locations today.

The case study on hip hop culture illustrated the pivotal function of place in constructing individual and group identities, locations of enunciation, and relationships of power. Hip hop emerged from the segregated space of the South Bronx—a forgotten and forsaken place. Fusing traditional communicative practices with contemporary technologies and postcolonial realities, the youth of the Bronx created a powerful cultural space. Hip hop cultural spaces give rise to both pleasure and protest that challenge the conditions of marginalized people within societies around the world. Yet hip hop culture's counter-hegemonic messages of resistance and struggle are often defused through processes of commodification. As cultures and cultural spaces are deterritorialized and reterritorialized around the world in the global context, contested and hybrid cultural spaces develop. Segregated, contested, and hybrid cultural spaces expose the context of unequal power relations that structure intercultural communication in the global age. We discovered that hybrid cultural spaces are much more than the blending of multiple cultural traditions and practices. Rather, hybrid cultural spaces are sites of intercultural negotiation, sites of resistance where people reconstitute identities, and sites where creative alternatives challenge and transform oppressive hegemonic forces.

KEY TERMS

cultural space
avowed identity
ascribed identity
locations of enunciation
out-thereness
(dis)placing culture and cultural space
time–space compression
glocalization
deindustrialization
appropriation

segregated cultural space
polysemic cultural space
contested cultural space
hybrid cultural space
hybrid cultural spaces as sites of intercultural negotiation
hybrid cultural spaces as sites of resistance
hybrid cultural spaces as sites of transformation

DISCUSSION QUESTIONS AND ACTIVITIES

Discussion Questions

1. Think about the neighborhood you grew up in, the street you live on, and the place you work. What is the most significant building or landmark in your town and what does it communicate? How do these cultural spaces contribute to your avowed and ascribed identities?

2. In what ways is globalization changing our experiences of cultural space? What does it mean when corporations, such as Starbucks and McDonald's, develop stores around the world, creating physical spaces that are exactly the same?

3. Using specific examples from the chapter, discuss the tension between voluntary and involuntary segregation of cultural space. Is it fair to say ethnic enclaves are voluntarily formed when the lines are drawn by racial and class stratifications? How about gated communities? Why do we perceive certain cultural spaces (i.e. ethnic enclaves) as "segregated," and not others (i.e. gated communities)?

Activities

1. Creating a Cultural Map—Group Activity

   a. On a geographical map of the area around your university campus, identify types of cultural spaces using words, symbols, colors, and pictures. Identify what kind of schools, neighborhoods, museums, businesses, cultural/ethnic/religious sites, and so on, are located in the area.

   b. Address the following questions:

      i. What groups (race, gender, sexuality, ethnicity, age, class, nationality, etc.) are associated with the cultural space? What meanings are attached to the space and people?

      ii. How is the area segregated and/or integrated? How does the segregation translate into or reflect unequal access to resources, such as housing, education, and health care?

      iii. Where can you position yourself in the map? How does the way you navigate in the area reflect your identity, belonging, and privilege, or lack thereof?

      iv. Can you see the signs of globalization on the map? If so, what concepts from the chapter can you apply to the phenomena?

2. The Body and the Space—Group Activity

   a. Choose a specific cultural space (i.e., restaurant, neighborhood, nightclub, and workplace) you are familiar with.

   b. Describe in detail how you communicate verbally and nonverbally in the space, such as your language, greetings, gestures, eye contact, voice, clothing, and use of space.

   c. Address the following questions:

      i. How is your verbal and nonverbal communication shaped by the particular cultural space?

      ii. What are the "codes of conduct" in the cultural space, and what happens if you violate them? Are there different codes based on gender?

      iii. How is your body signified in the particular cultural space? How are your differences marked on the body?

      iv. What is the relationship between the body and the space?

CHAPTER 5

Privileging Relationships

Intercultural Communication in Interpersonal Contexts

In the global context, the proximity of people from different cultures increases the likelihood of intercultural relationships.

Learning Objectives

1. Identify the challenges and opportunities of intercultural relationships in workplace, friendship, romantic, and cyber contexts.

2. Explain how difference, power, privilege, and positionality are negotiated and transformed in intercultural relationships.

3. Describe the impact of exclusion, prejudice, and myths on intercultural relationships, historically and today.

4. Explore how intercultural relationships in the global context are potential sites of alliances for social justice in the global context.

Relationships with coworkers, among friends, within families and romantic partners, as well as acquaintances made in schools, service sectors, entertainment, and religious groups have become increasingly diverse and multicultural in the age of globalization. Enhanced mobility, economic interdependence, and advances in technology bring people from very diverse cultural, socioeconomic, linguistic, and social positions together in unprecedented ways, creating both opportunities and challenges for intercultural relationships (Burawoy et al., 2000). Values and norms regarding friendships, family relationships, gender roles, romance, and sexuality are often questioned, disrupted, and reconfigured as a result of escalating flows of people, capital, and cultural products occurring in the context of globalization (Bell & Coleman, 1999; Padilla, Hirsch, Muñoz-Laboy, Sember, & Parker, 2007).

One out of every 32 people in the world lives outside her or his country of origin, accelerating the potential for and necessity of developing intercultural relationships (International Organization for Migration, n.d.). In both physical and virtual spaces, workplaces have become increasingly diverse and multicultural. In the United States and globally, escalating migration, increased access for nondominant groups as well as policies removing barriers to global business have accelerated the opportunities for and challenges of intercultural relationships in the workplace. Intercultural families, friendships, and longer-term romantic relationships also result from improved access to travel and tourism as well as social media that epitomize the mobility of people and messages in the global context. In her book *Romance on a Global Stage,* anthropologist Nicole Constable (2003) investigated intercultural heterosexual romantic relationships noting that:

> meeting marriage partners from abroad is not new, the Internet has fueled a global imagination and created a time-space compression that has greatly increased the scope and efficiency of introductions and communication between men and women from different parts of the world. (p. 4)

The proliferation of advanced communication and media technology from cell phones to the Internet to social media has also revolutionized and transformed the lives and lifestyles of lesbian, gay, bisexual, transgender, and queer (LGBTQ) communities in Asia and around the globe. For example, cartoon toy Hello Kitty, global symbol of cute, hangs on mobile phones in Japan to signify queer identity—an icon of performative femininity for gay men and sisterhood for lesbians (Yano, 2013). Websites like Black Gay Chat Live create spaces for networking, sharing stories, expressing political views, and gathering information. Living with severe state-sanctioned punishment and harassment in Iran, LGBT Iranians use the Internet to build community, maintain their identities, and seek critical information on health and sexuality (LGBT Republic of Iran, 2012).

Clearly, globalizing forces—the integration of capital and markets, the implementation of neoliberal policies, and advances in technology—have magnified the frequency and intensity of intercultural relationships. Yet, the complexities and contestations surrounding and impacting intercultural relationships in the context of globalization are also deeply embedded in the history of colonization as well as the anticolonial and civil rights movements of the second half of the 20th century. To a great extent, the rise of intercultural friendships and intimate relationships in the United States is attributable to the historic and monumental changes brought about by the civil rights movement in the 1950s and 1960s that challenged long-standing, colonial era laws inhibiting interracial interactions and prohibiting interracial marriages.

As early as 1660, legislation was enacted in the United States banning interracial marriage between Whites and Blacks. **Miscegenation** comes from Latin roots meaning "mixed" and "kind" and was used historically to refer to "mixed-race" relationships, specifically intermarriage, cohabitation, and sexual relationships between people of different socially constructed races. **Antimiscegenation** laws, which prohibited marriage between people of different so-called "racial" groups, existed in over 40 states until 1967 when the laws were overturned in the landmark *Loving v. Virginia Supreme Court* case (Roberts, 1994). Antimiscegenation laws normalized and maintained the socially constructed categories of "race" based on physical characteristics and promoted a belief that intermarriage across racial groups was deviant and would taint the "racial purity" of the dominant White, European American "race" (Childs, 2005; Lopez, 1997). As recently as 1970, only 1 out of 1,000 marriages in the United States were interethnic or interracial (Kalmijn, 1993). In 2010, approximately 5.4 million married-couple households were interracial or interethnic, which is 9.5% of all married-couple households in the United States (Johnson & Kreider, 2010). Research suggests that attitudes toward intercultural marriage are changing toward great acceptance (Wang, 2012). Interracial and interethnic relationships, partnerships, and marriages are increasing in the United States with each generation. Yet, they continue to be shaped by deeply embedded myths, stereotypes, assumptions, and prejudices forged in historical and current relationships of inequitable power that impact the initiation, development, and maintenance of these relationships (Childs, 2005; Orbe & Harris, 2008).

In this chapter, relationships are "privileged" in the sense that we foreground interpersonal relationships in our study of intercultural communication. The chapter title, "Privileging Relationships," also draws attention to how intercultural relationships in the global context are sites where cultural differences, power, privilege, and positionality are negotiated, translated, and transformed. The term *intercultural relationships* encompasses a broad and complicated terrain, including relationships between people from different racial, ethnic, national, and religious as well as class and sexual orientation groups; so we begin by exploring a topography of intercultural relationships. Then, brief case studies are used to illustrate and discuss theories and concepts that help us understand intercultural relationships in workplace, friendship, and romantic contexts. The impact of computer mediated communication (CMC), specifically the Internet and social media, on intercultural relationships in various contexts follows. A central goal of this chapter is to understand the critical role intercultural relationships can play in improving intercultural communication, challenging prejudices and stereotypes held by individuals and communities, and building alliances that advance social justice.

TOPOGRAPHY OF INTERCULTURAL RELATIONSHIPS

Interpersonal relationships are a vital and dynamic aspect of human interaction. People in all cultures initiate, develop, and at times dissolve relationships with others. To a great extent, our blueprints for interpersonal relationships come from our families of origin, which are profoundly shaped by cultural dimensions. Along with personal and contextual differences, we bring different culturally informed expectations, norms, and assumptions about relationships as well as historical and political influences into our interpersonal relationships.

Interracial Intercultural Relationships

Intercultural relationships, as defined here, encompass **interracial relationships**, or relationships that cross socially constructed racial groups—for example, a friendship or romantic relationship between a person who is grouped racially as Black and a person who is categorized racially as White, or between a person who is considered racially as Asian and someone who is Native American. Historically, interactions between different racial groups in the United States, and particularly between Blacks and Whites, were vigorously discouraged, curtailed, and in many cases prohibited by law. While laws have changed and interracial contact has increased in the United States, attitudes, stereotypes, and prejudices passed along, sanctioned, and policed by families and friends as well as through media representations continue to present barriers and challenges for interracial friendships and intimate relationships today (Chen & Toriegoe, 2016; Orbe & Harris, 2008; Thompson & Collier, 2006). Notions and perceptions of "race," as well as the meanings and significance attached to race, differ across countries and regions in the world. Therefore, the impact of race on intercultural relationships varies in different locations around the globe.

Interethnic Intercultural Relationships

Interethnic relationships are relationships between people who identify differently in terms of ethnicity or ethnic background. **Ethnicity** refers to shared heritage, place of origin, identity, and patterns of communication among a group. A relationship between an Italian American and Irish American, between a Filipino American and Chinese American, or between a Serbian and Croatian in the former Yugoslavia would be considered interethnic. Lines that divide ethnic groups within the racial category of White in the United States—Anglo/English American, Irish American, or Italian American, for example—have blurred through generations of assimilation and admission to the dominant racial group, making the distinctions between ethnic groups within the racial category of White less significant today than in the past. Yet, it is important to note that people who avow or are ascribed an identity as White do have an ethnicity. While the distinct and specific languages, heritages, and histories may be lost or only faintly remembered, a shared ethnic/racial culture does exist for European Americans, which manifests in communication patterns, values, norms, and practices.

International Intercultural Relationships

International relationships refer to relationships that develop across national cultural and citizenship lines, such as a relationship between someone who is from Turkey and someone who is from Germany or between someone who is Brazilian and a U.S. American. Many international relationships are also interracial and/or interethnic and therefore must address a complex intersection of socially constructed differences, positionalities, and influences from society in their relationships. In many cases, international intercultural relationships enrich the lives of both partners through exposure and experience of multiple countries, languages, and cultures, yet international intercultural romantic long-term relationships are often challenged by questions of where to live, legal rights of citizenship, and power imbalances if one partner is perpetually perceived as a "foreigner." In addition, international intercultural relationship partners may confront differences in access to social and institutional power and assumptions of superiority (or inferiority) based on perceptions about countries of origin and race from the social networks surrounding the friends or partners.

Interreligious Intercultural Relationships

Interreligious or interfaith relationships refer to relationships where people from two different religious orientations or faiths, such as Judaism, Buddhism, Christianity, and Hinduism or Catholic Christians and Protestant Christians form interpersonal relations. Changes in immigration laws within the United States since the 1965 Immigration and Naturalization Act along with the forces of globalization have brought large numbers of practicing Buddhists, Muslims, Sikhs, and Hindus to the United States, dramatically increasing the religious diversity in the United States (Fredericks, 2007). While much attention is placed on the influx of immigrants from religious groups that differ from the dominant Christian religion in the United States, Christian immigrants from developing countries account for over 60% of all new immigrants. Interfaith and interdenominational marriages are on the rise in the United States. A recent study noted that 45% of marriages in the past decade involved two religions or two Christian denominations that clashed significantly (Riley, 2010). Research also suggests that interfaith marriages are correlated with less religious participation and higher divorce rates than same-faith marriages (Kosin, Mayer, & Keysar, 2001).

Class Differences in Intercultural Relationships

Differences in class culture and how class culture intersects with and manifests differently based on ethnic, racial, and national differences also impact intercultural relationships. Class culture is a significant dimension of intercultural relationships from seemingly mundane issues, such as where coworkers, friends, or partners choose to eat, hang out, and socialize, to manners learned as appropriate in given settings, and from versions of the language spoken at home to what is expected in the university classroom. Class also affects meanings and attitudes attributed to workplace attire, public displays of wealth, as well as norms of raising children. Class culture translates into social capital to which one has access and manifests in our everyday lives in terms of our *habitus*—our patterns of perceptions, actions, sensibilities, and tastes (Bourdieu, 1984). Communication scholars Dreama Moon and Gary Rolison (1998) analyzed forms of nonverbal communication, such as proxemics—the use of space—and fashion to illustrate how "styles of consumption come to define and communicate class and further posit that the roots of classism are partially to be found in the communication, contestation and evaluation of 'class-culture commodities'" (p. 123). While **class prejudice** refers to personal attitudes that individuals of any class culture may hold about members of other classes, **classism** is defined as the systemic subordination of class groups by the dominant, privileged class.

Sexuality in Intercultural Relationships

Intercultural relationships are often sites where notions of sexuality and sexual identities intersect, collide, and coalesce with ethnic, racial, religious, and national cultural differences. Attitudes, norms, stereotypes, and assumptions regarding sexuality vary along a vast continuum and are deeply shaped by culture; histories of colonization; imperialism; economic, political, and social interests; as well as by the emergence of religious fundamentalism in the global context (Chávez, 2013; Weeks, Holland, & Waites, 2003). Socially constructed sexual identities, such as heterosexual, homosexual, gay, lesbian, bisexual, transsexual, transgender, and queer—whether ascribed, avowed, or both—position us differently in our relationships to each other and to institutions. Our differing positionalities enable and constrain access to power, privileges, and resources with particularly salient consequences for intercultural communication.

Photo 5.1 Lesbian, gay, bisexual, and transgender (LGBT) couples experience varying degrees of acceptance and exclusion in different locations in the United States and throughout the world

Issues of sexual orientation in society and in interpersonal relationships are often experienced as either completely invisible or hypervisible. When dominant norms of heterosexuality—including socially constructed gender roles, opposite-sex romantic attraction, and displays of physical affection—are followed and practiced, sexuality is generally unquestioned and heterosexuality is assumed. Yet, when an individual or couple challenges the dominant norms of heterosexuality—in terms of gender norms, same-sex affection, or attraction—then their sexuality is marked, underscored, and made highly visible (Nakayama, 1998). **Heteronormativity** refers to the institutionalization of heterosexuality in society and the assumption that heterosexuality is the only normal, natural, and universal form of sexuality. Social, economic, educational, media, legal, and religious institutions—as well as family and cultural attitudes—establish, reinforce, and regulate heteronormativity. **Heterosexism** is an ideological system that denies and denigrates any nonheterosexual behavior, identity, or community. Like sexism and racism, heterosexism not only entails individual biased attitudes, but refers to the coupling of prejudicial beliefs with institutional power to enact systemic discrimination. For example, international lesbian or gay couples, who may experience homophobia on a daily basis, are also systematically excluded from marriage in many states in the United States; without federal recognition of gay marriage, couples do not have access to spousal petitions for citizenship.

Multidimensional Cultural Differences in Intercultural Relationships

As you no doubt can see, intercultural relationships can and often do involve multiple and intersecting ethnic, racial, national, religious, class, and sexual orientation differences. An intimate, long-term romantic relationship between a Malaysian Muslim woman, for example, and an African American Christian man is likely to entail ongoing negotiations over cultural differences in verbal and nonverbal communication styles, norms, and expectations of families, intimacy, sexuality, and gender roles, as well as social pressures, alienation, and sanctions from friends, family, and society regarding their interracial relationship. Depending on the various geographic, cultural, and national landscapes through which the couple moves, institutional and individual racism, exclusion, and differences in their access to power and privilege may test their relationship. The couple's relationship may require them to address questions of citizenship, where they will live as well as where they can create a shared home in this globally mobile world. Additionally, their interfaith relationship may be a contested site particularly during life transitions, such as marriage, birth of children, and death, which are often marked by cultural and religious practices and rituals.

As illustrated here, intercultural relationships do not occur in a vacuum. Interpersonal relationships between people of different racial, ethnic, religious, national, class, and sexuality groups take place within historical, cultural, and political contexts, which are instrumental in how we interpret and make sense of them. The meanings attached to intercultural relationships—whether they are considered taboo, tolerated, or celebrated—are socially constructed by individuals, families, coworkers, and communities with real consequences. Intercultural interpersonal relationships, therefore, become sites where we develop and communicate shared and contested meanings of our identities, our sense of belonging to and exclusion from groups, and where we learn through our communication how we are positioned in relation to others. In the next section, we investigate in more depth concepts and processes that guide us in understanding intercultural relationships in the context of globalization.

Communicative Dimensions
Intercultural Relationships in the Workplace

Marian is a senior executive in a Fortune 500 multinational organization. In a weekly update meeting, Hugo, the manager of one of her design teams, expressed serious concerns about his staff. He reported reduced productivity and increased frustration due to intercultural misunderstandings between employees in China and the United States. Unable to hide the tension in his voice, Hugo told Marian, "If we don't do something about this soon, we may risk the loss of one of our key customers."

After consulting with her Human Resources representative, Marian was persuaded to hire an external intercultural communication consultant to assist with the problem. The U.S.-based consultant designed a full-day training course for the local team and also suggested that a few employees from China fly in for the session.

Given your knowledge of intercultural communication, you have been hired as the consultant. Here are some comments made by the design team members regarding differences in cultural values and communication styles:

Judith Anderson: I like working with Li. She's always friendly and polite over email and she does a great job. But, she doesn't give me clear deadlines. I know I missed one last week because she never stated it directly in any of her emails.

Li Min: For me, giving a specific deadline, especially to a peer, seems rude and demanding. I would be more likely to say something about a general time frame when the project will move on to the next phase. But, if Judith asked me what day it would be good to have the project completed, I would tell her the best date. I wouldn't see it as imposing a deadline though.

Melvin Cole: I have to admit that I often get irritated during conference calls with the design team in Beijing. When I ask what seems like a simple question, they take a long time to confer with everyone on their end before responding. I just can't see why one person doesn't just blurt out an answer the way I would.

Lotte Berg: I feel pretty embarrassed right now. I'm from the Netherlands and when I came to the United Ststes to work for this company, I assumed the entire corporate culture would be completely Westernized. I've been trying to connect with the leader of the group I work with in China by joking around and being really informal with him. I also try to make quick decisions and be assertive about them.

Using your knowledge of differences in cultural values, how would you explain the miscommunication and misunderstandings described here? What suggestions, as the intercultural communication consultant, would you make to this design team?

INTERCULTURAL RELATIONSHIPS IN THE WORKPLACE

In the context of globalization, the workplace—in both physical and virtual spaces—has become increasingly diverse and multicultural. Interacting with and managing diverse workforces, developing custom service strategies for culturally diverse groups, negotiating multinational contracts, and tapping diverse local and global markets all entail intercultural relationships with vast uncertainty and likelihood of misunderstanding as well as possibilities for learning and growth.

Cultural Values in the Workplace

Interpersonal relationships are critical sites where we are socialized into and negotiate **cultural values**—ideas and beliefs about what is important to us, what we care about, what we think is right and wrong, and what we evaluate as fair and unfair, which are gained from our cultural group membership. Our cultural values are shaped from an early age as meanings are shared and contested in our interpersonal relationships with family and others around us. As we grow up, we engage with broader circles and networks of people, with whom we may share and negotiate cultural values. Research in anthropology, psychology, sociology, international relations and intercultural communication has identified differences in values among cultural groups. Noting differences in values across cultural groups can be useful as a starting point in navigating the complexities of intercultural relationships with acquaintances, coworkers, and friends. However, as noted in our discussion of culture and cultural identities in previous chapters, cultural values have also been displaced/replaced, fragmented, hybridized, and reconfigured in the global context. While cultural groups based on nationality, race, and ethnicity may share some common values, we must also attend to the ways these values are mediated and altered based on gender, class, age, and religious and sexual orientation.

In the late 1960s, Dutch psychologist Geert Hofstede (1980) was contracted by IBM to conduct research with over 100,000 employees in 40 countries worldwide to identify and understand differences in national cultures and their impact on workplace culture. Based on problems faced by all cultures, four dimensions were identified. In the 1980s, prompted by criticism from researchers that the dimensions failed to address the influences of Confucianism on Eastern cultures, a fifth dimension was added. **Hofstede's** (2001) **cultural dimensions** provide broad maps for comparing cultures, understanding the impact of national culture on interpersonal communication, and developing strategies to address differences. While the original research was conducted in international business organizations, the dimensions can guide us broadly in understanding cultural differences that impact relationships in intercultural workplace, friendship, and family contexts. The five dimensions are as follows:

1. **Individualism–collectivism:** Individualistic cultures are ones where the interests of the individual are placed before the interest of the group. Individual identity, personal autonomy, individual rights, and responsibility tend to be valued. Collectivistic cultures tend to focus on the needs, interests, and goals of the group. In collectivistic cultures, individuals are socialized from an early age into cohesive, lifelong in-groups where relational interdependence and harmony within the group are stressed. According to Hofstede's (2001) research, countries in Asia, Latin America, Africa, and the Middle East tend to be collectivist while northern European and North American countries tend to be individualistic.

2. **Power distance:** Power distance is the tendency of individuals with less power in an organization to accept the unequal distribution of power. Small or low power distance cultures tend to emphasize equality, self-initiative, and consultation with subordinates in decision-making. Rewards and punishment are expected to be distributed equitably based on individual merit and performance. On the other hand, high power distance cultures tend to accept unequal status among members, respect those in higher status positions, and expect authority figures—managers or parents, for example—to make decisions. High power distance cultures reward age, rank, and status.

3. **Uncertainty avoidance:** Uncertainty avoidance refers to the tendency to feel threatened by the unknown and the inclination to steer clear of such situations. High uncertainty avoidance cultures tend to be more formal and ritual oriented while low uncertainty avoidance cultures tend to be more informal and less structured. In high uncertainty avoidance cultures, innovation is less acceptable, and conflict is seen as a threat to both group harmony and effectiveness. Low uncertainty avoidance cultures tend to encourage new and creative approaches.

4. **Masculinity–femininity:** According to Hofstede's (2001) dimensions, masculinity refers to societies that emphasize distinct differences in gender roles between men and women. On the other hand, femininity refers to cultures where gender roles overlap and gender characteristics are shared. Sensitivity to distinct and complementary gender role norms and rules as well as a focus on work-related achievements and results is important in masculine cultures. Flexible and interchangeable gender norms and balancing work/life, community, and environmental issues are important in feminine cultures. In both family and organizational contexts, boys and girls or men and women in feminine cultures are socialized and expected to be concerned with caring and task accomplishment; whereas, in more masculine cultures, girls and women are expected to be nurturing and attentive to relationships while boys and men are expected to be assertive and goal oriented.

5. **Time Orientation–Confucian dynamism:** This dimension addresses cultural differences in orientation to time. East Asian countries, for example, are characterized by a long-term orientation to time, with value placed on persistence, status, humility, and collective face-negotiation strategies. The tremendous economic growth of Singapore, Taiwan, Japan, Hong Kong, and Korea in the 1990s and of China at the beginning of the 21st century is often attributed to Confucian values of perseverance, hard work, frugality, respect for elders, and hierarchical structures.

Hofstede's (2001) cultural dimensions have been used widely to understand interpersonal relationships in the workplace and in international management. The value dimensions help us make sense of ourselves, and our relationships with others in workplaces and with friends and families. For example, the cultural dimension of individualism–collectivism may provide insight into how we approach work, what motivates us, and what we hold as important. A person from a more individualistically oriented culture may prefer to work independently and to be rewarded individually for tasks accomplished, while someone from a more collectivistic orientation may prefer to work in a group and expect to be rewarded based on the group's accomplishments. The nature of the relationships between the boss and an employee are generally quite different in high power distance cultures than in low power distance cultures. Different cultural orientations to power distance can translate into varying assumptions, expectations, and behaviors regarding relationships among coworkers that impact decision making, systems of reward, and workplace climate.

Low to high uncertainty avoidance points to types of communication styles we are socialized to develop and with whom we are encouraged to communicate and build relationships. In high uncertainty avoidance cultures, people generally do not engage with strangers; rather, one is introduced to new people through coworkers, friends, or family members who are mutually known. On the other hand, engaging with strangers is a common activity in low uncertainty avoidance cultures. Autonomy in tasks, roles, and relationships is more highly valued in individualistic, low power distance, low uncertainty avoidance, and feminine cultures. Children in individualistic cultures learn independence and self-sufficiency in their family and educational environments, and thus, autonomy in work roles is more likely to motivate and serve as a reward for employees in the workforce. As outlined by Hofstede, cultural dimensions extend beyond the workplace impacting intercultural friendships and intimate relationships.

Critics of Hofstede's dimensions and other value orientations based on national culture point out that data gathered in the late 1960s and early 1970s as well as foundational assumptions may be outdated. Given the complexities of intercultural interactions in the 21st century, the diversity of cultural tendencies within nations, and the dramatic geopolitical shifts that have occurred particularly in the last 30 years, frameworks of cultural variation based on national culture can lead to overgeneralization and stereotyping. Cultural differences do exist impacting interpersonal relationships in workplace, friendship, and romantic contexts. Used as broad maps, Hofstede's dimensions can provide a first step toward understanding the effects of culture on human interaction. Attention to situational contexts and cultural histories is also needed (Osland & Bird, 2000).

FORMING AND SUSTAINING INTERCULTURAL RELATIONSHIPS

Intercultural Friendships

Scenario One: *Maggie Hernandez and Neda Kohen became friends in their public speaking class freshman year. At first, they bonded over their fear of public speaking and now, five years later, they are good friends. Maggie's parents came to the United States from Guadalajara, Mexico, a few years before she was born. Neda's parents came to the United States from Tehran, Iran. She was born in the United States and identifies as Persian Jewish. In the first months of their friendship, Maggie had many questions and being an outgoing and curious person, she just asked Neda: How can you be Iranian and Jewish? Aren't most people from the Middle East Muslim? Why do you call yourself Persian if you're from Iran? Neda was a bit surprised and a little offended by these questions.*

After getting to know each other better through long talks and visits to each other's homes, Neda admitted she had made assumptions about Maggie and her family as well. Learning that Maggie's family was from Mexico, she wondered if they were in the United States illegally. When Neda met Maggie at Maggie's home to study for an exam, she was surprised to find out they lived in a middle-class neighborhood and that Maggie's mother worked as a paralegal at a law firm. Maggie was hurt that her friend would think these things, but it was hardly a new experience. As their friendship developed, other misunderstandings and challenges emerged. Maggie complained that Neda was never free to go out with friends on Friday nights and Neda's friends couldn't understand why she wanted to be friends with someone who was not Persian. Through all of this, their friendship continues.

Intercultural friendships like Neda's and Maggie's are a unique type of interpersonal relationship. Today, in the context of globalization where we frequently come in contact with people from diverse cultures in person and through social media, we are more likely to have friends who are culturally different from ourselves. Intercultural friendships often require us to navigate unknown terrain where our comfort and familiarity with interpersonal norms, communication styles, values, and expectations, as well as our language and meaning-making systems, are thrown into question. As with Neda and Maggie, these differences can increase anxiety, uncertainty, misunderstanding, and conflict (Gudykunst, 1995; Sias et al., 2008). Maintaining intercultural friendships often means we have to negotiate deeply embedded stereotypes and assumptions held not only by ourselves, but also by our network of friends, families, communities, and society. Intercultural relationships may also expose us very personally and with great impact to the ways that privilege, positionality, and power operate within society to advantage and include some, while disadvantaging and excluding others.

Forming and sustaining an intercultural friendship like the one between Maggie and Neda requires curiosity about each other, a willingness to learn about cultural and religious differences and histories as well as differences in standpoints and positionalities. By communicating and sharing life experiences, Neda and Maggie are able to understand how they are positioned differently based on others' perceptions, assumptions, and stereotypes about each of them. Their challenges, like the experiences of others who develop and sustain intercultural relationships, can translate into both personal and societal benefits by increasing understanding of other ethnic, racial, and cultural groups as well as deepening understanding of one's own group; challenging and breaking down misconceptions, stereotypes, and prejudices; and developing skills and strategies for intercultural alliances that create a more just and equitable world.

Take a moment to consider other intercultural friendships like Maggie and Neda's that bring together different ethnic, racial, class, religious, and sexual orientation groups. How are the challenges, issues, and benefits of intercultural friendship different if, for example, one friend is White and the other African American? If one relational partner is Korean American and the other is an international student from Japan? If the friendship is between a Somali American who is straight and a White American who is a lesbian? How do friendship norms, expectations, and assumptions differ if the relational partners are men? Our cultural, racial, ethnic, sexual orientation, gendered, national, and religious identities intersect and interplay in our intercultural friendships in particular ways that create distinct challenges due to historical and current conditions, standpoints, and positionalities; our intersectional identities, as they combine in intercultural relationships, also offer unique opportunities and benefits. Additionally, the contexts within which intercultural friendship initiates, develops, and moves play significant roles in how the relationship is "read" and how others and those in the friendship make meaning about the relationship.

Cultural Notions of Friendship

Unlike relationships with family and relatives, friendships are typically characterized as voluntary—in other words, they involve some element of choice by relational partners. While this is frequently the case, the concept of friendships as "chosen relationships" assumes a typically Western, individualistic orientation to friendship. In more group-oriented or collectivist cultures, friendships are often recognized as growing out of group associations, longer-term connections to place, community, and a sense of mutual obligation.

Communication scholar Mary Jane Collier's (1991) research on African American, Latino/Latina, and European American students found that for all groups the notion of friendship revolved around qualities of trust and acceptance. Collier (1996) also found that while similar in many respects, conversational rules in close friendships among ethnic groups differ. Specifically, while European Americans reported that close friendships developed in a few months, Asian Americans, African Americans, and Latinos/Latinas report taking approximately a year for close friendships to develop. Collier (1996) further noted morality and cultural respect are important for Latinos/Latinas, family is critical for Asian Americans, while African Americans focus on pride in ethnic heritage. In Krumrey-Fulks's (2001) research comparing Chinese and American expectations of friendship, Chinese participants viewed friends as those who provided help or assistance while Americans tended to look toward friends as good listeners. Notions of what constitutes a friend, what behaviors are appropriate, and what we expect to share in friendship relationships are shaped by the various age, gender, ethnic, racial, cultural, class, and national groups in which we participate and with which we identify.

Intercultural Relationship Development Processes

It is useful to think about intercultural relationships developing in three phases composed of an initial encounter phase, an exploratory interactional phase, and an ongoing involvement phase. In the initial encounter phase, people who initiate intercultural relationships are drawn to each other based on (1) proximity to each other; (2) similarities in interests, values, and goals as well as cultural, racial, and socioeconomic backgrounds; (3) the ways in which the two complement and are different from each other; and (4) physical attraction to one another.

Given the increased proximity of people from different cultures in the context of globalization, we would expect an increase in intercultural encounters and interactions. In a study titled "Who's Interacting? And What Are They Talking About?—Intercultural Contact and Interaction Among Multicultural University Students," communication scholar Rona Halualani and her colleagues (2004) found that, rather ironically, in a context that promotes diversity, students have relatively limited intercultural interaction. In this study, students interact interculturally one to two times per week, yet their intercultural interactions revealed distinct patterns based on the following: (1) the racial/ethnic group involved in contact, (2) the location of contact, (3) the topic of interaction, and (4) their socioeconomic class.

The researchers (Halualani et al., 2004) noted that people from diverse ethnic/racial backgrounds enter into intercultural interactions from different starting points shaped by socioeconomic class, previous contact with ethnic/racial groups, and historical memory of intercultural encounters between groups, which position individuals and groups differently in relation to each other. Different positionalities—rooted in hierarchies of social, economic, and political difference—impact the amount and frequency of interaction as well as the nature of intercultural contact. The study further suggests that people from different ethnic/racial groups may use "different sense-making logics" when engaging interculturally. For example, African Americans/Blacks may view intercultural interactions as a site of differentiation where cultural distinction and uniqueness is emphasized whereas Asian Americans, Latinos/Latinas,

and Whites/European Americans may interact interculturally using a logic of similarities stressing sameness in the encounter (Halualani et al., 2004, p. 369).

The tendency to seek similarity in friendship formation presents an undeniable challenge
in the initial encounter phase of intercultural relationship development. Language barriers,
cultural differences in our orientation to strangers, and culturally coded conversational rules
about what is appropriate to discuss and how much to disclose make initial encounters difficult and anxiety-producing. Discomfort regarding the unfamiliar, ambiguity about what is
expected, and fear of difference may lead to confusion, mistrust, and retreat from intercultural encounters and friendships. Additionally, our socially constructed and learned distinctions of race may also inhibit intercultural interactions in the initial phase. As noted in the
scenario about Neda and Maggie's friendship, how others in our social network perceive our
relationship with someone from outside our racial, ethnic, or cultural group is also important.

In the **initial encounter phase** of intercultural relationship development, it is important
to challenge preconceived assumptions, stereotypes, and prejudices regarding racial, cultural, and ethnic differences. At the same time, we need to acknowledge, seek to understand, and learn from the differences in communication styles; interactional patterns; and
cultural, racial, and ethnic histories that do exist. If we do not take the risk to move outside
our comfort zones, we miss the opportunity to develop a more in-depth knowledge, understanding, and experience of the world from the position of those who are different from
us. Staying in conversation with each other—especially about difficult, unfamiliar, and
uncomfortable topics—allowed Maggie and Neda to move from the challenges of the initial
phase to the next phase in relationship development.

Intercultural Praxis
Learning From Intercultural Relationships

In intercultural relationship development, engaging in intercultural praxis through curious inquiry
about people who are different from oneself means that we suspend our judgments, challenge our
preconceived notions of others, and take risks to initiate interactions outside our comfort zone.
Misunderstandings that result from cultural differences, different histories, and different worldviews
can motivate us to use the points of entry of framing and positioning in intercultural praxis to
broaden our knowledge, deepen our empathy, and increase our understanding of the world.

While different experiences and resultant standpoints provide opportunities for learning in intercultural friendships, members of the dominant group often find it easier to excuse and rationalize
incidents of racism, sexism, or homophobia experienced by nondominant groups rather than grapple
with the reality of the differences and the underlying systemic inequity revealed. Lack of recognition
of White privilege, male privilege, heterosexual privilege, and U.S. privilege by dominant group members can be a source of tension and conflict in intercultural friendships. A willingness to understand
how forms of privilege operate to disadvantage nondominant groups and to normalize the standpoint of the dominant group is critical.

In the **exploratory interaction phase,** intercultural relationships move toward greater sharing of information, increased levels of support and connection, and growing intimacy. A significant challenge for intercultural friendship relationships at this stage is the different culturally coded ways in which individuals from different groups have been socialized to achieve support, connection, and intimacy. In a well-known cross-cultural study, psychologist Kurt Lewin (1948) identified three spheres of information that people share with each other regarding the personal/private self. Imagine three concentric circles that model levels of information about the self. The larger, outer circle contains superficial information about one's self, such as interests and regular activities. The middle circle contains more personal information about family and background. The inner circle holds even more personal and private information that we are likely to share with fewer people. What information is held in each of these spheres—what is considered superficial and shared more freely as compared to what is more protected—may vary across cultures. Additionally, the degree to which we self-disclose information from each sphere and the amount of time it takes in the relationship development process to reach the inner core may also vary across cultures. International students in the United States frequently comment on the ease with which U.S. Americans share and self-disclose personal information about themselves. Confusion often arises as international students in the United States are unsure how to make sense of high levels of self-disclosure, which are sometimes mistaken for increased intimacy and closeness, signaling a movement toward a deeper friendship. Additionally, those who are accustomed to a more rapid pace and higher degrees of self-disclosure, often common in the United States, may find the lack of reciprocal disclosure from their relational partner off-putting and unrewarding.

As connection and affinity grow in intercultural friendships, relational partners typically spend more time together sharing experiences that expose them to each others' cultures and offer opportunities for intercultural learning. In this phase, friendships are also more susceptible to external pressures and societal perceptions regarding race, gender, culture, and nationality, as well as differences in access to power and privilege that each friendship partner may experience. A friendship between a White American and an African American may reveal through firsthand experience the different positionalities afforded each friend within society and the consequent differences in standpoint each holds. Common experiences of people of color in the United States, such as being singled out for surveillance in a store, pulled over by police for no apparent reason, ignored in conversations, or passed over in hiring processes because "you just don't fit in" may not be shared by a person who is White. The friendship partners are likely to make sense of these experiences in different ways based on different personal and cultural histories, which contribute to their divergent standpoints. The success of continuing intercultural friendship relationships often depends on a willingness to "value difference and affirm the other person as a member of a culturally different group" (Collier, 2002a, p. 308).

As noted by Lee (2008) and others, the transition to the **ongoing involvement phase** in intercultural relationship development is often marked by a turning point that promotes greater connection, intimacy, and involvement between the relational partners. Turning points could include sharing a significant event, such as meeting family members, taking a trip together, or having conversations that engage greater levels of self-disclosure, vulnerability, and sharing.

Being willing to stay in difficult conversations, as Maggie and Neda did, where one's limited knowledge of others' experiences and vulnerability is exposed and where one's privilege is challenged is critical. As friendship partners move into the ongoing involvement phase, shared rules of engagement that guide their interaction with each other emerge. Julia Wood (1982) used the term **relational identity/culture** to refer to the system of understanding that is developed between relational partners as they coordinate attitudes, actions, and identities within the relationship and with the world outside the relationship. Collier (2002a) noted that intercultural relationships involve the constant and ongoing negotiation of both the friendship relational identity "while simultaneously maintaining divergent cultural identities" (p. 307).

Intercultural Romantic Relationships

Scenario Two: *Beverly Marshall and Guy Johnson, both in their late 20s, met three years ago through an online dating site where their mutual interest in acting, theater, and sports caught each other's attention. The pictures helped, too! Beverly, who identifies as White or European American and grew up in the South, works as a marketing manager at a theater in a medium size city in the Midwest. Guy, who identifies as African American or Black and grew up on the East Coast, works in human resources for a chain retail business in the same city. After dating for several years, the couple was married last year.*

When they first got involved, Beverly was aware they might face some challenges, but she figured they were two strong individuals and if they cared enough about each other, everything would work out. Guy tried to warn her sharing experiences he'd had in the past. After dating for a few months, she overhead some of her White friends making very sexualized comments about Guy; on another occasion, one of her coworkers, an African American woman, accused her of stealing "her" men. Out in public together at the theater or dinner, sometimes they noticed people giving them strange looks.

Guy tried to talk with Beverly about these incidents, but at first Beverly just wanted to ignore them or excuse them as misunderstandings or misinterpretations. She decided it was easier not to go out in public—they could meet at each other's apartments or go to dinner at a friend's house. Over time, they both realized they had to talk through this and come up with ways to face the challenges together, which meant learning more about each other and about themselves. Visits to each of their family's homes before the wedding were eye-opening and challenging. For the most part, immediate family members were supportive; yet, some extended family community members were not so inclusive.

The number of people in the United States similar to Beverly and Guy who are in intercultural romantic relationships as defined in this chapter—interracial, interethnic, international, and interreligious as well as interclass intimate relationships—is unknown given that existing research tends to study these groups separately. We do know that attitudes toward interracial marriage and intercultural dating are changing. In 2012, a Pew Research Center study revealed the highest approval rating ever with 83 % of Americans approving marriage among Blacks and Whites (Wang, 2012). Yet, even with the increased diversity within the United States and greater acceptance of intercultural relationships, most people still live, work, worship, and socialize in largely segregated groups (Childs, 2005). Even though legal barriers to integration and laws prohibiting intermarriage are relics of the past, borders between ethnic, racial, cultural, religious, and class groups still remain and challenges persist, as for Guy and Beverly. While interracial relationships are often held up as symbols of progress in a supposed "postracial" era, Amy Steinbugler (2012) argues in her book *Beyond Loving: Intimate Racework in Lesbian, Gay, and Straight Interracial Relationships* that interracial intimacy is an ongoing process that requires couples to navigate spaces of racial homogeneity and manage visibility as well as engage in **racework**. The spatial segregation based on race and culture of residential areas, places of worship, restaurants, schools, and organizations creates significant challenges for interracial and intercultural couples. As interracial couples move through monocultural and multicultural spaces, they must navigate hypervisibilty, where the mixed-race aspect of their partnership is accentuated and sometimes targeted as well as invisibility, where their relationship as a couple, particularly for gay and lesbian couples, is simply not recognized for what it is. Steinbugler (2012) argues that interracial partners engage in **racework**—everyday actions and strategies through which close relationships that cross racial lines are maintained. Racework requires emotional work as couples negotiate differences in privilege, power, and standpoints and boundary work as partners construct and re-construct their individual and relational identities in intercultural relationships.

Historically embedded prejudices held by those surrounding the couple—family, friends, and society—may force people to choose between family and partner. As Childs (2005) made clear and the scenario above illustrates, it is not only the couple who navigate borders in intercultural relationships; rather, friends, families, and racial/ethnic communities are central in monitoring and creating the experiences of and meanings about intercultural couples. Typically, research has focused attention on the intercultural or interracial couple—the characteristics of individuals who choose intercultural unions and their psychological problems—promoting the assumption that intercultural relationships are deviant and reinforcing beliefs that romantic relationships within the same culture should be the standard and norm. Childs (2005) proposed that interracial couples are significant not so much for what they tell us about the particular individuals, but rather for the meanings produced about them in society and the roles these meanings play in the constructing, maintaining, and dismantling racial borders.

Intercultural Romantic Relationships Development

Much of the early research on interracial romantic or intimate relationships from the 1960s and 1970s reflected the stereotypes of the time and reinforced myths about race and sexuality. In a review of literature on Black–White couples, communication scholars Foeman and Nance (1999) identified five myths that have informed research, societal perceptions, and media representations regarding interracial couples. Many of these myths originated during the colonial period, functioning then to rationalize and justify the inequitable and exploitative relationships of slavery, and operating now to shape perceptions of intercultural relationships as deviant. The first myth is that Black people have an extraordinarily potent sex drive. We see this stereotype playing out in the scenario with Guy and Beverly. Viewed as highly sexual, Black men are feared by White men and portrayed as wanting revenge for White wrongdoing by sexually exploiting White women. Black women are also depicted as highly sexual, which served to alleviate the guilt of White slave owners for their abuses and rape of Black women (Smith, 1966) and absolves White men of their sexual aggressiveness and stereotypes of women of color today (Collins, 1990). A second myth is that Blacks marry Whites for status, a type of socioeconomic trade-off. While this may happen in some cases, research suggests that Black and White couples come from similar educational and socioeconomic backgrounds (Schoen & Wooldredge, 1989). A third myth, often perpetuated in popular culture, but unsubstantiated through research, is that Whites choose Black partners out of rebellion, spite for their parents, or as an effort to act out (Childs, 2005; Foeman & Nance, 1999). The assumptions that underlie these myths are that individuals who choose interracial romantic relationships are deviant and disturbed seeking only social or economic advancement or sex. Another false assumption is that all interracial relationships are heterosexual. While absent from the literature until recently and often still invisible in society's heterosexual landscapes, interracial gay and lesbian relationships developed historically and today.

Other myths include the genetic inferiority of children from interracial marriages and the psychological problems, particularly in terms of identity, of biracial or multiracial children. Recent research advances a more positive interpretation of biracial individuals highlighting their receptivity and adaptability to multiple cultures (González & Harris, 2013). While biracial and bicultural people are often challenged by society's obsessive need to categorize them and may experience marginalization in both ethnic/racial/cultural groups, bicultural and multicultural people use their ambiguous positionalities in constructive and creative ways (Anzaldúa, 1991; Bennett, 1993). "In contrast to the misconception of irreconcilable identity confusion, researchers have found that most mixed-race people have a great deal of clarity about their racial identities" (Laszloffy & Rockquemore, 2013, p. 47). After interviewing hundreds of biracial/bicultural people, clinical psychologist Maria P. P. Root (1996) wrote the "Bill of Rights for People of Mixed Heritage" to resist racial and cultural myths, stereotypes, and hierarchies that have served to divide and oppress people and groups in the United States (see Figure 5.1).

Foeman and Nance (1999) proposed a four-stage model for understanding interracial romantic relationships and the role communication plays in the relational development process. While their research focuses specifically on interracial relationships, the model is extended here to address intercultural relationships as defined in this chapter. The first stage is **racial/cultural awareness**, where relational partners become aware of their similarities and differences and develop awareness of four coexisting perspectives: (1) their own, (2) their partner's, (3) their collective racial/cultural group's perspective, and (4) their partner's racial/cultural group's perspective. While these perspectives may not be discussed openly, the various individual and group-based viewpoints likely impact decisions, such as where to eat out and with whom to socialize. As we can see with Beverly and Guy, communication plays a critical role at this stage as partners negotiate new awareness of themselves and outsiders' perceptions of them as a couple, as well as the roles race, ethnicity, culture, or class play in their initial attraction. Race and/or culture may be highlighted or minimized in the way the couple talks about their relationship; they are nevertheless negotiating their racial/cultural/ethnic differences in this initial phase. Differences in the couple's assumptions, standpoints, and privilege may be revealed, requiring explanations, a willingness to see oneself and the world differently, and "sensitivity to a sometimes uncomfortable alternative perspective" (Foeman & Nance, 1999, p. 550). Initially, Beverly tries to

Figure 5.1   Bill of Rights for People of Mixed Heritage

Bill of Rights

for

People of Mixed Heritage

I HAVE THE RIGHT . . .

Not to justify my existence in this world.

Not to keep the races separate within me.

Not to justify my ethnic legitimacy.

Not to be responsible for people's discomfort with my physical or ethnic ambiguity.

I HAVE THE RIGHT . . .

To identify myself differently than strangers expect me to identify.

To identify myself differently than how my parents identify me.

To identify myself differently than my brothers and sisters.

To identify myself differently in different situations.

I HAVE THE RIGHT . . .

To create a vocabulary to communicate about being multiracial or multiethnic.

To change my identity over my lifetime—and more than once.

To have loyalties and identification with more than one group of people.

To freely choose whom I befriend and love.

Source: © Maria P. P. Root, PhD, 1993, 1994.

overlook and minimize the racialized comments and experiences the couple encounters as her sense of self, of Guy and his identity as well as of their relationship are challenged by others' attitudes and actions. Her standpoint as a White woman and her positionality of privilege are being tested. The comment by her coworker about stealing "her" men brings Beverly's racial identity to the forefront; it also challenges Guy's identity and belonging as an African American man.

The second stage is the **coping stage**, where the couple develops proactive and reactive strategies to manage the challenges of their intercultural relationship and to protect themselves as a couple and individuals from harmful external forces, such as negative attitudes, stereotypes, and actions of friends, family, and society. As with Guy and Beverly, intercultural couples use communication to develop a shared understanding of situations, develop various responses to hostile environments, and seek out support. While dealing with these challenges can be stressful and can lead to the dissolution of the relationship, working through the difficulties also strengthens the relationship to ensure its survival (Foeman & Nance, 1999).

The third stage, **identity emergence**, occurs as interracial or intercultural couples take charge of the images of themselves, challenge negative societal forces, and reframe their relationship. "Instead of looking at their differences as obstacles to be overcome, interracial couples view the unique racial configuration of the families as a positive source of strength (e.g. 'Being biracial is a gift')" (Foeman & Nance, 1999, p. 553). Interracial and intercultural couples may choose, in fact, to see themselves as unusual or different, but frame their uniqueness in positive and supportive ways instead of as "deviant" or "deficient." "Communication functions to provide the voice and words to recast their world: We are the inevitable family of a truly multicultural society" (Foeman & Nance, 1999, p. 553).

The final stage in the interracial/intercultural relationship development is **relational maintenance**. The communication skills, strategies, and perspectives that couples have developed through earlier stages are used to negotiate differences between themselves and with the society at large. Foeman and Nance (1999) noted that each individual within the couple may start the relationship at a different stage or revisit earlier stages as issues, internal or external to the relationship, emerge. As the couple moves through different life stages—having children, for example—new challenges and opportunities for increased awareness and deepened perspectives, additional coping strategies, and a sense of family identity also emerge.

Consider other intimate intercultural relationships like Guy and Beverly's that interconnect individuals, families, and communities of different ethnic, racial, class, religious, and national backgrounds. How are the challenges and benefits of intercultural romantic relationships different if, for example, the racial combination is the same, White and Black as with Beverly and Guy, but the gender changes, as with a couple composed of a Black woman and a White man? Or an intimate relationship between a Latino man and an Asian American women, or between an Asian American man and a Latina woman? Questions of race, ethnicity, and culture are present for intercultural gay and lesbian intimate relationships, even as others view the same-sex aspect of the relationship as salient. Other issues include varying levels of acceptance of same-sex couples across cultures and communities; hypervisibility of lesbian and gay couples, on the one hand and yet, lack of visibility or acknowledgment of the relationship, on the other; and access to the privileges and benefits afforded straight couples who are married challenge queer intimate relationships.

As people from different ethnic, racial, class, and national cultures maintain friendships and intimate relationships, complex and often contradictory issues and tensions arise based on differing intersectional identities, positionalities, and relationships to power and privilege. Negotiating variations in cultural notions of friendships and intimacy, different norms of relationship development and cultural meaning-making are key to sustaining intercultural friendships and intimate relationships. Attention to how power and privilege operate both within the relationship and in society; an awareness of the roles cultural group histories play and the varied importance placed on history; and affirmation of the relational partner's culture and cultural identities all advance intercultural friendships and romantic relationships (Collier, 2002a).

CYBERSPACE AND INTERCULTURAL RELATIONSHIPS

In the context of globalization, cyberspace interactions and relationships have become increasingly common as the Internet and social media provide new contexts and alternative ways to meet strangers, engage in dyadic conversations, develop relationships, and participate in virtual communities. Digital media and online communication are pervasive in the lives of youth functioning as sites for socializing, learning, playing, and for self-expression (Ito, 2010).

Approximately 43% of the 7.2 billion people inhabiting the planet are connected through virtual superhighways (Internet World Stats, 2014). Yet, a digital divide persists globally and within nation-states. While about 84% of the population in North America has access to the Internet, the rate of penetration in Africa is only 26.5%. Also, within countries, huge discrepancies in access exist. India has an estimated 240 million active Internet users, yet this represents only 19% of the population (Internet World Stats, 2014). A recent study shows the rise of mobile smartphone usage in the United States has enabled those historically excluded by the digital divide—Blacks, Latino/as, and Native Americans—to access the Internet in record numbers. Little difference in Internet access was reported across racial groups within the same economic level in the United States; yet, the Internet access gap persists for low-income households, those with no high school education, and the elderly (Pew Research Internet Project, 2012).

Social networking sites (SNS), online platforms to build social relations, have become a central part of mainstream culture where people construct and communicate their identities, initiate relationships, develop connections and a sense of belonging, as well as negotiate differences. In her cyber-ethnography of university students in the United States, Natalia Rybas (2012) found that users of online social networks assume and expect authentic representations of self and others; yet, she argues, ". . . authenticity, even though expected, becomes an illusion of the Facebook-ing process" (p. 99). Given the constraints of the software, the constant updating, editing, and decisions about what is posted and what is omitted, Facebook users intentionally accentuate or erase identity differences based on race, gender, and class to meet audience expectations (Rybas, 2012). Online and offline presentations of self and relationships with others intersect in the context of hierarchies of difference framing our understanding of ourselves, others' perceptions and interpretations as well as positioning us differently in relationships of power with each other.

In a comparative study of Korean and U.S. social networking sites, Cho (2010) found that Koreans, indicative of a collectivistic cultural orientation, maintained tighter and narrower SNS relationships than people in the United States. Stressing interdependence in face-to-face social relations, Koreans paid greater attention to self-presentation behaviors in SNS than people in the United States who tend to have a more individualistic cultural orientation. Cho's (2010) research suggests that culture influences the use of SNS and shapes user behavior; thus, assumptions of homogenous global populations of SNS users and uses need critical attention.

Chen and Dai (2012) note that new media in the global era reconfigures affinity groups and creates new relational communities allowing more fluid and dynamic experiences, negotiations, and constructions of cultural identities. As culture is deterritorialized geographically and socially, traditional notions of identity are challenged and reconstituted in new ways. While intercultural communication through new media may transcend physical boundaries, geopolitical power dynamics are inevitably present. In mediated interactions, Chen and Dai argue that the asymmetrical power geometry of globalization works to the advantage of the West. The pervasiveness of Western modernity, the digital divide between Western and non-Western nations, and the hegemony of the English language in new media all reinforce Western dominance. In the context of such imbalanced power relations, the exchange of cultural symbols, values, norms and practices that occurs through new media impacts Western and non-Western cultures differently. Western cultures may be enriched and energized by processes of hybridization with non-Western cultures; yet, the penetration of Western values often threatens the values and identities of non-Western cultures (Chen & Dai, 2012).

Users of social networking sites, like Facebook originating in the United States, Qzone and Sina Weibo used primarily in China with increasing global reach, and Vkontakte (VK) in Russia, communicate with others by posting personal information and photos, commenting on others' posts, as well as initiating and developing relationships through posts and private communication. SNS and other forms of new media also serve as platforms for learning about and addressing social issues. Reporters Lindsay Deutsch and Jolie Lee (2014) speak to the role of social media in shaping narratives about social issues:

> People in Ferguson, Mo., didn't wait for news conferences, petitions or legal action to bring national attention to their streets after a police officer fatally shot an unarmed black teen. They snapped a photo. They used a hashtag. And, in the span of five days, their growing, stinging social media cloud of real-time updates shaped a raw public discourse about the teen, Michael Brown, race relations and police force in the USA.

While social media is a growing force promoting intercultural awareness, dialogue, and activism regarding social issues, **flaming**, or hostile, impulsive, and abusive behavior online in chatrooms, forums, social network sites and game lobbies, also impacts intercultural relations. Shielded by anonymity, online comments, posts, and interactions can become even more racially and sexually offensive and attacking than in face-to-face interactions. Oliva Chow expected her 2014 bid for mayor of Toronto, Canada, would be challenging. During one public debate, her personal history as an immigrant was used to question her qualifications for the position, and in another debate, she was told to "go back to China." Yet these remarks paled in comparison to the vitriolic sexist and racist comments that accumulated on Twitter, Facebook, and other online sites during the election (Strashin, 2014). In another example, a commercial that aired in the United States in 2013 depicted a young girl asking her White mother about the health benefits of Cheerios and then dumping the contents of the box on her Black father. The seemingly ordinary commercial incited such malicious and hateful responses that remarks in the comment section on YouTube had to be disabled. The mere portrayal of a mixed race couple elicited comments that "devolved into an endless flame war, with references to Nazis, 'troglodytes' and 'racial genocide'" (Nudd, 2013).

Clearly, advances in communication technology in the global context facilitate intercultural communication allowing friends and intimate partners to meet, develop relationships, and maintain contact particularly at great geographic distance. Mediated communication through email, social networking sites, and virtual communities enables individuals and groups to connect, expand social networks, and build political alliances. Nonetheless, relationships in "virtual" space are not immune to the social, political, and economic barriers and geopolitical power asymmetries that detrimentally impact intercultural communication in face-to-face encounters. In fact, "virtual" environments can work to erase and amplify differences based on culture, gender, race, sexuality, language and nationality in both subtle and blatant ways that negatively affect intercultural communication.

INTERCULTURAL ALLIANCES FOR
SOCIAL JUSTICE IN THE GLOBAL CONTEXT

In the global context, intercultural relationships are sites where cultural differences, positionalities, and issues of power and privilege are negotiated, translated, and potentially transformed. Intercultural friendships and intimate relationships can play a critical role in improving intercultural communication, challenging prejudices and stereotypes, developing allies, and building alliances that advance social justice. An ally is a supporter or partner who can be counted on to work in collaboration with another person, group, or community toward a common goal. An **intercultural ally**, then, is a person, group, or community working across lines or borders of nationality, culture, ethnicity, race, gender, class, religion, or sexual orientation in support of and in partnership with others. Given that socially constructed categories of difference inevitably position individuals and groups unevenly within systems of power and privilege, intercultural allies work to challenge inequity and marginalization of nondominant groups. Communication scholar Mary Jane Collier (2002b) defined **intercultural alliance** as a "relationship in which parties are interdependent and responsible to and for each other. Intercultural allies recognize their cultural difference and their interdependence, and often seek similar goals, but they are not necessarily friends" (p. 2). Communication scholar Brenda Allen (2004), an African American heterosexual woman, described her alliance with her colleague and friend, Anna, a White lesbian woman:

> We swap stories and perspectives on the socially constructed aspects of our
> identity for which society would condemn us, and we find beauty and awe in our
> differences. We collaborate with one another. We report to one another. We share
> challenges, victories, and failures together . . . As I review my friendship with
> Anna, an interracial relationship that is much more than that, I notice that it
> contains many elements of the classic model of interpersonal attraction. Despite
> our similarities in personal style and background, Anna and I would probably not
> have been such good friends if she were straight. Because of her sexual orientation
> she can be empathetic with me in ways that my other white, straight friends
> cannot. Thus, I believe that our marginalized positions in society and academia
> have been a major factor in forming the center of our friendship. (pp. 200–201)

In a cyberdialogue, scholar–practitioners examine and share their personal experiences of building and facilitating intercultural alliances on interpersonal, community, and international levels (Allen, Broome, Jones, Chen, & Collier, 2002). The authors emphasized the importance of developing trust, a sense of interdependence, and dialogue, where the space to speak openly and the ability to sit with the pain and difficulties of others is critical in intercultural alliance building. Tremendous potential for personal growth as well as movement toward social justice can occur in intercultural alliances. Having the interest and skills to identify and work through misunderstandings, tensions, and conflicts are crucial to developing and sustaining intercultural alliances. All points of entry in intercultural praxis—inquiry, framing, positioning, as well as dialogue and reflection—can lead to collaborative action that serves the interests and needs of both or multiple individuals or groups.

Intercultural alliances often call on individuals to bridge and translate different cultural standpoints, positionalities, struggles, and histories. In the book *This Bridge Called My Back: Writings by Radical Women of Color*, a collective of women of color—scholars, poets, and activists—use the metaphor of serving as a "bridge" between and across socially constructed groups (Moraga & Anzaldúa, 1981). Serving as a "bridge" often means translating languages, values, norms, ways of thinking and being, as well as standpoints and positionalities between disparate groups.

Engaging in **intercultural bridgework** means developing sensitivity, understanding, and empathy and extending vulnerability to traverse multiple positions, creating points of contact, negotiation, and pathways of connection. Our "backs"—as the title of the book implies— our lives, our identities, our experiences, and our access to material, emotional, and spiritual resources are bridges that can carry us across worlds divided by culture, race, ethnicity, nationality, gender, class, religion, and sexual orientation. Yet, historically, the hard work, weight, and cost of intercultural bridgework have fallen disproportionately on the backs of nondominant groups. In a volume dedicated to intercultural alliances, Collier (2002b) drew three conclusions. First, there are more institutions, norms, practices, and ideological forces operating in society to maintain hierarchies of difference than there are ones that encourage and support intercultural alliances; therefore, analysis, reflection, and dialogue on power, privilege, and dominance are necessary first steps toward change. Second, intercultural alliances are complex and dynamic. Attention to the intersecting, overlapping, and multifaceted nature of individual and group identities and histories is needed. Third, intercultural alliances across lines of culture, race, class, gender, nation, and sexual orientation are hard work demanding vulnerability and risk taking. Yet, as sites of intercultural praxis, alliances have the potential to open up a range of new possibilities, dismantle inequitable relations of power, and move toward social justice on interpersonal, community, and global levels.

SUMMARY

This chapter examined the complicated, contradictory, and contested ways in which intercultural relationships in the global context are sites where cultural differences, power, privilege, and positionality are negotiated, translated, and transformed. A typology of intercultural relationships was offered. The cultural dimensions of interpersonal relationships in workplace, friendship, and intimate contexts as well as the roles of power, privilege, and history in intercultural relationships were presented to enhance our understanding, develop more effective strategies for relating across cultures, and increase our awareness of the benefits and challenges of intercultural relationships in the global context. The impact of the computer to mediate communication in initiating and sustaining intercultural relationships, constructing collective identities, and creating virtual communities as well as the challenges for intercultural relations was addressed. The chapter concluded with a discussion of intercultural relationships as potential sites of alliances for social justice in the global context.

KEY TERMS

miscegenation
antimiscegenation
intercultural relationships
interracial relationships
interethnic relationships
ethnicity
international relationships
interreligious or interfaith relationships
class prejudice
classism
heteronormativity
heterosexism
cultural values
Hofstede's cultural dimensions
individualism–collectivism
power distance
uncertainty avoidance

masculinity–femininity
Time Orientation–Confucian dynamism
initial encounter phase
exploratory interaction phase
ongoing involvement phase
relational identity/culture
racework
racial/cultural awareness
coping stage
identity emergence
relational maintenance
social networking sites
flaming
intercultural ally
intercultural alliance
intercultural bridgework

DISCUSSION QUESTIONS AND ACTIVITIES

Discussion Questions

1. What kind of intercultural relationships/friendships do you have?

2. What are the benefits and/or challenges of having intercultural relationships?

3. How do historical contexts and/or relations of power shape your intercultural relationships?

4. In what ways do you use computer mediated communication to develop and sustain intercultural relationships? What examples do you have of social networking sites (SNS) increasing intercultural understanding? How have you seen SNS accentuating or erasing differences?

5. How do you think intercultural praxis may help us have more effective and fulfilling intercultural relationships?

Activities

1. Unpacking the Relationship Development Process

    a. Using the stages of intercultural friendship/romantic relationship development models, consider how your intercultural relationships have developed over time.

    b. Describe specific incidents, feelings, and stages you and your friend/partner have gone through to develop the relationship.

    c. Now consider if you can make connections between your experience and any of the key concepts/issues discussed in the chapter.

2. Performing Intercultural Relationships—Group Activity

    a. In a group of five people, come up with a scenario similar to the ones presented in the chapter in which cultural differences function as either a challenge or an advantage in intercultural relationships.

    b. Act out the scenario in front of the class.

    c. Now discuss the following questions:

        i. What worked and/or what went wrong and why?

        ii. What historical issues and power relations shape the relational interactions in your scenario?

        iii. How does globalization influence the way people form intercultural relationships?

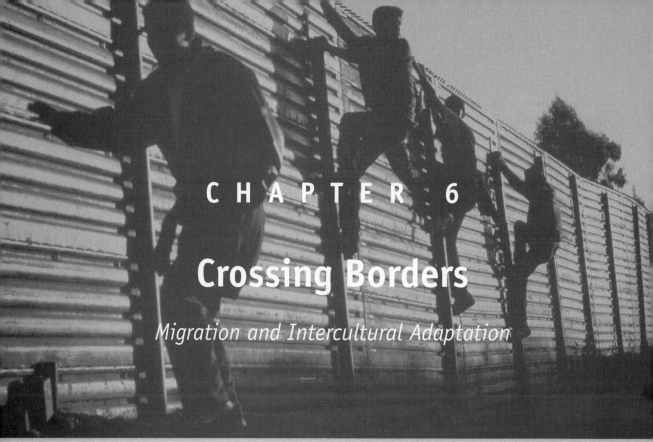

C H A P T E R   6

Crossing Borders

Migration and Intercultural Adaptation

Who can move freely across borders, and who is restricted?

Learning Objectives

1. Explain intercultural border crossing and adaptation within the context of globalization.

2. Identify the unique aspects of migration and intercultural adaptation today as well as the similarities with earlier waves of world migration.

3. Describe and apply a multi-level framework to analyze intercultural adaptation that accounts for micro-, meso- and macro-level factors and influences.

4. Gain knowledge and empathy for the challenges and rewards of migration and intercultural adaptation in the context of globalization.

Our world, in the first decades of the new millennium, is a world in motion. More people are on the move today crossing cultural boundaries and national borders than ever before in the history of humankind. The United Nations Population Division reported in 2013 that 232 million people live outside their country of origin. Migration and the multicultural societies created through the global movement of people are key issues facing individuals, communities, and nation-states today. In addition to migration, over a record 1.1 billion people crossed international borders as tourists (for leisure, business, visiting relatives, etc.) in 2014 despite major geopolitical uncertainty, health challenges, and a fragile global economic recovery (United Nations World Tourism Organization, 2014b). Globalization has dramatically altered the context for understanding the movement of people around the world. As Manuel Castells (1996) noted, we have moved from a space of "places" to a space of "flows." Why are so many people on the move today? What is unique about migration in the global context?

First, advances in transportation and communication technologies facilitate frequent, multidirectional flows and the creation of transnational networks of people. Second, the integration of global capital and markets has accelerated the concentration of wealth and exacerbated economic inequity both within and across nations, resulting in new patterns of rural to urban and South to North global migration as well as record migration within the global South. Third, the implementation of neoliberal policies has displaced millions of people who are compelled to move for jobs and livelihood. Fourth, escalation in intranational and international conflict has propelled unparalleled numbers of people across borders in search of safety, opportunity, and the spoils of war. Additionally, as the cross-border flows of people challenge the power and sovereignty of the nation-state, nation-states struggle to reassert control over national boundaries through increasingly restrictive and punitive immigration policies, by erecting walls, utilizing sophisticated surveillance, and mobilizing large numbers of people to police borders. We live in a world in motion driven and disrupted by powerful forces.

Nobel Prize–winning novelist Toni Morrison's theme, "A Foreigner's Home," chosen for a multidisciplinary, international conversation among artists and audiences at the Louvre Museum in Paris, France, requires "us to come to terms with being, fearing, and accepting strangers" (Riding, 2006). She focuses our attention not only on population mobility, but on the reception, adjustment, and impact of a world in motion for all of us. What role does intercultural communication play in the adaptation of migrants and in the social, political, and cultural transformations that result from the unprecedented flows of people crossing borders? This chapter begins with a brief discussion of different types of migrants and an overview of the three major waves of world migration, which provide a context for understanding contemporary patterns of migrant mobility, settlement, and the emergence of transnational migrant networks. Various theories of migration and cross-cultural adaptation are introduced and then applied to three case studies pertaining to the experiences of migrants in the global context. Throughout the chapter, the central role of communication in intercultural transitions is highlighted as people navigate the challenges and benefits of crossing borders.

MIGRANTS

Migrants are people who move from their primary cultural context, changing their place of residence for an extended period of time. It is useful to distinguish two dimensions when categorizing migrants. One important dimension is the degree of agency of a migrant in choosing to move or travel and a second is the length of stay or permanence of the relocation of migrants. Migrants who choose to leave home to travel or relocate are called **voluntary migrants. Sojourners** are voluntary migrants who leave home for limited periods of time and for specific purposes such as international students, business travelers, tourists, missionaries, and military personnel. Voluntary migrants who leave one country and settle permanently in another country are called **immigrants**. Europeans who moved along colonial routes during the first wave of world migration and to industrial centers in Europe and the Americas in the second wave are considered voluntary migrants. Migrants who are forced to leave due to famine, war, and political or religious persecution are called **involuntary migrants**. Africans who were traded as slaves during the colonial era, refugees who flee their countries of origin due to war and famine, or those seeking asylum for political reasons today are considered involuntary migrants. **Human trafficking** for sex work and other types of labor is another form of forced or involuntary migration, as people, particularly women, are transported against their will in increasing numbers in the global context. Involuntary migrants—refugees, asylum-seekers, and those forced into labor—may also, over time, seek or obtain permanent residence in the country of destination, making them immigrants.

The categories of voluntary and involuntary migrants underscore how the conditions of migration differ. Making a decision to leave one's place of origin and voluntarily settle in a new location suggests that the migrant has acted on their own agency with some desire to relocate, which establishes different conditions for relating to the country of destination compared to those who are forced to migrate. Yet, the distinction between voluntary and involuntary has always been somewhat ambiguous, and the difference blurs even more today for many people who leave their home countries and resettle either temporarily or permanently. For example, Mexican migrants may "choose" to leave their homes and migrate to the United States, but they often do so only under extreme duress when local economies collapse and jobs are lost. Migration is often the only viable alternative to provide food, clothing, and shelter for families. Let's take a look at how globalizing forces since the 16th century have resulted in three major waves of world migration. As you read, note the similarities and differences among the three migration waves.

HISTORICAL OVERVIEW OF WORLD MIGRATION

The **first wave of world migration** can be traced to the European colonial era from the 16th century through the 19th century. Thousands of migrants—sailors, soldiers, traders, missionaries, administrators, and later farmer–settlers—sailed out of ports of Europe for colonies in Africa, Asia, and the Americas, establishing sea trade routes that continue to structure migration flows today. While the experiences varied in different locations, a general pattern followed as colonizers appropriated the so-called "empty" lands and used indigenous peoples to extract the material wealth of the land. After indigenous labor was almost exhausted or annihilated through genocide and disease, the forced migration of over 15 million slaves from the west coast of Africa provided the labor for the production of commodities in mines and plantations (such as gold, silver, coffee, sugar, and cotton) in the colonies. The African diaspora dispersed people around the world to the Americas, Europe, and Asia. Also part of the first wave of colonial migration, after the abolition of slavery in the mid-19th century, some 12 million to 37 million people were transported internationally as indentured servants, representing a significant migratory flow to over 40 countries (Potts, 1990). Working under very poor conditions, indentured laborers were recruited—sometimes by force and sometimes voluntarily—and then transported great distances to fill the labor needs of European colonies. The wealth extracted from the colonies not only supported the lavish lifestyles of the ruling elite in Europe, but the exploitation of labor and land was crucial to the rise in economic and political power of European nations that spurred the second large wave of migration (Castles, de Haas, & Miller, 2014; Toro-Morn & Alicea, 2004).

Photo 6.1 Mrs. Finkelstein earns 75 cents a day working all day until 12 at night. Her daughters, Sofie, age 7, and Bessie, 13, also work long hours into the night making garters for Liberty Garter Works in New York, New York, in 1918. How do these conditions compare with sweatshops today?

Library of Congress

The **second wave of migration** took place from the mid-1800s to the early 1900s during the Industrial Revolution, when peasants from the rural parts of Europe, fleeing poverty and famine, migrated to urban areas in Europe and North and South America. Conditions in factories were severe—long hours, low pay, and unsafe environments—similar to conditions for workers in sweatshops today. Between 1846 and 1939, 59 million people left Europe for North and South America and Australia, first from Britain and Germany, and later from Spain, Italy, Ireland, and Eastern Europe (Castles, de Haas, & Miller, 2014). **Chain migration**, or linkages that connect migrants from points of origin to destinations, led to the segmentation of ethnic groups in the United States. For example, the Irish, Italians, and Jews tended to settle in the ports of the East Coast, while Central and Eastern Europeans were drawn to work in heavy industries in the Midwest. Until the 1880s, immigration to the United States was open; however, as racist campaigns increased, **nativist movements** emerged—movements that called for the exclusion of foreign-born people—Chinese and other Asian immigrants were targeted through the Chinese Exclusion Act of 1887 (Saenz, Morales, & Ayala, 2004). Italian and Irish immigrants, viewed as a threat to American values and as not capable of being assimilated, were also excluded. While the Irish and Italians are categorized racially as White today, in the late 1800s their differences from the dominant Anglo-Americans in terms of language and culture were used to classify them racially as non-White (Ignatiev, 1995). Throughout the history of the United States, immigration policy has served economic interests. The National Network for Immigrant and Refugee Rights (Cho, Puete, Louie, & Khokha, 2004) claims the following:

> Immigration policy in the U.S. has also served as a way to regulate the "character of the nation," limiting entry, citizenship, and economic access while enforcing racial divides. Because immigration can influence the demographic makeup of the nation, policy makers throughout U.S. history have admitted or excluded migrants based on qualifications such as national origin, race, class, gender, political ideology, and sexual orientation. (p. 40)

War, economic depression, and **xenophobia**—defined as the fear of outsiders—dramatically curtailed immigration to the United States until after WWII.

Communicative Practices
Rhetoric of Nativism

In April 2010, Arizona lawmakers passed anti-immigration legislation that spurred a nationwide protest and controversy. The law requires the state and local law enforcement to stop and interrogate people suspected as undocumented migrants. Massive protests and boycotts against the state ensued. The law, from the perspective of those who oppose it, is racist, normalizing racial profiling, and criminalizing undocumented migrants.

Supporters of this law deploy rhetoric of nativism and exclusion to justify their position. They argue that economic recession, increasing prison populations, an overburdened health care system, and unemployment result from the failure of the federal government to protect its border. In other words, undocumented migrants are a burden on U.S. society. Rhetoric of nativism not only leads to stricter laws, but also increases the militarization of the border and violence against migrants.

Post 911, nativist rhetoric continues to instill and incite fear of people of Middle Eastern and South Asian descent. Allegiance to Islam and one's ethnic community is assumed to be "un-American" and, therefore, threatening. Nativist rhetoric uses false dichotomies that perpetuate exclusion, mark citizens as "foreigners," and escalate fear of difference.

Nativist movements, whether today or in the past, show how people use language and discourse to create hierarchies of belonging and access in terms of citizenship and nation. The immigration debates also demonstrate the shifting and contested ideas about what is considered "criminal" and who is entitled to equal protection under the law. Such rhetoric often appeals to xenophobia and ethnocentrism, shaping historical and cultural contexts of intercultural communication.

The third wave of migration, often labeled the postindustrial wave, is more diverse and multidirectional than previous migrations and encompasses patterns of movement since WWII. Following WWII, large numbers of Jews left Europe for Israel, as well as South and North America. **Guest workers programs** brought workers from the periphery of Europe—Spain,

Italy, Turkey, Ireland, and Finland—to fill the labor shortages in industrialized Western Europe due to the war and declining population (Hammer, 1985). Another large wave of voluntary migration occurred as anticolonial movements across Africa and Asia led to independence for former colonies. Labor demands in the former European colonizing countries as well as political and economic instability in struggling recently independent nations resulted in **postcolonial migrants**, migrants who leave former colonies and relocate in colonizing countries. Postcolonial migrants include the movement of Indian, Pakistani, and Caribbean migrants to England; of North African, Tunisian, Moroccan, and West African migrants to France; and of migrants from Indonesia, a former Dutch colony, to the Netherlands.

Postcolonial migration patterns counter the directional flows of the first wave of colonial migration resulting in the unanticipated growth of significant non-White, ethnic minority populations within Europe. While guest workers and postcolonial migrants fueled the economies of host countries and played a major role in the rebuilding of Europe after WWII, their status and acceptance as immigrants within the host countries of Europe varies. Institutional and informal racism and discrimination often limit employment and educational options and create residential separation (Castles, de Haas & Miller, 2014). From the 1920s to 1965, immigration to the United States was severely restricted. Migrant workers from Mexico were recruited through a guest worker program called the **Bracero Program** in the 1940s to fill labor shortages during WWII. Migrants who participated in this program made tremendous contributions to the agricultural industry in the United States. They provided skilled, low-wage work until the mid-1960s when the program was ended due to protests over harsh working conditions and severe human rights violations. Migration to the United States declined until amendments to the Immigration and Nationality Act in 1965 challenged the discriminatory national origins quota system. The change was not intended or expected to instigate large scale migration from non-European countries. Yet, with the shift to kinship and family reunification with U.S. citizens as the main criteria, the number of Latin American and Asian immigrations increased dramatically (Borjas, 1990).

MIGRATION TRENDS IN THE CONTEXT OF GLOBALIZATION

In the later part of the 20th century and into the new millennium, migration is increasingly rapid, complex, multidirectional, and diverse. Countries in Europe that were, in the first and second waves of migration, primarily sending countries are now receiving migrants from Eastern European countries and from former colonies. While European countries depend on immigrants to fill labor needs and to support the negative population growth, ethnic, racial, and religious demographic changes have heightened cultural and political conflicts and increased anti-immigrant sentiment. Latin America was previously seen as a receiving continent during the colonial and industrial migration waves. However, as a result of macro-level changes, such as economic liberalization, Latin America is experiencing massive rural to urban migration within nations, international migration within Latin America (e.g., temporary migrants from Nicaragua to Costa Rica and from El Salvador to Mexico), and international migration to North America. These shifts create major challenges as divided and displaced families and communities struggle to maintain connections and construct regional and transnational networks.

As global economic integration concentrates wealth in more developed countries, Africans from less developed and poverty-ridden countries are driven to more affluent neighboring countries, such as the Ivory Coast and South Africa. Africa has a very large refugee population due to unstable political and economic conditions in the struggling former colonies. **Refugees** are people who are forced to flee for safety reasons from their country of origin due to war, fear of persecution, or famine. According to the United Nations High Commissioner for Refugees (UNHCR) (n.d.), in 2014 the number of forcibly displaced people (official refugees, asylum seekers, and the internally displaced) exceeded 50 million for the first time post-WWII. War, human rights violations, and ethnic cleansing in the Balkans, Rwanda, and the Soviet Federation in the 1990s; in Sudan, the Congo, Afghanistan, and Iraq since 2000; and more recently in Syria have displaced hundreds of thousands of people who move from the poorest and most politically unstable countries in the world. By the end of 2013, the war in Syria had forced 2.5 million into becoming refugees and internally displaced over 6.5 million people. While the official refugee count worldwide has risen in the last few years, the number of **internally displaced persons,** refugees within one's own country of origin, has increased significantly to a record 33.3 million.

Migration patterns within and to the Arab region are propelled primarily by the magnet of oil rich countries that draw laborers from India, Pakistan, Sri Lanka, Bangladesh, the Philippines, Thailand, and Indonesia to the Middle East. Most Asians come as **contract workers** through labor agreements established between the governments of the sending and receiving countries. Conditions for employment are often severe and exploitative and do not allow for permanent settlement or family reunification. Known as the "tiger economies," the Asia Pacific region holds half the world's population and two thirds of the world's workforce (Castles, de Haas & Miller, 2014). While often the case in the global era, migrants within and from Asia can be divided into **high- and low-skilled laborers.** Economic liberalization, the entry of multinational corporations into formerly closed areas, and the creation of free-trade zones have promoted rural to urban movement in China, India, Thailand, and Vietnam as low-skilled laborers and particularly women, driven by poverty, seek factory work in export processing zones. Regional economic disparities draw low-skilled workers from poorer countries—the Philippines, Bangladesh, India, and Sri Lanka—to wealth-concentrated Asian countries—Japan, Hong Kong, Singapore, and Malaysia—who often perform what is known as the three Ds in Japan: work that is (1) difficult, (2) dangerous, and (3) dirty, such as factory, agricultural, food processing, sex industry, and domestic labor. On the other end of the spectrum, educated, high-skilled workers migrate from Asia, primarily from India and China, to developed countries, such as the United States, Canada, England, and Australia to work in high-tech and medical professions. Toro-Morn and Alicea (2004) noted that these migratory flows are two sides of the same coin:

> Global restructuring has led to a global division of labor, where periphery economies have become the source of production and assembly lines while core economies such as the United States, Canada, and Europe have become centers of high finance and technology. (p. xxix)

In summary, multidirectional migration is a central feature of globalization resulting in an increase in and intensification of intercultural interactions, alliances, and conflicts. As areas of the world join and are forced into the interconnected global economy, people are thrust into unparalleled migration flows. The lives of those who are uprooted, the lives of those who remain, and the lives of those in places where people resettle are dramatically transformed. Second, advances in communication and transportation technologies create the conditions for migration networks to form that enable transmigrants to maintain, hybridize, and change the "host" cultures and "home" cultures through global migration flows. Third, approximately 59% of all international migration is to highly developed countries of the north. As south-to-north migrant flows concentrate in urban centers of Europe, the United States, Canada, Australia, and Japan, significant changes and tensions emerge, fueling anti-immigrant campaigns, mobilizing immigrant rights groups, and igniting intercultural tensions and conflicts. Fourth, women across the economic spectrum are entering the paid labor force in unprecedented numbers leading to the **feminization of the workforce**. Women joining the workforce in developed countries create demand for women from developing countries to migrate great distances to serve as caretakers and surrogate mothers, often leaving their own children with relatives. In export processing zones, women are often preferred for low-skilled work because they can be paid less and are more easily exploited. Today, one half of the 232 million international migrants are women, exacerbating the familial, social, and economic impact of migration and displacement.

The three waves of migration have produced the multicultural societies in which we live today, affording opportunities to engage with and benefit from diverse cultural groups and individuals. Yet, many of the challenges faced by societies around the world—racial and ethnic discrimination and tension, intensified economic inequity, and increasing poverty, as well as disputes over immigrant rights and immigration policies—are also embedded in and structured by racist, classist, and ethnocentric ideologies forged and institutionalized through the past 500 years of global migration. We turn now to a range of theories that assist us in making sense of the complex, multidirectional patterns of migration and cultural adaptation in the context of globalization.

THEORIES OF MIGRATION AND INTERCULTURAL ADAPTATION

To understand the experiences of migrants as they move around the globe today, we need to consider migration patterns and intercultural adaptation from three interrelated levels or frames: (1) the macro or large scale economic-political level of nation-states and global transnational structures; (2) the micro or individual level of migrant adaptation; and (3) the meso or intermediate level of migrant networks and sociocultural group ties that link the macro, structural level and the micro, individual level. While much of the research on cultural adaptation in the field of communication focuses on the individual level of migrants' adaptation to new environments, the micro-level experience is inevitably impacted by social networks on the meso-level and by macro-level political and economic global structures. A multilevel analysis accounts for the structural inequities and sociocultural networks that circumscribe migrants' process of cultural adaptation as they cross borders in the context of globalization.

Macro-Level Theories

Many of the traditional macro-level explanations of migration are variations of the **push-pull theory**, first articulated by a British geographer in the late 1800s, which proposes that circumstances in the country of origin "push" people toward migratory paths—economic hardship, famine, war, or persecution, for example—and conditions in the country of destination "pull" people toward particular locations. The conditions that pull people may be a higher degree of economic opportunities relative to what is available in the country of origin, the opportunity for family reunification, or political stability. While the push-pull theory is useful today, the complexities of migration and migratory patterns in the global context defy simple explanation. **World-systems theory** argues that international migration today is a result of the structure of global capitalism (Sassen, 1994; Wallerstein, 2000). Migration flow from less developed, or Third World countries, to more highly developed, or First World countries, is a result of global structural inequity grounded in colonization. Nation-states and global institutions that act on behalf of capitalists drive migration as they take advantage of land, labor, resources, and markets in peripheral or Third World countries (Massey et al., 1993). Decisions, policies, and treaties made at the global institutional level—the World Trade Organization (WTO), the International Monetary Fund (IMF), and the World Bank (WB)—create conditions where people cannot survive in their countries of origin, propelling migration.

Where migrants are "pulled" to or where they go is also affected by nation-state immigration policies and transnational economic and political agreements on the macro-level. The orientation of the "host" or "destination" country toward migrants and migrant groups in official and informal terms impacts migrants' processes of adaptation in the new country (Castles, de Haas & Miller, 2014). Are the nation-state's immigration policies and practices directed toward assimilation, exclusion, or integration in a multicultural society? Historically, the primary orientation toward migrant adaptation in the United States has been assimilation to the dominant culture with the **melting pot** serving as the metaphor. The melting pot ideology, popularized by Jewish immigrant Israel Zangwill in his play in the early 1900s, assumes that the migrants' adaptation to a new culture requires and allows newcomers to "melt" or "blend" into the mainstream to form a cohesive whole (Postiglioni, 1983). While the notion of the melting pot was, to some extent, descriptive of the experiences of some Europeans who immigrated to the United States, it has never adequately captured the diverse experiences of exclusion and adjustment of non-White migrants, migrants with strong ethnic ties, or many immigrant groups who have lived in the United States for generations. The myth of the melting pot prevails today, masking the ways that some migrants are not allowed to "melt" and casting suspicion on those who do not want to shed their cultural norms, values, and practices. More recently, an ideology of **pluralism** that emphasizes the maintenance of ethnic and cultural values, norms, and practices within a multicultural society has emerged as a result of the civil rights movement, anticolonial movements, and immigrant rights movements, challenging the inaccurate myth of the melting pot.

Cultural Identity
Home, Family, and Culture

Leo is a Chinese American man in his late 20s. He explains his changing relationship to his home, family, and culture:

Growing up in San Francisco, all I wanted to be was anything but Chinese. All my life I tried my best not to be associated with Chinese culture.

Things changed drastically when I took a trip to Shanghai to attend my grandmother's funeral when I was 25. I was welcomed by my cousins, relatives, and friends of my parents. To my greatest surprise, I felt like I belonged for the first time in my life. It was so strange that I felt at "home" in a place I had never been or really cared about. The experience in Shanghai made me think about my cultural identity in a completely new way.

I ended up moving to Shanghai for a year. Things were great, but over time, it became clear that I didn't really belong there—I didn't speak the language and I didn't have a job. Although I looked liked them, I began to realize I am still an American. Now I visit Shanghai every year to see my relatives and friends. I hope someday my children will appreciate the history of transnational migration that has shaped my Chinese American identity.

Micro-Level Theories

While macro-level theories provide a map for understanding the large scale dimensions of migration and cultural adaptation in the global context, micro-level theories focus our attention on the smaller scale individual and interpersonal dynamics (see Table 6.1). The **U-curve model** of adaptation, based on research conducted with Norwegian international students who traveled to the United States on study abroad programs in the 1950s, was one of first models developed that focused on short-term adaptation. The research measured the level of contentment or happiness experienced by sojourners over time. Norwegian researcher Sverre Lysgaard (1955) noted three significant stages in the cultural adaptation process. The first stage was one of **anticipation**, where excitement about the new culture characterizes the sojourner's experience. The second stage is marked by **culture shock**, or the disorientation and discomfort sojourners experience from being in an unfamiliar environment. Originally theorized as a disease because it is often accompanied by physical symptoms (Oberg, 1960), culture shock has been reinterpreted as a type of transition shock that leads to growth, learning, and personal change (Adler, 1987). The third stage is one of **adjustment** to the new environment as the sojourner learns to negotiate the verbal and nonverbal codes, values, norms, behaviors, and assumptions of the new culture. Adjustment varies considerably based on a range of factors including the sojourner's desire to adapt, the host culture's receptivity, the degree of similarity or difference between home and host cultures, as well as age, gender, race, and socioeconomic background.

Table 6.1 Multilevel Approach to Intercultural Adaptation

Level/Frame	Theories/Concepts
Macro: Economic–political level of nation-states, global, transnational structures	Push-pull theory World-systems theory
Meso: Intermediate level of migrant networks and sociocultural group ties	Migrant networks Social capital Transmigrants
Micro: Individual level of migrant adaptation	U-curve W-curve Migrant–host relationships Integrative theory

Noting the experiences of sojourners and other types of migrants as they return to their countries of origin, the U-curve model has been extended to the **W-curve model**, which addresses the challenges of reentry into one's "home" culture (Gullahorn & Gullahorn, 1963). Reentry, or return, may follow a similar pattern of anticipation, culture shock, and adjustment, yet the changes that an individual has gone through in the cultural adjustment process away from home as well as the fact that the culture the sojourner is returning to has also changed may exacerbate culture shock and adjustment on return (Martin, 1984).

To understand the cultural adaptation of longer-term migrants, social psychologist John Berry (1992) considered the attitudes of migrants toward their host and own cultures, outlining four **migrant–host modes of relationship**, which include assimilation, separation, marginalization, and integration. **Assimilation** occurs when a migrant values the host's culture more than his or her own culture. Historically and today, Europeans who migrate to the United States generally have developed a migrant–host relationship of assimilation, facilitated by the similarities between their own cultures and the dominant host culture and the receptivity of the host culture to them, along with the migrants' desire to assimilate. **Separation** describes the migrant–host mode of relationship when the migrant values their own or home culture more than the host culture. The desire to maintain one's cultural values, norms, and practices leads some migrants to voluntarily choose separation as a mode of relationship with the dominant host culture, yet, in other cases, migrants have been forced by law or informal discriminatory practices into a migrant–host relationship of separation, such as the historical segregation of Chinatowns in major U.S. cities and real estate covenants that excluded minorities. Economic stratification in the host country can also lead to separation of migrants in terms of housing, education, and employment. **Marginalization,** according to Berry (1992), occurs when the migrant places little value on either her or his own culture or the host culture. Migrants, who experience a sense of distance from and lack of acceptance by both their culture of origin and the dominant culture, live on the borders of both cultures. Marginalization is often characterized as psychologically isolating and stressful, yet it is also potentially a creative and empowering migrant–host mode of relationship (Bennett, 1993). Someone who is on the margins of both the home and host cultures occupies a unique position that allows for the emergence of fluid and multifaceted standpoints, as well as creative hybridization of the two cultures. **Integration** describes the migrant–host mode of relationship when the migrant values both his or her own culture and the host culture. Migrants who sustain their cultural identity by maintaining their language and cultural practices through social networks and participate in the dominant host culture develop a migrant–host mode of integration. While integration may appear to be the ideal migrant–host mode of relationship, many factors influence the relationship a migrant adopts at any given time.

The attitudes of the migrant to adaptation are not the only factors that influence the migrant–host mode of relationship. The host nation's immigration policies, the institutional practices, and the attitudes of the dominant culture toward the migrant and her or his group also impact migrants' experiences. Racism and ethnocentrism also play central roles in host culture's receptivity to migrants and their culture. In the global context, representations of immigrants as threats to national security and national cultural identity galvanize anti-immigrant, nationalist rhetoric and policies as well as incite conflict and violence. A far-right radical Norwegian man committed a mass shooting at a youth camp in 2011 claiming the victims were traitors who embraced multiculturalism and Muslim immigration, which was leading to the destruction of Norwegian culture (Anders Behring Breivik, 2012). Low pay, long hours, and demoralizing work conditions can also lead to conflicts between migrants and "hosts." Regarding changes in immigration policies in Japan, a leading labor organizer states, "Japan's immigration policy refuses to treat migrant workers as people with rights that must be protected. The new move is a clear example of a 'use and discard foreign labour' goal" (Kakuchi, 2014).

In the context of globalization, as migrants move more frequently and rapidly between "host" and "home" cultures, the modes of relationship that migrants maintain with their own culture *within their country of origin* is increasingly significant in the intercultural adaptation process. "Host" and "home" are put in quotes here to note the complicated nature of labeling the various locations where migrants live, work, develop affinities, and build community in the global context. Traditionally, the host country designated the country of destination where migrants settle either temporarily or permanently. Host carries a connotation of visitors who are treated with hospitality, which does not adequately represent the experiences of many migrants historically or today. The notion of home culture or country is also problematic as migrants today increasingly maintain strong connections to their country of origins, and yet may consider their country of resettlement (host country) more their home than their country of origin.

Communication scholar Young Yun Kim (2001, p. 15) noted "that the individual and the environment co-define the adaptation process." She argued for an **integrative theory of cultural adaptation** that addresses the attitudes and receptivity of the host environment, the ethnic communities within the majority culture, and the psychological characteristics of the individual. Taking a general systems perspective, Kim (2001) identified three assumptions about the nature of human adaptation: (1) humans have an innate self-organizing drive and a capacity to adapt to environmental challenges, (2) adaptation of an individual to a given cultural environment occurs in and through communication, and (3) adaptation is a complex and dynamic process that brings about a qualitative transformation of the individual. Kim's process model of cultural adaptation, emphasizing the role of communication as individuals adapt across cultural boundaries, states that individuals experience a process of stress, adaptation, and growth as they interact with and adjust in new and different cultural environments. Encounters with new cultures often challenge our assumed and taken for granted ways of thinking, behaving, and understanding ourselves, our communities, and the world around us. As migrants gain new information and insight about the norms and values and adapt their behaviors to the host culture in a process of **acculturation**, migrants also go through a process of **deculturation**, or the unlearning of some aspects of their culture of origin. This dynamic and ongoing movement between stress and adaptation, disequilibrium and readjustment produces growth. Kim (2001) postulated that **intercultural transformation** occurs as a result of this stress-adaptation-growth process and identifies three outcomes: (1) increased functional fitness of the migrant's ability to engage effectively with the host culture; (2) improved psychological health of the migrant in coping with the environment; and (3) a shift toward an intercultural identity, which allows the migrant to connect and identify with multiple cultural groups. All three micro-level theories—the U- and W-curve model, the migrant–host relationship model, and the integrative theory—provide insights that allow us to explain and navigate the challenges and rewards of intercultural adaptation.

Meso-Level Theories

Meso-level theories of migration and cultural adaptation seek to bridge macro-level theories that emphasize structural issues and micro-level theories that focus on individual attributes in the cultural adaptation process. A critical feature of intermediate level theories examines the role migrant networks play in global migration patterns and adaptation processes (see Figure 5.3). **Migrant networks** are defined as "sets of interpersonal ties that connect migrants, former migrants and non-migrants in origin and destination areas through ties of kinship, friendship and shared community origin" (Massey et al., 1993, p. 448). Attention to migrant networks highlights how social groups and collective cultural relationships motivate, sustain, and give meaning to migration and cultural adaptation processes. Meso-level analyses reveal how migrant social networks provide information and support for travel, housing, employment, education, and health care, which are instrumental in mediating both the macro-level structural conditions of global migration and the micro-level individual challenges that migrants face in their cultural adaptation process.

Migrant network approaches draw attention to the ways that migration and cultural adaptation in the context of globalization are embedded in webs of interlocking political, cultural, community, and familial relationships, environments, and locations, where social capital develops and is exchanged. **Social capital** refers to the sense of commitment and obligation people within a group or network share to look after the well-being and interests of one another (Gold, 2005). Today, migrants maintain connections to more than one nation, community, and location, reinforcing, breaking, and reconstituting collective identities and migrant networks across national boundaries. A new category of migrants has emerged in the global context often referred to as **transmigrants,** or migrants who move across national boundaries to new locations for work and family reunification, and yet also maintain cultural, social, economic, and political ties with their country, region, or city of origin (Basch, Blanc, & Schiller, 1994; Portes, Guarnizo, & Landolt, 1999). Transmigrants are able to maintain transnational bonds in the global context through frequent communication, travel, and through migrant networks that enable the construction of transnational homes, or transnational spaces where collective identities, economic support, and empowerment are nurtured and where political resistance across national borders is possible. For example, when a transmigrant from India who lives in the United States is invited to join Facebook by a friend from home, she is instantly added to the Facebook pages of old classmates and relatives, linking her to an expansive transnational network where past, present, and future friends around the world are connected.

Using a multilevel approach that integrates macro-, micro-, and meso-level theories of migration and cultural adaptation allows us to understand the challenges, choices, losses, opportunities, and rewards migrants face as they cross borders and negotiate "homes" in the global context. In the following pages, three case studies are presented. After each, theories of migration and cultural adaptation are used to critically analyze each case. The goal is to develop a process of analysis to make sense of the complex web of individual, social, and geopolitical factors that impact migrants and the globalized environments as we all adapt to a world in motion. I encourage you to empathize with the tremendous challenges migrants face, and recognize the relationships among macro-, micro-, and meso-level issues facing migrants today.

Intercultural Praxis and the "American Dream"

As a deeply-held cultural ethos of the United States, the American Dream both unites and divides those who strive for the promise of a better life. Using Intercultural Praxis, consider the following narratives by three students whose positionalities and standpoints provide very different pictures of the American Dream:

Mahad, whose parents migrated to the United States as refugees from Somalia, views the American Dream as upward mobility that promises a better life. He grew up being taught the importance of education and hard work by his parents. While some may still view him as an outsider, it is his drive for success and opportunity that defines his identity as an American.

Sarah, a White American woman, was raised by her mother in a single-parent household. She is a hardworking student, but she expects to have over $30,000 in student debt by the time she graduates from college. She proclaims that her American Dream is "a college degree without debt." She worries that the financial strains will hold her back after leaving school, particularly in the unstable job market.

Nina is a Hmong American first generation college student. For her, the American Dream is about creating a society free of discrimination, prejudice, and racism with a greater respect and appreciation

(Continued)

(Continued)

for cultural tradition and diversity. She believes that the traditional notion of the American Dream is increasingly unattainable for many families, but we shouldn't give up on the Dream because hope keeps us going.

As Mahad, Sarah, and Nina reflect on their views on the American Dream, they position themselves within the broader narrative of hope and progress (or the lack thereof). The way they frame the American Dream says a great deal about their positionalities in the United States and what is at stake when we imagine and strive for a "good life."

What does the "American Dream" mean to you?

How does your response to this question reflect your positionality and cultural frame(s)?

What were/are the systemic barriers to realizing the "American Dream" historically and today?

CASE STUDIES: MIGRATION AND INTERCULTURAL ADAPTATION

The case studies that follow tell the stories of migrants with a focus on the conditions of migration and the complexities of intercultural adaptation in the global context. As you read these stories, notice the ways in which the experiences of migrants today are both similar to and different from the experiences of migrants in the first and second waves of world migration. Also consider what factors influence migrants' experiences of intercultural adaptation.

Villachuato, Mexico, to Marshalltown, Iowa: Transnational Connections[1]

In 1989, laborers—primarily men—began traveling from the small town of Villachuato in the state of Michoacán, Mexico, to work in a meatpacking plant in Marshalltown, Iowa. As economic conditions in Mexico worsened, larger numbers made the 2,000 mile trek to *el norte*. By the late 1990s, more than half of the employees at the third largest pork processing plant in the world were Latinos/Latinas and about half of those workers were from Villachuato. The meatpacking plant would shut down if not for the migrant laborers. Through remittances and fund drives organized by migrant networks that link several locations in the United States, wages made by workers in the United States are used to improve the Mexican community, such as installing water and electricity, paving roads, and renovating the town plaza and church. Workers return to Villachuato frequently for annual religious events, weddings, and funerals often quitting their jobs and returning for rehire. While these practices benefit the plant economically, White American managers view them as disruptive and criticize Latinos/Latinas for being "irresponsible," for not learning English, and

---

[1]Case based on Grey & Woodrick (2002) and Woodrick (2010).

for not wanting to settle permanently in the United States. Tensions between Anglos and Latinos flared when the plant was raided by the Immigration and Naturalization Service (INS) with the knowledge of plant supervisors, and undocumented workers were deported. Efforts to build sustainable relations between the two communities improved when Marshalltown community leaders, the chief of police, and others visited Villachuato. Increasingly, as children of migrant families are born in the United States, families make decisions to seek permanent residence.

How can we make sense of the complex dynamics occurring in this scenario? The macro-level push–pull theory explains that high unemployment and poverty in Mexico relative to the United States "pushes" migrants from Mexico and "pulls" them to the United States. But, why is there such great economic disparity between Mexico and the United States? A world systems approach argues that, historically, colonization and military force were used to establish conditions for the accumulation of capital by European and U.S. powers. Today, the conditions are established and maintained by "free-trade agreements" (i.e., North American Free Trade Agreement [NAFTA] and Central America Free Trade Agreement [CAFTA]), negotiated through global governance bodies, such as the IMF, WB, and WTO. NAFTA has displaced hundreds of thousands of people in Mexico. Seeking employment, about 6 million people, just over half of the 11.2 million unauthorized migrants living in the United States are from Mexico (Krogstad & Passel, 2014). While working conditions are harsh—difficult, dangerous, and dirty—and legal status for some workers perilous, basic self-survival and the survival of family members remaining in Mexico propel them to their northern neighbor. The globalization of capital, goods, and labor has linked Villachuato and Marshalltown to a global economy dominated by the United States. These communities are no longer marginal to the world economy; rather, they are part of an uneven global capitalist expansion (Grey & Woodrick, 2002). Like towns across the United States and Mexico, the lives and livelihoods of people from Villachuato and Marshalltown are intertwined and interdependent in the global context (Woodrick, 2010).

How is migration between Villachuato and Marshalltown and cultural adaptation sustained? Meso-level approaches to adaptation suggest that migrant networks pass along knowledge and experience about safe migration routes, work, housing, and other services through interpersonal communication with friends, family relations, and community connections. The establishment of migrant networks clearly support and promote migration and the creation of a transnational community. **Transnational communities** are constructed by transmigrants whose density of movement and social ties over time and across geographic space form circuits of exchange, support, and belonging (Goldring, 1996). Sociologist Luin Goldring noted that transnational communities are characterized by intertwining familial relationships across locations, identification with "home" or sending locations, and the ability to mobilize collective resources. The Villachuato–Marshalltown transnational community exemplifies all three characteristics.

Interestingly, the characteristics that define transnational migration are often the source of intercultural misunderstanding and conflict. First, the transmigrants' social, cultural, economic, and political allegiance to and sustained contact with their community in Mexico challenges the migrant–host mode of relationship of assimilation, where migrants from Europe in previous waves assimilated to the dominant culture (even if it took several generations of struggle). These new patterns of transmigration disrupt and resist hegemonic assumptions of U.S. superiority and the desirability of living in the United States, which further escalates tensions between the dominant group and migrant workers. The individual and collective agency of Villachuato migrants expressed through frequent travel between the two communities, remittances and fund drives to support the community in Mexico, and the ability to quit work are all strategies that challenge and subvert the assumed unidirectional power of U.S. national and corporate interests.

Second, the migrant–host mode of relationship in this case is initially one of separation as migrant laborers and their families from Villachuato are separated from the Marshalltown community. A level of voluntary separation based on migrant networks that affords social, economic, and political support combines with subtle and more blatant forms of segregation in housing and employment as well as social exclusion through stereotypes, prejudice, and racism by the "host" or receiving community. The transmigrants' mode of relationship with the host culture that is sustained through migrant networks is often viewed negatively by the dominant or host culture, commonly giving rise to statements like "they don't want to assimilate." Yet, as children of transmigrants are born in the United States, a sense of allegiance to and connection with their Marshalltown home shifts the migrant–host relationship for some to one of integration. Additionally, as community members from Marshalltown take an interest in the community in Villachuato, Mexico, a process of intercultural adaptation occurs not only for migrants, but also for Marshalltown residents. Kim's (2001) integrative theory of cultural adaptation explains that through an ongoing process of stress, disequilibrium, and adaptation growth takes place. It is not only the transmigrants from Mexico who are involved in a process of adaptation. As a transnational community is forged, the residents of both Marshalltown and Villachuato as well as the communities are also changed over time by the interactions and experience a process of intercultural adaptation characterized by stress, adaptation, and growth.

Challenging U.S.-centric approaches to transnational migration, communication scholars Gerardo Villalobos-Romo and Sachi Sekimoto (2016) focus on the experiences of Mexican families who remain in Mexico after their family members and relatives have migrated to the United States. Interviews with residents in Aguascalientes, Mexico, reveal how transnational familial identities and relational dynamics are mediated through communication technologies and media. The cultural space of "home" is transformed and reconfigured through computer mediated communication (CMC), mass media, and migration. Intercultural contact with relatives in the United States and with U.S. culture evokes desire as well as a sense of ambivalence, and in some cases resistance among those who remain at home. The return of migrant relatives accentuates the asymmetrical power relations between the two countries as well as the growing cultural and economic distance between those who stay and those who immigrate to the United States. In the context of globalization, transnational migration disrupts and dislocates cultural and familial identities (Villalobos-Romo & Sekimoto, 2016).

Fujian, China, to New York, New York:
Human Smuggling of Low-Skilled Workers[2]

In the early 1990s, Ms. Zhang and her husband arrived in New York and immediately started working long hours for little pay at different Chinese restaurants in Chinatown, organized by the smuggling network that had arranged their transportation. After agreeing to pay a considerable amount of money ($30,000 each) for the illegal 17,000 mile, 3-month journey, although excited to finally be in New York, for several months Ms. Zhang experienced anxiety and fear. She was able to communicate with other Chinese migrants, but found the different languages, regional accents, and ways of life in this new urban setting disorienting. For months, she took the same route to and from work, stopping only briefly to purchase food at the same shop each day. Over time, she became more familiar with her surroundings, developed contacts with people in her new environment, and learned some English. Ms. Zhang and her husband came to the United States from a rural area in the Fujian province in southeastern China where they worked in a factory that afforded them enough money to live, but no extra money. Three years after coming to New York, she gave birth to their son. Since she could not afford to stop working and one income would not support the family, Ms. Zhang decided to go back to China with her son. She and her husband hoped she could return to the United States with their child when he was old enough to enter public school. In China, she was welcomed home, but found it difficult to adjust.

What theories of cultural adaptation shed light on this situation? What conditions of globalization allow for and lead to such risk-taking actions on the part of Fujian Chinese migrants? Clearly, Ms. Zhang experienced the stages of the U-curve model as she progressed through excitement and anticipation, the disorientation and anxiety of culture shock, and an extended period of cultural adjustment as she familiarized herself with her new environment, made connections with people, and gained a degree of intercultural competence. Her story illustrates the processes of entry into new cultural contexts and reentry into familiar and yet changed cultures of origin, reflecting the W-curve model. Her experience also points to the potential for ongoing cycles of departure and arrival to and from various "homes" that characterize migration in the global context.

On a macro-level, "push" and "pull" theories of migration provide insight, and yet do not explain the whole story. Workers in China, on average, can make about three times as much in cities than in rural areas and as much as eight times more in coastal cities. In the United States, the average income is four to five times that of earnings in coastal cities of China. Yet, on relatively low wages as undocumented workers, migrants work long hours to cover basic needs and pay off debts to their smugglers (Liu, 2007). Chinese migrants often dream of becoming wealthy in the United States, known as "the Golden Mountain," based on the relative difference in wages between the United States and China.

---

[2]Case based on Y. Zhou (2004).

In the context of globalization, media images of wealth, lavish lifestyles, and material success circulate around the world creating dissatisfaction with what one has and instilling desires for greater wealth and status. Author of *Smuggled Chinese: Clandestine Immigration to the United States*, Ko-lin Chin (2000) commented, "When people get together they always talk about how their sons or daughters or relatives or husbands or brothers are doing in the United States." Having a family member living in the United States is seen as a status symbol among relatives and neighbors. People are often pressured into making the risky journey and are ridiculed if reluctant. Once in the United States, Chinese migrants are often too embarrassed to talk about their devastating conditions, preferring to appear "successful" even as they toil night and day in miserable conditions. Migrant networks that link people on the interpersonal, familial, and community level compel migration even as they facilitate it (M. Zhou, 2009). While the Zhangs in the vignette are by no means wealthy, they are also not poor compared to other regions of China. However, China's transition to a market-oriented economy has dramatically increased overall income inequality (Xie & Zhou, 2014). The increased disparity between income levels combines with heightened exposure to actual and media images of material wealth such that poorer people, people in the lower economic ranks, feel a sense of **relative deprivation.** In other words, in absolute terms, they are not poor. Rather, in a world with increasing inequity, the difference between oneself and those who have more motivates a desire to find ways to leave and make more money. While economic mobility has improved for some in China, going to the United States, even with the level of risk and suffering involved, is perceived as a way of getting rich (Keefe, 2008).

On the other end of the economic spectrum, Chinese immigrants to the United States in the past 20 years who have had access to educational and monetary resources have become highly successful professionals in the sciences, technology, medicine, and other fields in the United States. Chinese entrepreneurial families view the United States as an important destination for one or more sons to cultivate links in a growing global web of capital connection and accumulation. Anthropologist Aihwa Ong (1999) noted, "For over a century, overseas Chinese have been the forerunners of today's multiply displaced subjects, who are always on the move mentally and physically" (p. 2). High-skilled migration to the United States from India, China, the Philippines, or Canada has increased since the late 1980s as the elevated demand for knowledge workers, particularly in the areas of information technology, medicine, and science combines with insufficient supply in the United States.

A controversial aspect of high-skilled migration has been the **brain drain** that results when high-skilled workers migrate temporarily or permanently from one country to another. The movement of high-skilled workers away from their countries of origin represents a huge loss in terms of knowledge, skills, investment, and capital for the sending countries (Blake & Brock, 2014) The large numbers of Indian scientists, doctors, and computer programmers who migrated to the United States and other First World countries in the 1980s and 1990s are an example of brain drain. Yet, today, with the phenomenal growth of high-tech industries in India, many Indian migrants are returning to India. Additionally, there is a new pattern of U.S. migrants going to India to set up branch offices and to serve as English instructors in call centers on one- to two-year contracts. High-skilled workers are often accepted more easily than low-skilled workers into the dominant society in host countries due to their educational and economic levels, affording them the option to integrate into the host culture. The formation of ethnic, religious, and national cultural communities within host, or receiving, countries as well as transnational networks supported by communication and transportation technologies allow migrants to maintain connections with their cultural communities while they also develop association and acceptance with the dominant host culture. The migrant–host mode of relationship of integration best describes these migrant experiences.

Directphoto Collection/Alamy

North Africa–France: Postcolonial Immigrant Experience[3]

"You live in France so you MUST adapt to our laws and principles." Karima, a 20-year-old French citizen of Algerian descent, hears remarks like this almost every day. Her identity and nationality are questioned simply because she wears a *hijab*, Arabic for headscarf or covering. Her parents were displaced by the Algerian war of independence and moved to France in the 1960s. Recently, she faced a terrible humiliation when one of her university professors stopped his lecture and ordered

Photo 6.2 Protesting heightened restrictions on women wearing headscarves in public in France, a young woman uses the French flag as a headscarf. Her sign reads: "The veil covering your eyes is more dangerous than the one covering my hair"

her to take off her *hijab*. The professor publically declared that her attire symbolizes the decline of the France he knows and loves and had Karima escorted out of the building.

Karima struggles daily with how her religion and Algerian culture are portrayed. It was *her* decision to wear the *hijab*; the men in her family and community tried to dissuade her knowing how she would be treated. To her, the *hijab* symbolizes religious devotion and spiritual humility; wearing it is an act of empowerment countering Western hypersexualized and objectified images of women. Others around her, including many of her classmates, interpret her decision to wear the *hijab* as a symbol of men's power over women, and see the *hijab* as a sign of women's oppression in her culture. Media commentators cast Karima and women who wear such religious symbols as less French. Youth ask why are you doing this? Why not try to blend in and adapt to the secular values of France? She has been called anti-French, and an Islamic extremist. Karima feels it is her right as a French citizen to decide what she can and cannot wear. She has now joined a nonprofit organization fighting for French Muslim women affected by discriminatory laws and practices.

What role do colonial and diasporic histories play in this scenario? How is culture—in this case, what it means to be "French," to be "Algerian," to be a "Muslim woman," and to be a "woman"—a contested site where meaning is negotiated? As the daughter of immigrants, is France a "host" country for Karima or "home" country? In what ways, as suggested by Karima's case, is citizenship a contested site with unequal benefits?

---

[3]Case based on Floc'h (2014).

Viewing the scenario from a macro-level, Karima, like many who have been deterritorialized/reterritorialized in the past 50 to 60 years, is a postcolonial migrant or, more accurately, a second generation postcolonial immigrant. Born into an Algerian family in France, she constantly negotiates national, cultural, religious, racial, and class borders. The colonial relationship between her family's homeland of Algeria and her current "home" of France structures her life, opportunities, and future. Prior to Algeria's independence from France in 1962, Algerians who migrated to France were French *subjects*, but not *citizens*. While filling major labor gaps in post–WWII France, Algerians were often represented in the media as criminals, uncivilized, and poor. Algerians fought a long, bloody war of independence from France between 1954 and 1962 in which a half million Algerians died. Bitter memories and untended wounds scar the fabric of both nations fueling prejudices and hindering the integration of Algerians into French society.

For much of the past thousand years, France was a primary Catholic country of Europe, where Christian beliefs, norms, and practices formed the nation-state. A secular state since 1905 when laws were passed to officially separate the State from the Church, today, approximately 58% of French people identify as Christian, predominantly Catholic, 35% claim no religion, and 4% identify as Muslims. Nationalist discourse today pits French secularism against religious practices, like wearing a *hijab,* a headscarf or *niqab*, a face veil, that are perceived as uncivilized and oppressive. Former French President Sarkozy claims the veil is ". . . 'a sign of enslavement and debasement,' the ultimate symbol of Islam's oppression of women" (Harris, 2010). While public discourse frames second and third generation Muslim immigrants as "disruptions" to traditions of French secularism, anthropologist Mayanthi Fernando (2014) argues that Muslim French unsettle and expose taken for granted assumptions of national unity revealing the contradictions, discontinuities, and instabilities of the French secular republic.

On a meso-level, Algerian migrants' segregation from and stigmatization within mainstream French culture was intensified after the war of independence by discriminatory housing and employment practices, as well as repressive and prejudicial treatment by law enforcement, legal, and educational systems. Since the 1970s, second generation immigrants like Karima, the daughters and sons of Algerian migrants, have been targeted in media and governmental discourses as "problems." Young women are represented as "passive," "submissive," while young men are depicted as "criminals" and "not capable of being assimilated." The rise in France of nationalist, racist, Islamophobic, and anti-immigrant sentiment in recent years make it increasingly difficult for postcolonial immigrants like Karima to call France "home," strengthening their connection and adherence to their parents' cultural and religious heritages. In 2004, a law was passed banning conspicuous religious signs in public schools. More recently, in 2010, a controversial law banned garments that cover one's face in the public sphere (Jamet & Ceilles, 2014). Some Muslims and Muslim women in particular who choose to express their religion by wearing a *niqab* feel singled out and targeted. The rationale for the law was that hiding one's face behind a garment is a matter of national security.

The clash between Karima's French and Algerian cultural and religious heritages was always present, but with her decision to wear the *hijab*, she feels even more stuck between two worlds. The public anti-Islamic rhetoric regarding Muslim women covering their hair or face obscures the lively and ongoing debate among Muslim women and feminists about the *hijab*. Coopted by "us versus them" rhetoric, attacks from outside take away the freedom of choice Muslim women want to exercise over their own clothing and bodies. As a result of institutionalized forms of discrimination and anti-immigrant rhetoric, she and other postcolonial migrants like her around the world join organizations and develop networks that provide cultural, religious, and political support. Drawing on both Islamic and secular republican traditions, Muslim French, like Karima, create "new modes of ethical and political engagement, reconfiguring those traditions to image a future for France" (Fernando, 2014, p. 6)

On a micro-level, marginalization best describes the migrant–host–home relationship that Karima experiences in France. Karima's attachment to and expression of her parents' cultural and religious heritage marginalizes her in relation to the dominant French culture where she was born and has lived her entire life, and to some extent, within the immigrant Algerian community in France. As the experiences of Karima illustrate, marginalization occurs in the complex intersection of the host culture's attitudes and practices toward migrant groups, the migrant or immigrant's desires and choices regarding both the host and home cultures, and the histories—in this case, colonial and postcolonial legacies—between the two countries and cultures. While marginalization often has a negative connotation and does indeed carry significant challenges, living in or being on the margins of social, cultural, and national groups can be an empowering and creative position.

As illustrated by the case studies, understanding migration and cultural adaptation in the global context requires that we address the intricate web of individual, social, and geopolitical factors that compel and constrain as well as empower and transform migrants and their surroundings. A multilevel analysis that attends to the macro-level historical, political, and economic issues; micro-level individual attributes; and meso-level migrant networks account for the intersection of complex and contradictory conditions that shape a world in motion.

Based on these case studies, a number of factors influence the experiences of migrants crossing borders today. Clearly the history of relations between nations that extends back to the first wave of colonial migration influences the direction of migration and the reception of migrants in host countries. The globalization of capitalism, integration of markets, and the implementation of neoliberal polices have exacerbated economic inequity within countries and across nations catapulting people from the Global South into migratory paths. Legal and economic status affects migrants' experiences and adaptation as well as educational level, language abilities, gender, age, and familiarity with the "host" culture. The reception of the "host" culture to the migrant group also has a tremendous impact. The migrant–host modes of relationship of assimilation, separation, marginality, and integration are directly impacted and shaped by the attitudes and policies as well as the histories of interaction between the host and home countries. In addition, migrant networks impact the cultural adaptation of people who cross cultural borders, offering social and economic support, recreating collective regional and cultural identities, and providing political alliances.

SUMMARY

In this chapter, we defined various types of migrants from voluntary and involuntary migrants to postcolonial migrants and transmigrants. The purpose of identifying different types of migrants is to highlight the particular conditions that shape the experiences of migrants and draw attention to commonalities and differences across the three waves of migration. World migration from the first wave to the current wave has been integral to the growth of capitalism. Migrants—on a continuum from voluntary to involuntary—have fueled and resuscitated First World economies from the colonial to the industrial and into the postindustrial wave of migration. Viewing migration through a capitalist–labor lens highlights the varying degrees of exclusion and inclusion migrants experience in "host" countries, which significantly affects their ability to participate in "host" countries.

As the forces of globalization converge, unprecedented numbers of people have been displaced, dramatically impacting those who are uprooted, those who remain, and those in places where people resettle. Advances in communication and transportation technologies have created the conditions for migration networks to form that enable transmigrants to maintain, hybridize, and change the "host" cultures and "home" cultures. As south to north migrant flows concentrate in urban centers of Europe, the United States, Canada, Australia, and Japan, significant social and cultural changes as well as economic and political tensions emerge. Anti-immigrant campaigns rally and immigrant rights groups mobilize, fueling racial, interethnic, and intercultural tensions and conflicts. Questions of human rights, civil rights, and immigrant rights coalesce in the global context with complex and unparalleled implications.

Theories of migration and cultural adaptation from macro-, meso-, and micro-levels were introduced that enable us to understand the dynamic and multifaceted nature of migration and cultural adaptation today. Macro-level theories provide insight into the large scale historical, political, and economic structures that shape patterns of migration and adaptation. Micro-level theories enable us to describe and explain individual migrants' experiences of cultural adjustment and intercultural transformation. Bridging these two, the meso-level approach focuses on the role of migrant networks in supporting migration and facilitating the creation of transmigrant communities. As Toni Morrison pointed out, our world in motion requires "us to come to terms with being, fearing, and accepting strangers" (Riding, 2006).

KEY TERMS

migrants

voluntary migrants

sojourners

immigrants

involuntary migrants

human trafficking

first wave of world migration

second wave of migration

chain migration

nativist movements

xenophobia
the third wave of migration
guest workers programs
postcolonial migrants
Bracero Program
refugees
internally displaced persons
contract workers
high- and low-skilled laborers
feminization of the workforce
push-pull theory
world-systems theory
melting pot
pluralism
U-curve model
anticipation
culture shock

adjustment
W-curve model
migrant–host modes of relationship
assimilation
separation
marginalization
integration
integrative theory of cultural adaptation
acculturation
deculturation
intercultural transformation
migrant networks
social capital
transmigrants
transnational communities
relative deprivation
brain drain

DISCUSSION QUESTIONS AND ACTIVITIES

Discussion Questions

1. How do voluntary and involuntary migrants (sojourners, immigrants, refugees, guest workers, transmigrants, postcolonial migrants, etc.) experience cultural adaptation differently? What are the factors that influence their experience, attitudes, and outcome?

2. How do voluntary and involuntary migrants (sojourners, immigrants, refugees, guest workers, transmigrants, postcolonial migrants, etc.) experience cultural adaptation differently? What are the factors that influence their experience, attitudes, and outcome?

3. Why is the metaphor "melting pot" problematic and/or inaccurate to describe U.S. society? Can you think of other metaphors that describe the United States as a country of people with diverse backgrounds?

4. In the context of globalization, we witness complex formations of transnational communities, transmigrants, and global migrant networks. How do these contemporary conditions of migration impact the U- and W-curve models of migration? What kind of models would best describe the conditions of migrants' cultural adaptation today?

5. Why is it important to use micro-, meso-, and macro-level theories to understand the dynamics of global migration?

6. In a previous chapter, we discussed the notion of cultural space. How does global migration impact the construction and transformation of cultural space?

Activities

1. Crossing Borders: Case Study Analysis

   a. Provide a description of someone you know (including yourself, if appropriate) who is a migrant. Address the following questions:

      i. What kind of migrant is she or he?

      ii. What was the social, political, historical, and economic context in which she/he migrated to another country? How did the context shape his or her experience?

      iii. What theories of migration are useful to understand her or his experience as a migrant?

      iv. What role does communication play in his or her process of cultural adaptation?

2. Negotiating Immigration Policies—Group Activity

   a. The class is divided into two independent nation-states located next to each other.

   b. First, name your country and assign each group member to be one of the following categories: political leaders, wealthy elites, educated middle-class, working/lower class, and immigrants.

   c. As a group, decide immigration policies toward the other nation-state to maximize the national interest. Address the following questions, and make sure to include opinions of all citizens:

      i. Who and how many should be allowed to enter the country?

      ii. What are the terms and conditions for migration?

      iii. How can migrants become permanent residents and/or citizens?

      iv. Do you enforce any requirements or restrictions on language skills, educational background, religious beliefs, sexual orientation, nation of origin, and so on?

   d. Share your immigration policies with the other nation-state.

   e. Address the following questions to discuss and debrief the process:

      i. Whose opinions were more powerful and influential in determining the policies, and why?

      ii. What factors were the most important in making the policies?

      iii. How will the immigration policies shape the international relations between the two countries?

      iv. How will the immigration policies shape intercultural interactions between migrants and natives of the country?

      v. What kind of "multicultural society" do you think your country will be?

CHAPTER 7

Jamming Media and Popular Culture

Analyzing Messages About Diverse Cultures

How do you know what you know about cultures that are different from your own?

Learning Objectives

1. Explain the impact of media and popular culture on intercultural communication in the context of globalization.

2. Describe how global and regional flows of media and popular culture influence intercultural communication and cultural identities.

3. Explain the role of power and hegemony in mediated intercultural communication and the representation of nondominant groups.

4. Gain skills and strategies to critically consume, resist, and produce media messages in the global context.

Did you know that five students protesting the military coup in Thailand in November 2014 raised the *Hunger Games* salute, the hand gesture freedom fighters popularized in the *Hunger Games* symbolizing solidarity, unity, and defiance? (Olarn & Bothlho, 2014). What does this example of repurposing say about the relationship between popular culture and "real" life?

Did you know that when Jason Collins came out in 2013, he was the first publicly gay athlete to play in any of the four major professional sports leagues in North America? In 2014, Michael Sam was the first publicly gay athlete drafted by the National Football League (NFL); he was cut at the end of training camp. Does being gay have an impact on his opportunities in the NFL?

Did you see Katy Perry's geisha-inspired performance of "Unconditionally" during the 2013 American Music Awards? What are the implications for intercultural communication of her cultural appropriation? Is there a relationship between her performance and the emergence of Japanese popular culture, including *anime* (animation), *manga* (comic books), JPop, and JRock on the global scene?

Did you know that social networking sites, particularly Facebook and Twitter, were critical during the Arab Spring as youth posted pictures, videos, and text to expose repressive regimes and mobilize activists?

Along with the fast-paced and multidirectional movement of people in the global context discussed in the previous chapter, mediated messages and popular culture as noted above also circulate more rapidly, more widely, and with greater degrees of saturation today than ever before. The forces and factors that have given rise to globalization—advances in communication technology and social media platforms, the integration of global markets, as well as the privatization and deregulation of media outlets in much of the world—combine to intensify the role of media and popular culture in shaping our communication with and understanding of cultures different from our own. Media and popular culture also play pivotal roles in how we make sense of and construct our own cultures and identities.

Often the assumptions, stereotypes, and attitudes we hold about people from different cultures or distant countries come solely or primarily through media and popular culture forms, such as movies, TV and cable network programs, and celebrities. Take a minute and write down everything you know about the cultures of India, Greece, Brazil, or China. Consider how you know what you do about the cultures of these countries. You may have traveled to one or more of these places or perhaps know someone from there, yet it's likely that much of the information you use to construct your "knowledge" about people and places different from your own comes through mediated forms of communication and popular culture sources. Now imagine people in India, Greece, Brazil, and China watching popular U.S. TV programs, such as *The Big Bang Theory, Breaking Bad, Modern Family,* or *American Idol.* What stereotypes and assumptions might people hold about the United States if their primary exposure to the culture is through these mediated texts?

Media and popular culture play central roles in intercultural communication. First, media and popular culture facilitate communication across cultural and national boundaries escalating the flow of information and images interculturally. Second, media frame global issues and normalize particular cultural ideologies. By 2015, five to seven major media monopolies dominated the distribution of mediated images and messages around the globe. The broad reach and global control by a small number of media giants places a few transnational corporations in a position to exert tremendous power over the perspectives, standpoints, and ideologies that are available. Third, the global spread of mass media and popular culture fragments and disrupts national and cultural identities, leading to resistance, opposition, and conflict. Finally, media and popular culture forge hybrid transnational cultural identities in the global context by re-collecting diasporic identities, constructing a global semiculture, and creating intercultural political and social alliances. These four roles of media and popular culture in intercultural communication are addressed throughout the chapter.

The title of this chapter ("Jamming Media and Popular Culture") is used to connote the improvisational and emergent nature of intercultural communication in the technologically advanced, global age—the rapid absorption, adaptation, appropriation, and fusion of verbal and nonverbal languages, and visual and musical codes—that characterizes the mediated popular culture scene, as well as new social movements in the context of globalization. We begin by defining media and popular culture and discussing their impact on intercultural communication in the context of globalization. From there, processes of encoding and decoding media messages, questions of power and hegemony, and the representation of nondominant groups are explored. The chapter concludes with steps to heighten our awareness and skills for consuming media and popular culture messages, strategies to resist mainstream corporate messages, and ways to actively produce media messages, such as alternative and citizen media that are emerging in the global context.

MEDIA, POPULAR CULTURE, AND GLOBALIZATION

Defining Media

In the broadest sense, the word *media* (note that "media" is the plural form of the singular "medium") refers to the modes, means, or channels through which messages are communicated. For example, a telephone or cell phone is a medium of interpersonal communication connecting one point to another; newspapers, magazines, TV, movies, and music recordings are types of mass media, where a source disseminates messages to large audiences. The term *network media* refers to media like the World Wide Web, which connects multiple points to multiple points in addition to serving interpersonal and mass media functions. Technology is a critical feature of media, and advances in technology have dramatically magnified the impact of media on global communication today. Yet, media as channels of communication are not only technologies; media—TV, films, the World Wide Web, and email—do not exist "independently of the concepts people have of them, the uses people make of them, and the social relations that produce them and that are organized around them everyday" (Grossberg, Wartella, Whitney, & Wise, 2006, p. 8). The authors of *MediaMaking* (Grossberg et al., 2006) posited that the media are composed of three elements: (1) technology; (2) social relationships or institutions, such as broadcasting organizations and music and film companies; and (3) cultural forms. **Cultural forms** refer to the products' format (newscasts, sitcoms, action dramas, or thrillers), structures, languages, and narrative styles that are produced when media technologies and institutions come together.

Media bring together technologies, institutions, and cultural forms to create and convey meaning-making products that reflect, construct, and reinforce cultural ideologies. Political scientist Lane Crothers (2013) argued that the popularity of *Titanic*, the second highest grossing film of all time, rested on its embodiment of cultural ideologies of American civil society, such as the presumed irrelevance of class distinctions, a tolerance for difference, the centrality of individualism, and the attraction to and fascination with capitalism. Given this, we can see how the global sale, distribution, and consumption of media are not merely economic transactions. When one nation's cultural products—namely, the United States—dominate the world market, the appeal and fascination as well as the concern and resistance focus on the effects on national cultural values, behavior, and identities.

Defining Popular Culture

The term *media* is often confused and conflated with the term *popular culture*. While the media are the source of much of popular culture today and serve to advertise and distribute a broad range of popular cultural forms, the two are not interchangeable. Popular culture as a term has come into common usage in recent years to replace the term *low culture*, which carried a negative connotation as compared to "high culture" as discussed in Chapter 1. Scholars have argued since the 1960s that the mass production of products—TV programs, Barbie dolls, iPhones, or hip hop music, for example—does not take away their meaning; rather, groups of people, cultures, and subcultures use mass produced products as a way to make meaning in their lives. People use mass produced forms of popular culture to reflect and construct identities as well as display and enact values. **Popular culture** refers to systems and artifacts that the general populous or broad masses within a society share or about which most people have some understanding (Brummett, 1994). Hamburgers and fries, baggy jeans and bling, tattoos, celebrities, music videos, sports, reality shows, Disneyland, TV evangelists, tourism, video games, and pornography are all forms of popular culture. Three characteristics help define popular culture: (1) Popular culture is central and pervasive in advanced capitalist systems, (2) popular culture is produced by culture industries, and (3) popular culture serves social functions. In a world where most everything is commodified, very little is outside of popular culture. From entertainment, fashion, and health to religious rituals, the environment, social causes, and cultural identities, almost everything has been turned into commodities that are packaged, bought, and sold.

Isolated pockets of what in the past were referred to as **folk culture**—localized cultural practices that are enacted for the sole purpose of people within a particular place—still exist. However, as these practices are sought out by tourists for their "authenticity" as folk culture, such as ritual feast days, dances at the Pueblos in New Mexico, or hula dances in Hawaii, they too become commodities in the nostalgic search for the "pure," the "real," and tourist destinations of "authentic" culture (Root, 1996; Sorrells, 2002). As U.S. cultural celebrations, such as Halloween, Valentine's Day, and Mother's Day, and culturally rooted coming of age rituals, such as quinceañeras and bar mitzvahs, are commodified, they become part of popular culture.

The term *culture industry* refers to industries that mass produce standardized cultural goods, such as the Disney Corporation, Time Warner Inc., and Viacom. It is easier to understand these megacorporations as culture industries when we consider the range of products that Disney, for example, produces—amusement parks, adventure tours, cartoons, cable networks, clubs, movies, music, games, toys, clothing, concerts, phones, product tie-ins, and virtual communities. Critical theorists Theodor Adorno and Max Horkheimer (1972), who initially coined the term in the middle of the 20th century, were concerned that culture industries could easily manipulate the masses into becoming docile and passive consumers. Certainly, in a media-saturated culture produced by culture industries, popular culture is a central and pervasive element of advanced capitalist societies. On the streets, airports, buses, subways; in school, in the workplace, and in restaurants; on the Internet; in the dentist and doctor's waiting room; and most especially in our homes and on our bodies, popular culture permeates and penetrates every corner of our lives. The average adult in the United States consumes a tremendous amount of media through TV, computers, phones, and radio. In 2008, Americans listened to and viewed media an average of 11 hours per day. By 2013, that number had increased to 13.6 hours per day per person. Data from the study indicate that in 2015, the average adult in the United States consumes 15.5 hours of media per day (Short, 2013). Given the pervasive consumption of popular culture through increasingly varied forms of media, what functions does it serve?

Sociologist Dustin Kidd (2007) noted that the primary function of popular culture within advanced capitalist societies is to generate profit. Yet, he argued it also serves to establish social norms, constitute social identities and maintain social boundaries, and create meaning through shared rituals of consumption. Finally, popular culture functions as a site of innovation and social change. Popular culture—whether through TV dramas, radio talk shows, magazine articles and advertisements, sports events, or celebrity stories—is the most central and effective means of defining and disseminating social norms. Portrayals and enactments of interpersonal, intergenerational, gender, and intercultural relationships in popular culture normalize culturally informed ways of interacting, social practices, and hierarchies of power. U.S. dominant cultural values of consumerism, individualism, and competition as well as White American middle-class ideologies of what is proper, acceptable, and desirable are reinforced through popular culture. Note how hip hop culture or heavy metal are demonized as abhorrent and distasteful within the broader cultural discussion while other forms of popular culture are considered acceptable.

Popular culture is a key component in the production of social identities, such as class, race, culture, and age where the consumption of popular culture creates and marks social boundaries of inclusion and exclusion (Dines & Humez, 2015; Kidd, 2007). Consider how the clothes you buy, the hairstyle you pay for, the music you consume, and the TV programs you enjoy constitute your identity. Additionally, when people collectively participate in the shared consumption of popular culture through rituals—by attending the Coachella Music and Arts Festival; going to watch the Atlanta Hawks, Detroit Pistons, or San Antonio Spurs; or participating in video gaming communities or fandoms based on the *Hunger Games* or *Sherlock Holmes*—the shared sense of meaning of the ritual provides the basis of group solidarity and identity. In other words, in advanced capitalist cultures, the consumption of popular culture serves as shorthand for sets of values, practices, and goals; for individual and group identities; and for inclusion and exclusion in social groups.

Cultural Identity
Cultural/Self-Expression Through Fashion and Popular Culture

Cultural Identity

Rachel, a White American student from Minneapolis, Minnesota, spent a semester teaching English to Somali women who came to the United States as refugees. Minnesota has the largest Somali population in North America. Rachel discusses her observations of how Somali women use popular culture—especially fashion—to express themselves and maintain their culture:

Before I started working with Somali women, I had this stereotype that they are not very fashion-conscious. Because they have to cover their head and dress modestly for religious reasons, I thought they didn't really care about how they dressed. After getting to know some Somali women, I began to realize they actually take great pride in what they wear. They have amazing collections of skirts and dresses. The designs are more subtle than American fashion, but certainly detailed, well-made, and fun in their own way.

A young Somali woman told me that she would never leave Minnesota because the latest Somali fashions come to Minneapolis first. There are three Somali shopping centers where she buys the latest trends from Somalia. To my surprise, she has never lived in Somalia. She was born in a refugee camp in Kenya and then moved to the United States. She is still deeply connected to her homeland, and fashion is one way for her to maintain her connection as a second generation, diasporic Somali American.

Finally, popular culture can function as a platform for discussion or as an initiating force for social change. When Ellen DeGeneres, star of the popular sitcom *Ellen,* came out in 1997 as a lesbian (both as the actress and the character she played), an international discussion of lesbians and gay men on prime-time TV and the social acceptability of lifestyles that differ from the heterosexual norm ensued. The fact that the enormously popular show—one of the highest rated TV shows ever and winner of an Emmy Award—was cancelled by ABC also generated tremendous discussion about the power of networks to control and censor popular culture. When Don Imus made his now infamous racist and sexist remarks about the Rutgers women's basketball team in 2007, a nationwide discussion and debate about race, gender, and hip hop culture in the United States followed. The story about *The Interview*, a Sony Pictures comedy about a plot to assassinate North Korean leader Kim Jong-un, and the cyberhack of Sony attributed to North Korea by U.S. intelligence agents and used to shut down the release of the film, exploded on media outlets in late 2014. Questions and discussions about "cyberterrorism" and censorship among media pundits, professors in classrooms, and people across social media sites proliferated.

Additionally, popular culture celebrities have been instrumental in raising awareness and mobilizing economic and political support for natural and social crises through events, such as Live Aid, a rock concert known as the "global jukebox" that provided support for famine victims in Ethiopia in 1985; the Rock the Vote campaign that began in the 1990s and has continued in the 2000s and today; and the internationally broadcast benefit concert for Hurricane Katrina victims in 2005. During this event, hip hop artist Kanye West improvised off script saying, "George Bush doesn't care about Black people," generating discussion in public and private spaces about the historically and institutionally embedded racial discrimination in the United States, which was exposed when the levies in New Orleans broke (Dyson, 2006). In 2011, Japanese popular culture celebrities and animators used their influence to gain support for earthquake and tsunami victims. These examples illustrate how popular culture, in addition to generating profit, defining social norms, and constituting social identities, provides a stage for discussion of social issues and can be instrumental in initiating social change. Given its centrality both socially and economically, let's take a look at how popular culture impacts intercultural communication in the context of globalization.

POPULAR CULTURE, INTERCULTURAL COMMUNICATION, AND GLOBALIZATION

From the first pages of his book *Globalization & American Popular Culture,* political scientist Lane Crothers (2013) noted the seemingly odd juxtaposition of popular culture, which is often characterized as light, fun, and "just entertainment" with the weighty and important set of issues associated with globalization. Yet, he argued that what may appear at first glance as inconsequential forms of entertainment—films, TV programs, and popular music—are, in fact, key elements in contemporary globalization that alternately promote deeply felt desires for global integration and also mobilize adamant resistance to integration.

Consider the fact that American television programming, movies, and music are the dominant forms of entertainment globally and that more than 70% of the revenue for U.S. films is generated from international sales (Crothers, 2013). Given its position as a global leader in the production of popular culture, the United States has led the international battle to reduce or remove restrictions on the flow of popular culture around the world, claiming popular culture is a commodity like any other. Yet, popular culture forms are not simply commodities like corn, cars, or computers. Many, including representatives of nation-states as well as local culture industries argue that popular culture products are embedded with cultural values, norms, and ideologies. What may seem like harmless and frivolous entertainment actually disseminates core U.S. cultural values, such as individualism, personal freedom, and consumerism around the globe; through the distribution and consumption of U.S. popular culture globally, particular cultural views on gender norms and gender relationships, sex, sexuality, and violence, as well as racial stereotypes and intercultural relations are normalized (Dines & Humez, 2015; Durham & Kellner, 2012). Thus, in addition to purely economic objections to U.S. global dominance of popular culture that drives national and local producers of cultural products out of business, various countries, notably France, Canada, and Australia initially, and Iran, Venezuela, and Hong Kong more recently have resisted the unregulated flow of cultural products arguing that popular culture can lead to cultural corruption, cultural homogenization, and cultural imperialism (Crothers, 2013).

Cultural corruption refers to the perceived and experienced alteration of a culture in negative or detrimental ways through the influence of other cultures. **Cultural homogenization** is the convergence toward common cultural values and practices as a result of global integration, and **cultural imperialism** is the domination of one culture over others through cultural forms, such as popular culture, media, and cultural products. All three objections—cultural corruption, cultural homogenization, and cultural imperialism—focus on the dominance today of U.S. popular culture globally and the potentially significant ways this dominance may contribute to the loss, change, and/or undermining of national and local cultural practices, values, and identities. In 1993, French president François Mitterrand captured the rising fear, stating the following:

> Creations of the spirit are not just commodities; the elements of culture are not pure business. What is at stake is the cultural identities of all of our nations—it is the freedom to create and choose our own images. A society which abandons the means of depicting itself would soon be an enslaved society. (Shapiro, 2000)

Globalization has often enabled and sometimes forced the integration of markets, politics, and cultures globally. Integration on a global scale has led to the fragmentation and disruption of economic, political, and cultural cohesiveness within nation-states and communities. Just as the massive and multidirectional migration of people around the globe discussed in the previous chapter has disrupted and fragmented economic, political, and social norms, so too the increased movement of cultural products and popular cultural forms has fragmented local and national cultural identities, values, norms, and practices. Political scientist James Rosenau (2003) has coined the word *fragmegration* to describe the dual and simultaneous dynamic of integration and fragmentation that has emerged in the context of globalization. The term *fragmegration* helps explain the dual, simultaneous, and often contradictory tensions of integration and fragmentation that accompany the spread of and resistance to U.S. popular culture in the context of globalization. Having defined basic terms and highlighted the contested intercultural issues of popular culture and globalization, we turn now to a discussion of global and regional media circuits.

Communicative Dimensions
Popular Culture, Fragmentation, and Globalization

The following examples of fragmegration, the simultaneous dynamic of integration and fragmentation, illustrate how popular culture is experienced in the context of globalization. Many in France are outraged by what they experience as the corrosive influence of U.S. popular culture. English is increasingly part of casual conversations and daily business practices in France as evidenced by terms, such as *le deal* and *le cash flow*. "Bazinga" is becoming as common in France as *bonjour* as a result of the popularity of the *Big Bang Theory*. Outcries that U.S. popular culture is an assault on French language and national identity exemplify the concern about *cultural corruption*.

In Iran today, where more than two thirds of the population is under the age of 30, U.S. popular culture and messages are very alluring. Adaption by youth of cultural practices and values expressed through music, movies, and fashion from the United States and the West illustrates the tendency toward *cultural homogenization* as a result of global integration. Social networking sites, particularly Facebook and Twitter, played central roles in Iran and subsequently during the Arab Spring as youth posted pictures, videos, and text to expose repressive regimes and mobilize activists. The Egyptian government attempted to stop the use of social media for revolutionary purposes by shutting down the Internet across the nation. Thus, U.S. popular culture and new media are both desired and resisted for social and political reasons.

In a move to resist what was seen as *cultural imperialism*, in April 2014, the Chinese government banned *The Big Bang Theory* and several other popular U.S. television programs, including *NCIS*, *The Good Wife*, and *The Practice*, which were accessed in China via the Web for multiple seasons. Part of broader efforts to clean up the Web, Chinese President Xi's campaign targeted the increasing influence of foreign popular culture. Ironically, as conflict escalated between the Chinese and the U.S. governments, journalist Evan Osnos (2014) noted the convergence of lived experiences in China and the United States as youth share similar jokes, tastes, anxieties, and aspirations.

GLOBAL AND REGIONAL MEDIA CIRCUITS

Remember *Avatar*, the most commercially successful film ever made? Communication scholar Tanner Mirrlees (2013) noted *Avatar* was touted by many as a quintessentially "American" film, a product of Hollywood, at the center of American cultural industries; yet, *Avatar* is not only an American film. It is the product of News Corp, a transnational media corporation with stockholders from many countries, including Saudi Arabia, the United Kingdom, and the United States and is owned by Rupert Murdoch, a binational citizen of Australia; the U.S. Twentieth Century Fox corporation is owned by News Corp and has transnational distribution subsidiaries in Finland, Czech Republic, Portugal, Japan, and Latvia among other countries. James Cameron, the director of *Avatar*, has binational citizenship in New Zealand and Canada. While many of the film's stars are U.S. born and the production and post-production were managed by U.S. companies, the male star, Sam Worthington, was born in England and raised in Australia; firms around the world (Canada, France, New Zealand, Japan, and the United States) participated in the creation of the film. Parts of the movie were shot in the United States, but it was primarily filmed in New Zealand with government subsidies. So, is *Avatar* an American film?

Avatar has been interpreted as an allegory of Western and U.S. imperialism and critiqued as a neocolonial view of naïve, innocent, and pure indigenous "others" who are rescued and liberated by yet another White male "savior." Still, activists have repurposed Avatar, finding parallels and identification with the experiences of oppressed people around the world (Jenkins, 2010). Marginalized people in China, India, Bolivia, South Africa, and Palestine have appropriated Avatar as a sign of resistance to capitalism, neoliberalism, and militarization that destroy natural environments and local cultures, and violate human rights. Mirrlees (2013) contends that Avatar, open to multiple and often contradictory readings, is a form of global popular culture rather than distinctly American.

Jeremy Tunstall (2008), author of *The Media Were American,* argued that we need to understand global flows of media today in terms of Euro-American dominance rather than focusing solely on the United States as the primary force. He used the term *Euro-American* to refer to the continents of Europe and South and North America, which are the main importers and exporters of media around the globe. While the United States remains central to the production of media and popular culture, many of the films made in Hollywood are collaborations with British and Canadian partners. In the past decade, a number of TV programs immensely popular with U.S. audiences did not originate in the United States. Programs such as *Who Wants to Be a Millionaire?* and *The Weakest Link* were British, and the reality show *Big Brother* was created in the Netherlands. Additionally, over the past decades, South American **telenovelas** produced in countries with large viewing audiences, such as Brazil, Mexico, Venezuela, Argentina, and Chile, are now imported to over 125 countries around the world; they are especially popular in Italy, Greece, Spain, Portugal, France, and Sweden as well as Eastern Europe, Russia, India, Philippines, and Vietnam (Aldama & Rojas, 2013). While U.S. soaps are still shown regularly around the world, Tunstall (2008) noted that Latin American telenovelas, despite or perhaps because of their rags-to-riches plots, are finding greater appeal than depictions of glitzy affluence in U.S. soap operas.

As telenovelas are exported around the globe, they not only expose people in distant places and different cultures to the narratives, social realities, and cultural practices of Latin America, but they also serve a central function for diasporic Latin American communities. Forms of popular culture, such as TV programs and movies from migrants' countries of origin, allow migrant communities to stay in touch with, remember, and recreate their cultural identities. While telenovelas produced in Latin America have long been popular among U.S. Latinos/Latinas, in 2006, TV executives from the top two Spanish-language networks—Univision and Telemundo—began writing and producing shows in Miami. *Washington Post* writer Peter Whoriskey (2006) reported that executives hope to hook more Hispanics "by depicting the realities of U.S. life, where dating and class distinctions—the staples of many a melodrama—adhere to different rules than in other countries." Whoriskey quoted Telemundo President Don Browne:

> A lot of our audience came from Mexico, they're Mexican, but their life experiences are much different than people who haven't emigrated. The humor is different. The pacing is different. It was critical for us to be more relevant. Everyone reduces their appeal down to language—and it's not just language. It's cultural relevance.

Increasingly, the 50 million Latinos/Latinas in the United States, including bilingual viewers who could be watching the major U.S. networks, are drawn to telenovelas, such as Univision's blockbuster *Amores Verdaderos* (True Love) and *La Madrastra* (The Stepmother).

While Euro-American media and popular culture remain dominant in the global flow of media today, the world's most densely populated countries—India and China—represent significant audiences of regional importance, especially when combined with the large diasporic communities from each country living around the world. Tunstall (2008) noted that large population countries like India and China as well as the United States, Mexico, and Brazil are much less likely to import media because they have the capacity to produce media for their internal audiences. Large population countries, however, do generally export their media regionally and increasingly, in the current context, globally. International communication scholar Daya Kishan Thussu (2010) noted that India is one of the only non-Western countries that has impacted the global cultural market. In terms of production and viewership, India's film industry, based in Mumbai (formerly Bombay giving rise to the name "Bollywood"), is the largest in the world. Annually, 1 billion more tickets are sold to Indian films than Hollywood films (Thussu, 2010). In 2013, the United States produced about 620 feature films while India produced roughly 1,325 films, yet Indian superstar Shah Ruhk Khan remains relatively unknown outside India and the diasporic Indian communities around the world. Nevertheless, the popularity of films like *100-Foot Journey, Heaven and Earth, My Name is Khan,* and *Namesake* suggests that as Indian films address the challenges of diasporic communities in France, Canada, and the United States, they increasingly appeal to a broader crossover audience.

Like telenovelas for the Latino/Latina audiences living outside Latin America, Indian films play a critical role in the lives of many diasporic Indians. A participant in communication scholar Anjali Ram's (2004) research commented that Hindi films allow "our children to be educated in their own culture, to know about our own childhood, how we grew up—children get to understand about our culture and that in reality, we are foreigners here" (p. 128). Ram noted the following:

> . . . it is clear that Hindi cinema functions as much more than entertainment. Rather, it facilitates and shapes recollections, it allows the past to be reconstructed within the present context, and it provides an emotionally charged technicolor medium through which the past can be shared and communicated with others, both in everyday contexts and shared commemorative events. (p. 129)

China, like India, represents a large viewer and consumer audience for media and popular culture, with much of its media produced either within China for national and regional consumption or imported from geographically and culturally close countries, such as Taiwan and Hong Kong in the 1990s and increasingly from Singapore, Japan, and South Korea. With a population of 1.4 billion—850,000 of whom speak one language, Mandarin—China remains self-sufficient as a media producer and relatively impenetrable to Western imports (Tunstall, 2008). Called "The Great Firewall of China," the Chinese government exercises stringent control over media outlets restricting rebroadcasting and satellites, jamming shortwave broadcasts, and blocking websites. The astronomical number of Internet users—more than 618 million by the end of 2013—is the world's largest online population, Chinese access is primarily for instant messaging and news (British Broadcasting Corporation, 2014).

In contrast, small population countries in Central America, the Caribbean, Africa, and Asia are solely dependent on media imports. More than one third of the countries of the world produce no films at all and are dependent on regional and global sources for much of their TV programming. Interestingly, in both small and large population countries, people around the world prefer to watch the news, soap operas, and dramas in their own languages, with culturally relevant content and culturally familiar formats when possible.

The predominance of the Euro-American media circuit combines with regional and diasporic media circuits to create dynamic and contradictory challenges for intercultural communication in the global context. Tunstall (2008) stated the following:

> Most people in almost all other countries spend a tenth or more of their media time with media imported, typically, from the United States and/or from one or two other countries. Consequently, most of the world's people have some sustained exposure to the history, culture, and mythology of one or two other countries. (p. xiv)

Clearly, the circulation of media regionally and globally escalates the flow of information and images interculturally, which exposes people to different cultures, yet this exposure can fragment and disrupt local and national cultural identities. Also, as noted in the examples of Latinos/Latinas in the United States and the diasporic Indian communities, the circulation of media and popular culture creates hybrid transnational cultural identities in the global context by re-collecting and reconstituting diasporic identities. Additionally, the predominance of U.S. media and popular culture internationally has been instrumental in constructing a global semiculture where people from far-reaching countries and cultures—in France, India, Guatemala, Iran, Thailand, South Korea, China, and the United States, for example—share some aspects of U.S. popular culture, yet the pervasiveness of U.S. popular culture and English (more particularly American English) has led to the decline and hybridization of local cultures and languages, threatening cultural and linguistic diversity around the world. Tunstall (2008) succinctly articulated another concern:

> The United States remains unique in that most Americans are exposed almost entirely to their own nation's history, culture, and mythology. What do they know (of a supposedly global reality) who only American media know? (p. xiv)

While the dominance of the United States in terms of media and popular culture may appear beneficial to the United States and to Americans, a lack of understanding of other cultures' perspectives, histories, lifestyles, values, and ideologies is a distinct disadvantage and disturbing danger of this asymmetrical flow. The one-sided view that many people in the United States have as a result of consuming only or primarily U.S. media and popular culture can and often does lead to misperceptions, misunderstanding, ignorance, stereotypes, and prejudice about other ethnicities/races as well as national cultural groups. One of the contradictions of globalization for people living in the United States is that while the world is increasingly interconnected and integrated, Americans can and do live relatively uninformed about the perspectives, and insulated from the conditions, of others around the world due to the inequitable and uneven flows of media and popular culture. Now that we have a broad picture of how media and popular culture circulate globally and regionally, we examine in greater depth the processes of meaning-making involved in the production and consumption of popular culture.

PRODUCING AND CONSUMING POPULAR CULTURE

When studying popular culture, media, and communication, scholars often look at three areas: (1) the production or encoding of popular culture, where the institutions, the people, and the relationships of power involved in making popular culture products or texts are studied; (2) textual analysis, where the actual product or text—the TV program or film, such as *The Big Bang Theory* or *Avatar,* for example—is analyzed for symbolic meaning and narrative content; and (3) audience analysis, where the meanings and interpretations that viewers/readers/listeners decode from popular culture text are investigated. It may seem a bit odd to ask what meanings are constructed by particular forms of popular culture, yet the production and consumption of popular culture involves ongoing meaning-making processes that establish social norms, constitute identities, disseminate dominant ideologies, and allow for oppositional meanings to emerge. Given the asymmetrical distribution of popular culture around the globe that has led to claims of cultural corruption, cultural homogenization, and cultural imperialism, it is important to understand the meaning-making processes and their consequences in the production and consumption of popular culture.

Cultural studies scholar Stuart Hall (1980), in his article titled "Encoding/Decoding," offered a model that helps us understand the processes of meaning-making that occur as popular culture is produced and consumed. His original research in the 1970s focused on understanding the meanings people made of TV programs in Britain. He examined the ways in which people in England decoded mass mediated messages that were encoded by program producers. Hall noted that **decoding**, or the active interpretative and sense-making processes of audiences, is as important as **encoding**, or the construction of mass mediated meaning by culture industries. Further, Hall (1980) argued that "decoding does not necessarily follow from encoding" (p. 136), emphasizing the interpretative agency audiences have in producing meaning. Let's take a look at his model (see Figure 7.1).

According to Hall, "meaning structures 1" and "meaning structures 2" may not be the same. Agreement between the meanings that are encoded and those that are decoded depends on the degree of symmetry between the social and institutional positions of the encoder–producer and the decoder–receiver. The structural differences of relation and position between the media/popular culture producer (meaning structures 1) and the audience (meaning structures 2) may lead to the creation of different meanings. While Hall argued that all stages of the meaning-making are imprinted within complex structures of dominance, he stressed the important role that social, economic, cultural, and political positionality play in both the encoding and decoding of popular culture texts. Hall outlined three broad ways of "reading" popular culture texts: (1) a dominant or hegemonic reading, (2) a negotiated reading, and (3) an oppositional reading. A **dominant reading** is one where the viewer or reader shares the meanings that are encoded in the text and accepts the preferred reading, which generally naturalizes and reinforces dominant ideologies. A **negotiated reading** is one where the reader or viewer generally shares the codes and preferred meanings of the texts, but may also resist and modify the encoded meaning based on her or his positionality, interests, and experiences resulting

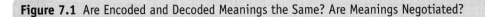

Figure 7.1 Are Encoded and Decoded Meanings the Same? Are Meanings Negotiated?

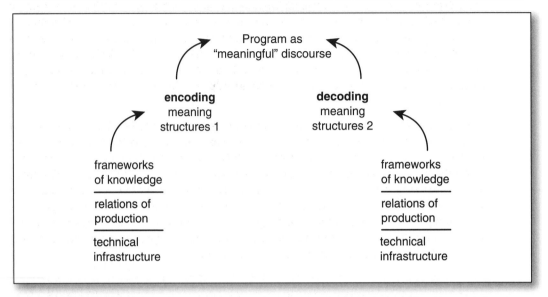

Source: From Culture, Media, Language by Stuart Hall. Copyright © 1980 Taylor & Francis. Reproduced by permission of Taylor & Francis Books UK.

in a contradictory reading of the text. An **oppositional reading** is one where the social position (in terms of class, race, gender, religion, nationality, ideology, etc.) of the viewer or reader of the text places them in opposition to the dominant code and preferred reading of the popular culture text. The reader understands the dominant code yet brings an alternative frame of reference, which leads him or her to resist the encoded meaning. An oppositional reading is not simply the negation of the dominant reading; rather, it is a reading that opposes the ideologies that are taken for granted in the dominant reading. An oppositional reading generates alternative ways of understanding and making sense of the text creating new possibilities for living and being in the world.

Let's take the Spider-Man film series (*Spider-Man* was released in 2002, *Spider-Man 2* in 2004, and *Spider-Man 3* in 2007) to illustrate the concept of dominant, negotiated, and oppositional readings of popular culture texts. The Spider-Man film series is based on the Marvel Comics character created in the 1960s—a groundbreaking comic in that the main character was a teenage superhero with all the insecurities of rejection and loneliness to which a growing adolescent comic book market could relate (Wright, 2001). In the three films to date, the "geeky" Peter Parker from Queens struggles to balance choices and responsibilities presented by his human desires and his superhuman abilities. As he transforms into Spider-Man to fight an array of evil villains that threaten New York City, including Green Goblin, Dr. Octopus, Sandman, New Goblin, and Venom, he also negotiates a romantic relationship with his childhood crush, Mary Jane Watson. The monstrous villains are human-made mistakes. They are accidents produced when exaggerated ambitions and inflated egos of men combine with futuristic science and technology. Parker's best friend, Harry Osborn, is torn between friendship and avenging the death of his father, a scientist and CEO of Oscorp who morphed into the Green Goblin and died in a duel with Spider-Man. Mary Jane is "the girl next door," a victim of domestic abuse and an aspiring actress who plays the role of girlfriend to four different men in the three films as her love for Peter Parker waxes and wanes. As the true love of Spider-Man, she is the target of numerous captures by various villains and heroic rescues by Spider-Man and Harry (who has become the New Goblin).

• A dominant reading of the Spider-Man film series is as follows: The world we live in is a dangerous and treacherous place divided between forces of good and evil. People need protection from evil or villainous forces, which can take many different forms—even science, which is usually considered a force of progress and good, can be turned to disastrous ends. Fortunately, however, average or even nerdy, working-class boys can grow up to be superheros and can serve as role models if they believe in themselves and take responsibility for the power they have. Making the right choices is difficult in the complex, competitive, capitalist-driven world, but individuals, by making the right decisions, can succeed, saving and protecting others less capable or fortunate.

• A negotiated reading of the Spider-Man film series is as follows: Yes, the world is a dangerous place divided between good and evil, but why is the superhero always a boy/man, and why are all the main characters in the film White? Are the only people who can save or destroy the world White men? The female characters in the film—from Mary Jane to the secretaries in the newspaper office—are presented as passive "damsels-in-distress" in stereotypically domestic roles or revered and prized for their beauty and bodies. Fortunately, Mary Jane *is* represented as making some choices in her dedication to her career, as well as which boyfriend she wants. Women, apparently, do have choices—just more limited ones than men.

• An oppositional reading of the Spider-Man film series is as follows: All the evil or "bad" things that are presented in the films—from the demonic villains, to the misrepresentation of Spider-Man in the media, to the foreclosure of Aunt May's house—were caused by the greed for money, power, and fame in a capitalist, corporatized, militarized society. The situations people were in had less to do with their individual decisions and more to do with the oppressive and exploitative corporate, media, criminal, and military systems that are depicted as "normal" in the films. The emphasis on individual choice masks the systemic oppression that creates the "evil" from which Spider-Man—the young, White, superhero male—must rescue and protect the vulnerable masses.

This example illustrates how dominant, negotiated, and oppositional readings of the text differ. The varied readings of the Spider-Man film series also demonstrate how ideologies central to U.S. culture—such as individualism; freedom of choice; equality; the irrelevance of class, gender, and race; and the valorization of capitalism—are encoded and normalized in the text. Consumers of media and popular culture texts can make decisions to resist or challenge dominant readings; however, the ability to develop a negotiated or oppositional reading depends on being conscious of how one's individual or group-based interests are undermined by the passive acceptance of dominant ideologies. People or groups for whom the dominant reading is less than beneficial—people who are disadvantaged or oppressed in the capitalist system, non-White people and women, for example—may be more likely to negotiate and oppose the dominant reading. Now that we have a general overview of the process of producing and consuming popular culture, let's look more closely at how cultural and racial groups are represented in popular culture and the ways individuals and groups negotiate these representations.

Cultural Identity
Race, Gender, and Sexual Orientation in Professional Sports

Similar to many institutions, professional sports, historically, has a long history of excluding people of color and women. Jackie Robinson broke the baseball color line in 1947; Black players were excluded from the NBA until 1950. The Women's Sports Association was not formed until the 1970s; Billie Jean King, who created the Association, was one of the first women classified as a professional athlete. Even today, most female athletes throughout the world are not paid enough to support themselves. Yet, the athletic playing field has come to signify a place and space where social change occurs even as it remains a site where dominant ideologies persist. With professional athletes like 2013 Southeastern Conference Defensive Player of the Year Michael Sam, WNBA basketball superstar Brittany Griner, and long-term NBA veteran Jason Collins coming out while pursuing their athletic careers, gay and lesbian professional athletes are increasingly acknowledging their sexual orientation publically. In light of recent political victories for LGBT rights, the public is slowly moving from disapproval to tolerance of gay men and lesbians in sports. Yet, famed players like Kobe Bryant and managers like Ozzie Guillen, among others, have made anti-gay slurs leading to their participation in diversity sensitivity training. NFL punter Chris Klume concluded he has been blackballed for publicly supporting gay marriage and challenging the homophobic environment of the NFL.

Interestingly, heterosexual identities are assumed for men when participating in highly combative sports characterized by speed, strength, and stamina; the performance of masculine heterosexuality has long been promoted through clothing, tattoos, hairstyles, and physique in the world of professional sports. Yet, many women athletes, regardless of their sexual orientation, are, at some point, assumed to be lesbian—because they play sports. The different expectations and assumptions made about men versus those made about women in sports illustrate the intersecting heteronormative and patriarchal basis of institutional sports in society.

How can professional sports promote a space inclusive of all identities and one that is free of stigma? How does the intersection of race, gender, and sexual orientation affect the inclusion of athletes in professional sports?

POPULAR CULTURE, REPRESENTATION, AND RESISTANCE

Media and popular culture serve as primary channels through which we learn about groups who are different from ourselves, as well as make sense of who we are. Through the consumption of media and popular culture, children, teenagers, and adults are fed a steady diet of images that often promote and reinforce stereotypes and misinformation about cultural groups. A study conducted at the University of Southern California (Smith, Choueiti, & Pieper, 2013) found that minorities are still underrepresented in film. Evaluating 500 top grossing films from 2007 to 2012, researchers found that 76.3% of all speaking roles were White, 10.8% were Black, 5% were Asian, and 3.6% were from other racial/ethnic backgrounds. Latino/as or Hispanics were particularly underrepresented with only 4.2% speaking roles. A strong relationship was found between the race of the director and the race of the cast. Communication scholar Pieper noted, "At the core, this is a visibility issue. Who we see in film sends a powerful message about who is important and whose stories are valuable, both to international audiences and to younger viewers in our own country. . . . Are films communicating to audiences that only certain stories are worth telling?" (Keegan, 2013). In addition, researchers found that Latina/Hispanic women are most likely to be shown in sexy clothing or nude, while Black men are the least likely to be depicted in committed relationships.

Limited representations of non-White groups in the United States media have damaging effects as nondominant groups are more frequently represented as criminals, crime victims, and in limited roles in terms of work. While the number of representations of Blacks has increased on TV and in films over the past 30 years, the preponderance of images of African American males in stereotypically negatives roles, such as criminals, pimps, drug dealers, and gang members continues a 200-year tradition of denigrating, dehumanizing, and devaluing Blacks in the U.S. media. Education scholar Darron Smith (2013) notes that other typical roles for Black men include the White protagonist's sidekick, the comic relief, the athlete, the over-sexualized player, or simply the token Black. Popular shows on prime-time TV and cinematic films overwhelming cast White characters and reflect the interest of White people. The predominantly White film and TV industry, and White screenwriters and directors, who write and direct from their perspective, often limit and marginalize the lived experiences and standpoints of people of color.

Latinos/Latinas, Asian Americans, Native Americans, Arab Americans, and other non-dominant groups have been relatively invisible in U.S.-produced TV programs and films. When appearing, non-White groups are frequently cast as socially deviant elements; as less moral, less intelligent, or "primitive"; as comic figures; or as threats to dominant U.S. or White cultural norms, values, and superiority. Latinos appeared early on in TV history in programs, such as *I Love Lucy* and *Cisco Kid*, in a few situational comedies appearing in the 1970s (*Chico and the Man* and *Viva Valdez*), in star roles in the 1980s and 1990s (notably Edward James Olmos in *Miami Vice* and Jimmy Smits in *L.A. Law*); however, the first network series featuring an all-Latino/Latina cast, *Kingpin,* appearing in 2002, depicted "a Mexican drug lord and his family of stereotypical characters" (Wilson, Gutiérrez, & Chao, 2013). Representations in popular culture depict Asians and Asian Americans alternately as dangerous, crafty, devious, and sadistically violent (especially in the use of martial arts), as the "yellow peril"—serving political ends during WWII, the Korean War, the Cold War, and the Vietnam War—and as subservient and comic or as model minorities. Interestingly, while Asian men are depicted as feminized with their sexuality all but erased, images of Asian women as exotic, sexual, and submissive continue to serve the erotic fantasies of White men.

In *The Guardian* newspaper, cultural critic Priya Elan (2014) comments on the cultural stereotypes rampant in pop music. In 2004, Gwen Stefani released her first solo album, including a poignant song "Long Way to Go" about the challenges faced by mixed race couples; yet, the album featured girls, identically dressed backup dancers who never spoke, an "ethnic posse" for Stefani to use like decoration. Comedian Margaret Cho (2005) sarcastically commented on Stefani's Harajuku girls saying:

> . . . racial stereotypes are really cute sometimes, and I don't want to bum everyone out by pointing out the minstrel show. I think it is totally acceptable to enjoy the Harajuku girls, because there are not that many other Asian people out there in the media really, so we have to take whatever we can get. Amos 'n Andy had lots of fans, didn't they? At least it is a measure of visibility, which is better than invisibility. I am so sick of not existing, that I would settle for following any white person around with an umbrella, just so I could say I was there.

Ten years later, Katy Perry's performances with selected cultures as her backdrop exemplifies cultural stereotyping, appropriation, and fetishism. What are the intended and received messages of her carefully applied makeup, kimono, and rather eclectic array of pan-Asian props in "Unconditionally," performed during the 2013 American Music Awards? And what of her reimagined world of Cleopatra's Egypt in "Dark Horse," one of the most frequently viewed videos in 2014? Priya Elan (2014) commented:

> The road of cultural insensitivity leads very quickly to the slipstream of racism, because racism isn't just someone calling you a name in the street or in the playground; it's a subtle, creeping thing that hangs about in words left unsaid and moments not challenged when they should be. As Maya Angelou said: "The plague of racism is insidious, entering into our minds as smoothly and quietly and invisibly as floating airborne microbes enter into our bodies to find lifelong purchase in our bloodstreams."

The nondominant group with the longest history of being targeted for stereotypical and dehumanizing treatment in the media in the United States is American Indians. Centuries ago, images appeared in print media, paintings, and literature that vilified Native Americans; then, films and TV programs depicted American Indians as brute and primitive savages who were barely considered human (epitomized by films, such as *The Searchers*, released in 1956, featuring protagonist John Wayne). More sympathetic depictions of Native Americans have appeared in the past 20 years. Yet, such portrayals as those found in Disney's animated film *Pocahontas,* which claimed to challenge racism and intolerance and promote respect for other cultures, were criticized for masking the brutal realities of the intercultural encounter between Europeans and Native Americans and for reinforcing racial and gender stereotypes (Buescher & Ono, 1996). To evaluate Disney's claim of positive representations of Native Americans and women and to explore possible readings of the movie from the standpoint of different cultural groups, communication scholar Amy Aidman (1999) compared the responses of Native American girls ages 9 to 13 from both urban and rural settings and European American girls from an urban setting to the movie. She concluded the following:

> While the Euro-American girls produced a reading that could be labeled as "negotiated" in some respects, they appeared to accept the colonist lesson about U.S. history and to view the movie as somewhat comical. For the urban Native American girls, "Pocahontas" was an important movie to which they related strongly. The Native American girls from the reservation were not as enthusiastic about the movie, perhaps because the culture of their everyday lives strengthened their personal and cultural identities in such a way as to make media representations of Native Americans less significant to them. (pp. 154–155)

Aidman's research highlights the ways our positionality in terms of culture, race, class, and geographic location impact our reading of a movie text. It also demonstrates the significant role media representations play in making sense not only of groups that are different from our own, but also in how we make sense of our own identities. The Native American girls who had few real-life role models that reflected and embodied their cultural identities in their urban setting showed a high level of identification with *Pocahontas*. As anthropologist S. Elizabeth Bird (2014) noted in *Imagining Indians*:

> For most White Americans, to live in a media world is to live with a smorgasbord of images that reflect back themselves, and offer pleasurable tools for identity formation. American Indians, like many other minorities, do not see themselves, except as expressions through a cultural script they do not recognize, and which they reject with both humor and anger. (p. 209)

In the wake of U.S. military invasions in the Middle East in the 1990s and 2000s and the catastrophe of 9/11, a series of films featuring Arabs, Arab Americans, and Muslims have reflected and fueled negative racial, cultural, and religious stereotypes against these groups. Tremendous controversy, protest, and debate accompanied the debut of *The Siege* in 1998 as the Arab Americans Anti-Discrimination League argued that the film was "insidious, incendiary and dangerous," and proponents of the film claimed it provided a platform for discussing stereotyping, terrorism, and the balance between personal freedoms and collective security (as quoted in Hasian, 2002, p. 227). Communication scholar Marouf Hasian (2002) noted that by the 1980s, depictions of Islamic fundamentalists and Muslim fanatics had become stock characters in media and popular culture. By the mid-1990s, Arabs, Islamic fundamentalists, and Muslims had replaced communism as the perceived threat to Western democracy to the extent that Arabs were immediately assumed to be responsible for the bombing of the Federal Building in Oklahoma City in 1995. The bombings were, in fact, perpetrated by two European American members of an antigovernment militia movement, yet White Americans have not been represented collectively as "terrorists," subjected to racial profiling, and been targets of hate crimes for their racial or national identities.

Anthropologist Suad Joseph's (2006) study of the *New York Times* and the *Wall Street Journal* from 2001 to 2003 points to the critical role media outlets play in racializing and essentializing Arabs and Muslims in general and Arab and Muslim Americans by association. Joseph's research found that media representations of Arab and Muslim Americans in the two most prominent, agenda-setting print media sources in the United States erase the diversity and humanity within Arab and Muslim groups while emphasizing their distinctiveness and "otherness" from Americans. For example, Arab Americans are depicted in the U.S. media as Muslims. Yet, the majority of Arab Americans are Christian. Muslims are represented in the U.S. media as Arabs. Yet, fewer than 15% of Muslims worldwide are Arabs. Indonesia has the largest Muslim population in the world and over 60% of all Muslims live in Asia (Pew Research Center, 2009). Further, Muslim Americans are depicted as Arabs when in fact the largest group of Muslims in the United States is African American Muslims. In an analysis of the interaction of organizations—those with pro-Muslim and anti-Muslim agendas—with the media, sociologist Christopher Bail (2012) found that emotional messages released to the press emphasizing fear and anger had the best chance of getting media attention. While 85% of press releases went unnoticed, the least representative messages received the most attention. Muslim organizations condemning terrorism with what was perceived as a dispassionate tone rarely received attention. Yet, emotional and angry responses to discrimination from Muslim organizations were much more likely to receive attention leaving the impression on non-Muslim media viewers that Muslims cared little about terrorism and were over sensitive to Islamophobia. Continuous and repeated misrepresentation and misinformation in the media fuels ignorance and stereotypes about vastly diverse populations of Muslims and Muslim Americans, resulting in discrimination, violation of civil rights, and hate crimes.

As previously illustrated, media and popular culture representations of nondominant groups are often negative and stereotypical. While negative representations of dominant group members also exist, these representations appear as attributes of the individual within the group among a broad range of other options. For example, White men are, in some instances, represented as criminals, yet they are also represented as doctors, lawyers, political leaders, teachers, and in other positive roles. Therefore, the element of criminality is attributed to the individual character of the person rather than to the racial or ethnic group as a whole. The final section of the chapter offers examples and concrete strategies for analyzing, challenging, and re-creating media and popular culture.

RESISTING AND RE-CREATING MEDIA AND POPULAR CULTURE

Given the issues presented in this chapter, concern that culture industries can manipulate the masses into docile and passive consumers is understandable. What are the consequences of the consolidated control of the media by a few powerful multinational corporations and the asymmetrical distribution of popular culture around the globe? To what extent are you an active interpreter of popular culture and media texts as Hall (1980) suggested?

What actions can individuals and organized groups take to make a difference? The following three-step process is designed to develop our competence as "readers" or decoders and as "producers" or encoders of media and popular culture texts.

Step One: Increased Awareness

An initial and significant step in improving our competence is to become conscious of the role of the media and popular culture in shaping our views of the world, in normalizing dominant ideologies, and in perpetuating denigrating stereotypes and misrepresentations. Lessons from media literacy offer a framework that can help us navigate and make sense of the media-saturated culture in which we live in the context of globalization. Table 7.1, modified from the Center for Media Literacy (n.d.), identifies five keywords and core concepts with corresponding key questions that assist us in critically analyzing the production and consumption of media and popular culture messages or texts.

Step Two: Informed Action

As we develop a critical process of analysis, we have choices about how we consume and act in relation to media and popular culture. Engaging in intercultural praxis, we may continue to consume the same media and popular culture texts that we have

Table 7.1 Core Concepts and Key Questions for Media Literacy

	Key Words	Core Concepts	Key Questions
1	Authorship	Media/popular culture messages or texts are constructed.	Who created the message?
2	Format	The form or format of media/popular culture messages/texts is cultural.	What cultural messages are conveyed by the media/popular culture format?
3	Audience	People read the same media/popular culture text differently.	What is a dominant, negotiated, and oppositional reading of this text?
4	Content	Media/popular culture are embedded with values, points of view, and ideologies.	What values, points of view, and beliefs are represented or omitted from this text?
5	Function/Purpose	Media/popular culture messages are created for profit and establish social norms, constitute identities, and create shared meanings and sites of innovation.	What purpose does the media/popular culture text serve?

Source: Adapted from Center for Media Literacy (n.d.).

before, yet with our increased awareness, we bring a critical reading of these texts to our consciousness. When we share our critical analysis with others and present our alternative readings to friends, family, coworkers, and others, we take informed action. We may also choose to seek out alternative points of view or media and popular culture texts that offer perspectives that differ from the dominant view. **Alternative media or independent media** refers to media practices that fall outside of or are independent from the mainstream corporate-owned and controlled mass media (Waltz, 2005). In recent years, due to the consolidation of media ownership and the publishing industry and the alignment of mass produced forms of media with multinational corporate interests in the global context, obtaining perspectives independent from corporate interests is increasingly difficult. Accessing news from radio and Internet sources that are independent from corporate interests, searching for news stories and commentary from countries outside the United States, and seeking information from nondominant groups can provide insight into negotiated and oppositional readings that question and challenge dominant perspectives on current and historical events and issues.

Making a decision *not* to consume media or popular culture that reinforces stereotypical and dehumanizing portrayals or that presents racist, sexist, classist, and ethnocentric messages is another type of informed action. It may not seem like individual acts, such as refusing to consume media and popular culture can make a difference. However, when organized collectively—such as the boycott campaign launched against Apple for labor practices in China, or against Chick-fil-A for the CEO's anti-gay marriage stance—the act of not consuming products, brands, or popular culture forms can and does make a difference in a capitalist-driven world. Historic examples, such as the boycott of British goods by Philadelphia merchants in 1769 who opposed "taxation without representation"; the bus boycott in Montgomery, Alabama, in 1955 that initiated the civil rights movement; and the boycott of grapes and lettuce organized by the United Farm Workers Union to protest inhumane working conditions for Mexican migrants in the 1970s attest to the power of collective action to promote change. More recent illustrations of collective consumer resistance include the People for Ethical Treatment of Animals (PETA) "McCruelty" campaign against McDonald's; the Just Do It! Boycott Nike Now campaign to bring attention to and change Nike's sweatshop working conditions in Vietnam and other Asian countries; campaigns at universities across the United States to investigate the working conditions for laborers within and outside the United States who make campus and athletic apparel; and the No Sweat campaign in Canadian public institutions. Educating yourself and others, organizing with people who agree that opposition is necessary, and implementing a plan to challenge media and popular culture can lead to social change. By writing letters; signing online petitions; addressing local, state, national, and international officials; and targeting corporate/multinational interests, people's actions—particularly by organized groups of people—can result in movement toward social justice.

Step Three: Creative Production

The first two steps outline our progress from passive consumers to informed actors as we develop increased awareness and skills to critically analyze and consume media and popular culture. A third step in the process of developing strategies for intercultural praxis

Thinner than ever.

Courtesy of Adbusters Media Foundation

Photo 7.1 The transgressive practices of "culture jamming" are creative efforts to block or jam and subvert mainstream messages. Culture jamming challenges dominant readings or interpretations of mainstream popular culture and media texts by producing and negotiating oppositional readings that "talk back to" centers of economic, political, and symbolic power, such as multinational corporations. Through increased awareness, informed action, and creative production, we transform ourselves into active interpreters and producers of media and popular culture texts as opposed to passive consumers.

in relation to media and popular culture is to redefine ourselves as creators who can and do produce texts. With advanced technologies in the global context, average citizens in many parts of the world increasingly have access to producing media and popular culture texts. **Citizen media or participatory media** are media texts created by average citizens who are not affiliated with mainstream, corporate media outlets (Rodríguez, 2001), including videos that appear on YouTube, zines (web-based and print fan magazines), blogs (weblogs) and vlogs (video blogs), podcasts, and digital storytelling. Citizen or participatory media texts document and provide commentary on current events and issues that produce alternative viewpoints to mainstream media (Atton, 2002). New technologies and social media enable people to become active producers—participants in constructing meaning through a range of media resources. Blogs and tweets from Ferguson, Missouri, influential social media posts on the war in Syria, and podcasts demanding open nominations for top leaders in Hong Kong suggest the power of participatory media to contest the hegemony of mainstream media.

Culture jamming, or the act of altering or transforming mass media and popular culture forms into messages or commentary about itself, is another way to resist dominant mainstream media and produce alternative popular culture texts. The publisher of *Adbusters,* a magazine aimed at challenging and disrupting the "media trance" of our consumer addicted world and author of *Culture Jam,* Kalle Lasn (2000) argued that culture jamming is a form of public activism that challenges, subverts, and redefines dominant, hegemonic meanings produced by multinational culture industries. Consider the examples of culture jamming in Photo 7.2.

SUMMARY

This chapter title ("Jamming Media and Popular Culture") suggests the spontaneous, creative, and evolving nature of intercultural communication in the technologically advanced global age. In the context of globalization, media and popular culture are venues for entertainment, information, and social change that are characterized by rapid adaptation, appropriation, and fusion of verbal and nonverbal languages, as well as visual and musical codes. Amidst this vibrant, constantly changing context, the chapter highlighted the central role of media and popular culture in intercultural communication. Undoubtedly, media and popular culture *facilitate* communication across cultural and national boundaries escalating the flow of information and images interculturally. Media also *frame* global issues and normalize particular cultural ideologies. Popular culture forms like *Spider-Man* may seem like innocent entertainment, yet they are encoded with dominant ideologies that normalize and naturalize particular ways of being, thinking, and understanding the world. The global distribution of Euro-American and particularly U.S. media and popular culture—embedded with cultural values, beliefs, and norms—has disrupted and *fragmented* national and cultural identities, leading to resistance, opposition, and conflict. Yet, the global distribution of media and popular culture has also *forged* hybrid transnational cultural identities in the global context.

The process of encoding and decoding media messages was outlined to assist us in understanding how media and popular culture messages are produced and consumed. Dominant, negotiated, and oppositional readings were illustrated to reveal the ways prevailing ideologies are represented and reinforced through popular culture and to bring to awareness the possibility of alternative interpretations based on the positionality of readers of media and popular culture texts. The links between power and hegemony in mediated intercultural communication and the representation of nondominant groups were explored. Stereotypical and negative representations of nondominant groups serve to maintain the supremacy of dominant groups in terms of race, culture, class, gender, sexuality, and other forms of socially constructed difference. Borrowing from media literacy, the chapter concluded with steps to heighten our awareness and skills for consuming media and popular culture messages, strategies to resist and redefine mainstream corporate messages and ways to become active producers of media in the global context.

KEY TERMS

media
network media
cultural forms
popular culture
folk culture
culture industry
cultural corruption
cultural homogenization
cultural imperialism
fragmegration

telenovelas
decoding
encoding
dominant reading
negotiated reading
oppositional reading
alternative media or independent media
citizen media or participatory media
culture jamming

DISCUSSION QUESTIONS AND ACTIVITIES

Discussion Questions

1. Why is popular culture an important aspect of intercultural communication in the context of globalization?

2. Why is cultural appropriation (i.e. Gwen Stefani's and Katy Perry's use of Asian femininity in their performances, or Native American mascots in sports) problematic? How does it impact intercultural interactions between dominant and nondominant groups?

3. American people are exposed to the media images produced almost entirely by the U.S. media industry. What are the negative consequences of this asymmetrical flow of popular culture on intercultural communication?

4. In the age of media globalization where hybrid cultures are produced and commodified, how can we remain sensitive to cultural differences and honor other groups' cultural identities? How can we raise our awareness of how media representations (or the lack thereof) marginalize, silence, or stigmatize certain groups?

5. Adorno and Horkheimer (1972) argued that culture industries can manipulate the masses into docile and passive consumers. How do you think social media can change or challenge this? Do social media provide a platform for media democracy, or is it just an extension of media monopoly?

6. How is popular culture a site of resistance and power negotiation? How can the definition of culture as resource (Chapter 1) be applied to the process of culture jamming?

Activities

1. Critical Analysis of Media Representation

   a. Choose a movie, and analyze it for its authorship, format, audience, and content using the table of media literacy in the chapter.

   b. Address the following questions:

      i. Who created the message?

      ii. What cultural messages are conveyed by the media/popular culture format?

      iii. What is a dominant, negotiated, and oppositional reading of this text?

      iv. What values, points of view, and beliefs are represented or omitted from this text?

      v. What purpose does the media/popular culture text serve?

2. Producing Alternative Media—Group Activity

   a. Create a list of specific problems you see in how different groups are represented in media and popular culture today.

   b. Assuming a position as a producer and writer, create a proposal for a new TV program, movie, song, novel, magazine, website, and so forth, that provides alternative views and representations.

   c. Propose the plan to your class, and vote on the best proposal that challenges, resists, and transforms existing views, stereotypes, and misrepresentations.

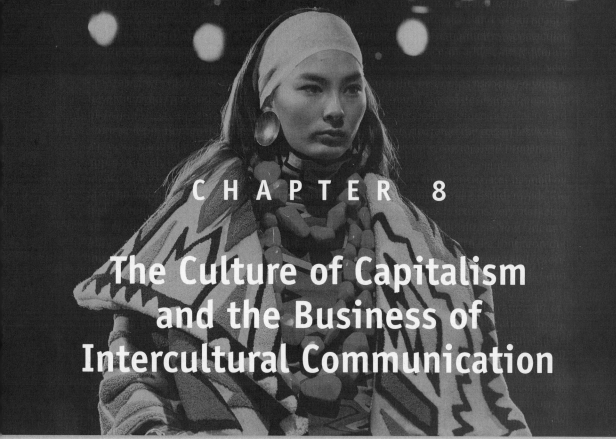

CHAPTER 8

The Culture of Capitalism and the Business of Intercultural Communication

©Zeduce/Corbis

Culture for sale! What is the impact when cultures and cultural forms are commodified?

Learning Objectives

1. Describe how the culture of capitalism impacts intercultural communication.

2. Explain the history, values, and ideologies that constitute the culture of capitalism and the effect on cultures in the United States and globally.

3. Explain the impact of the commodification of culture and tourism on intercultural communication.

4. Identify concrete strategies for economic and social responsibility as intercultural actors in the global context.

The financial crisis that erupted in the United States in the fall of 2008 sent shock waves throughout the entire global financial system with devastating consequences for billions around the world. The economic crisis effectively illustrates the intricate web of financial interdependence, the frailty of the global economic system, and the ubiquitous yet uneven impact of economic globalization. At the epicenter of the collapse in 2008 were U.S. financial giants, such as Bear Stearns, Morgan Stanley, and Lehman Brothers, which led to devastating declines and ongoing volatility in stock markets around the world. This precipitated the withdrawal of international capital from global circulation, which put tremendous pressure on developing nations and necessitated the emergency intervention of the International Monetary Fund (IMF) (2009) in Iceland, Hungary, the Ukraine, Pakistan, and other countries.

Around the globe and in the United States, the economic crisis dramatically increased the ranks of the unemployed and the number of people living in poverty. By 2015, the unemployment rate in the United States was just under 6% recovering from 10% unemployment in 2009, which was the highest in the last 30 years (U.S. Department of Labor, 2015). Yet, globally, unemployment continues to rise as the world economy enters a new phase of sluggish growth, widening inequities, and greater instability. Youth and particularly young women in all regions of the world are disproportionately impacted by unemployment (World Employment Social Outlook, 2015). In 2013, approximately 50 million people or 16% of the people in the United States lived under the poverty line (U.S. Census Bureau, 2014). Worldwide, 1.6 billion people or 23% of the world's population live in poverty (Global Multidimensional Poverty Index, 2013). The World Employment Social Outlook (2015) reported:

> The world economy continues to expand at rates well below the trends that preceded the advent of the global crisis in 2008 and is unable to close the significant employment and social gaps that have emerged. The challenge of bringing unemployment back to pre-crisis levels now appears as daunting a task as ever, with considerable societal and economic risks associated with this situation. (p. 3)

Increasing unemployment, lost and vulnerable jobs, diminished investments, corporate closures, global employment gap, reduced remittances that increase hardship for people dependent on money from migrants, a dramatic slowdown in world trade, a world where 1% of the population owns more wealth than the other 99%: What does all this have to do with intercultural communication? An immediate and obvious connection is the differential impact of the economic crisis and sluggish recovery on racial, class, and national cultural groups around the globe. The Great Recession of 2007 to 2009, as it is often called, devastated the wealth of all families in the United States except the very rich. While many in the United States, particularly Whites, think that racial discrimination ended during the 1960s civil rights movement, the racial wealth divide continues. With historic underpinnings, the inequity, perpetuated and exacerbated by current laws, policies, and practices that favor the rich results in striking wealth gaps between White households and households of color. On average, White households own approximately 20 times more wealth than Black and Latino households (Shapiro, Meschede, & Osoro, 2013). Globally, the economic crisis squeezed advanced and emerging economies from Europe and Japan to Brazil, India, and China. Slow economic recovery, widening inequity within and across nations, and tenuous employment opportunities heighten mistrust of governments, increase intercultural conflict, and intensify social unrest.

In a longer-term and more deeply rooted sense, economic realities, material conditions, and the culture of capitalism provide an ever-present backdrop for intercultural communication (Tomlinson, 1999). From the basics of food, clothing, and shelter; to the construction of identities, pleasure, and desire; to the ways we show love, celebrate holidays, engage in conflict, and fight wars; commodities are central to all cultures and intercultural interactions in the context of global capitalism. James Ridgeway (2004), author of *It's All for Sale: The Control of Global Resources* noted the following:

> Commodities seldom draw much attention in the interpretation of today's world events. And yet they played an important role in the evolution of colonialism and empire, and in the waging of small and large wars. They have influenced the flow of migration and emigration. People were enslaved to exploit commodities. They have always been at the heart of things. (p. ix)

The trade of commodities has brought people and things from different cultures into contact and collision since antiquity. From the ancient Silk Road to Columbus's expeditions in the New World, and from the 19th-century British opium trade to the U.S. support of coups and military interventions, commodities have been integrally linked to intercultural exchange, nation-state building, and international conflicts.

This chapter addresses the linkages between intercultural communication and capitalism historically and today in the global context. We begin with a history of capitalism and discuss the emergence of the culture of capitalism in the United States and globally. The global intercultural marketplace is our next stop where we explore the commodification of culture and the consumption of cultural "Others." We then examine tourism as a site of intercultural interaction and contestation, considering the impact of transforming cultural practices and urban spaces into spectacles. The chapter concludes with a discussion of economic responsibility and intercultural communication in the context of globalization.

HISTORICAL CONTEXT: CAPITALISM AND GLOBALIZATION

French economist Michel Beaud (2001) argued that **capitalism** is a complex social logic that cannot be reduced to economic dimensions alone; rather, in order to understand capitalism, we must take social, cultural, political, ideological, and ethical issues into account. While some argue that capitalism has evolved naturally, the assumption in this chapter is that capitalism is a product of historical processes. Capitalism is best understood as sets of relationships between capitalists, laborers, and consumers. Robbins (2014) noted the following:

> The culture of capitalism is devoted to encouraging the production and sale of commodities. For capitalists, the culture encourages the accumulation of profit; for laborers, it encourages the accumulation of wages; for consumers, it encourages the accumulation of goods. In other words, capitalism defines sets of people who, behaving according to a set of learned rules, act as they must act. (p. 12)

There is nothing "natural" or "inevitable" about these roles, behaviors, and goals. Human beings are not driven by "nature" to accumulate wealth or to continuously acquire things. The culture of capitalism, like all cultures, has developed over time through historical processes where behaviors, beliefs, and values as well as relationships of power are learned and normalized. At times, the culture of capitalism has been equated with "civilization" and with "modernization" implying that nations or groups who do not participate are "uncivilized" or "primitive" (Robbins, 2014). Capitalism has provided relative comfort for large numbers of people; spurred advancements in medicine, food production, communication, and transportation technologies; and engineered or forced global economic integration. Yet ethnocentric assumptions that the culture of capitalism is superior to all others mask the exploitative and dehumanizing consequences of the culture of capitalism. These assumptions ignore how capitalism is central to many of the world's problems today, such as unparalleled inequality, unprecedented hunger, poverty, racial and ethnic conflict, as well as irreversible environmental degradation (Beaud, 2001; Harvey, 2005; Robbins, 2014).

Capitalism 101: The Historical Emergence of the Culture of Capitalism

In precapitalist or noncapitalist societies, people make or obtain commodities for use. If you need food, clothing, or shelter, you grow, gather, or make it out of the materials available to you. According to economists, these commodities have **use value**. If you need something you cannot make or grow, you trade for it. Yet, the main purpose of the trade is for the *use* of the commodity. Precapitalist forms of commerce, where goods are bought in one place at a certain price and then sold at another site for a profit, extend far back into human history in many societies around the world. In this case, the commodity has what economists call **exchange value**. The purpose of the exchange is not for use, but to get money or capital. While this type of exchange involves a critical element of capitalism—the goal of obtaining capital rather than the commodity itself—it is still commonly considered precapitalist. A unique element in capitalism—the way of combining labor and the means of production—is still missing.

Capitalism and Colonialism: Capital Accumulation and the Nation-State

At the beginning of the 1400s, China was the most technologically advanced society in the world with sophisticated trade practices, and military as well as political and social organization (Robbins, 2014). While Europe was still under a feudal economic and political system, China and India were likely the wealthiest countries in the world. By the 16th century, economic dominance shifted to Europe. As outlined in Chapter 3, the extraction of immense wealth in the form of raw materials from the New World and later from colonies like India financed Europe's emerging economic and political power. Slavery provided the exploitable mass labor to extract raw materials to produce commodities, which were sold for profit developing the modern capitalist economy (Winant, 2001). This profit, then, was recycled to extract more raw materials, finance the movement of more slave labor, and exponentially expand the coffers in the centers of colonial power. The world racial hierarchy was foundational to the accumulation of capital and the concentration of wealth in Europe and the United States.

By the 17th century, the nobility and merchant class in European nation-states enacted policies and practices, which economists refer to as **mercantilism**, to enhance and control economic prosperity for the state and to keep the wealth acquired through trade in the nation-state. Mercantilism involved the implementation of protectionist polices that excluded foreign goods and subsidized cheap labor in certain industries. At this time, trading companies like the East India Trading Company and the Hudson's Bay Company, precursors to today's corporations, joined forces with nation-state militaries to ensure the continued extraction of wealth around the world. Intercultural encounters with trading companies dramatically altered the way of life, economic livelihood, and social organization of indigenous communities in the New World and Africa. Material things made locally, such as pottery, clothing, tools, and weapons were, over time, replaced by imported goods, which increased dependence on world trade and contributed to the loss of cultural knowledge. Integration into the world economy, then as now, has a significant and irreversible impact on cultures.

Mahatma Gandhi, the preeminent political and spiritual leader of the Indian independence movement, understood well the link among world trade, exploitation, and colonial power. He used the spinning wheel, a locally available tool, as the symbol for the independence movement. Gandhi recognized that in order to resist the economic hold of the British Empire, Indians needed to spin their own cloth instead of depend on British imports. His famous Salt March in 1930, which opposed British taxation of salt, is another illustration of how Gandhi's strategy of nonviolent resistance to the British Empire was based on Indians reclaiming the means of production for goods produced and consumed by Indians (Ackerman & Duvall, 2000).

Capitalism and the Industrial Revolution: Creating the Working Class

The Industrial Revolution in England between the 1800s and 1900s initiated a new means of capital accumulation. Wolf (1982) argued that for capitalism to exist, money must be able to purchase labor power by severing the link between producers and the means of production. Control of the means of production—land, materials, tools, and equipment—must be taken from peasants, craftspeople, and workers. Consequently, workers have no alternative, but to negotiate agreements to use the land and the tools they need, receiving wages for their labor. Since capitalists control the means of production and the goods that are produced, laborers who produce the goods must buy what they need from capitalists. Therefore, people not only become laborers, but also consumers. Thus, through the Industrial Revolution of the 19th century, the working class was forged.

Robbins (2014) identified four characteristics of the working class. First, members of the working class must be mobile, allowing them to move, unfettered by property ownership, to places where work is needed. In 19th-century Europe, the sale of common domain land to large landowners forced the movement of peasants to urban centers—a story similar to what is occurring today in Mexico, Latin America, and parts of Asia. The second characteristic of members of the working class is that they are segmented by race, ethnicity, gender, religion, and age. For example, Irish were pitted against English workers in British factories and Black workers against Irish in the U.S. workforce. A third characteristic is that the working class must be disciplined. Modeled after prisons, the factory was a central site of control. Through constant supervision, rewards, and punishments, laborers were disciplined in new concepts of work and time with far-reaching implications for the whole society. The culture of capitalism established a distinct orientation to time as ruled by the clock, equated with money, and exploited like commodities and laborers for maximum profit. The fourth characteristic is that members of the working class often resisted the conditions imposed on them by the capitalist class (Robbins, 2014).

Capitalism and Consumption: Creating the Consumer

By the late 1800s, capitalism had reached a defining moment with panic gripping businesspeople and governments. The construction of the capitalist and labor classes led to the overproduction of goods and economic depression loomed. Thus, in the early 20th century, the consumer was born. The consumer culture that envelops the United States today—a culture where more and bigger is better, where identities and lifestyles are constructed through consumption, and where human value is measured by the acquisition of things—has not always characterized U.S. culture.

> In fact, the culture of nineteenth century America emphasized not unlimited consumption but moderation and self-denial. People, workers in particular, were expected to be frugal and save their money; spending, particularly on luxuries, was seen as "wasteful." People purchased only necessities—basic foodstuffs, clothing, household utensils, and appliances—or shared basic items when they could. (Robbins, 2014, p. 14)

In essence, to accommodate the excess production of goods accomplished through the Industrial Revolution, luxuries had to be transformed into necessities. Novel marketing strategies like department stores designed for consumer enjoyment were introduced transforming spending from an act of necessity to one of pleasure (Leach, 1993). Advertising in the form of company catalogs, newspaper ads, celebrity promotions, and fashion were all unleashed in the early part of the 20th century constituting the consumer.

Americans had to be socialized through rewards and enticements to consume and the desire for things developed through the culture of capitalism. Dan Neil (2009) of the *Los Angeles Times* noted the following:

> Longtime Chairman Alfred Sloan's program of "planned obsolescence"—making annual, often minor changes in the products in such a way as to make last year's model hopelessly unfashionable—put Americans on the acquisitive treadmill they are panting on yet today. (p. A1)

Institutions, such as universities, museums, governmental agencies, and financial organizations also facilitated the advance of consumer capitalism by incorporating education and training on how to market and consume and by extending credit to increase the buying power of consumers (Robbins, 2014).

> **Intercultural Praxis**
> **Culture and Consumerism**
>
> Using intercultural praxis, we can understand how the construction of the consumer in Western industrial countries, which took about a century, is replicated within decades in much of the rest of the world.
>
> Adiya Metha (2009) reporting in *Nazar*, a South Asian online magazine, classified Indian consumers into four broad categories. The first group, born before Indian independence in 1947, are reluctant consumers who may even feel guilty enjoying things on a regular basis that were previously considered luxuries. The second group, born between 1947 and 1965, is very frugal saving and recycling consumer products whenever possible. A third group, born from 1965 to 1988, was old enough in 1991 when India opened its economy to see and experience the tremendous social changes that resulted. "They generally believe in working hard and spending hard, and are responsible for the current boom in consumerism. They have no qualms about borrowing and spending money, showing it off, or being materialistic." The fourth group, born since 1988, is described as being:
>
> > culturally closer to the developed world and unfortunately will spend like them too once they start earning money in the next three to five years. For instance, most urban kids play less cricket and more video games than the third group. They have tremendous choice in what they want to eat, wear, play with and study. They have add-on credit cards that their parents give them.

Capitalism, Corporations, and Global Bodies of Governance

Corporations have their origins in the trading companies of the 17th century, which allowed groups of investors to avoid the risk of individual debt and loss though backing by the nation-state. "Corporations used this power, of course, to create conditions in which they could make money. But, in a larger sense, they used this power to define the ideology or ethos of the emerging culture of capitalism" (Robbins, 2014, p. 85). Today, corporations exercise power through campaign contributions, lobbying for legislation, such as "free" trade agreements, environmental, health care, and labor policies, as well as military contracts that serve corporate interests, and by using the media to influence public opinion (Beaud, 2001).

At the end of WWII, President Roosevelt invited government financial leaders from 44 countries to Bretton Woods, New Hampshire, to lay out plans to rebuild war-torn economies and to insure economic stability. Out of these meetings, three very significant bodies of global governance, with far-reaching implications, were formed: (1) The IMF, established to ease currency exchange across nations, provides short-term loans to member countries that face debt crises; (2) the World Bank (WB) provides loans to developing countries to support economic growth; and (3) the General Agreement on Tariffs and Trade (GATT), later the World Trade Organization (WTO), negotiates free-trade agreements and disputes among nations.

While providing needed financial assistances, these financial bodies have forced the integration of recipient countries in Latin America, Asia, Africa, and eastern Europe into the global economy (Stiglitz, 2002). Loans are accompanied by stipulations that require indebted countries to increase exports of designated products and reduce or eliminate support for social services, education, and health care. The IMF and WB admit they have only had limited success. After trillions of dollars in loans, indebtedness in developing nations has increased and the social, economic, and environmental impact of the imposed policies has been devastating (Stiglitz, 2002).

Capitalism, Neoliberalism, and Globalization

At the end of the 20th century, neoliberalism, an economic and political ideology endorsed by Prime Minister Thatcher of England and President Reagan of the United States in the 1980s, dramatically increased the movement of capital, commodities, services, information, and labor around the globe. **Neoliberalism**, or the reassertion of liberal ideologies, advocates reducing state intervention, deregulating all aspects of the market, privatizing public resources, decreasing social protection, and dismantling labor unions (Harvey, 2005). Historically, colonization and military force were used to establish conditions for the accumulation of capital by European and U.S. powers; today, in the context of globalization, political leaders, capital controllers, and global financial institutions, such as the IMF, WB, and WTO create conditions for multinational corporations to accumulate capital, exploit mobile labor, and create consumers around the world (Wallerstein, 2000). Corporations benefit from the **surplus value** or the profit that is made by reducing labor costs as they move their manufacturing and assembly sites offshore to countries like Mexico, China, and Indonesia where cheaper labor is available and where few if any labor laws or environmental restrictions exist. Dispossessed of their land and means of production, similar to the Industrial Revolution in Europe, farmers and craftspeople in developing nations have no choice, but to seek work in factories at less than living wages. The labor force is segmented or stratified based on various forms of social discrimination—most notable is the increased flow of women into the workforce who are paid lower wages than men (Naples & Desai, 2002). In the logic of capitalism, sexism, racism, bias against immigrants, and exploitation of the working class are profitable.

The historical emergence of capitalism from its embryonic phase in the colonial era to its full-blown manifestation in a globalized world has transformed human culture. As a result, today we live in a vastly unequal world with immensely productive and destructive powers where asymmetrical intercultural interactions and international relationships are the norm. Capitalism, as a continually transforming social logic, integrally shapes and informs U.S. culture, and cultures that are touched or engulfed by its catalytic and consuming powers.

THE CULTURE OF CAPITALISM

As it has evolved historically in the United States, the culture of capitalism promotes individualism, competitiveness, and the pursuit of personal goals and interests. It encourages an orientation to life where the fundamental purpose and meaning is focused on consumption. In the current culture of capitalism, consumer relations structure social relations. Interpersonal relationships are theorized, assessed, and experienced in terms of costs and benefits. Often human relationships are mediated and expressed through commodities, where relationships with people are secondary to relationships with things—the house, car, wedding ring, vacation, credit card, or HDTV. Students see themselves as consumers or customers, term papers and curricula are called "deliverables," universities market themselves as desirable playgrounds, and graduates are encouraged to "brand" themselves to commence into the global job market. The power and control of commodities is not only in the accumulation of things; "the commodity's reign is evident, rather, in the submission to market forces of all aspects of mankind's [sic] life and all aspects of society's functioning" (Beaud, 2001, p. 292).

In capitalist culture, segmentation and stratification of labor as well as consumers is normalized. While the culture of capitalism reinforces and profits from sexism, racism, classism, and other forms of social discrimination, today these deeply embedded systems of inequity are masked and rationalized through the rhetoric of "colorblindness," "cultural difference," and the market logic of capitalism. Due to geographic distance and production fragmentation, no relationship exists between consumers of commodities and those who labor to produce them, which further mystifies the practices that sustain capitalism.

In the postindustrial capitalist society of the United States, identities are defined through the things we consume. Inundated with marketing strategies aimed at grabbing our attention and coding our sense of self through consumer items and consumable experiences— T-shirts, shoes, cars, computers, package tours, cell phones, accessories, and music—our identities and worldviews are constructed and branded by corporations. For example, are you a PC or a Mac person? We are simultaneously laborers, consumers, products, and advertisements thoroughly articulated in capitalism. The concept of "citizen" in democratic societies is appropriated and conflated with consumer identities with deep-seated implications for democratic participation. Clearly, the values we often identify as U.S. cultural values are deeply intertwined with and influenced by the culture of capitalism as it has emerged historically in this country. We turn now to a look at intercultural dimensions of the contemporary workplace.

Communicative Dimensions
Communication and Ideology

"Greed is good," Gordon Gekko proclaimed in the movie *Wall Street* (Stone, 1987). The infamous or now famous phrase exemplifies the values and norms that have shaped U.S. financial markets and culture since the 1980s. The sequel of Wall Street was released in 2010 after the biggest financial crisis since the Great Depression. Mr. Gekko commented on his remark: "Someone reminded me I once said greed is good. Now it seems it's legal."

Our everyday cultural communication is embedded with capitalist ideologies. With a hint of sarcasm, phrases on bumper stickers, such as "He who dies with the most toys wins," "When the going

(Continued)

(Continued)

gets tough, the tough go shopping," or "Keep Calm and Continue to Consume!" point to the underlying belief in material possessions, wealth, and consumerism.

The following proverbs from different parts of the world also communicate beliefs about the power of money to shape social and cultural realities: "When money speaks, the truth keeps silent" (Russian). "When gold speaks every tongue is silent" (Italian). "The saving man becomes the free man" (Chinese). "One hand full of money is stronger than two full of truth" (Danish).

THE INTERCULTURAL MARKETPLACE

Today, culture, cultural forms, and cultural experiences—from music, cuisine, art, and sports; to religious holidays, weddings, bar mitzvahs, and funerals; as well as places and communities—are commodified. The **commodification of culture** refers to the ways culture and cultural experiences—local practices, festivals, arts, rituals, and even groups—are produced and consumed for the market. As cultural practices and cultural groups circulate within the logic of capitalism, they become sites of contestation. Both constrained and propelled by market forces, cultural commodification gives rise to questions of authenticity, appropriation, identity, and resistance. Journalist Jeremy (2000) wrote this in the *Los Angeles Times:*

> A great transformation is occurring in the nature of capitalism. After hundreds of years of converting physical resources into goods, the primary means of generating wealth now involves transforming cultural resources into paid-for personal experiences and entertainments. (para. 1)

Commodification of Culture

Today, culture is a product that is invented, packaged, and consumed. Take for example cultural practices, such as pow wows, hip hop, or dancehall music along with the material aspects of these cultures—clothing or regalia that signify a particular native tribe; fashion, rhymes, and nonverbal performances that signify hip hop culture; or improvisational rituals enacted through language and the body in dancehall music from Jamaica. When articulated into the logic of capitalism, these practices, performances, and objects are accessed and packaged as "experiences" and "products" to be consumed, which inevitably alters the experience and the meanings associated with these cultural practices. The marketability of cultural practices, material culture, and cultural identities frequently depends on constructing culture and cultural practices as different—different from the dominant culture. "It has been argued that under conditions of globalization, difference rather than homogenization infuses the prevailing logic of accumulation" (Yúdice, 2003, p. 28). This "difference" between the culture that is commodified and those who consume it must be constructed as "real," offering the consumer a taste of what is supposedly authentic and exotic.

Discourses of authenticity become particularly salient, often in paradoxical ways, as culture is commodified. **Authenticity** trades on the notion that a "genuine," "pure," "untouched," and "sacred" culture exists or existed at some point. The "authentic" contrasts with and is distinct from modern or postmodern culture that is "affected," "contaminated," "profane." Authenticity presumes an association of particular people with particular places and particular practices that are distinct, "native" and "different" (Shepherd, 2002). When the dynamics of cultural commodification are in play, representations of cultural Others are often "fixed" or "frozen" in the past, and their difference from the dominant group is made hypervisible. The valorization of the past as the site of authenticity couples with the **exoticization of the Other**—a process by which "difference" from the dominant norm is exaggerated and constructed as mysterious, strange, and alluring—perpetuating stereotypical and limiting images of the cultural Other. Exoticization is an aspect of Orientalism, a way of thinking that justified colonialism, and the rescue by the West of the "exotic," "backward," and "uncivilized" Other.

In the commodification of culture, monetary and sign value is placed on the "authentic" cultures, cultural forms and practices. **Sign value** (Gottdiener, 2000) is the symbolic value of commodities conveying social meaning and social positioning within the political economy of late capitalism. "Authentic" culture is assumed to have existed in the past and has been lost; thus, nostalgia propels desires to recover, possess, and consume "authentic" cultures, cultural forms, and cultural practices. What has been lost in the modern or postmodern world can be found in the cultural Other, which is constructed as "primitive" and "exotic" therefore, "natural," and "authentic." This Western construction of the Other is highly romanticized, essentialized, and colonial. Let's unpack the underlying premises of cultural commodification in some more depth.

First, cultures have never existed bounded by space or suspended in time; cultures, cultural forms, and practices have always been heterogeneously influenced and changed by interactions with others—even if not as dramatically as today—through trade, invasion, and migration. Second, discourses of authenticity that advance a romanticized version of the past—a "pure" cultural Other—depend on erasing the very intercultural encounters of the colonial past and postcolonial present that have deeply and devastatingly impacted non-Western cultures. Paradoxically, the process of commodification, like colonization, participates in the very destruction it alleges to protect, salvage, and preserve. Third, in the commodification of culture, the construction of the cultural Other through discourses of authenticity and exoticization, neutralize and mask the agency of the people and cultural groups negotiating and participating in processes of commodification.

The commodification of culture promotes and reifies particular constructions of race, culture, gender, class, and sexuality. Returning to our examples of pow wows, hip hop, and dancehall music, particular racialized, gendered, class, and heteronormative representations are advanced as local and situated cultural practices are turned into products—events for which one purchases tickets and for which corporations make profits, through musical lyrics and dance moves that exaggerate difference, violence, and sexual dominance, and through cultural practices that are romanticized and fetishized as antidotes to modern or postmodern ills.

In addition, the commodification of culture endorses and normalizes a particular relationship to materialism and ideologies regarding desire, consumption, and culture. Through the process of commodification, culture is often reduced to a buffet of material objects that can be consumed—like *sushi*, *tapas*, and *masala* to exoticize and spice up life; culture is experienced as an accessory effortlessly put on and taken off at whim—as if wearing hijab, a bindi, or dreads is solely a fashion statement devoid of material conditions and consequences; and culture is constructed as a playground—like Las Vegas, Santa Fe, or Disneyland—where admission to performances of cultural fantasies are gained through money and the suspension of lived experiences of difference. Learning about and experiencing cultures through food, film, clothes or travel itself is not problematic. Yet, it is important to develop a conscious awareness of how the commodification of culture conditions and normalizes particular ways of understanding and experiencing culture; how the commodification of culture is a contested site where individuals and cultural groups actively negotiate issues of representation, identity, survival; and how participation in the commodification of culture—as consumers, laborers, or capitalists—occurs today within unequal relations of power that are historically rooted. Let's take a look at a few case studies that illustrate and illuminate the intercultural communication dynamics inherent in the commodification of culture.

CASE STUDY 1: CONSUMING AND ROMANTICIZING THE "OTHER"

The first case examines the commodification of cultural forms made by Pueblo and Navajo women in New Mexico (Sorrells, 2002). For generations, Pueblo and Navajo women have represented themselves and their cultures through their pottery and weaving, respectively. Pueblo women gather the earth around them molding vessels that hold their culture as well as represent the complex intercultural interactions that characterize the colonial history of New Mexico. Navajo women collect material from their environment transforming it into weavings that tell cultural stories of the Navajo people as well as visually depict the dynamics of power in the southwest region of the United States. Today, in upscale galleries in Santa Fe and well-publicized street markets, in gas stations and curio shops, and on websites accessible around the world, Pueblo pottery and Navajo weavings are packaged, bought, and sold as iconic representations of these cultural groups and of New Mexico.

In face-to-face "sales" interactions, the most common questions Pueblo potters and Navajo weavers receive from consumers or tourists are, "Did you make these?" "Are they made by hand?" and "Are they traditional?" Emma Yepa (personal communication, April 23, 1999) from Jemez Pueblo said that sometimes when she makes her more contemporary designs, customers ask her to make them more traditional: "We want more tradition. And I say, 'This is traditional.' You know? . . . You're telling me what is tradition and what is not." Discourse of authenticity operate here as Emma Yepa, a Pueblo potter, and her artistic work are questioned when perceived as not conforming to the consumers idea of Indian art. The commodification of indigenous cultural forms in New Mexico is not new. Anthropologist Evelyn Hatcher (1967) observed that by the early 1900s, Navajo weavings showed "the Indian's idea of the trader's idea of what the white man thought was Indian design" (p. 174).

In the early part of the 20th century, the successful commodification of New Mexico's cultures depended on creating an image of an exotic and unusual yet safe place to consume the Other. Ambivalence and anxiety toward cultural difference—the combination of fear and fascination—was neutralized and palatably packaged for tourists from the eastern United States to purchase a glimpse of the exotic (Howard & Pardue, 1996). Through advertisements, museum exhibits, and scholarship, an idealized view of the "picturesque," the "authentic," and the "spiritual" aspects of indigenous cultures was constructed and touted as offering aesthetic, moral, and spiritual salvation from the depravities of contemporary life.

Thus, New Mexico was reimagined and re-created to present a "romantic" image with a distinctively "exotic" regional and cultural identity. Through their articulation into the marketplace, Pueblo pottery and Navajo weavings are viewed as symbols or signs of their respective cultures. Yet, the creative forms are as much a representation of the dominant culture's notion of the Other as they are representations of the cultures for which they are marketed. Difference, or Otherness, from the dominant group is what signifies and sells (Hall, 2013). The stereotypes of Indian people as "quaint," "primitive," and "traditional" produced through processes of commodification reduce the complexity of individuals and groups to easily identifiable and often denigrating characteristics.

The "cultural" art created by Pueblo and Navajo women is a contested site where issues of representation, identity, and notions of tradition are negotiated and transformed. Even as difference is marketed as exotic and enticing for the consumption of the dominant culture (hooks, 1992), women artists in New Mexico exert personal, cultural, and economic agency as they challenge the restrictive stereotypes and characterizations as the Other.

The commodification of cultures often creates barriers for intercultural communication. As anthropologist Dean McCannell (1976) argued, commodification of cultural symbols "represents an end to the dialogue, a final freezing of ethnic imagery which is both artificial and deterministic" (p. 375). When consumers from nonnative cultures demand that cultural forms of representation fit their notions of what Indian art is, a superficial level of engagement is established that can preclude intercultural exchange. The relationship is defined by and often limited to the consumption of one group by another within a system of inequitable power. What could be a space for intercultural connection—the shared appreciation of beauty between consumer and artist, the recognition of struggle and survival in a changing world, and the layering of cultural influences manifest in artistic forms—is frequently reduced to a monetary exchange. Travel to new places, whether international or domestic, offers incredible opportunities for intercultural communication. Yet, the ways that cultures, communities, and cultural spaces have been commodified through the logic of capitalism often works against intercultural exchange and genuine intercultural dialogue. As Yúdice (2003) noted, in the context of globalization, culture plays a greater role today than in the past because of the ways it is linked to local and transnational economies and politics. Culture, as it is commodified in the marketplace, is a resource that is exploited for economic and political power and agency.

Communicative Dimensions
The Commodification of Sports

Commodification is a process of transforming goods (not usually considered goods) and services, as well as ideas and practices, into products. The commodification of cultural practices, for example, dance, rituals like weddings, and sports, converts social meanings and social functions into financial terms. Historically, sports have functioned as rehearsals for war, as in the original Olympic Games in Ancient Greece, as leisure activities that satisfy human needs for competition and community, and as forms of fitness, entertainment, and pleasure. Yet, through processes of commodification, sports have primarily become economic endeavors where goods and services are marketed and sold, sponsorships are expanded, and where salaries for players, profits for team owners and league officials are continually increased. Sports now are giant billboards for corporate advertising.

Institutions like the National Collegiate Athletic Association (NCAA) have been accused of engaging in practices that parallel capitalist industries. In addition, the corporatization of sport is now a global phenomenon. Major League Baseball (MLB) teams like the New York Yankees and Chicago Cubs, and club soccer teams like Manchester United have expanded their markets by signing athletes from overseas to promote their teams and merchandise transnationally. The steroid era in MLB, where several athletes used performance-enhancing drugs to increase their physique and strength, not only resulted from pressure to perform; it also contributed to the commercial interests of the MLB, whose popularity dwindled during and after the work stoppage of the 1994 to 1995 season. While many professional athletes make millions of dollars for participating in sports, male athletes are valued as commodities possessing hypermasculine physiques and even "postracial" aspirations. For example, Tiger Woods and Michael Jordan, at one time, were represented in mass media accounts as "postracial" commodities. Thus, while the commodification of sports advances capitalist interests, it also serves to normalize hegemonic ideologies.

The commodification and corporatization of sports, where profit and spectacle are prioritized, diminishes the historical, cultural, emotional, and aesthetic appeal of sports. In contemporary society, the influence of corporate interests on sports creates captivating spectacles, yet disconcerting conditions within sports. Sport—like many cultural forms—is a contested site where processes of commodification for profit compete with and often obscure other social roles and meanings.

CASE STUDY 2: CONSUMING AND DESIRING THE "OTHER"

The second case focuses on the *Bratz* doll line, a collection of "hip" fashion dolls and merchandize produced by MGM, which steadily gained popularity, and by the mid-2000s owned over 40% of the fashion doll market. Four original dolls were released in 2001— Cloe, a White doll; Sasha, an African American doll; Jade, an Asian American doll; and Yasmin, a seemingly mixed race doll—with additional products, including *Bratz Kidz*, *Bratz Babyz*, as well as a movie, music albums, video games, and a TV series. The dolls are outfitted with trendy, urban-inspired clothing along with all sorts of accessories, including miniskirts, platform shoes, and fur coats as well as props, such as a sushi bar, karaoke club, and e-café. The *Bratz* can shop at the mall transported by mini-Cooper, low rider, or motorcycle, or go out with their boy band counterparts on the private party jet. Challenging the long-standing dominance of Barbie—for the hearts and minds of little girls world-wide and of course, market share—American Studies scholar Lisa Guerrero (2009) argues that *Bratz* dolls

Photo 8.1 Bratz dolls: Transformed, yet problematic constructions of race, gender, sexuality, and notions of the Other

offer transformed, yet problematic constructions of race, gender, sexuality, and notions of the Other.

The *Bratz* line is clearly invested in and capitalizing on racial identities offering a plurality of images of youth of color rarely seen in the past. Much of the popularity of the doll line depends on its representation of racial difference as desirable, normal, and hip. Yet, as Guerrero notes, the appeal of racial difference only works by centering traits and characteristics that are recognized as signifiers of "Otherness," which is, paradoxically, accomplished by exaggerating physical characteristics and using hypervisible stereotypes. Nevertheless, in contrast to Barbie and other fashion doll lines where non-White dolls are simply cast as darker versions of White dolls, the *Bratz* line reflects demographic shifts in the United States and the destabilization of racial categories. Guerrero (2009) noted:

> Beauty and race have a very different relationship in the *Bratz* line than they do in Barbie's world; racial difference is made both visible *and* beautiful through these dolls, though the reliance on certain stereotypes and the transitory nature of commodification do also make these new models of racial identification problematic.
>
> Within the doll line, as within much of today's American popular culture phenomena where race plays a central role, race, for the *Bratz*, exists in a social, political, and material vacuum. Race merely serves as another kind of "accessory" that signifies "hipness," without incurring the actual costs and consequences of real-world racial signification. (p. 190)

In other words, race is constructed as something you can put on and take off—like clothes or a hairstyle—and produced as something that is chosen as if one could choose to or not to be racialized within a society with a long history of institutionalized racism and systemic marginalization based on race. Markers of difference in the real world cannot simply be removed any more than the social, economic, and political consequences of being positioned as racially "Other" can be removed.

Guerrero (2009) argued that the construction of gender identities in the *Bratz* line is also paradoxical and problematic. While the dolls, like Barbie, are intended to embody independence, femininity, power and sexuality, *Bratz* depart from more confining gender roles tied to traditional middle-class values of family, home, and career represented by Barbie toward a world of desire, indulgence, and gratification. The dolls are presented as sexy; yet, their femininity lies in their ability to play with gender identities as they accessorize to perform tomboy, punk girl, girly girl, athlete, and others. Their fluidity across various feminine identities as well as their mobility—unfettered by family, children, or home—is central to the construction of their agency and power in terms of gender.

Confined to heteronormative performances, representations of sexuality in the *Bratz* dolls are less fluid, and yet, quite controversial. Called "Hooker Barbie" and "harlots," complaints from parents and criticism from organizations, such as the American Psychological Association have decried the impact on young girls of the hyper-sexualized clothing of the *Bratz* dolls. Interesting, Barbie is re-centered as the paradigm of feminine sexuality and the "street-wise" and edgy *Bratz*—girls of color—are seen as "tarty," and "obscene."

The *Bratz* line also valorizes commodities, branded items used to construct identities, as well as children's relationships to desire consumerism and social acceptance as hipsters. Undoubtedly, a line of dolls alone does not advance an ideology of consumption; rather the *Bratz* dolls contribute to and normalize at a very young age a prevailing aspiration for wealth. At the same time that commodities and wealth take on a central role in the line of dolls, the labor and hard work to attain such is erased. "This disconnected relationship to wealth that increasingly consumes American youth is reflected sharply in toys like the *Bratz*. The complexities of this isolated formation of class-consciousness become especially highlighted when placed in contrast to the manufacturing realities of the line of dolls" (Guerrero, 2009, p. 192). The dolls, like so much that is consumed in the United States are made in China, primarily by women in arguably exploitative labor conditions. In addition to erasing the conditions of production in China, which result from and represent global inequities, the *Bratz* doll line also masks the unequal access to wealth experienced by people of color.

Tourism and Intercultural Communication

In 2014, 1.1 billion people travelled abroad generating over $1.4 trillion through the global travel industry. Recovering from the economic crisis, the tourism industry projects an increase of 3.3% annually from 2010 to 2030 with an estimated 1.8 billion people travelling abroad by 2030. One out of every eleven jobs worldwide is associated with the tourist industry (United Nations World Tourism Organization [UNWTO], 2014b). Tourism plays a particularly significant role in economically underprivileged nations, where global bodies of governance introduced in Chapter 2, such as the International Monetary Fund (IMF) and World Bank (WB), promote tourism as a means of economic development and recovery. Yet, mass travel and tourism often exploit unequal relationships of wealth and power as people from richer, more economically advantaged countries travel to poorer, more economically disadvantaged countries. Frequently, colonial patterns of exploitation and displacement, as well as notions of authenticity and exoticization are re-inscribed in contemporary intercultural encounters in tourist contexts. "Tourism propels environmental transformation, cultural commoditization, and sexual consumption—all processes that are actually felt in many countries still grappling with the legacies of western colonization" (Carrigan, 2011, p. xi).

Young people, predominantly students, from the ages of 15 to 30, account for approximately 20% of annual travel, which represents a huge market for governments and tourist industries to target their appeals (Mohn, 2013). A study released by the *World Youth Student and Educational Travel Confederation* surveying over 34,000 young travelers from 137 countries found that youth travel is increasingly complex appealing to larger and more diverse populations than ever before. Motivations for and orientations to travel for youth have changed in recent years as youth travelers aim to immerse themselves in local cultures, learn new languages, and see traveling as a way of life. With rising youth unemployment in many advanced capitalist countries, young people with some access to resources travel for work, education, and cultural experiences. Less focused than in the past on traditional leisure destinations, 22% of young people travel to learn languages, 15% to acquire work experience, and 1% to study abroad. Youth travelers are also spending money at higher rates than ever before; **flashbackers**, or backpackers who travel with laptops, tablets, smartphones, and other electronic devices, are changing youth tourism as travelers develop friendship networks and travel plans through the Internet and social media (Mohn, 2013).

Travel can provide opportunities for intercultural engagement, learning about the unknown, and appreciation of the different ways human beings around the world live and make sense of their lives. Yet today, the majority of tourists choose options that limit their exposure and access to the very places they pay to visit. Pat Thomas (2009), British editor of the *Ecologist,* observed the following:

> Most of us are not travelers at all—as vulnerable to processes of commodification as the places we visit. . . . The smaller the world gets, the more we seem to want it to be as much like home as possible (but with cleaner sheets and towels and without the washing up). (p.2)

According to surveys administered by Halifax Travel Insurance, British tourists on international vacations spent less than 8 hours a week outside of the hotel; three quarters of the 2,000 surveyed made no effort to learn the local language, and 70% never visited a local attraction (Thomas, 2009). Similar to tourists to New Mexico in the early 1900s, package tours to Spain for the British, and to Jamaica or Mexico for U.S. tourists offer exotic yet often limited and sanitized experiences of the cultural Other. In addition to questioning the goal of looking for "home" when one travels, which often precludes intercultural exchange, it is important to note finding "home" when traveling (in the sense of finding what is familiar from your culture around the world) is not even an option for much of the world. Today, the cultural and economic hegemony of the West is experienced in contradictory ways by Western tourists. On the one hand, Western tourists desire and often demand the familiarity of "home," yet simultaneously, complaints abound that other cultures are too "Americanized," too "Westernized," or too much like home.

Tourism is one of the world's largest industries employing more than 266 million people worldwide (World Travel & Tourism Council, 2013). TV, magazine, and Internet ads; billboards; and travelogues present tourism as good for local economies. The travel industry purports that tourism brings in foreign capital, provides jobs, and preserves local cultures. Undoubtedly, international tourism is a source of foreign capital for many economies around the world; in cases like Mexico, tourism is a significant economic resource. Yet, slick advertisements that display cultural and natural resources in alluring and desirable ways gloss over the economic, environmental, and social conditions just below the surface. Vying for the attention of consumers, city, state, and national governments collaborate with the tourist industry to offer ever-growing enticements, which frequently draw on natural and cultural resources as different, authentic, exotic, titillating, and romantic. Culture, within the equation of tourism and profit, is most often seen as an unimportant backdrop or as a commodity for capitalization (Carrigan, 2011). Either way, the impact of tourism on local cultures and people is transformative. The framing of cultural practices, forms and spaces as well as cultural histories as commodities to be "preserved" and "marketed," trades on colonial and postcolonial stereotypes that fix and essentialize local cultures. Presented as "pure" or "authentic," local cultures are constructed as if they exist or once existed as homogenous entities suspended outside of time and history, completely erasing pre-colonial, colonial, and postcolonial intercultural encounters. This framing in tourist literature and at cultural sites and performances for tourists masks the decimation, hybridization, and adaptation local cultures have engaged in and survived for centuries and continue to negotiate today (Carrigan, 2011).

In his book *The Society of the Spectacle*, Guy Debord (1973) introduced the concept of the **spectacle** to refer to the domination of media images and consumer society over the individual, which obscures the conditions and effects of capitalism. Seduced through leisure, entertainment, and consumption, the spectacle serves to pacify and depoliticize society. Happiness and fulfillment are found through consumption of commodities and spectacles.

Cultural Identity
I "Like," Therefore, I Am

What did you "like" on Facebook today? What massages or articles did you tweet and retweet most recently? What blogposts did you make or "reblog" on Tumblr? In the past decade, we have witnessed a spread of social media that is both explosive and revolutionary. Social media, such as Facebook, Twitter, and Instagram allow us to keep in contact with friends and family in real time. Social media provide a more participatory and democratic platform of communication than traditional mass media, such as television and radio. The participatory nature of social media seems to fundamentally alter the separation between producers and consumers of media messages. Despite its growing significance, can we equate the revolution in social media with a promise of empowerment for all? In the documentary *Generation Like*, producers and writers Douglas Rushkoff and Frank Koughan (2014) follow the lives of adolescent social media "celebrities" who enjoy social and financial capital by virtue of their online popularity. Their investigations reveal the paradoxes of social media "empowerment" shaped by the intricate connection between youths' online activities and corporate marketing. Your personal identity is now inseparable from your consumer profile—what you "like" on Facebook not only becomes a part of massive consumer data, but also your online activity itself becomes a form of advertisement to your friends and followers. Rushkoff points out how young people's seemingly self-empowered and self-initiated online activities ultimately serve as corporate marketing strategies. When you make a post about your favorite movies, shops, and athletes on social media, your self-expression never escapes the corporate interest in commodifying your personal life. What does this all mean for our identities? What are the promises and pitfalls of social media? What are the consequences of reducing our identities to "I 'like,' therefore I am"?

CASE STUDY 3: CONSUMING CULTURAL SPECTACLES

In his analysis of the Mardi Gras celebration in New Orleans, urban studies scholar Kevin Gotham (2002) illustrated the impact of transforming cultural practices and urban spaces into spectacles. Mardi Gras—wild parties, exotic costumes, masked marauders, spectacular floats, lots of skin, nudity, and much more—is marketed as a once-in-a-lifetime "cultural" experience not to be missed. While Mardi Gras celebrations have taken place in New Orleans since 1857, the reasons for the celebration and the meanings associated with it have changed tremendously. A pre-Christian version of Mardi Gras dates back thousands of years as a pagan celebration of spring and fertility. As Christianity gained popularity and dominance in Rome, religious leaders appropriated and incorporated the pagan festival as a time of feasting before Lent, a Christian observance of penance, fasting, and preparation approximately six weeks prior Easter.

Brought to what is now known as Louisiana in the 1700s by the French, later banned by Spanish colonizers and then re-introduced by and for locals, Mardi Gras existed outside the logic of market exchange and capital circulation. Today, Mardi Gras is extensively marketed and promoted as part of a broader strategy to increase tourism to the city of New Orleans. All year long, local and national companies produce and sell paraphernalia that promote the celebration as a site of desire and fantasy. Divorced from its religious roots and reconstituted as part of Sin City's advertising package, many locals feel the celebration has been devalued (Gotham, 2002).

Corporate and trade conventions are scheduled at the time of the celebration; international media, including crews from the British Broadcasting Corporation (BBC), Japan, and Playboy package the celebration for a global audience. Corporations like Bacardi, Coors, and Kool use their Mardi Gras–themed advertisements not only to sell their products during the celebration, but as a means to shape their brand image nationally. As noted by Debord (1973), the process of commodifying areas of social life, such as culture, religion, and leisure trivializes and destroys them. Mardi Gras, originally a celebration of rich and deeply rooted religious and cultural symbolism, is now leveraged to expand capitalism, remake desires, boost demand, and cultivate new needs (Gotham, 2002). When themes, motifs, and cultural symbols are created and circulated in ways that are easily identifiable by consumers, the commodity—in this case the cultural experience of Mardi Gras—has sign value, in addition to exchange and use value.

Over 100 years ago, Karl Marx argued that when commodities are endowed with powers, such as status, success, fame, and identity in a process of **fetishization,** the underlying social relations that govern the production and exchange of commodities are hidden or masked (Gottdiener, 2000). In this case, the marketing and consumption of Mardi Gras serves both to accumulate profits for commercial interests and at the same time constructs demands for and attempts to satisfy the tourists' desires for experiences—experiences that satisfy needs for self-expression and identity. Yet, the fetishization of commodities and society's spectacles hide the exploitation of labor, damage to the environment, and the impact on culture that make them possible. In the case of New Orleans, tremendous social problems, including population flight, loss of jobs, increased racial segregation, and poverty have accompanied the city's move from an industrial site to a tourist destination (Gotham, 2002). Mardi Gras—now celebrated in many cities in the United States and around the world—illustrates the global market for cultural experiences made possible through the exploitation of labor, culture, and the environment within inequitable relations of power.

ECONOMIC RESPONSIBILITY AND INTERCULTURAL COMMUNICATION

United States Americans—4.4% of the world's population—accounted for 33% of the global consumption. The residents of high income countries—17% of the world's population—consume more than 80% of the global total; whereas, the other 5 million people live on the remaining 20%. Today, more than one fifth of the world's population lives on the brink of hunger and death. Spread of disease, degradation of the environment, exploitation of workers, global conflicts, and militarization impact the lives of billions of people daily. Robbins (2014) questions the underlying and pervasive assumption of capitalism:

> Growth will solve environmental problems, so this reasoning goes, reduce poverty, lead to advances in medicine that will save lives, and reduce conflict. Yet it gets more difficult to maintain this assumption when, in spite of a more than tenfold increase in economic activities over the past seventy years, environmental problems are getting more severe, inequity is growing, conflict over scarce resources is increasing, and environmental destruction is leading to the emergence of new and more lethal disease. (p. 354)

Global problems are most often framed as economic ones, and solutions are proposed through financial means. Yet, overlooked in the analysis is the central role of culture—the shared and contested beliefs, values, norms, and practices of the culture of late capitalism. A central feature of the culture of capitalism is the masking of negative consequences that result from the operation of the market (Robbins, 2014). By virtue of living in the culture of capitalism, we all knowingly and unknowingly participate to varying degrees in this obscuring process. Corporations spend billions of dollars to distance themselves and consumers from the 3Ds of labor—dirty, dangerous, and difficult—the exploitative conditions in which much of the world works. Commodities are represented in advertisements as shiny, appealing things that consumers must have, concealing human and environmental conditions of abuse and destruction. Legislative and legal measures advanced by corporations limit, control, and manipulate information presented to the public about the social, health, and environmental consequences of the market. Uprisings, ethnic cleansing, and genocide are blamed on long-standing hatred among groups concealing the economic and political causes directly tied to the market. Through language, representation, and discourse, developing countries are blamed for population growth; the poor are blamed for their poverty; migrants are blamed for all kinds of social ills, including leaving home to survive. Yet, in each case, constructing the challenges in this way ignores the relationship to the historic expansion of capitalism. It is also important to consider the racialized and class-based dimensions of discourses that blame global problems on those who experience the most devastating impact of capitalism in the global context. As Robbin's (2014) notes, we "develop ideologies that seek to explain global problems in ways that distance the problems from the operation of the market" (p. 131).

As noted earlier, the values, practices, and discourses of conspicuous consumption and perpetual growth are actually quite new to much of the world and less than a century old in the United States—the country most identified with consumer culture (Nandy, 2004). Given that people construct the culture of capitalism through historic processes, people can also challenge and change it. Resistance to the culture of capitalism has been an important factor in history and continues today throughout the world in local sites and in national and international movements (George, 2004). Discussion of alter-globalization (alternative globalization) movements and resistance to global capitalism are addressed in the following two chapters. However, at this point, it is useful to think about our role in the culture of capitalism and consider what steps, small as they may seem, we can take toward changing a culture that promotes economic, political, social, and cultural injustice as well as threatens the sustainability of our home—planet Earth. Here are four steps you can take to get started:

1. Observe your consumption patterns.

   - Keep a journal of the things you purchase.
   - Note where you shop.
   - Note where the goods—things, entertainment, and experiences—are produced.

2. Educate yourself about the circumstances and impact.

   - As a consumer: Find out about the working conditions of the people who make the goods you consume; engage in dialogue with the people who provide services for you while on vacation or when consuming a cultural experience.
   - As a laborer/worker: Learn about the relationship between owners and workers in your organization/corporation; educate yourself about the norms, behaviors, and attitudes that have enabled the success (or lack of it) of your company/organization.
   - As a capitalist: If you have a savings account, investments, stocks, or other means of making money from money, learn about how this works. Investigate who benefits and who is exploited through your investments.

3. Act responsibly based on your knowledge.

   - Make conscious and responsible consumer choices: For example, when you find out that the megastore where you prefer to shop is only able to provide such low prices because of exploitative labor and unsustainable environmental practices, seek out alternatives.

- Transform sites of consumption into sites for intercultural praxis: Along with purchasing an object or experience, actively engage in intercultural dialogue.
- Act to challenge inequities in the workplace.

4. Join others in challenging inequity and injustice.

- Consider your spheres of influence: Make a point of talking with others about your decisions, and find others who support your values of social and economic responsibility.
- Join consumer groups or activist organizations: One of the greatest losses of advanced capitalist societies is human connection, engagement with others, and civic contributions. Join or start your own group that creates alternatives and challenges the dehumanizing conditions of the culture of capitalism.

SUMMARY

In the context of globalization, everything, including culture, has been commodified. This chapter focused on the pivotal, yet often unacknowledged linkages between intercultural communication and capitalism in the global context. The purpose of providing an overview of the culture of capitalism was threefold: The first goal was to situate the culture of capitalism historically to understand how we find ourselves where we are today; the second aim was to unmask what is seen as "normal" and "just the way things are" by revealing the values, assumptions, and ideologies that underlie and constitute the culture of capitalism; the third purpose was to understand how the culture of capitalism impacts intercultural interactions. Given that most everything today circulates within the market, we explored the commodification of culture, tourism and the impact on intercultural communication. We discussed key concepts, such as authenticity, exoticization, sign value, and fetishization to better understand the impact on intercultural communication as cultural Others are produced and consumed through the commodification of culture. The final section offered steps to move toward increased economic and social responsibility as intercultural actors in the global context.

KEY TERMS

capitalism
use value
exchange value
mercantilism
neoliberalism
surplus value
commodification of culture

authenticity
exoticization
  of the Other
sign value
flashbackers
spectacle
fetishization

DISCUSSION QUESTIONS AND ACTIVITIES

Discussion Questions

1. How is diversity approached in the culture of capitalism? Is diversity profitable, or is it a barrier to capitalist development?

2. In the culture of capitalism, how are identities commodified? What does it mean when identity is commodified, and how does it influence intercultural communication?

3. What are the differences among use value, exchange value, and sign value? Think about a relatively expensive purchase you made recently; which type of value does the product most have?

4. What happens when cultures and cultural experiences are commodified? Discuss examples of how we produce, sell, and/or purchase culture and cultural experiences.

5. What are the challenges and opportunities of tourism from an intercultural perspective? How can you engage with other cultures respectfully and responsibly as a tourist?

6. What is fetishization? Discuss examples of how people give symbolic power to commodities and the impact on cultures.

Activities

1. Watch the video *Not Business as Usual* (Le Lam, 2014):
   a. What are the successes of capitalism?
   b. What is the price/costs of capitalism?
   c. What is your role in the culture of capitalism?
   d. How can you join with others to address the costs of capitalism?

2. Watch the documentary *The Corporation* (Achbar & Abbott, 2005), and discuss the following questions:
   a. What is the relationship between the corporation and commodification of culture?
   b. What is the relationship between the corporation and globalization?
   c. How does neoliberalism shape the corporate business practices across the world?
   d. Do you think the goal of corporations to accumulate wealth can coexist with economic responsibility and sustainable economy?

3. Watch the documentary *Wal-Mart: The High Cost of Low Price* (Greenwald, 2005), and discuss the following questions:
   a. What did you find most problematic about Wal-Mart's business practices?
   b. How do Walmart's business practices impact local cultures?

   c. How do you think Wal-Mart deals with issues of diversity? How does "culture" matter in their business goals?

   d. What can you do to become a more economically responsible consumer?

4. Exploring Economic Responsibility:

   a. Keep a list of things you purchased for a week, including the price, store, manufacturer, and the location of production.

   b. Based on your list, discuss the following questions:

      i. What did you learn about yourself as a consumer?

      ii. What can you learn about the culture of capitalism from your list?

      iii. How does the culture of capitalism affect intercultural communication?

      iv. How is your identity connected to or expressed by what you consume?

      v. What would you change in your consumer activity in order for you to become a more economically responsible consumer?

I CHAPTER 9

Negotiating Intercultural Conflict and Social Justice

Strategies for Intercultural Relations

epa european pressphoto agency b.v./
Alamy SEAN DRAKES/Alamy

"I can't breathe," Eric Garner yelled eleven times as he died from a police chokehold on Staten Island, New York, in 2014. The slogan has become a symbol of protest against institutions such as law enforcement and the judicial system that treat people unjustly and inequitably based on race and class.

Learning Objectives

1. Describe how people from diverse groups engage in conflict differently and explore the conditions that lead to intercultural conflict.

2. Explain and apply a multi-dimensional framework of analysis for addressing the complexities of intercultural conflict in the global context.

3. Describe how micro-, meso- and macro-level issues impact interpersonal, intergroup, and international intercultural conflicts.

4. Identify communication skills and strategies to increase effectiveness in addressing intercultural conflicts.

Scenario One: *They met through friends in Southern California spending long days together getting to know each other. When Josh visited Patrice in Florida at her parents' house where she lives, he had a hard time feeling the closeness he had experienced in California. While her parents were gracious to him, her Haitian immigrant family seemed formal and structured compared to the close-knit, laid-back environment of his Jewish family in California. Josh's displays of affection in public made Patrice uncomfortable. And then, Josh wanted to talk about everything—whether there was a slight disagreement between them or a moment of closeness, he always wanted to express it.*

Scenario Two: *One hot day in early September during the crowded lunch period at a high school in Los Angeles, Tina bumped into Marta causing Marta's lunch tray to spill all over her blouse. Marta, embarrassed, looks up at Tina and yells, "What are you doing? I can't believe you did that. You did that on purpose." Tina laughs and shouts, "It was an accident . . . but if you don't stop yelling at me, I'm going to get my friends over here to prove it." A crowd surrounds the two girls, Armenian students backing up Tina and Latina/o students behind Marta each side hurling ethnic insults and yelling that the other is disrespecting their group.*

Scenario Three: *Around the turn of the previous century Jews began to immigrate to Palestine with the goal of establishing a national homeland. There were many arguments about the appropriateness and availability of this land, but early Zionists sought to establish a Jewish State on what they claimed was their ancient holy land. On the same land, however, lived Arabs with historic and family claims to the land. This resulted in a clash over ownership and issues of self-determination, statehood, and identity. These two adversaries pose increasing obstacles and impediments to peace including settlement expansion, terrorism, assassination, religious fanaticism, and general recalcitrance.* (Ellis, 2005, p. 49)

The scenarios point to the likelihood of intercultural conflict as our lives, resources, and everyday experiences become increasingly interconnected with people from diverse cultures. Greater proximity, increased competition, diminishing resources, post/colonial histories, exploitative conditions, and rising religious fundamentalism as well as exacerbated social and economic inequity fuel conflicts among individuals and groups from different cultural, ethnic, racial, religious, and national backgrounds. In the context of globalization, migrants who are driven from their homes as refugees of the global economy and asylum seekers fleeing conflict areas increase the presence of "foreigners" in locations all around the world, escalating intercultural tensions. According to the Southern Poverty Law Center, extremist groups, which have grown exponentially in the United States especially since 2005, use immigration debates to incite violence toward immigrants, particularly Latinos/Latinas. The rise in nativism, or anti-immigrant sentiment, has reached a level not seen in the United States in over a century. Provoking hatred and often conflict, anti-immigrant groups assert, without evidence to support their claims, that Latin American immigrants are responsible for a whole host of social ills, including poverty and crime, as well as environmental and cultural degradation (Beirich, n.d.).

Anti-immigrant sentiment, which often combines with and masks deeply embedded prejudices based on race, religion, and class is not unique to the United States. A Gallup poll revealed that Europeans have the most negative attitudes toward immigrants worldwide with over 50% calling for a decrease in immigration (Faiola, 2015). The anti-Islamic movement PEGIDA (Patriotic Europeans Against the Islamization of the West) initially took root in Dresden, Germany in 2014 and spread across Western Europe by 2015, amid soaring anti-immigrant sentiment. Drawing over 25,000 people in weekly rallies after gunmen inspired by ISIS (the Islamic State of Iraq and Syria) killed 17 people in Paris, France, in January 2015, PEGIDA emerged during a surge across Europe in asylum seekers arriving from war-torn countries, such as Syria and Libya. To understand conflicts in countries, such as Syria, Sudan, and the Congo today, sociologist Andreas Wimmer (2013) argues for a broad historical view focusing on the formation and development of the nation-state. First, violence often accompanies the formation of the nation-state as evident with the American Revolution, and more recently with the Balkan states. Second, bloody struggles often result over which ethnic or national groups will hold power as well as the borders of the state. One third of present day countries fought violent wars of independence temporarily unifying diverse groups; yet, colonial-era favoritism and inequities advanced the interests of certain ethnic groups over others resulting in great internal conflicts as seen in Rwanda as well as postcolonial conflicts among ethnic elites, such as in Syria today. "It is not diversity, but political inequity, that breeds conflict" (Wimmer, 2013).

Yet, people from different ethnic, racial, cultural and national groups have joined together historically and are uniting today around the globe in unprecedented ways to challenge inequity and injustice by building intercultural alliances. For example, *United We Dream* is a multiracial coalition of undocumented students working for educational access and citizenship for immigrants in the United States; *The Climate Justice Alliance*, a coalition of over 35 community-based organizations rooted in indigenous, Latino/a, African American, Asian Pacific Islander, and working-class White communities in the United States, addresses the twin crises of economics and the environment converging today; and Boycott, Divest, and Sanctions (BDS) is a global movement campaigning for Palestinian rights and Israeli compliance with international laws.

Intercultural conflict is defined here as the real or perceived incompatibility of values, norms, expectations, goals, processes, or outcomes between two or more *interdependent* individuals or groups from different cultures (Hocker & Wilmot, 1998). In the context of globalization, increased interdependence—economically, culturally, socially, and politically—has created unprecedented opportunities for and threats of intercultural conflict. While conflict is often characterized negatively, it's likely that most of us have experienced conflicts that were resolved in ways leading to positive outcomes or creative solutions—even if the paths to these outcomes were challenging. In interpersonal contexts, conflicts, if handled effectively, can clear the air and result in stronger bonds between two people. Workplace conflicts, if managed successfully, can result in better programs, products, or presentations. Movements for independence from colonial rule and social movements for human rights, such as the civil rights movement, women's rights, and gay rights movements and the anti-apartheid movement in South Africa have used conflict to move toward more equitable and just ends. Conflicts, while inevitably messy and infused with emotions, can lead to personal growth, creative and alternative solutions, as well as social change.

This chapter focuses on conflict, which is a central feature of human interaction and intercultural relations. Our goal is to understand how and why people from diverse groups engage in conflict, the conditions that lead to conflict, and the communication strategies that can increase effectiveness in addressing intercultural conflicts. In doing so, the relationship among intercultural conflict, communication, and social justice is highlighted. Histories of interaction between groups and the increasingly asymmetrical relationships of power today are critical dimensions to take into account. We begin by outlining a multidimensional framework for analyzing intercultural conflicts to grasp the complexities in the context of globalization. Following this, the multidimensional analysis is applied to three case studies. The chapter concludes with a discussion of strategies for addressing and negotiating intercultural conflicts using intercultural praxis.

INTERCULTURAL CONFLICT: A MULTIDIMENSIONAL FRAMEWORK OF ANALYSIS

Using the intercultural praxis entry point of framing, we explore intercultural conflict from three interrelated frames: (1) the micro-frame that examines cultural orientations to conflict and communication styles; (2) the meso- or intermediate frame that broadens our view to address cultural group prejudices, cultural histories, and cultural identities; and (3) the macro- or geopolitical frame that expands our viewpoint to include the impact of media and discourse as well as political and economic factors on intercultural conflict.

Micro-Frame Analysis of Intercultural Conflict

The micro-frame analysis focuses on the individual-based interactional dimension of intercultural conflict. All intercultural conflicts, whether in the interpersonal context where neighbors argue over what is perceived as loud music, the intergroup context where two ethnic groups fight over entitlement to government resources, or the international/global context where two nation-states engage in combat, have micro-frame components. Cultural orientations to conflict, communication, and facework impact the management of intercultural conflict. Differences across cultures in these areas can be sources of conflict themselves.

Cultural Orientations

Across cultures and historic times, tremendous variation exists in orientations to conflict as well as the styles and strategies for dealing with conflicts. For example, Taoism, a philosophical religious tradition rooted in ancient China, views conflict as arising from an imbalance of opposites. Conflicts, from a Taoist perspective, are natural responses to disharmony in the flow of life and can be resolved by rebalancing what is out of proportion. Confucianism, Buddhism, and Taoism, which influence many Asian cultures, all emphasize harmony, selflessness, and an interdependent worldview. Broadly speaking, collectivistic cultures tend to cultivate an **interdependent orientation**, where the self is understood as relational and conflict is seen as a part of life that is managed in relationship with others. Ting-Toomey & Oetzel (2001) noted that in conflict situations, people from collectivistic cultures tend to present opinions or ideas of the group, refrain from expressing personal emotions, and protect in-group members from accountability. Interdependent worldviews, such as in China, Japan, and Korea tend to take indirect approaches to conflict, where maintaining harmony and accord in relationships is critical.

From an **independent orientation**, the individual is seen as an autonomous agent pursuing personal goals based on his or her beliefs. Individualistic cultures that promote an independent worldview, such as the dominant U.S. culture tend to emphasize individual initiative and self-directed action, socializing people to assert personal opinions and hold individuals accountable for problems or mistakes. An individualistic, independent orientation often translates into approaches to conflict that use direct communication and generate multiple solutions to a problem. In cultures with an independent worldview, such as the European–American culture, conflict is seen as resulting from competition between personal interests of two or more people and as an incidental intrusion or infringement on individuals' autonomy or rights. Conflict is often viewed as a problem that must be overcome quickly, rationally, unemotionally, and directly. In contrast to interdependent-oriented cultures that stress relationship maintenance, the goal of mediation and conflict resolution in independent-oriented cultures is often to remove obstacles to the pursuit of individual goals (Markus & Lin, 1999).

The two approaches sketched out are generalizations that alert us to ways that cultural assumptions, beliefs, practices, and institutions orient people to make sense of and manage conflict differently. Yet, diversity of approaches and preferred orientations exist within groups as well. Today, rapid and circular migration; the depth and penetration of international media; and increases in intercultural relationships in homes, workplaces, and international settings blur distinct lines that categorize national and ethnic cultural orientations to conflict.

Communication and Conflict Styles

Varying styles of communication shaped by culture can be sources of misunderstanding and conflict in intercultural communication. Edward T. Hall (1976) introduced the concept of low and high context communication. **Context**, in this case, refers to the information that surrounds a communication event, which is closely tied to the meaning of the event. **High context communication** is "one where most of the information is already in the person, while very little is in the coded, explicit, transmitted part of the message" (Hall, 1976, p. 79). In other words, people rely on shared knowledge, the situation, and nonverbal cues to give meaning to communication. High context communication tends to be indirect. **Low context communication** is communication where the "mass of the information is vested in the explicit code" (Hall, 1976, p. 70). Low context communication is more direct, specific, and literal with less attention placed on gathering meaning from unstated contextual cues. Collectivistic cultures that have more interdependent worldviews and share close networks of relationships over long periods of time tend to display high context communication; on the other hand, individualistic cultures that are more independent in terms of worldview, and separate and compartmentalize personal and work relationships often require more explicit detailing of information to communicate and therefore tend to display low context communication.

Facework

The notion of "face" has roots in both Eastern and Western traditions and is used across cultures, yet the meanings associated with face differ in different historical and cultural contexts. In research in intercultural communication studies today, **face** can be defined as favorable social self-worth in relation to the assessment of "other-worth" in interpersonal relationships (Ting-Toomey & Kurogi, 1998). Face, which can be threatened, lost, protected, maintained, and saved, is a critical resource that is negotiated through communication in social interactions. **Facework** refers to the communication strategies used to negotiate face between the self and other. Ting-Toomey and Oetzel (2002) argued that people from individualistic or independent cultural orientations tend to be more concerned with protecting or saving their own face, and therefore often use conflict styles that are more confrontational, controlling, and aimed at finding solutions. On the other hand, people from more collectivistic and interdependent orientations are more likely to be concerned with accommodating the other person's face or finding ways for mutual face-saving. Facework in more interdependent-oriented cultures leads to conflict styles that are more avoiding, obliging, or integrating.

Communication scholars Noorie Baig, Stella Ting-Toomey, and Tenzin Dorjee (2014) examined *izzat*, the notion of "face" in South Asian Indian culture, among first- and second-generation immigrants to the United States. *Izzat* refers to respect, honor, and prestige and is understood as "a complex set of societal and personal conduct rules that an individual learns in order to protect the family honor and one's personal conduct with the community" (p. 166). In both the older and younger generation of South Asian Indian Americans, respect was the predominant meaning of *izzat*. Respect is shown through verbal and nonverbal performance rituals, such as showing deference to elders through linguistic formality; staging family face by avoiding bringing shame on the family, and protecting others' views of one's family; and by reacting to the complexity of emotions associated with *izzat*. The study found differences across generations where the older generation showed more concern for the extended family's *izzat* and the complex emotionality within the community, while the younger generation were concerned with the *izzat* of the immediate family and were more disconnected from the other-oriented affective concerns. Both older and younger generations connected "face" with the notion of respect, but with much less emphasis on the deeply rooted and emotionally charged aspect of honor suggesting the acculturation of South Asian Indians to more individualistic orientations of the United States.

Situational Factors

A wide range of situational and relational factors also contribute to decisions individuals make in conflict situations. Brew and Cairns (2004) found that cultural orientation alone did not explain or predict communication choices in conflict situations with East Asian and Australian employees at five Western organizations in Bangkok and Singapore. Situational constraints modified the expected communication strategies based on cultural norms. Australians are generally described as individualistic, low context communicators who are independent-oriented and egalitarian, valuing transparency, honesty, and direct communication. These characteristics may be experienced as blunt by those from more collectivistic cultures. Thais and Singaporeans are generally described as collectivistic, high context communicators who tend to avoid conflict, open displays of criticism, or dissent, which are seen as rude or damaging. Saving "face" is seen as a particularly important concern, which results in skirting challenging issues to avoid embarrassment to self and others (Chi-Ching, 1998).

Brew and Cairns (2004) argued that these broad generalizations may be useful as a guide to understand cultural orientations to communication and conflict, but in interpersonal communication in workplace settings individuals make decisions about how to act and respond that are also highly contingent on situational factors. The situational constraint of time urgency, which is an increasing pressure in the context of globalization, may explain why Thai and Singaporean employees used more direct communication than expected based on their cultural orientation. Additionally, Australians used more indirect communication when interacting with Thai and Singaporean workers who were both superiors and subordinates, suggesting that Australians modified their communication strategies based on the cultural identity of the person with whom they interacted. The situational factor of the status of the other was significant for East Asians as they chose to communicate indirectly with superiors and more directly with subordinates.

The micro-frame draws our attention to cultural orientations to conflict, communication, and conflict styles, as well as different facework strategies. Additionally, we note how situational factors may play an important role along with cultural norms in determining individuals' choices and actions in conflict management. From the micro-frame of analysis of intercultural conflict, we now broaden our viewpoint to the meso- or intermediate frame of reference.

Meso-Frame Analysis of Intercultural Conflict

The meso-frame allows us to address the influence of group-based prejudices and ethnocentrism as well as cultural histories and identities on intercultural conflict. Attitudes, beliefs, perceptions, and attributions held by groups are often grounded in cultural group histories and are integral to cultural group identities. The perceived and real access to power or the group's positionality within hierarchies of power also plays a role in how conflicts unfold, entrench, and transform.

Prejudice, Ethnocentrism, and Racism

All intercultural conflict involves some degree of biased in-group perceptions and attributions as individuals or groups make sense of conflict situations. **In-groups** are groups of individuals for whom we feel concern, with whom we are willing to cooperate and from whom separation creates anxiety (Triandis, 1995). **Out-groups** are groups of individuals who are seen as separate and different from us, are often perceived as unequal to our group, as well as potentially threatening. Stereotypes, ethnocentric attitudes, or long-held prejudices from in-groups inform interpretations and experiences as well as the degree to which meaningful relationships can be formed with out-group members.

The degree to which distinctions between in-groups and out-groups are apparent and how these distinctions inform actions varies across cultures, contexts, and situations. However, conflict situations tend to tap into and bring out latent in-group/out-group distinctions, prejudices, and ethnocentric attitudes. As conflict situations escalate, "us versus them" dichotomies often become entrenched (Ting-Toomey & Oetzel, 2001). For example, in the 1980s before the fall of the former Yugoslavian nation-state, Serbia and Croatian immigrants in Seattle, Washington, frequently engaged in social activities together and paid little attention to the ethnic distinctions between them. However, with the collapse of Yugoslavia in 1991 and the ensuing violence and ethnic cleansing, the immigrant communities in Seattle drew distinct lines between themselves, severing communication, and in a few cases even sending death threats to members of the other group.

Racism, sexism, classism, and heterosexism are sources of intercultural conflict as well as ubiquitous backdrops that play into differing interpretations of conflict in intercultural situations. In historical and contemporary contexts, where everyday interactions and institutions provide systemic advantages to some and disadvantages to others, relatively small instances of exclusion based on race, gender, class, or sexual orientation can provoke conflict.

Cultural Identity
Intercultural Conflict

In some situations, the initial source of conflict may appear to have little to do with cultural differences. However, once the conflict is triggered, hidden stereotypes and prejudices surface. Consider the following example.

A multicultural group of university students is assigned to work together to research a topic area and present their findings in class. The project requires students to meet outside of class on numerous occasions, and initially all members attend. Yet, over time, one member, Marissa, stops coming. She tries to contact her group members to let them know she is ill, but gets no response. As the group makes final preparations, a heated argument develops. Some students think Marissa should be excluded from presenting and others argue that she should be allowed to share her part. A few students worry that her lack of participation will hurt their group grade. In the midst of the conflict, one group member says, "She's Hispanic. That's why she didn't do her work." Another Latino/ Hispanic group member objects to the comment saying he won't present with a bigot. Clearly, our cultural identities, cultural histories, and the way cultural groups have been targeted historically combine to impact interpersonal and intergroup conflict.

Cultural Histories and Cultural Identities

Cultural histories are shared stories and interpretations of cultural groups that are often passed along in written or oral form from generation to generation. While cultural histories often intersect with national histories, cultural histories explain events and experiences from the perspectives of the cultural group. Cultural histories of nondominant groups— whether groups based on ethnicity, race, gender, religion or sexual orientation—may complement or contradict the received national history and are viewpoints on history that are often hidden or silenced from the mainstream culture. Cultural histories provide cohesiveness for cultural groups and a foundation for sustaining unified group-based identities. People from nondominant groups generally know more about the cultural histories of dominant groups than the reverse (Kivel, 1996). Lack of knowledge of others' cultural histories or a refusal to validate the importance of cultural histories can limit intercultural understanding, increase the likelihood for misunderstanding, and exacerbate conflicts.

Shared cultural histories, experiences of exclusion, and struggles for recognition by nondominant cultural groups are often inextricably intertwined with the definition and protection of cultural group identities. Disrespect or rejection directed at individuals or groups based on their cultural identity can be a source of intercultural conflict and can exacerbate conflicts that are not primarily focused on identity. Lack of respect and validation for a group's cultural identity often provokes efforts to regain face and respect for the group's identity. Ting-Toomey and Oetzel (2002) noted that validation–rejection, respect–disrespect, approval–disapproval, and valuing–disconfirming are identity-based issues that are linked to cultural values, beliefs, and assumption and can play a critical role in conflict situations. For example, once the perpetrator of the tragic massacre at Virginia Tech in April 2007 had been identified as a Korean alien resident in the United States, the president of Korea, representing the collective shame and loss of face of all people of Korea, expressed his sorrow and apologized to the families who had lost loved ones (Shim, Kim, & Martin, 2008).

Passage of legislation like Proposition 8 in California in 2008 that denied same-sex couples the right to marriage harnessed and perpetuated a climate of disrespect and rejection of lesbian, gay, bisexual, and transgender (LGBT) communities across the United States. While questions of access to rights and privileges equal to those afforded heterosexuals were the fundamental source of conflict, disapproval and rejection of the collective identities of LGBT people were necessarily interwoven with the passage of this legislation. As evidenced during the civil rights and the feminist movements, threats and attacks on cultural group identities also serve to define, unify, and mobilize group-based identities. The LGBT movement, punctuated by conflicts over civil rights across the United States in the past 40 years, has been instrumental in constituting a collective "queer" identity (Archer, 2004).

The non-indictment of White police officers in multiple grand jury cases where unarmed Black men were killed in 2014 in cities across the United States punctuated long-standing claims of police brutality among communities of color, galvanized protestors across racial groups, and stimulated organizing based on Black identities. The Twitter post #Black Lives Matter, co-founded by Black organizers and activists Alica Garza, Patrisse Cullors, and Opal Tometi, is a U.S.-based international movement that started after the acquittal of George Zimmerman in the fatal shooting of Trayvon Martin in 2013, and gained momentum in 2014. Demanding an end to racial profiling, police brutality, mass incarceration, and the demilitarization of U.S. police departments, the movement has garnered attention globally for its broad scope and inclusiveness of intersectional Black identities, including queer and trans Black people and undocumented Black people. "In the Black tradition of call and response, #Blacklivesmatter is both a call to action and response to the ways in which our lives have been de-valued" (#Blacklivesmatter, n.d.)

In intractable ethnopolitical conflicts, such as the historically entrenched clashes between the Sinhalese and Tamils in Sri Lanka, or between Israeli Jews and Palestinians, communication scholar Donald Ellis (2005) noted the following:

> Identities are strong, rigid and stable. They do not change easily. In fact, identities are so strong the conflict threatens the individual's sense of self. This threat evokes a powerful response. Typically, this response is aggressive and can escalate. Ethnopolitical conflicts usually involve polarized negative identities where one's sense of self is dependent upon being in opposition to another. (p. 47)

To varying degrees, intercultural conflicts involve issues of cultural identity, cultural histories, racism, ethnocentrism, and prejudice, which are linked to inequitable relations of power.

Religious Fundamentalism

In recent decades, religious fundamentalism has increasingly impacted political, legal, social, and intercultural relations in many areas of the world. The assumption that modernization inevitably results in secularism has not held up; rather, technological development and the promise of progress have often led to alienation, loss, and resentment. The undermining of "traditional" values and social systems, the rise of consumer culture worldwide, and the uneven distribution of resources and wealth in the context of globalization has produced disaffection and isolation stimulating the search for a sense of identity and belonging (Hayes, 1995). Christian fundamentalism is on the rise in the United States, Latin America, Central America, and Africa. Jewish fundamentalism has exacerbated conflict and instability in the Middle East. Islamic fundamentalism is on the rise in Pakistan, Afghanistan, and parts of the Middle East, Africa and Europe. Nearly a third of the 198 countries in a Pew Research Center study (2014) had a high level of social hostilities involving religion. The sharpest increases from previous years were in the Middle East and North Africa as well as in the Asia-Pacific region.

The term *fundamentalism* was first used to refer to Christians in the United States who demanded strict adherence to specific theological beliefs in the early part of the 20th century. Reacting to modernist theology, which proposed new scientific approaches to the Bible, fundamentalism became a movement among conservative Protestant communities. The term was originally used to connote a return to basic irreducible tenets or beliefs within the Christian religion; yet, fundamentalism is used more broadly today, primarily, but not exclusively in regard to religion to refer to literal interpretations of doctrines or texts. Fundamentalists draw strong distinctions between in-groups and out-groups relying on notions of "original" and "pure" interpretations of doctrine and a return to an ideal from the past. Diversity of opinions, perspectives, and approaches to the "fundamentals" is not acceptable within the group.

In a nationwide study of U.S. Muslim-Americans, political scientist Rachel Gillum (2013) found that while religious fundamentalism among Muslim immigrants in Europe is much greater than among Christian Europeans, religious fundamentalism among Muslims and Christians in the United States is nearly identical. Christians in the United States are more religious and socially conservative than European Christians, and U.S. Muslims expressed lower levels of adherence to fundamentalist beliefs than European Muslims explaining the difference in the gap between fundamentalists and non-fundamentalists in the United States and in Europe. Based on studies in Europe, Gillum also noted that fundamentalism is associated with feelings that "ones own group is threatened by outside enemies." According to this expectation, the general population in the United States is more fundamentalist, therefore more likely to believe Islam encourages violence compared to native Europeans. In a similar way, European Muslims, as more fundamentalist, are more likely to believe the West is out to destroy Islam as compared to U.S. Muslims (Gillum, 2013).

Power Imbalance

Imbalances in power are often pivotal features in conflicts in interpersonal, intergroup, and international/global contexts. Through the meso- or intermediate frame, we focus attention on group-based power. Power is always relational and can take multiple forms. Group-based power can be gained in a variety of ways, including force and domination; majority representation; and control of economic, political, and social institutions, as well as control of resources considered valuable. In the United States, White European Americans represent a numeric majority (approximately 70% of the population) and have historically controlled access to institutions and resources. Nondominant or cocultural groups are expected to adapt and assimilate to European American values, communication styles, norms, practices, and standards due to this power imbalance. Increased numbers may augment group-based power, for example, the gains in political power made by Latinos/Hispanics in the United States as this group's population increases. Yet, numbers of people do not necessarily translate into power as was evident in apartheid in South Africa.

Inequitable relations of power and lack of access to power within society often lead cocultural or nondominant groups to make clear distinctions between those in the dominant group who hold power and those in nondominant groups who do not have access to power (Orbe, 1998). In the context of these power differentials, cocultural or nondominant groups tend to enact strong group-based cultural identities to preserve their languages, customs, practices, and identities. Dominant group members often find it hard to understand the need to preserve cultural identities, are bothered by cocultural groups' enactments of cultural difference, and are sometimes affronted by the lack of willingness to assimilate into the dominant culture. Real and perceived imbalances in power are sources of resentment and misinterpretation for both nondominant and dominant groups, which can lead to conflict. Hierarchies of power within societies also lead cocultural groups to fight with each other over access to limited resources.

The meso-frame highlights the role that group-based prejudices, cultural histories, and identities, as well as imbalances in power, have on intercultural conflict. Influences on conflict revealed through the meso-frame are undoubtedly interconnected to and impacted by issues made evident through the macro-frame.

Communicative Dimensions
Mediating Intercultural Conflict

For 25 years, Mexican and Central American laborers gathered to look for work in the parking lot of a paint store on the corner of Beverly and La Jolla in Los Angeles. When the store ownership changed, the laborers were forced to stand on the corners. Some of the neighborhood residents, who were mostly elderly and Jewish, complained to the police. While the laborers had committed no crime and were on public property, the police harassed and arrested them. The laborers enlisted the help of a local organization, Day Laborer Leadership Program of the Coalition for Humane Immigrant Rights of Los Angeles (CHIRLA), who went door to door to talk with residents. While a small group of residents were upset about the laborers, others had hired workers in the past. Some of the older residents were also threatened by new Russian and Asian residents. CHIRLA used a wide range of communication strategies to negotiate the intercultural conflict. They talked and listened to residents, laborers, and the police; they worked to address the stereotypes each group held about the other. Through dialogue at a community forum, residents and laborers were able to come to an agreement about the use of neighborhood space.

Source: Cho, Puete, Louie, & Khokha (2004).

Macro-Frame Analysis of Intercultural Conflict

From the meso-frame of analysis of intercultural conflict, we broaden our view further to encompass the macro-frame, which allows us to consider the impact that media, economic factors, and geopolitical power asymmetries have on intercultural conflicts.

Media

Events, decisions, and discourse at the macro-level may seem distant from our everyday life experiences. Yet, discourses and media representations about controversial issues such as U.S. immigration, the rise of the Islamic State of Iraq and Syria (ISIS), protests over law enforcement and justice systems, the global economy and the deadly massacres in Nigeria to name only a few examples, have direct and indirect impact on our intercultural interactions. As discussed in Chapter 6, media representations are primary sources of information about groups of people, nations, and conflicts with which we have little or no contact or knowledge. Stereotypical or biased portrayals of nondominant groups in the media perpetuate prejudices and ethnocentrism.

In conflict situations, ethnic minority groups are often depicted as criminals and as threats to national security. The case study of Algerian Muslim immigrants in France presented in Chapter 6 illustrates this point well. The media often play a significant role in interethnic and international conflicts furthering divisiveness between groups by using **oppositional metaphors**, or metaphors that use rigid and polarized dichotomies, such as "us versus them," "good versus evil," and "civil versus barbarian." Media representation of interethnic conflicts in the former Yugoslavia, Rwanda, and Zaire in the 1990s relied heavily on shocking scenes that reduced the complexities of the conflicts to fighting between different "tribes" and often presented ethnic groups as "wild," "mad," and "volatile." Allen and Seaton (1999) argued that such representation "enables the governments of rich industrialized nations to absolve themselves of responsibility for what was happening, and helped them to adapt increasingly oppressive measures against immigrants and refugees" (p. 2).

During the growing unrest in Ukraine in 2014, media representation from Ukraine, Russia, and the West diverged greatly. Both the Western/U.S. and Russian media were accused of propagandizing and waging information wars through media coverage. Media representation of the Islamic State of Iraq and Syria (ISIS) has been overwhelmingly negative and sensationalizing. For example, Prime Minister Abbott of Australia said, "This [Islamic State] is a movement—as we've seen on our TV screens and front pages of our newspapers—of utter ferocity, medieval barbarism allied to modern technology—that's how serious and dangerous this movement is" (Bedford, 2014). While the actions and intent of ISIS are unquestionably egregious and abhorrent, media representation in the West problematically conflates ISIS with Islam. Writer Kavita Bedford argued that the disproportionate attention given in the media to radicalism feeds into misrepresentations of Muslims in the West. Despite governmental assurance to the contrary, ". . . 'radicalism' is treated in the public debate as though it were exclusively bound up with the menace of Islamism. It's a dangerous game fueled by the media" (Bedford, 2014). The use of oppositional metaphors in media representations of ISIS also obscures the historic and current role of the United States and other countries in the emergence of ISIS.

While media often exacerbate conflicts and are frequently monopolized to advance the interests of powerful ethnic/racial and national groups, Melone, Terzis, and Beleli (2002) suggested that media can also be a vehicle for conflict transformation. The nonprofit organization The European Centre for Common Ground has worked in collaboration with local media owners, journalists, and reporters in Angola, Burundi, Greece, Iran, the United States, and the Middle East using a wide variety of media forms creating a common base among adversarial groups to cultivate conditions for conflict transformation. Common Ground has produced TV and radio programs, used street theater and comics, recorded peace songs from rival political groups, as well as facilitated intercultural dialogues to address interethnic and international conflicts. Additionally, average people around the world are using tools of new media, such as smart phones, social networking sites, and blogs to further peacemaking and conflict resolution (United States Institute of Peace, 2011). Citizen journalists in conflict zones, such as Syria, Nigeria, and the Republic of Congo, use cell phones, blogs, and social media to share first-hand local knowledge of situations offering vital information otherwise not reported in mainstream media.

Intercultural Praxis
Freedom of Expression, Religion, and Intercultural Conflict

On January 7th, 2015, two brothers, trained by an al-Qaeda branch in Yemen, attacked the French satirical magazine *Charlie Hebdo* (Charlie Weekly). The editor in chief, several famous caricaturists (known for their controversial depictions of Islamic prophet Muhammad and other caricatures), as well as other employees of the magazine were violently killed by the individuals who claimed to seek revenge for the disrespectful and blasphemous representations of Muhammad that had appeared in the magazine. *Charlie Hedbo* was under fire and had been sued in court for reprinting images of the Islamic prophet Muhammad that had caused controversy in Denmark when first published. The world watched as French citizens took to the streets to demonstrate their alarm, solidarity, and strong commitment to two of the most central values of French democracy: freedom of expression and freedom of the press. Over 4 million demonstrators congregated in the streets to display a unified front against radical thought and for democratic rights. Demonstrators chanted a slogan that quickly became the symbol of their fight, "*Je suis Charlie*," or "I Am Charlie," which implied that by killing the *Charlie Hebdo* journalists/caricaturists, every French citizens' fundamental rights had been threatened.

The event and demonstrations triggered a national debate about multiculturalism, secularism, the rise of Islam fundamentalism, and freedom of expression. Some extreme right politicians used this event to promote anti-Muslim and anti-immigration policies. Others showed a strong desire to maintain a united front against radical thought (specifically radical Islam), which they found divisive and detrimental to the secular state of France. Days after the demonstrations, others noted that while the attack was in no way justified and should be condemned, a double standard exists regarding whose freedom of expression is protected. Indeed, while speech that promotes racial hatred (e.g., anti-Semitic comments) is banned, magazines such as *Charlie Hebdo*'s "blasphemous" discourse is not. Some French Muslims feel that when anti-Muslim or racist discourse is expressed (as it was with *Charlie Hebdo*'s caricatures), their concern and shock is met with criticism and seen as unjustified. Under the guise of the freedom of the press and expression, *Charlie Hebdo* has been notorious for pushing the envelope and offering provocative caricatures often portraying religious, political, and/or public figures. While its editors in chief and staff have always held that their work was to highlight current events, it is undeniable that in some ways their drawings also have offended, provoked racial hatred, and created more division.

Famous comedians such as Dieudonné have been chastised for their anti-Semitic comments that were deemed to promote racial hatred, and banned in France; however *Charlie Hebdo*'s satirical representations are not only seen as acceptable, but crucial to the survival of a democratic state. These recent events have exacerbated intercultural tensions in an already anti-immigrant and racist climate in Western Europe. Is freedom of expression for and about some groups more valued and protected than others? How are some messages censored and deemed "racial hatred" while others—equally divisive and seen as malicious by many—are deemed vital for the survival of democracy? Using intercultural praxis, what other questions need to be asked to understand this situation? How do framing and positioning help make sense of whose voices are heard and whose censored? Who is included and who is excluded in "*Je suis Charlie*?"

Economic and Political Factors

As noted and discussed throughout the book, neoliberal policies implemented in the context of globalization have magnified economic disparity within nation-states and across nation-states, which often translates into a greater likelihood of intercultural conflict. Struggles over limited resources, such as money, jobs, or land are primarily economic and political in nature. Yet, animosity and conflict are often framed in terms of ethnic, racial, religious, and cultural differences. In the context of the global economic crisis and recovery in the United States, fear and hostility toward immigrants has escalated and immigrants have become easy targets to blame for the nation's problems resulting in legislation, such as Arizona's SB 1070, the most far-reaching and severe anti-immigrant measure in decades. Racial slurs and verbal attacks hurled on radio talk shows and violent crimes against Latinos/ Hispanics have increased impacting individuals and cultural groups as well as educational, health care, and criminal justice institutions. The passage of SB 1070 in Arizona led to similar legislation in other states in 2011. The states of Alabama, Georgia, Indiana, South Carolina, and Utah have passed comparable laws, which target Latino/as, Asian Americans and others who are assumed to be "foreign" based on how people look and sound.

Deepa Fernandes (2007) brought to our attention the deeply troubling ways that economic and political factors have aligned since 9/11 in regard to national security, immigration, and intercultural conflict:

> Today, enforcing immigration policy has become the latest way to make a buck. . . . I call it the immigration-industrial complex. There is big money to be made as the government dramatically increases its reliance on the private sector to carry out its war on terror. On the home front, the prime targets of this war are immigrants. (pp. 169–170)

The **immigration industrial complex** refers to the "confluence of public and private sector interests in the criminalization of undocumented migration, immigration law enforcement, and the promotion of 'anti-illegal' rhetoric" (Golash-Boza, 2009, p. 295). The immigration industrial complex uses the following: (1) rhetoric of fear, (2) the confluence of power interests, and (3) otherization discourse. A culture of fear targeting "illegals" as undesirable Others, racialized as Mexicans in the current context, justifies massive government expenditures. In an industrial complex, the marginalized group pays the biggest price while the powerful and well-connected are enriched (Golash-Boza, 2009).

Geopolitical Power Inequities

As noted throughout the book, the configuration of geopolitical influence and the asymmetrical relations of power that characterize the current context of globalization are rooted in histories of colonization, Western imperialism, and U.S. hegemony. In the first decades of the new millennium, 31 to 37 significant armed conflicts were ongoing around the world (Koffmar, 2014). Many of these conflicts, lasting two, three, and even four decades, are in non-Western postcolonial states in Africa, Asia, and the Middle East (Eller, 1999). United States military intervention in countries from China, Korea, Iran, Guatemala, Vietnam,

Cambodia, Laos, Haiti, Chile, Grenada, Nicaragua, Panama, Afghanistan, and Iraq, to name only a few, over the past 70 years have caused the deaths of millions and disrupted the lives and livelihoods of millions more (Blum, 1995). Criminology and public policy scholars Mullard and Cole (2007) noted the following:

> The wars in Iraq and Afghanistan are replays of colonial "civilizing missions" in Africa, clouded by deceit, corruption and corporate invasion of pacified homelands. Like the concessionaire and charted companies in nineteenth-century Africa, the International Monetary Fund (IMF), the Word Bank, the Development Fund for Iraq (DFI), and other international financial institutions (IFIs) are, as a consequence of the war on terror, actively involved in the corporate takeover and economic occupation of Iraq. (p. 1)

Intervention, war, armed conflict, and occupation—whether justified by rhetoric attacking the barbaric actions of the enemy, defended by claims of political and moral inferiority of the Other, or warranted by assertions of human rights violations—foster deep and long-standing resentment and animosity. Since the global war on terror, initiated by former U.S. president George W. Bush following 9/11, U.S. citizens traveling abroad have experienced firsthand the role geopolitics plays in the reception and treatment of individuals and national cultural groups. One's real or perceived membership in a national cultural group or in an ethnic, religious, or racial group positions each us of differently in the complex web of global geopolitical relationships of power. Moustafa Bayoumi (2008) captured the struggles and challenges of seven young Arab Americans in the United States since 9/11 in his book titled *How Does It Feel to Be a Problem?* Bayoumi told the stories of Arab Americans, the newest minority in the United States identified as communities of suspicion and targeted as the latest "problem." Yet, Bayoumi argued, "What you will find are seven Arab American narratives that are in the end very American stories about race, religion, and civil rights and about how the pressures of domestic life and foreign policy push on individual lives" (p. 11).

The macro-frame draws our attention to how intercultural conflicts are shaped by media representation, economic factors, and asymmetries in geopolitical power. Intercultural conflicts in the context of globalization are complex, often deeply rooted in history and situated within inequitable relationships of power. The multiframe model allows us to highlight the linkages and interplay between the micro-, meso-, and macro-frames. Three case studies of intercultural conflict from interpersonal, intergroup, and international contexts are presented next to illustrate the utility of a multidimensional framework of analysis (see Table 9.1).

CASE STUDY 1: INTERPERSONAL CONTEXT

Patrice, a Haitian Christian immigrant, lives in south Florida and is in a long-term, intimate relationship with Josh, a Jewish multigenerational resident of Southern California. Conflict is not unusual in their long-distance, interracial, and interreligious relationship affording both opportunities for growth and potential threats to their relationship. They met through

Table 9.1   Multidimensional Framework of Analysis for Intercultural Conflict

Frames	Micro-Frame (Individual-Based)	Meso-Frame (Group-Based)	Macro-Frame (Discourse and Representation)
	Cultural orientation Communication style Language Conflict style Facework Situational factors	Prejudice Ethnocentrism Racism, sexism, homophobia, religious discrimination, etc. Cultural histories Cultural identities Religious fundamentalism Power imbalance	Media Economic factors Political factors Geopolitical power inequities
Context of conflict: Interpersonal conflict	Independent/interdependent orientation Low/high context Indirect/direct Protecting own/other's face	Strong in-group/out-group orientation History of exclusion Lack of knowledge of others	Stereotypical/misrepresentation in media Discriminatory discourse/actions Perceived/real inequity in resource distribution
Context of conflict: Intergroup conflict	Defense of group-based face Communication style differences Conflict style differences Historically based mistrust/enmity	Group-based stereotypes Racism, religious discrimination History of conflict Defense of cultural identities Resistance to assimilation Religious fundamentalism	Systemic inequities Lack of/misrepresentation in media Historic genocide Perceived/real inequity in resource distribution
Context of conflict: International/global conflict	Language and communication style differences Value differences Facework	Ethnocentrism/prejudice In-group bias/pressure Negative identity Trauma of violence/long-standing conflict Religious fundamentalism	Differing historical accounts Geopolitical pressure/power asymmetry Oppositional metaphors/discourse

Source: Kathryn Sorrells.

friends in Southern California spending long days together getting to know each other. When Josh visited Patrice in Florida at her parents' house where she lives, he had a hard time feeling the closeness he had experienced in California. While her parents were gracious to him, her family seemed formal and structured compared to the close-knit, laid-back environment at his home. Josh's displays of affection in public made Patrice uncomfortable. And then, Josh wanted to talk about everything—whether there was a slight disagreement between them or a moment of closeness, he always wanted to express it. He wanted to deal with the issue right then and there and later say "I love you."

One day Josh met Patrice after she got off work. She was furious. In separate incidents, a customer and a coworker had treated her in demeaning ways. "It's because I'm a young, Black women. I can't believe these people. They're so racist." Josh listened to her explanation of what had happened and offered several reasons other than race that could explain what had happened. Frustrated, Patrice sat there quiet and fuming.

Four years into the relationship, as Patrice and Josh manage the conflicts that arise from their differences, two issues remain central: (1) religion, and (2) children. Josh wonders how it will be for his children if their mother is not Jewish and if he will be able to sustain a Jewish home environment. Will he be able to relate to the experiences of his children as biracial kids in a racialized U.S. society? Patrice worships at a fundamentalist Christian church in the Haitian community. While the preacher claims non-Christians are doomed to hell, Patrice doesn't think it's a big deal that Josh is Jewish.

Using the multiframe analysis introduced in the previous section, let's explore the range of intercultural communication issues confronting Patrice and Josh. Through the micro-frame, we see that the two have differing orientations to conflict and communication. While Patrice prefers a high context form of communication, Josh is more comfortable with low context communication. In conflict situations, Josh, operating from an individualistic, independent worldview, wants to "get it all out on the table," have each of them share their opinions and come up with solutions. Patrice, enculturated into a more interdependent worldview, would rather let some things go instead of making every issue a conflict by talking about it. Her approach to conflict is more indirect, where she assumes building a strong relationship between them will safeguard against threatening conflicts.

From the meso-frame, questions of race, prejudice, cultural histories, and group-based power differences come into play. According to Patrice and Josh, neither racism nor ethnocentrism play central roles in the relationship between the two of them, yet how their relationship is perceived by others in society as well as their differing experiences of race in the world are sources of conflict. When Josh finds other explanations for what Patrice experiences as discrimination and racism, Patrice feels invalidated and dismissed. Josh is certainly aware of the history of discrimination against Blacks in the United States, yet, from the perspective of a White man shielded by White privilege, he resists Patrice's interpretation of the events. Their different interpretations, informed by their standpoints and positionalities, are sometimes hard to bridge.

Religion plays an important role in both Patrice's and Josh's lives offering each a set of beliefs that guide their daily lives as well as communities of belonging with long-held cultural traditions, histories of suffering, and survival. Understanding the purpose of religion in the life of their partner has been an important step toward reconciling their religious differences. As an immigrant, church connects Patrice on a weekly basis with her Haitian heritage, sustains and deepens her cultural ties, and offers her support from her cultural community. Josh sees his Jewish faith as a way to connect on a spiritual level with all people regardless of race, religion, or creed. Separating institutional religious beliefs from their individual interpretations of their respective religions was a significant step in building tentative bridges across their differing religious orientations.

The macro-frame brings into view the role of media, discourse, economic, and political factors in intercultural conflict. Josh's concern about raising biracial children stems primarily from depictions of non-Whites in the U.S. media and popular discourse. The realities of racial prejudice and injustice in U.S. society add an extra level of care and tension to their decision-making process about marriage and children. Additionally, Patrice has to deal on a regular basis with stereotypes perpetuated in the media about Haiti. While the realities of poverty in her country of origin are disturbing, what troubles Patrice the most is the lack of information provided to U.S. audiences about the history of struggle of her country, the role the United States has played in undermining economic growth and democratic processes in Haiti, and the portrayal of Haiti as corrupt, poor, and unable to manage itself.

Macro-, meso-, and micro-framed issues intertwine in Patrice and Josh's relationship shaping a context for communication, which often leads to misunderstanding, tension, and conflict. Yet, sorting through their differences and staying in the difficult dialogues that emerge also provide opportunities to learn from each other and enrich their understanding of their cultures and the globalized world they inhabit.

CASE STUDY 2: INTERGROUP CONTEXT

Grant High School is a large, multicultural public school in the heart of the San Fernando Valley in California. Like many high schools in the United States, students from different ethnic and racial groups tend to segregate themselves from each other. In the past years, the quad in the center of the school has been divided spatially—the Armenian students congregate around the tree at the north end and Latinos/Latinas gather near the open-air lunch area. While the school has students from a wide range of different cultural backgrounds, the tensions and conflicts revolve primarily around the two groups with the largest representation: Latinos/Latinas and Armenians.

One hot day in early September during the crowded lunch period, Tina bumped into Marta causing Marta's lunch tray to spill all over her blouse. Marta, embarrassed, looked up at Tina and yelled, "What are you doing? I can't believe you did that. You did that on purpose." Tina laughed and exclaimed, "It was an accident . . . but if you don't stop yelling at me, I'm going to get my friends over here to prove it." A crowd surrounded the two girls, Armenian students backing up Tina and Latino/Latina students behind Marta each side yelling that the other was disrespecting their group. Ethnically derogatory names were hurled, food trays were used as weapons, and fists started punching whoever was in sight.

The most salient feature in the analysis of the conflict from the micro-frame is the question of face and facework, which is inseparable in this case from the meso-frame issues of cultural histories, cultural identities, and power. The two groups at the high school have drawn clear lines between in-group and out-group based on cultural identities and histories. In the conflict previously described, Armenian and Latino/Latina students defend their cultural group's face. When their collective face is threatened, each group's facework strategies are limited to dominating and denigrating the other. Each group's stereotypes and long-held prejudices toward the other feed ethnocentric attitudes of superiority of their in-group and inform their interpretations of experiences.

The two cultural groups share much in common, including their experiences as relatively recent immigrant groups in the United States, yet the uniqueness of their cultural histories is also significant. The Armenian Genocide, which began in 1915, was a systematic and organized destruction of approximately 1.5 million Armenians by the Ottoman Empire. Acknowledged as the first modern genocide, the Armenian Holocaust spurred the Armenian diaspora, where Armenians fled to destinations in Eastern Europe, the Middle East, and South America (Bournoutian, 2002). Since the 1970s, Armenian communities have grown in the United States and Canada as later generations of Armenians left the Middle East. The Armenian students at Grant High School are part of the most recent wave of Armenian immigration prompted by the fall of the former Soviet Union in the early 1990s and the economic conditions in the Republic of Armenia.

The horrific genocide defines and marks the cultural history of Armenian communities worldwide. At Grant High School, this manifests as expressions by students of intense pride in their culture and history as they learn from their community to vigilantly protect their Armenian cultural identity from external threats and from mainstream forces of assimilation. Perceived as "old world," "traditional," and "resistant to assimilation" by administrators and teachers at the school, Armenian students are taught by their families to maintain close-knit Armenian cultural bonds and friendship ties.

On the other hand, generally the Latino/Latina students at Grant High School were born in the United States into migrant families from Mexico and Central America. While these students are grouped together, officially and informally referred to as "Hispanic" at the school, most prefer to identify as Mexican, Honduran, or Salvadoran often espousing bicultural, hybrid identities that acknowledge both their family's country of origin and their U.S. cultural backgrounds. Their collective identity as "Hispanic" is less salient due to their national culture differences and the varied political and economic circumstances that propelled their family's migration to the United States. Yet, the students are targets of stereotypes and misperceptions held by some administrators and teachers that claim Hispanic students are "lazy" and "not interested in education."

Meso-frame issues are intertwined with the broader historical, political, economic, and media issues revealed through the macro-frame of analysis. Lack of official recognition of the Armenian Genocide by both the United States and Turkish governments for political and economic reasons dismisses and devalues the cultural history and struggles of Armenian communities worldwide (Payaslian, 2005). Commemorative events, scheduled each year on April 24th in Los Angeles and around the world, serve to educate the broader public about the genocide and also galvanize Armenian solidarity. The pride and protection Armenian youth at Grant High School take toward their culture today is impacted by these geopolitical dynamics. Administrators, teachers, and students are also influenced by stereotypical representations of Latinas/Latinos in movies, TV programs, and news as well as anti-immigrant rhetoric. Additionally, the historic segregation and current hostilities and violence in U.S. schools provide a backdrop that normalizes intergroup conflict.

Addressing the conflict at Grant High School requires an understanding of how different in-group/out-group perceptions and prejudices, cultural group histories, and inequitable geopolitical power relations intertwine in complicated and layered ways to shape, provoke, and sustain the intercultural conflict. The multiframe analysis draws attention to the linkages between issues highlighted by each frame that are critical for addressing the intergroup conflict.

CASE STUDY 3: INTERNATIONAL AND GLOBAL CONTEXT

Around the turn of the previous century, Jews began to immigrate to Palestine with the goal of establishing a national homeland. There were many arguments about the appropriateness and availability of this land, but early Zionists sought to establish a Jewish state on what they claimed was their ancient holy land. On the same land, however, lived Arabs with historic and family claims to the land. This resulted in a clash over ownership and issues of self-determination, statehood, and identity. There was violence between these two groups from the early 1920s with various degrees of intensity. The United Nations partitioned the land in 1947 and established two states—one Arab and one Jewish Israeli. The Palestinians rejected this partition and war broke out in 1948. Israeli Jews refer to this war as the War of Independence and claim the Arabs started it. Palestinians refer to the same war as "the disaster" and accuse the Jews of predatory territorial acquisition arguing that the United Nations had no right to partition the land in the first place. Israeli Jews and Palestinians have fought numerous wars since 1948 with Israel on one side and Arab nations on the other. The 1967 war led to additional land under Israeli control and created the conditions for Israeli occupation of territories and violent opposition by Palestinians to this occupation. The Oslo peace accords of 1993 was hailed as a breakthrough, but ended in failure. These two adversaries pose increasing obstacles and impediments to peace, including settlement expansion, terrorism, assassination, religious fanaticism, and general recalcitrance (Ellis, 2005, p. 49).

The magnitude, the long-term intractable nature, and the geopolitical dimensions of this conflict suggest a macro-frame analysis as a starting point for making sense of the conflict. One of the pivotal aspects of the Israeli–Palestinian conflict is the vastly different perceptions and interpretations held and promoted by each group regarding the historic and ongoing episodes of the conflict. Each group marks the origins, causes, and experiences of successive conflicts in vastly different ways and holds firmly to their group's perceptions, often to the exclusion of the other's. Thus, questions of representation—how the events are represented—in interpersonal interactions; in popular discourse; and in local, national, and international media are central in maintaining the oppositional metaphors, fueling the intractable nature of the conflict, and inhibiting movement toward solutions.

The previous description is a representation of the conflict. Both sides of the conflict would undoubtedly argue this representation leaves out information critical for understanding the conflict. For example, the scenario does not mention that Judea, home of the Jews in ancient times, was captured and renamed Palestine by the Romans. The scenario does not address the role of Britain, following the Balfour Declaration in 1917, in establishing Palestine as a national home for the Jews as a League of Nations mandate. Additionally, the scenario does not detail the 700,000 or more Palestinians who were displaced in the 1948 War (United Nations Relief and Works Agency, 2007); nor does it mention that the number of Palestinian refugees has grown to over 5 million with refugee camps in Gaza, the West Bank, Jordan,

Lebanon, and Syria (United Nations Relief and Works Agency for Palestine Refugees, 2014). The scenario also neglects to address the role of the United States in providing military support and funding for Israel. Clearly, a critical aspect of all conflicts and particularly ones with international and global implications is the role of representation—whether in interpersonal interactions or media—in framing the conflict, in interpreting and constructing meaning about the conflict, as well as in choices made about what information is disseminated and to whom. Additionally, the macro-frame analysis draws our attention to how the geopolitical power inequities between Palestinians, who are seen as nonstate actors and Israel, which is officially recognized as a nation-state, entails both political and economic ramifications. As nonstate perpetrators of violence, Palestinians are labeled "terrorists," while Israel's violent use of force is framed as "national defense" or "national security."

The meso-frame analysis reveals how differences in Jewish Israeli and Palestinian cultural histories and identities not only fuel the deeply entrenched conflict, but have become deeply intertwined with and dependent on the conflict. In-group biases support ethnocentric attitudes and perceptions as well as perpetuate stereotypes and lack of trust. Ellis (2005) argued that both groups hold "harmful stereotypes, mutual delegitimization, and negative identity. Their identities are rooted in a conception of the land as sacred, and supported by religion, historical narratives of persecution, and myths" (p. 49). **Negative identity** refers to group identity that is "based on being the opposite of the other, or 'not' being the other" (p. 51). The identities of Israeli Jews and Palestinians are structured in opposition to each other such that the positive identity of one entails the negative image of the other.

Intractable conflicts take place in the context of power imbalances (Coleman, 2003). The dominant group, Israeli Jews, in this case, competes with the less powerful group, Palestinians, over what constitutes violence, morality, criminal behavior, legal rights, and self-definition. As Ellis (2005) noted, these contestations are institutionalized by the dominant group in ways that further disenfranchise and victimize the nondominant group. Intractable conflicts are also characterized by groups who are interrelated geographically, politically, and economically yet have very little contact with each other, which exacerbates misinformation and stereotypes. In addition, protracted ethnopolitical

Photo 9.1 Israeli and Palestinian conflict: In this on-going intercultural conflict, whose version of the story is privileged and agreed on as true?

conflicts engender extreme emotions including humiliation, indignation, self-righteousness, and defensiveness. The trauma of violence and the concomitant emotions are long-standing and are often passed along from one generation to the next making them highly resistant to change (Coleman, 2003; Ellis, 2005).

Issues highlighted through the macro- and meso-frames are intertwined with and exacerbated by differences in cultural norms of communication and interaction between Israeli Jews and Palestinians that are made evident through a micro-frame. Greifat and Katriel (1989) identified the Arab linguistic term *musayara*, which refers to the act of accompanying one's conversational partner in dialogue. This cultural communication style, broadly shared by Arab cultures, is aimed at maintaining and promoting harmony and is often accomplished through flourishing language, use of repetition, and metaphors. The style is generally characterized as high context, indirect, rhetorically complex, and aimed at the preservation of the listener's face. Interruptions in many situations are interpreted as a lack of respect for the speaker (Greifat & Katriel, 1989). In contrast, Jewish Israeli communication style, characterized by the term *dugri,* or straight talk, is described as direct, simple, forceful, and concerned with the preservation of the speaker's face. Jewish interactional styles are described as polyvocal and fast-paced, where turn-taking is rapid and where participation by multiple speakers and interruptions are experienced as forms of bonding, not as disruptions.

Yet, in mediated dialogue sessions between Israeli Jews and Palestinians, situational factors, such as the political context of the event as well as the erosion of culturally held patterns of communication modify and mitigate cultural communication styles. Research conducted during political dialogue groups suggested that Israelis modified their communication style to allow for and listen to the perspectives of Palestinians while Palestinians tended to adopt a style that included interruptions to a degree similar to Israeli Jews, suggesting the contextual nature of communication styles (Zupnik, 2000).

As illustrated through the case studies, intercultural conflicts are compelling, contentious, and complex. The multiframe analysis enables us to see how intercultural conflicts operate on multiple levels and how each level informs the other. To navigate intercultural conflicts in the context of globalization, we need to be aware of how communication styles, orientations to conflict, and facework strategies differ across cultures. The meso-frame brings into view the role of group-based prejudices, stereotypes, cultural histories, and cultural identities that impact intercultural conflict. Intercultural conflicts are also influenced by macro-frame factors, such as media, discourse, and economic forces that are situated in the context of asymmetrical geopolitical power. The multiframe analysis brings to our attention the potential short- and long-term causes of intercultural conflicts and the conditions that escalate and entrench conflict among cultural groups. We turn now to a discussion of strategies to address intercultural conflicts in our everyday lives.

STRATEGIES FOR ADDRESSING INTERCULTURAL CONFLICT

Intercultural praxis discussed throughout the book is used here to provide strategies for addressing intercultural conflicts on interpersonal, intergroup, and international levels. Engaging in intercultural praxis in intercultural conflict situations raises our awareness, increases our critical analysis, and develops our socially responsible action. Intercultural praxis is applicable to conflicts among individuals, groups, communities, and nations. The model is intended to assist in understanding the complex intersections of cultural differences and historically situated yet changing structures and contexts of power. The goal of engaging in intercultural praxis is to develop our individual and collective critical consciousness to create a more equitable and socially just world—everyday, one action and interaction at a time.

Inquiry

One of the greatest challenges in intercultural misunderstandings and conflicts is cultivating an interest in and empathy for seeing the situation from the other person's point of view. Our tendency is to hold firm to our own position and defend it from alternative perspectives. The entry point of inquiry requires that we suspend our judgments about others, loosen our posture of defensiveness, and have a willingness to know the experiences of the other. There are risks involved as our way of viewing the situation may be challenged by hearing and acknowledging the views of others. Further, through inquiry, we may actually change our position, which if long-held and deeply intertwined with our identities can be scary.

In some conflict situations, asking questions with a sincere desire to know can be enough to shift the contentious nature of the conflict toward one of mutual understanding. In other situations, inquiry may be accomplished more effectively through careful observation of those who are culturally different from us or who are positioned differently from us. Through observation, we can begin to see the patterns of engagement that make sense from the other's perspective; the ways our approach, attitudes, or beliefs may cause friction; and how we can make adjustments to ease the misunderstanding or conflict. For example, in Josh and Patrice's situation, their differing communication and conflict styles exacerbate the tension between them. However, over time, they have both learned to balance direct inquiry and explicit expression of feelings with more implicit forms of inquiry. In the case of interethnic conflict at the high school, classroom activities and structured learning exercises provided an opening for all students, including Latino/Latina and Armenian students to gain knowledge about each others' backgrounds and recognize commonalities as well as differences (Sorrells, 2003).

Framing

As demonstrated in the case studies, it is critical to have the capacity to intentionally analyze intercultural misunderstanding and conflicts from micro-, meso-, and macro-frames as well as appreciate how issues on different levels impact each other. Conflicts between Israeli Jews and Palestinians can and do occur on a daily basis. It is important to look at the micro-level differences in communication and conflict styles. As we broaden the frame, we see how the history of conflict, cultural identities, and patterns of inequities, as well as broader relations of power affect the particular and situated intercultural conflict. As we focus in and foreground the micro-frame of intercultural communication, we need to keep the wider background frame in mind as it provides the context in which meaning about the particular is made. Also our perspectives, our views on ourselves, others, and the world around us are always and inevitably limited by frames. Our goal in engaging in intercultural praxis is to recognize the frames of reference that allow for and limit our view and experience of the world.

Positioning

In intercultural conflict situations, awareness of how and where we are positioned in relation to others in terms of socially constructed hierarchies of power is critical. Our gender, ethnicity, race, class, religion, nationality, and sexual orientation all inform the locations from which we speak, listen, act, think, and make sense of the world. Our positionality within these categories also offers and limits our access to privilege and power. Recognizing how Josh's positionality impacts his perceptions and interpretations may allow him to reevaluate his responses to Patrice and listen with greater empathy to her interpretation instead of minimizing her experiences. Awareness of his positionality enables Josh to use his position of privilege as a White male to intervene in situations where discrimination and systemic inequity occur.

Positioning as a strategy in conflict situations also directs us to attend to who can speak and who is silenced; whose actions have the power to shape and impact others; and whose actions are dismissed, unreported, and marginalized. As illustrated in the Israeli–Palestinian conflict, it is critical to investigate whose version of the story is privileged and agreed on as true, and whose knowledge is deemed unworthy, insignificant, or unnecessary.

Dialogue

Dialogue, informed by inquiry, framing, and positioning, is a central strategy for managing and negotiating intercultural conflicts. Dialogue provides the opportunity to reach across differences and creatively engage with points of view, ways of thinking, and beliefs different from our own. Yet, dialogue with people who hold perspectives, beliefs, and worldviews that are different from our own is often quite difficult. Communication scholars Sonja Foss and Cindy Griffin (1995) proposed **invitational rhetoric** as a form of communication committed to equality, recognition, and self-determination. Instead of entering or engaging in conflict situations with the intention of changing, persuading, or conquering the other, the goal of invitational rhetoric is to shift the frame of the engagement to one of invitation, cooperation, and coordination. In the initiative to address the ongoing conflict between Latino/Latina and Armenian students at Grant High School, university students were trained to facilitate dialogue sessions with students at the school, which included conversations, group activities, and role plays to reframe their differences as opportunities for learning and building upon their commonalities (Sorrells, 2003).

Additionally, the notion of cooperative argument can be a useful strategy in intercultural conflict situations. **Cooperative argument** refers to a model of argument that manages the resolutions of disagreement within a set of rules that are responsive to intercultural differences (Ellis, 2005). Shifting from an adversarial and competitive model of argument, cooperative argument seeks understanding and the formulation of solutions for groups whose livelihoods and existences are interdependent.

The participants see themselves as members of a deliberative community; that is, the process is one of ethical dialogue with a concern for relational integrity, empathy, and using the arguments and information of the other culture to make decisions built on a common framework of understanding. (Ellis, 2005, p. 60)

Reflection

Reflection is central to learning, growth, and change in all situations, yet the ability to be self-reflexive and to see oneself as a creative, flexible subject with the capacity to change is essential to effectively manage intercultural conflict. The ability to employ the strategies of framing and positioning requires that we consciously observe ourselves and critically analyze our interrelationships with others. Reflection is necessary to initiate, maintain, and sustain dialogue across bumpy, unknown, and difficult terrain of intercultural conflicts. Sometimes reflection takes place on its own. We think back over a conversation, a misunderstanding, or a conflict we had and consider how we can act and engage differently to encourage understanding and meaningful exchanges. Sometimes reflection occurs in dialogue with the person with whom we are in conflict or with a third party. At other times, we need structured environments, such as dialogue groups, conflict resolution, or formal negotiations to access, express feelings, develop empathy, and reframe conflicts in constructive ways. Reflection informs our actions. Reflection that incorporates critical analyses of micro-, meso-, and macro-frames of intercultural conflicts, that recognizes our own and others' positioning, and that engages us in genuine dialogue enables us to act in the world in meaningful, effective, and responsible ways.

Action

Intercultural praxis is not only about deepening our understanding; rather, intercultural praxis means we join our increased understanding with responsible action to make a difference in the world—to create a more socially just, equitable, and peaceful world. In conflicts, the intercultural praxis entry point of action can take the form of doing research to learn more about the background and history of the individuals or groups in conflict. It can involve speaking up and using your access to power or privilege to challenge discrimination or prejudice among friends and coworkers. It could also entail joining with others to move initiatives, policies, or practices forward that create equitable access and benefits for all in your organization, community, or state.

Action can also entail joining an intercultural coalition or activist group aimed at creating systemic change toward greater equity and justice. In the early 2000s, students on campuses across the country used sit-ins, rallies, and marches in campaigns to end the use of sweatshop labor in the $2.5 billion collegiate clothing industry. Students from over 70 universities across the country formed the Campus Antiwar Network (CAN) organizing actions, such as national demonstrations, direct aid to victims of Hurricane Katrina, referendums like the "College Not Combat" ballot measure in San Francisco, as well as collaborations with international peace organizations (Campus Antiwar Network, n.d.). Diverse undocumented immigrant youth leaders from across the United States, known as DREAMers, have been instrumental through their coalition *United We Dream* formed in 2007 in building an immigrant youth movement to promote equal access to education and pathways to citizenship for undocumented immigrant youth (United We Dream, n.d). Intercultural praxis offers us points of entry for critical, reflective thinking and acting that enable us to navigate the complex and conflictive intercultural spaces we inhabit interpersonally, communally, and globally.

SUMMARY

Conflicts among individuals and groups from different cultural, ethical, racial, religious, and national backgrounds are propelled today by greater proximity, increasing competition, and diminishing resources. Colonial histories, exploitative conditions, and magnified social and economic inequity also shape the causes and consequences of intercultural conflict. A multiframe model was presented in this chapter to analyze the complexities of intercultural conflict, to inform our understanding of how and why diverse groups engage in conflict, and to guide our awareness of the situational factors that lead to and exacerbate conflict in the global context. The model highlights the interplay between the micro-, meso-, and macro-frames that impact intercultural conflicts. Case studies of intercultural conflict from interpersonal, intergroup, and international contexts were used to illustrate the multiframe analysis. Intercultural praxis provides an approach for effective communication strategies to address and negotiate intercultural conflicts.

KEY TERMS

intercultural conflict
interdependent orientation
independent orientation
context
high context communication
low context communication
face
facework
in-groups
out-groups

cultural histories
oppositional metaphors
fundamentalism
immigration industrial complex
negative identity
musayara
dugri
invitational rhetoric
cooperative argument

DISCUSSION QUESTIONS AND ACTIVITIES

Discussion Questions

1. What is your orientation to conflict? Using the key concepts from the chapter (i.e., independent/interdependent orientation, facework, low/high context, invitational rhetoric), discuss how you are inclined to act in conflict.

2. As the world becomes more globalized and each nation more multicultural, why do we continue to witness intercultural conflicts across the world? Is conflict innate to human nature? Is conflict inherent in the process of globalization? Is conflict profitable? If so, who benefits from conflict and how?

3. What is the relationship between intercultural conflict and social justice? Why is social justice important when we address intercultural conflict?

4. Think about the most recent or difficult conflict you had with others. How did culture or cultural differences shape the conflict? How do you think intercultural praxis might help you and others address the conflict effectively?

Activities

1. Applying the Multidimensional Framework of Analysis

   a. In groups of 3 to 4 people, select an incident of intercultural conflict (interpersonal, intergroup, or international).

   b. Apply the multidimensional framework used in this chapter to analyze the micro-, meso-, and macro-levels of the conflict.

   c. Discuss how the micro-, meso-, and macro-frames interrelate with and influence each other.

2. Using Intercultural Praxis

   a. Using the intercultural conflict analyzed in Activity 1, discuss how you can use intercultural praxis to manage the conflict.

   b. Discuss specific ways in which you can engage both individually and collectively in the process of addressing intercultural conflict.

3. Different Definitions of Culture in Conflict Negotiation

   a. In groups of 2 to 3 people, create a list of how intercultural conflict can be understood and addressed differently through various definitions of "culture" discussed in Chapter 1.

   b. In your list, discuss how culture as (1) shared meaning, (2) contested meaning, and (3) a resource shape the ways we approach and manage intercultural conflict.

   c. Finally, discuss in your group the role of culture in producing and/or resolving conflict.

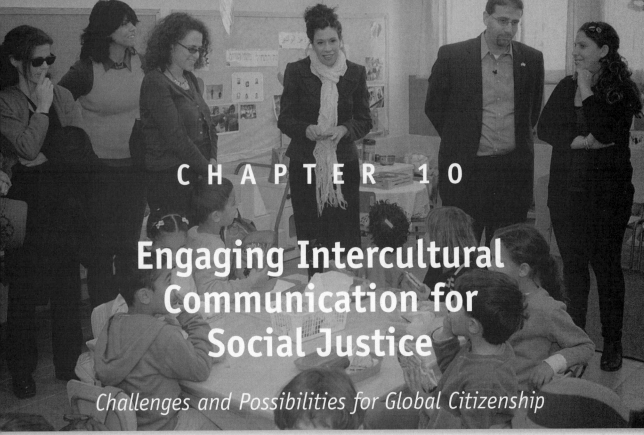

CHAPTER 10

Engaging Intercultural Communication for Social Justice

Challenges and Possibilities for Global Citizenship

Flickr.com/U.S. Embassy Tel Aviv

The Hagar School in Be'er-Sheva, Israel, is a bilingual, multicultural school where Arab and Jewish children join together to learn and to create a peaceful and shared future. The association, Hagar: Jewish-Arab Education for Equality, *founded the school as a catalyst for social change.*

Learning Objectives

1. Describe the capacities necessary for global citizenship today.

2. Engage intercultural praxis as a model for intercultural competence.

3. Describe how we can transform apathy into empowerment for social change.

4. Explain how intercultural alliances can challenge inequities and create a more equitable, socially just, and peaceful world.

We began our conversation about intercultural communication in this book by acknowledging the increasing interconnectedness and interdependence of the nearly 7 billion people who call planet Earth "home." From the start of our dialogue through this concluding chapter, the emphasis has been on "we," the 7 billion people of the world. As noted throughout, the accelerated interrelationship among people from diverse cultures, fueled by advances in communication and transportation technologies, and forged through neoliberal economic and political policies, has dramatically impacted intercultural communication in the context of globalization offering both challenges and possibilities.

The challenges are many. Neoliberal economic and political polices have reconstituted colonial and imperial relations of power. Inequities in and across countries and cultures have magnified. Interethnic and interracial tensions and conflicts have escalated. Poverty and hunger have increased with devastating impact on human health. The environmental health of our planet is in peril (Robbins, 2014). These are real challenges affecting each of us to varying degrees in observable and hidden ways.

Possibilities, in the context of globalization, also abound. Potential for democratization and the spread of human rights is at hand (Armaline, Glasberg, & Purkayastha, 2011). We need only look to the "people-powered" movements across Latin America and the Middle East in the last 10 years for evidence of this. Knowledge to address and ensure the basic human needs of food, shelter, health, education, and cultural maintenance for all 7 billion people is obtainable. Consciousness of a world where benefits are shared broadly rather than funneled for the advantage of an elite few is rising. Networks to build coalitions that resist injustice and establish new terms of engagement are available (Collier, 2014; George, 2004). Many opportunities to take action not only for ourselves, but socially responsible action in collaboration with others are available (Boggs, 2011). The knowledge, attitudes, and skills learned by studying intercultural communication and engaging in intercultural praxis prepare us to build connections, alliances, and coalitions. Thus, we must join our knowledge, capacities, and skills with intention and commitment to manifest a more equitable and socially just world.

In a world saturated by media spectacles, where scenes of violence, corruption, and human and natural devastation replay 24/7, it is easy to become apathetic and think of social justice as unrealistic and idealistic. It is tempting to let indifference or despair overcome us when we are inundated by daily demands and struggle in a climate of reduced resources and limited access. We may think: What can one person do? There've always been the "haves" and the "have-nots"; I just have to look out for myself; Things are never going to change; or It's not my problem. Yet, the people throughout history and today who are the most actively involved in organizing for change, challenging injustice, and seeking alternatives for a more equitable world are the ones who are most hopeful.

As we culminate our exploration together, this chapter focuses on applying and embodying our intercultural knowledge, skills, and attitudes to create a more equitable, just, and peaceful world. **Social justice**, as defined, illustrated, and used throughout the book, is both a goal and process. The overarching goal of social justice, as incorporated in our daily lives, in our workplaces, our homes, communities, organizations, nations and globally, is equal access to, participation in, and distribution of opportunities and resources among all members and groups to meet their needs. While the word "social" is highlighted, the term "social justice" implies economic, political, and cultural, as well as social dimensions of human interaction. Social justice includes a vision of resource distribution where social actors experience agency with and responsibility for others. The process of moving toward social justice is as important as the goal. Processes where social actors engage with democratic, participatory, and inclusive practices and values that uphold our individual and collective capacities and agency to create change are central to social justice (Adams, Bell, & Griffin, 2007).

We begin this chapter by identifying the capacities necessary for global citizenship in the 21st century. The model of intercultural praxis introduced and developed throughout the book is used here as the basis for our discussion of intercultural competence. Following this, personal testimonies from people who are active in community-based advocacy and international activism illustrate how we can move from apathy to empowerment as we engage in intercultural praxis. We then turn our attention to a case study to learn how intercultural alliances in the context of globalization are sites where injustice is challenged and responsible action creates possibilities for a more equitable, just, and peaceful world. The chapter concludes with a review of four principles that have provided the foundation for engaging in intercultural communication for social justice throughout the book.

BECOMING GLOBAL CITIZENS IN THE 21ST CENTURY

Daisaku Ikeda, Buddhist leader, educator, peace activist, and founder of the Boston Research Center for the 21st Century, has identified three **qualities of global citizens**. First, he proposed that wisdom is necessary. Specifically, Ikeda (2005) referred to the wisdom to perceive the interconnectedness of all life. As shown throughout this book, the slow economic recovery from the 2008 crisis; political unrest in Ukraine, Thailand, Hong Kong, and the Middle East; and the fallout from natural disasters in the Philippines and Japan do indeed impact our lives in the United States. At the macro-level, our foreign policies and economic strategies are affected. Yet, events and actions on the global stage also influence the micro-level. Experts from the Carnegie Endowment for International Peace noted that "the annexation of Crimea by Russia and possible incursions into eastern Ukraine in the future could reshape the geopolitical map of Europe and derail cooperation between Moscow and the West for years to come" (Rumer, Weiss, Speck, Khatib, Perkovich, & Paal, 2014). The implications go far beyond Europe affecting the United States as Europe's central security partner, impacting international efforts to address the war in Syria, and exposing the economic interdependence around the globe.

The second quality of a global citizen is courage—"the courage to respect one another's differences and use them as impetus to creative living, rather than rejecting or excluding others on the basis of culture, nationality and race" (Ikeda, 2005, p. x). The third quality is compassion, which "means being a true friend who hears the anguished cries of others, striving with them to overcome and surmount suffering" (Ikeda, 2005 p. x). Compassion is often associated with empathy. **Empathy** refers to the ability to share the pain of others and the capacity to know the emotional experience of others from within their frame of reference.

Commonly, the notion of citizenship has been used to refer to membership in and identity associated with a nation-state. For example, you may identify yourself as a U.S. citizen or a citizen of Sweden, Brazil, or Turkey. People recognized as citizens are seen as having specific rights, duties, responsibilities, and privileges that go along with citizenship. Citizenship in certain nations, namely, wealthy First World nations, confers benefits and privileges of international mobility that are denied many in the global context. The notion of national "citizenship" is problematic given the racialized, classist, and heteronormative policies that prescribe inclusion and exclusion in nation-states.

Today, we live in a world where interactions, commerce, communication networks, media representations, and conflicts are increasingly global. Yet, no single global government exits to which we can swear allegiance, call on for protection, or access for defense of rights (Noddings, 2005). Given this, Peggy McIntosh (2005) argued for a redefinition of the notion of "citizenship" in the context of globalization. She suggested that conceiving of and enacting global citizenship requires a sense of belonging in the world that goes beyond loyalty, responsibility, and protection based on one's city, region, or nation. "Within this vast world, the marks of a global citizenship would need to include affection, respect, care, curiosity, and concern for the well-being of all living beings" (McIntosh, 2005, p. 23).

Capacities for Global Citizenship

McIntosh (2005) proposed a set of capacities of mind, heart, body, and soul that reimagine citizenship based on "needs" rather than "rights." **Capacities for global citizenship** are capacities that reimagine citizenship based on human needs rather than rights. The capacities of mind she outlined for global citizenship provide a foundation for intercultural competence for the 21st century:

1. The ability to observe one's self and the world around one

2. The ability to make comparisons and contrasts between these worlds

3. The ability to see "plurally" as a result

4. The ability to understand that both "reality" and language come in versions

5. The ability to see power relations and understand them systemically

6. The ability to balance awareness of one's own realities with the realities of others (p. 23)

Understanding the world as complex, multifaceted, and plural is critical for global citizenship in the 21st century. Having the capacity to see the interrelationship between various perspectives; to validate multiple perspectives, realities, and experiences; and to see how these perspectives are shaped by relations of power are all necessary capacities for effective global citizenship.

McIntosh (2005) identified the following capacities of the heart that are essential for global citizenship:

1. The ability to respect and delve into one's own feelings

2. The awareness of others' feelings and the ability to validate others' feelings

3. The ability to experience a mixture of conflicting feelings without a loss of integrity

4. The ability to experience affective worlds plurally while keeping one's core orientation

5. The capacity to wish competing parties well

6. The ability to understand how the "politics of location" affects one's own and others' positions and power in the world

7. The ability to balance being heartfelt with the knowledge of how culture is embedded in ourselves and others (p. 23)

In intercultural interactions, misunderstandings, and conflicts, we have a tendency to allow our own feelings and perceptions to eclipse the emotional experiences of others. Awareness of the feelings of others as well as our own is critical. Having the capacities to hold and validate both—a plurality of affective worlds—is essential. Poet and essayist Terry Tempest Williams (2005) noted the following:

> The human heart is the first home of democracy. It is where we embrace our questions. Can we be equitable? Can we be generous? Can we listen with our whole being, not just our mind, and offer our attention rather than our opinion? And do we have enough resolve in our heart to act courageously, relentlessly, without giving up, ever—trusting our fellow citizens to join us in a determined pursuit of a living democracy? The heart is the house of empathy, whose door opens when we receive the pain of others. This is where bravery lives, where we'll find our mettle to give and receive, to love and be loved, to stand in the center of uncertainty with strength, not fear, understanding this is all there is. The heart is the path to wisdom because it dares to be vulnerable in the presence of power. (p. 39)

Additionally, "the politics of location," as used by McIntosh and discussed throughout the book as "positionality" and "positioning," refers to our awareness of how we are positioned or "located" differently in relation to others within systems of power. Our positionality as individuals and members of socially constructed groups affords and limits our access to power, privilege, and resources. Awareness of the "politics of location" provides insight into who is advantaged and privileged within interlocking systems and who is disadvantaged or targeted systemically.

Interestingly, McIntosh (2005) noted that people who have a great deal of formal education often manifest weaker capacities of the heart than those who have less education. In strengthening the abilities to compete successfully in the competitive world of capitalism, have we lost our capacities for emotional connection, empathy, and compassion? McIntosh (2005) coupled the capacities of the mind and heart with those of the soul and body. The capacities of the body and soul include respect for our own and others' physical needs and the pursuit of nondestructive ways to preserve and enhance all people physically and spiritually. Finally, the capacities of the global citizenship include engaging rather than withdrawing from tensions, conflicts, and contestations. Global citizens serve the greater good by acting to alleviate both danger and suffering.

The capacities previously outlined are often gendered as "feminine" and thus are devalued, diminished, and seen as "weak" and insignificant in societies infused with "masculine" values. McIntosh (2005) advocated a shift in paradigm from "human rights," invented by 18th-century European thinkers, to "human needs," which are empirically verifiable and universal.

> Water, food, clothing, shelter, and meaningful connection with other human beings are basic needs without whose fulfillment we die. The ethos of global citizenship, I believe, must start with providing, and caring about providing, these basic human necessities and the protections for sustaining ecosystems that humans depend upon. (McIntosh, 2005, p. 26)

Intercultural Competence

Intercultural competency refers to the knowledge, attitudes, and skills needed to engage effectively in intercultural situations. The model of intercultural praxis presented throughout the book provides a blueprint for developing intercultural competencies for global citizenship in the 21st century. As described along our journey, intercultural praxis is a way of being in the world that joins critical, reflective, and engaged analysis with informed action for socially responsible action and global justice. All moments in our day provide opportunities to practice and develop our communication competence by engaging in intercultural praxis. The competencies discussed here elaborate on the points of entry for intercultural praxis.

Inquiry, as an intercultural competency for global citizenship, is characterized by an "interrogative" mode of being in the world (Gadamer, 1989; Heidegger, 1962). The interrogative mode both challenges and complements the received Western tradition of advancing statements or assertions as truth claims. Curious inquiry about those who are different from ourselves leads us to engage with others, learn about how they are both different from and similar to ourselves, and recognize, as McIntosh (2005) proposed, the plurality of perceptions, experiences, and feelings among ourselves and others.

As an intercultural competency, inquiry requires motivation to know about others and ourselves. Often, it is easier to stay with what is comfortable and familiar instead of taking risks to learn about others. Seemingly, it takes much less effort to hold on to our judgments about others and take refuge in old stereotypes rather than suspend judgments and question our preconceived ideas of those who are different from us. On the surface, it seems much less painful and disruptive just to stick with our received assumptions and perceptions about the world than being receptive to challenging and changing the way we think, feel, see, and act in the world. Frequently, people who are in dominant groups—for example, Whites, men, heterosexuals, people in middle and upper classes, and Christians in the United States—do not feel the need or incentive to step outside their comfort zones. Today, the rapid and increasing movement of people; demographic shifts in neighborhoods, schools, and workplaces; as well as local and international events can and do prod people from their comfort zones. However, inquiry, as an intercultural competence for the 21st century, is not only a reactive capacity; inquiry means that individuals and groups are *motivated* and take the initiative to engage with people who are different from themselves, recognizing both the challenges and benefits of intercultural interactions, relationships, and alliances.

Framing as an intercultural competence entails an awareness that our perspectives, our views on ourselves, others, and the world around us are always and inevitably enabled and constrained by frames. We see things through multiple frames or lenses—individual, cultural, regional, and national—that necessarily include some things and exclude others. Not only does this process of "highlighting" and "hiding" impact our everyday perceptions of the world, but our frames also represent and advance certain dominant or oppositional interests. Thus, frames serve political ends as well as sense-making functions.

As demonstrated in previous chapters, framing also means we have the competency to shift among micro-, meso-, and macro-frames of perception and analysis. Shifting frames, we are able to map out the ways that particular and situated intercultural interactions, misunderstandings, or conflicts are positioned and contextualized within interpersonal, local, and national as well as broader geopolitical and global relations of power. The flexibility to shift perspectives between the particular, situated dimensions of intercultural communication and the broader, global dimensions while maintaining awareness of multiple frames is an important intercultural competence for global citizenship.

Positioning, as an intercultural competence for the 21st century, entails understanding how we are positioned in relation to others. As noted throughout the book, the world in which we live is stratified by socially constructed categories based on culture, race, class, gender, nationality, religion, age, and physical abilities, among others. These categories not only serve to divide and group us; categories of difference also position us socially, politically, and materially in relation to each other and to hierarchal configurations of power. Awareness of positioning as an intercultural competence not only draws attention to the material and symbolic consequences of our differing positionalities, but also requires us to use our access to power, privilege, and resources to challenge inequitable systems that disproportionately advantage some and disadvantage others.

Additionally, positioning, as an intercultural competence, reminds us to investigate who can speak and who is silenced in any given situation. It is critical to be cognizant of whose communication styles, both verbal and nonverbal communication, and whose behaviors are seen as "normal" as well as how communication is used to marginalize and exclude. We need to examine whose actions are dismissed or criminalized and who are in positions of power to make decisions. Attending to positioning as a competency for intercultural communication reveals the relationship among positionality, power, and what we regard as "knowledge." Instead of accepting what is presented to us as "true" in the media, by government leaders, teachers, parents, or friends, positioning requires that we ask what interests are served by a particular version of a situation, event, or crisis. We also ask who benefits if we believe and act in accordance with a particular version of "truth."

Dialogue, as an intercultural competence, may seem easy. However, as conceptualized here, dialogue entails bringing the competencies of inquiry, framing, and positioning to bear on our conversations, interactions, and engagements with others. Dialogue in intercultural interactions inevitably requires the ability to stretch ourselves; to extend into unknown territory; and to stay in conversation even when it is difficult, painful, and challenging. This is no easy task. Cultural differences as well as differences in power and positionality in intercultural interactions require us to imagine, experience, and engage creatively with points of view; ways of thinking, being, and doing; and beliefs different from our own while accepting that we may not fully understand or come to common agreement. Intercultural dialogue—from initial encounters to the development of intercultural friendships to resolving intercultural conflicts—requires an ability to deal with ambiguity. **Managing ambiguity** refers to an individual's or group's ability to handle the uncertainty, anxiety, and tension that arises from the unknown in intercultural situations.

Communication scholar Sara DeTurk (2006) argued that structured dialogue among individuals from diverse cultures and positionalities can facilitate intercultural alliances as perspective-taking personal agency and responsibility develop among people. Additionally, when individuals are exposed to muted and silenced voices, dialogue can diminish intercultural conflict.

Reflection, as an aspect of intercultural competence, is central to each of the intercultural competencies already addressed. To engage in curious inquiry, one must be able to reflect on oneself as a subject—a thinking, learning, and acting subject. Self-reflection allows for awareness and knowledge of self to develop. **Self-awareness** in intercultural communication refers to an awareness or consciousness of oneself as a cultural being, whose beliefs, assumptions, attitudes, values, and behaviors are contoured by culture. Self-awareness gained through reflection allows one to critically analyze one's positionality and interrelationship with others, which are essential for the competencies of positioning, framing, and dialogue. Critical self-awareness gained through reflection is important as we initiate, maintain, and sustain dialogue across the new and often difficult intercultural terrain of the 21st century.

As Paulo Freire (1998) observed, reflection can itself serve political functions. Through reflection, we can intervene in uninformed actions that may otherwise be normalized as "the way things are" and "the way things must be." By disengaging from the taken-for-granted and the nonreflexive flow of everyday actions, knowledge systems, and value commitments, the act of reflection allows us to reposition and reframe what may well be oppressive conditions or relations of power (Sorrells & Nakagawa, 2008).

Action, as an intercultural competence, joins analysis and reflection. Having the competence to deepen our understanding of ourselves, others, and the world in which we live is critical; however, as we strive toward global citizenship in the 21st century, we must actualize and manifest our increased understanding through responsible and liberatory action that makes a difference in the world. Each of us takes actions every day both individually and collectively that can bring about change toward a more just and equitable world. Our actions and decisions in educational, work, and relational contexts provide opportunities for informed engagement and critical intervention. In a capitalist society, our consumer choices about what media we view, how we entertain ourselves, and what we purchase and consume are all actions that can and do impact the world we live in. When we recognize our complicity in furthering inequities, we have the opportunity to confront ourselves and others about the choices we make through our consumer actions. We can also join others to organize and take collective action. Everyday actions informed by the intercultural competencies of inquiry, framing, positioning, dialogue, and reflection can be catalysts for actions that engage and produce social justice and global transformation.

Developing the intercultural competencies outlined here enable us to use our multi-faceted identity positions and shifting access to privilege and power to identify allies, build solidarity, imagine alternatives, and intervene in struggles for social responsibility and social justice. One of the founding theorists of critical pedagogy, Henry Giroux (2004) noted:

> As a critical practice, pedagogy's role lies not only in changing how people think about themselves and their relationship to others and the world, but in energizing students and others to engage in those struggles that further possibilities for living in a more just society. (pp. 63–64)

In her book *Another World Is Possible If* . . . , scholar and activist Susan George (2004) asserted the following:

> My answer is that another world is indeed possible—but only when the greatest possible number of people with many backgrounds, viewpoints and skills join together to make it happen. Things change when enough people insist on it and work for it. No one should be left out and feel they can not contribute. No one who wants to help build another world should, for lack of knowledge or connections, remain on the sideline. (pp. xii–xiii)

Too often, people in positions of greater social, economic, and political power develop visions and actions with the intent of "helping" disenfranchised groups. Yet, if the voices, perspectives, needs, and experiences of marginalized groups are not at the table, the process and outcome of the effort repeat and reinforce rather than rectify injustices. The involvement of multiple and diverse points of view and social actors with different positionalities is critical to envision and enact another world, a more socially just world.

"HOPE IN THE DARK": FROM APATHY TO EMPOWERMENT

News of current events and forecasts of the future often depict dark realities and project dire prospects. In her book titled *Hope in the Dark: Untold Histories, Wild Possibilities*, activist and cultural historian Rebecca Solnit (2004) noted that few people recognize the radically transformed world in which we live. Undoubtedly, the world has been changed by the devastating consequences of global capital and global warming. Yet, what often goes unnoticed is the ways in which our world has also been altered "by dreams of freedom and justice—and transformed by things we could not have dreamed of" (Solnit, 2004, p. 2). Mainstream media frequently focus on violence, crises, and disasters creating spectacles that serve to distract or entertain rather than inform. In an effort to ferret out the untold side of the stories of conventional outlets, alternative media often focus on misrepresentations and distortions in the mainstream media revealing even deeper realities and consequences of devastation. Both sets of stories are incomplete. What stories are missing? What accounts of the current realities and everyday experiences of the 7 billion people on planet Earth are left out?

The stories of students, teachers, and workers who decide to take action in ways that work toward collective social and economic good are often missing. The reports of consumers who change their patterns of consumption to challenge their complicity with practices that exploit and dehumanize others are passed over. The accounts of soldiers, corporate managers, and citizens who refuse the use of violence to force others' submission, who challenge systems that benefit a few and abuse the less powerful, and who take stands against social injustice are rarely told.

Intercultural Praxis
Communication for Social Justice

Reverend James M. Lawson Jr., a close associate of Dr. Martin Luther King Jr. and leading architect of the civil rights movement, worked closely with the California State University, Northridge campus community on the *Civil Discourse and Social Change Initiative* from 2010 to 2015. Now in his 80s, Reverend Lawson has devoted his life to nonviolent social change, working to dismantle racism and sexism and gain living wages for workers and equal rights for lesbian, gay, bisexual, and transgender (LGBT) communities. Informed by the philosophy of nonviolence practiced by Mahatma Gandhi, Reverend Lawson has trained students and activists in the United States and around the world on strategies for nonviolent direct action. Nonviolence does not mean passivism. Rather, the 20th century concept of nonviolence refers to the use of people power for political action. Nonviolent direct action means engendering another view of power—an alternative to violent, destructive power—where people power is used to create equity and justice. History books often focus on wars and bloody revolutions, yet the 20th century provides ample evidence of the extraordinary power of nonviolence to overcome colonial rule, the suppression of human rights, and dictatorial control. In the book *A Force More Powerful*, Ackerman and DuVall (2001) documented history altering reforms created through nonviolent struggle in Russia, Denmark, India, the United States, Poland, and Chile to name only a few. The revolution in Egypt in 2011; United We Dream, the DREAM student movement promoting equal access to education for undocumented immigrant youth; and the nonviolent groups organized across the United States to challenge police brutality and the militarization of the police as well as mass incarceration of people of color are recent examples of the power of nonviolent direct action.

In the context of globalization, our narratives of intercultural alliances for social change—small and big—need to be told. We need to hear the stories of how our world has been transformed by dreams, hopes, and actions for social justice and peace. Solnit (2004) commented on the role of hope on the path to empowerment and social change:

> Causes and effects assume history marches forward, but history is not an army. It is a crab scuttling sideways, a drip of soft water wearing away stone, an earthquake breaking centuries of tension. Sometimes one person inspires a movement, or her

words do decades later; sometimes a few passionate people change the world; sometimes those millions are stirred by the same outrage or the same ideal and change comes upon us like a change of weather. All that these transformations have in common is that they begin in the imagination, in hope. To hope is to gamble. It's to bet on the future, on your desires, on the possibility that an open heart and uncertainty is better than gloom and safety. To hope is dangerous and yet, it is the opposite of fear, for to live is to risk. (p. 4)

"Hope"—as envisioned by Solnit—is not blind hope. Rather, hope is a belief in a way forward, a belief in finding a door to walk through. If no door exists, then hope is the possibility of creating a new one. Despair is easier, safer, more predictable, and less demanding. Hope requires risk in uncertain times and the courage to act against unpredictable odds.

Drawing from various sources, **intercultural activism** is defined here as engagement in actions that create a democratic world where power is shared; diversity is protected and valued as a resource; and where discrimination, domination, and oppression based on race, ethnicity, class, sexual orientation, religion, and nationality are challenged (Broome, Carey, De La Garza, Martin, & Morris, 2005; Solnit, 2004). Intercultural activism can take many forms, including protests, boycotts, canvassing, sit-ins, teach-ins, and street theater. Intercultural activism can also take the form of intervening through consciousness-raising in classrooms, churches, and at family gatherings as well as in emergent opportunities in informal settings—where pressure is exercised "on the fault lines of a network of power" (Yep, 2008, p. 196).

In the following pages, the narratives of individuals who have the wisdom to see their interconnectedness with others, the courage to respect and use cultural differences as resources, and the compassion to feel the pain and suffering of others are told. Through engagement in intercultural activism, people move from apathy and fear to empowerment and hope.

Another World Is Possible: Student to Student Empowerment for Change

In Chapter 9, we analyzed the intergroup conflict at Grant High School in Los Angeles, California, in a case study. Narratives and reflections from Communicating Common Ground, a nationally sponsored project initiated to address the conflicts at Grant High School, are drawn on here to illustrate how university students developed and used their intercultural competencies to intervene in intercultural conflict (Sorrells, 2003). By the late 1990s, relations between Latino/Latina and Armenian students had worsened at Grant High School to the point where annual riots were a tradition at the school (Sauerwein, 2000). In an effort to break the cycle of violence, students in intercultural communication courses were brought into the high school over a period of 5 years to work with 9th and 10th graders to address the escalating tensions. Many university students reported that facilitating dialogue groups, community building activities, and conflict resolution sessions across ethnic and racial groups at Grant High School was the most powerful learning experience of their educational careers. By creating a cycle of empowerment—student to student—the tradition of violence was challenged and changed. Here are a few student accounts of the experience:

Teresa Ramos: What I learned at Grant High School will stay with me throughout my life. Not only have my experiences helped me to grow as an individual, I think we helped the high school students grow. Despite the negativity from the racial tension, I think the time we spent with the students has opened their eyes to exactly how powerful they really are. At the end of the sessions, I felt as if we had made a difference. I did not expect to make an impact on these students. I truly believe that [Grant students] do realize there are alternatives to racial tension . . . they acknowledge that another way—a way without violence—is possible.

Sachi Sekimoto: The visit to Grant High School started with excitement, nervousness, and surprise since it was my first time to visit a high school in the United States. From the beginning, the oppressive atmosphere of the school intimidated me; the school buildings surrounded by ugly fences, security guards at the entrance and the schoolyard where invisible lines separated [Latino/Latina] and Armenian students. As we walked around campus, the students stared at us with skeptical eyes that were by no means eyes of curiosity. Their eyes reminded me of my race as Asian—not a source of pride or privilege, but as a source of fear and racial hatred. . . . As the weeks passed, it became such an enjoyable and rewarding experience to visit Grant High School and work with the students. When I look at each student, they are not racist. It is the system of racism in the school and the communication produced by fear and power struggles that make them stereotype and hate people of other races. The only way to break the system is through interaction and communication with others. It is so rewarding to see students engaging in the sessions and learning new things. Being about to assist their learning and learn myself was an empowering experience.

Justin Weiss: During one of the group sessions, one of the high school students, Charlotte, stated that the teachers are against the students and "we can't do anything to change it." I learned that these students may not be getting the tools at home or school that they need so maybe that's why their initial thought is that they can't change anything. But, by helping the students understand that they are meaningful and by reinforcing their sense of agency through encouragement and positive examples, they were able to see that they could make a change. I noticed that the high school students really do want to make a change. I also realized and understand that there is power in numbers and by sending a clear message that change starts with "You," it can spread to others like a ripple and multiply. One person who believes in their abilities will turn into two people who believe change is possible, which will become four people, then ten and then one hundred people. And before you know it, there will be a large and significant representation of people who believe in their abilities to create positive change.

The narratives point to the powerful experiences of both university and high school students who were involved in the Communicating Common Ground project. While initially skeptical and hesitant, their willingness to engage in intercultural praxis and use the competencies of curious inquiry, framing, positioning, dialogue, reflection, and action enabled them to serve as role models, teaching the benefits and challenges of intercultural communication and intercultural activism to the high school students. The narratives illustrate how the university students used their knowledge, skills, and attitudes—their intercultural competencies—to empower the high school students and in the process were empowered themselves.

Another World Is Possible: Individual and Collective Action for Change

Photo 10.1   Multicultural identity collage created by students at Grant High School, Los Angeles

The brief stories included next reveal how individual actions and collective alliances can make a difference in creating a more equitable and just world. Acting in alignment with beliefs in social justice and struggling to overcome historically embedded divisions, the narrative provides examples of hope in the dark and the realization that another world is possible, as George (2004) claimed, if people from diverse backgrounds join together and insist on change.

Tam Tran and Cinthya Felix grew up in undocumented immigrant families in Los Angeles. The two UCLA students became close friends and nationally recognized leaders in the movement to pass the Development, Relief, and Education for Alien Minors (DREAM) act. "The movement to pass the DREAM Act arose in the hearts and minds of thousands of young immigrants who claim America as their home; the movement has created powerful bonds among these young activists who are assuming leadership roles and shaping the nation's future" (Wong & Ramos, 2012, p. 3). Tam was born into a Vietnamese family in Germany, refugees of the Vietnam War, and then immigrated with her family to the United States when she was six. Refused asylum in the United States, Tam was Vietnamese, but had never been to Vietnam and did not have citizenship in Vietnam, Germany, or the United States. She was not only undocumented, she was stateless.

Cinthya Felix was born and lived in Sinaloa, Mexico, until her family moved to the United States out of economic necessity when she was fifteen. Cinthya attended high school in East Los Angeles and was an excellent student and basketball player. She worked hard, saved her money and bought a car, and yet like so many other undocumented youth, was unable to get a drivers license in California. Cinthya organized a trip to Washington State with other undocumented students where it is easier for immigrants to obtain a drivers license, and her friend Tam made the film, *The Seattle Underground Railroad,* documenting the experience (Wong & Ramos, 2012). While often stereotyped and misrepresented as the silent minority, Asian Americans like Tam have spoken out in

Photo 10.2   DREAM students stand in solidarity for education for all.

words, films, and protest on undocumented student issues. "From her own family's refugee experience, she [Tam] understood that silence was not an inherent Asian characteristic, but rather a learned practice, conditioned by larger social, historical, and political contexts" (Chen & Buenavista, 2012, p. 47). Tragically, while on the east coast pursuing graduate degrees, Cinthya and Tam were killed in a car accident.

Approximately 2 million of the 11 million undocumented people in the United States are minors who had no input into the decision to come to the United States, and yet they face the consequences of a failed immigration system daily. The goal of the DREAM act is to provide a pathway to legal status for young people through the completion of two years of higher education, or through service to the U.S. military.

> Dream activists like Tam and Cinthya became advocates for their own legal status as part of the broader fight for immigration reform. The rise in visibility of such activists challenged the pejorative labels of "illegal" and "law-breaking" frequently used in congressional and media debates on immigration. Tam and Cinthya and others like them showed American a different, more accurate image of undocumented youth that exemplified all that we value and hope for in our children: leadership, courage, articulateness, civic-minded commitment, and profession skills. They epitomized the motto of the DREAM Act movement: Undocumented and Unafraid. Breaking the habit of fear and anonymity by sharing their stories, they advanced a powerful movement for social justice. (Wong & Ramos, 2012, p. 4)

Rose Kabute was raised in a Ugandan refugee camp after her parents fled the conflict between Hutus and Tutsis in Rwanda. She joined an opposition movement and army, the Rwandan Patriotic Front; served as mayor of a city in Rwanda; and from 2003 to 2010 served as an advisor to government leaders, including President Paul Kagame. She was awarded The Rwandan National Liberation Medal and the Campaign against Genocide Medal for contributions to the liberation of her country (Institute of Inclusive Security, 2014). In an effort to bridge the conflict between Hutus and Tutsis after the massive genocide that occurred in the mid-1990s, the Rwandan government set up a Unity and Reconciliation Commission so that members of both groups could learn about each other as well and the perspectives and experiences of the other group. With this model in mind and the goal of addressing the ongoing conflict between Rwanda and the Congo, a group of women from both countries attended conflict resolution training in the United States in 2000. Here are Kabute's (2005) words about the process:

> In the beginning we listened to each other with a mediator. Later, we learned how to listen on our own. We also learned that each one of us had a point. We were already in a better place. And we tried to figure out a solution together: they couldn't arrest the militia members in the Congo, but they could lobby the Congolese government to stop supporting them. And we could lobby the Rwandan government to pull out of their territory. When we went back home, I was able to talk to my leaders about what Congolese and Rwandan women, together, thought might work. Some people think it is strange that I work for peace, because I am in

the army. But others are glad. They say to me, "You waged war and now you are waging peace!" I know how terrible wars can be. That's why I want to leave behind a safer world for our children. (p. 40)

In her book, *Community Engagement and Intercultural Praxis: Dancing With Difference in Diverse Contexts*, communication scholar Mary Jane Collier (2014) featured a case study based on research conducted with facilitators who work toward conflict resolution and peacebuilding in Northern Ireland. Violent conflict in Northern Ireland has roots in a long history. Formerly a colony of the United Kingdom, the Irish War of Independence or the Anglo-Irish War, fueled primarily by the Catholic majority in Ireland, was fought between 1919 and 1921. The island was partitioned in 1922 as the Protestant majority in the northern part of Ireland sought to preserve its economic, cultural, and national interests by separating from the southern part. The southern part with a Catholic majority favored independence from the United Kingdom; the northern part, primarily Protestant, did not. The Catholic minority in Northern Ireland supported a unified independent Ireland. The partition of Ireland established the terrain in Northern Ireland for on-going political and ethno-cultural conflict, including what is known as the "Troubles," starting in the late 1960s and officially ending in 1998 with the Belfast "Good Friday" Agreement—even though sporadic violence still occurs.

While the Agreement "created the political foundation for sustainable peaceful relations between the two major communities in Northern Ireland," a voluntary sector emerged focusing on the social needs of people and intergroup relations, which were not addressed through formal political structures (Collier, 2014, p. 64). Today, Northern Ireland is increasingly diverse as immigrant populations are drawn by a strengthening economy. Racism and other forms of discrimination directed at ethnic minority groups now compound the challenges of long-standing political and religious differences. Drawing on a long history of community and peace building organizations, a "new generation" of facilitators has emerged with a commitment "to the potential of community engagement processes, such as intergroup dialogue to develop more inclusive, equitable, and just relations (Collier, 2014, p. 67). A "new generation" facilitator interviewed in the study noted:

> The facilitation needs from the last generation, they were quickly and easily identified. With the conflict here one of the main things that needed facilitation was the bilateral approach to dialogue, promoting understanding, looking at the issues in a safe environment. . . Facilitation has become inherently so much a part of the process these days. . . . It's very much about trying to build the capacity of people . . . promoting understanding on a variety of issues . . . creating the opportunity for people, experiences which they might not otherwise get. It's about creating new opportunities for people to meet someone from a different culture, whether that's someone from a different ethnic culture or from the inherently traditional Catholic or Protestant cultural communities here. (p. 73)

Each story and case illustrates the potential of intercultural activism—collaborative actions taken by individuals and groups across cultural, racial, and national lines—to challenge and dismantle systems of domination and discrimination, to build relationships that respect and use diversity, and to create a more democratic and equitable world.

INTERCULTURAL ALLIANCES FOR SOCIAL JUSTICE

Intercultural alliances are increasingly necessary and frequent in the context of globalization. As discussed in Chapter 5, intercultural alliances are sites where cultural differences, positionalities, and issues of power and privilege are negotiated, translated, and potentially transformed. Intercultural alliances in interpersonal relationships and political organizing play critical roles in improving intercultural communication and challenging prejudices and stereotypes. Importantly, alliances that form and sustain among groups across ethnic, racial, cultural, and religious differences threaten social, economic, and political systems that have historically divided and isolated groups pitting each against the other. Intercultural alliances offer alternatives to the status quo "divide and conquer" paradigm by applying pressure in public and private arenas, advocating for policy changes, accessing and channeling resources, and empowering communities to create a more equitable and socially just world. The goal in intercultural alliances is to address root causes of injustice rather than simply providing temporary relief from symptoms. Collier (2014) calls for reflexivity, acknowledgement of the roles of power, privilege, and positionality as well as the ability to frame issues to engage the experiences and material conditions of those most impacted by injustices while recognizing structural constraints.

Using participatory action research, communication scholar Sara DeTurk (2015) documented the success and challenges of intercultural alliance building at the *Esperanza Peace and Justice Center* in San Antonio, Texas, a multi-issue social justice organization committed to holistic approaches to social change. *Esperanza's* vision statement:

> The people of *Esperanza* dream of a world where everyone has civil rights and economic justice, where the environment is cared for, where cultures are honored and communities are safe. The *Esperanza* advocates for those wounded by domination and inequality--women, people of color, queer people, the working class and poor. We believe in creating bridges between people by exchanging ideas and educating and empowering each other. We believe it is vital to share our visions of hope . . . we are esperanza. (p. 269)

Esperanza emphasizes systemic approaches to oppression and justice highlighting intersectionality, relationship building, and belonging to build effective intercultural alliances. Building alliances at *Esperanza Peace and Justice Center* means recognizing the interconnectedness of various forms of social and economic injustices; thus the organization attends to deeply connected structures of culture and power as they take political action across a range of issues and concerns. Growing out of a network of civil rights organizations, *Esperanza* has worked historically and today with many social justice groups locally and internationally. The center's "unrelenting rhetoric" and "unabashed confrontation" of multiple forms of injustice is both critical to the mission and a challenge to maintaining relationships with allies. Sometimes, single-issue allies resist the multi-issue focus of *Esperanza*. The concerns and priorities of different single-issue organizations may differ. For example, a group focused on environmental rights may lack concern for racial justice; a male-orientated gay organization may have difficulties addressing gender issues. The organization also experiences resistance from individuals who have privilege based on race, gender, or class and who are unwilling to have their privilege challenged. Esperanza's commitment to challenging systems of power on individual and institutional levels through political confrontation can also clash with individuals and groups with social privilege who would rather not risk the loss of their privilege. De Turk concludes, ". . . the success of the *Esperanza Peace and Justice Center* reflects hard work, savvy communication tactics, fidelity to its values, and also changes in the broader culture (e.g., increasing acceptance of sexual minorities and expanding power of Latinos), which the center itself has helped bring about" (p. 278).

As noted in other chapters, intercultural alliance building requires a sense of mutual interdependence among allies, processes to develop trust and dialogue, where people can speak openly and authentically as well as hear and empathize with the pain and difficulties of others. Having the motivation and skill to identify and work through misunderstandings, tensions, and conflicts is crucial to developing and sustaining intercultural alliances (Allen, Broome, Jones, Chen, & Collier, 2002). While inevitably challenging and uncomfortable, cultural differences are viewed as necessary, vital, and productive resources in intercultural alliances. Intercultural alliances require that we engage in intercultural bridgework, as discussed in Chapter 5, where we traverse multiple positions, identify points of intersection, and negotiate pathways of connection. When our intercultural competencies—inquiry, framing, positioning, dialogue, and reflection—inform collaborative action, intercultural alliances have the potential to create more humane, equitable, and just communities and societies. A case study is provided here to illustrate what can be accomplished through intercultural alliances.

CASE STUDY: COMMUNITY COALITION OF SOUTH LOS ANGELES

The Community Coalition of South Los Angeles was founded in 1990 by a group of dedicated community leaders to address the devastation wrought on South LA from the crack cocaine epidemic in the 1980s. The initial goal was to provide preventative community-based solutions to the drug problems. Karen Bass, elected speaker of the California Assembly in 2008, and re-elected for a third term as U.S. representative for California's 37th District in 2014, was one of the original founders. The Community Coalition has distinguished itself as an intercultural alliance of African Americans and Latinos/Latinas working together to build a prosperous, safe, and healthy South LA community where educational, social, and economic opportunities are available to all. The Community Coalition serves all ethnic/racial groups in South LA with a wide representation of cultural groups functioning in leadership roles in the Community Coalition (Community Coalition, 2015a).

The Community Coalition accomplishes their goals through a variety of programs focusing on keeping families together, creating healthy and safe neighborhoods, strengthening safety nets, and fighting for better schools. The Prevention Network works to create a strong safety net for a healthy, thriving community. In the past, the Community Coalition worked to remove the disproportionate number of liquor stores, motels, and recycling centers in South LA that lead to a concentration of criminal activities. In 2008, they won support from the city of LA to pass the Nuisance Abatement Ordinance giving residents more power to challenge negligent businesses. The Prevention Network is an alliance of social service providers who advocate for proactive policies that increase and improve services to the most vulnerable residents, such as ex-offenders transitioning from prison and those precluded from welfare.

Families Helping Families is a program that connects relative caregivers with services that meet the needs of families. While children often do much better in the care of extended family members, relatives do not receive the same resources and support that is offered through traditional foster care. The Community Coalition trains family and community members how to advocate on their behalf for increased and equitable resources to provide care for children of the community. The South LA community struggles to raise healthy children in an environment challenged by drugs, violence, and limited resources. In 2014, the Community Coalition received a $3 million grant from the Center for Disease Control to identify, develop, and disseminate strategies for addressing health disparities across a range of "at risk" health areas (Sentinel News Agency, 2014).

The Community Coalition recognizes that political power is central to developing public policy and leadership that serves the community. The Coalition works to build political power to serve the community of South LA by strengthening residents' civic engagement and developing strong leadership in areas, such as voter registration initiatives, town hall meetings, and leadership training. The leadership training addresses issues of race and racism, perspectives and challenges of unifying Blacks and Latinos/Latinas, as well as strategies for community organizing. In March 2011, Community Coalition mobilized over 200 parents, relative caregivers, residents, social service providers, youth and community leaders for the "Be the Change: South LA Action Conference," a call to action to involve residents in progressive work to improve South LA.

Approximately 60% of the youth who attend schools in South LA "disappear" from school before graduation. To address this startling reality that leaves young people of color with few options, and to break the school to prison pipeline, the Community Coalition formed the Architecture, Construction, and Engineering Academy (ACE Academy) to train students for high-skilled and high-paying careers. The Coalition recognizes the critical role youth can play in organizing for change and how the knowledge and skills gained through organizing for community change can enhance the academic and life goals of youth. South Central Youth Empowerment Through Action (SCYEA) brings African American and Latino/Latina youth together to create the next generation of leadership for positive change in the schools and community of South LA. SCYEA provides academic mentoring for youth, college preparation, and an annual road trip to colleges and universities, as well as training in community organizing and opportunities to work collaboratively to make positive change in the community. SCYEA youth organizers led a fierce campaign calling for the L.A. Unified School Board to invest resources in the highest-need schools. In June 2014, the District Board passed the precedent setting "Equity in Justice Resolution," a policy directing millions of dollars to the highest-need schools in the district.

The Community Coalition's "Freedom Schools," part of a nationwide effort organized by the *Children's Defense Fund,* celebrated its fourth year of success in the summer of 2014. Freedom School programs teach 3rd to 12th graders academic and leadership skills as well as health, wellness, and political education. Marion Wright Edleman, founder and President of the *Children's Defense Fund*, took the idea of Freedom Schools from the Summer Project of 1964, which provided safe places for children to receive citizenship education during the Voter Registration drive (Community Coalition, 2015b). Here is the story of Latino youth, Christian Molto, a participant in the SCYEA Freedom School:

> Chris came to South LA from Ontario, California and began his freshman year at Dorsey High. Although he jumped into school life by getting involved in wrestling and swimming, Chris quickly described himself as shy. "I didn't really talk or express myself. That ninth grade year, I wasn't very social. . . . I hung around people who looked like me and [if anything went down] could protect me.
>
> Things began to change when he met youth leaders from his school's chapter of South Central Youth Empowered through Action—also a program of Community Coalition—who had been involved with the Freedom School. "Whatever they were doing I wanted to be a part of it," recalls Chris. For him, being around his African-American peers broke down barriers, ". . . there was no tension. We're all people of color and have commonalities." Seeing his peers as leaders inspired him and as he spent time around other South L.A. youth and discussed issues that touched all of their lives, it hit him. "I saw that none of us come from perfect families and none of us went to perfect schools . . . but that doesn't put limits on where we can go." By the end of the school year, Chris was ready to take on a leadership role in the upcoming Freedom School.
>
> Chris immediately felt the difference between his school and the Freedom School. For him, one major difference was the School's emphasis on the African-American and Latino experience. "At [regular] school, our history is spoon fed," notes Chris, "here, I learned about the Black Panther Party." While mainstream narratives of the historic organization might focus on guns and violent encounters with the police, Chris was captivated by the benefits the group provided to their community, such as the Free Breakfast for Children program. "They brought a whole people together . . . and provided services that the government couldn't."
>
> Unity is one of the biggest takeaways from his summer long experience. "We [South Central youth] can fight for common goals. We can win campaigns for students, like the Student Need Index" [the "Equity in Justice Resolution" referred to above]. Chris' passion to be an active change agent, in his own life and in his surrounding environment, isn't being dampened anytime soon. "I want to be a leader who works with groups . . . I'll return to Freedom School and leave my own footprint." In his personal life, Chris has his sights set on attending either the University of California at Berkeley or San Francisco State University and majoring in Sociology. The goal? To take the knowledge he accrues to serve his neighborhood as an organizer for Community Coalition. For him the reason is simple, "I know that it is with our grasp to create change." The fact that Chris now

sees himself as an active change agent is remarkable considering he was a youth mired in diffidence only a few months ago. (Community Coalition, 2015b)

The Community Coalition has had tremendous success. These successes have been attained through the long-term commitment of key members, the strength in organizing the powerful voices of large numbers of people, and the sustained vision that a better world is possible if people work collectively across racial and ethnic lines. The challenge to move residents from despair to empowerment is ongoing. The struggle to build bridges across diverse identities, cultural differences, and cultural histories is continuous. The effort to create networks across vastly different positionalities using the influence of individuals and the collective power of groups is constant. The Community Coalition uses many forms of intervention—protests, training on race and racism, advocacy and organizing, educational and support programs, and public policy initiatives—to create change in South LA.

As noted by Collier (2002b), there are many more institutions, practices, and ideological forces operating in society to maintain hierarchies of difference than ones that encourage and support intercultural alliances. The Community Coalition is an example of an organization that recognizes the importance of analyzing, reflecting, and dialoguing on power, privilege, and dominance as a necessary first step toward change. Given the complex and dynamic nature of intercultural alliances like the Community Coalition, attending to the multifaceted nature of individual and group identities and histories is critical. Building and sustaining intercultural alliances is hard work, yet intercultural alliances have the potential to map out new possibilities, dismantle inequitable relations of power, and move toward social justice on interpersonal, community, and global levels.

SUMMARY

Closing the Conversation

As discussed throughout the book, our current context—the context of globalization—has dramatically altered the conditions that shape, enable, and constrain intercultural communication. The context of globalization is characterized by an intensification of intercultural interaction and exchange in an increasingly dynamic, mobile world. Changes in economic and political policies, governance, and institutions have escalated global intercultural interdependence ushering in an era of shared interests, needs, and resources, as well as tensions and conflicts. The financial crisis in the United States in the fall of 2008 launched shock waves from which the entire global financial system is still recovering illustrating clearly the intricate web of interdependence and the ubiquitous yet asymmetrical impact of globalization.

Global interdependence has also intensified intercultural, interethnic, interracial, and international tensions and conflicts. The forces of globalization have magnified inequities within and across nation-states exacerbating already existing injustices that limit and exclude access to education, jobs, services, and opportunities. Increased disparities structure and bind intercultural relationships in terms of power, privilege, and positionality. Importantly, injustice forged through colonization, Western domination, and U.S. hegemony, while reconfigured today, continues to define and shape intercultural relations. Yet, as described in this chapter, intercultural alliances occur more frequently than ever before and collective calls for justice echo around the globe. The popular uprisings to end authoritarian rule and demand democracy in 2011 reverberated far beyond the Middle East. Occupy Wall Street popularized the slogan "We are the 99%" drawing attention to the economic and social inequities between the wealthiest 1% and the rest. The growing movement to protest and resist police brutality, mass incarceration, and a justice system that has failed people of color, particularly African Americans, is gaining momentum and attention not only in the United States, but worldwide.

Our global interdependences coupled with the inequitable distribution and access to resources present current and future generations an imperative to envision new relationships of engagement and innovative strategies for sustainability in the 21st century. Taking up our responsibilities as global citizens, developing our intercultural competencies, and engaging in intercultural activism offer opportunities to challenge systems of domination, question hierarchies of power, and create a more equitable world.

Perspectives and approaches for imagining and enacting a more equitable and socially just world have provided the foundation for understanding and engaging in intercultural communication in this book. Let's review the principles that have guided our journey together in our exploration of intercultural communication in the context of globalization. First, throughout, we defined *culture* as a site of contestation where meaning-making is a struggle and not a static entity that remains fixed and stable. Understanding culture from a critical perspective as "contested meanings," along with more traditional notions of culture as "shared meanings," we are able to question the ways that dominant perspectives, values, and practices are privileged. Viewing culture as a site of contested meaning allows alternative, nondominant, and competing standpoints and voices to be valued and heard. Numerous examples and case studies throughout the book exemplify this definition of culture. The historical construction of "race," how race has signified differently over time and location, and the way race is rearticulated today illustrate the dynamic and negotiated nature of cultural meaning-making processes. Contested and hybrid cultural spaces, migrants' actions that challenge dominant assumptions about the superiority of the United States, as well as readings of popular culture texts that negotiate and resist hegemonic cultural ideologies also demonstrate how culture is a contested site.

Additionally, the concept of culture as a "resource" that is exploited for economic development and harnessed for empowerment was introduced and elaborated throughout the book. Hip hop culture with its origins in the Bronx, its deterritorialization and reterritorialization globally, and the commodification of hip hop culture all illustrate how culture is a resource in the global context. In the world today, as our discussion of Pueblo pottery, Mardi Gras festivals, the Bratz dolls, and tourism typify, culture is packaged, bought, and sold in the global intercultural marketplace. The notion of culture as a resource draws attention to the production and consumption of cultural "Others"; it also highlights the cultural agency and empowerment used in intercultural activism and movements for social justice. Defining culture as a resource reveals the symbolic and material realities of cultural inequality, difference, marginalization, and empowerment in the context of globalization.

The second principle that informs this book is the role history and relations of power play in intercultural communication. The broad historical context of the past 500 years of colonization, Western imperialism, and U.S. hegemony, which include the anticolonial and independence struggles, the civil rights movements, and the alterglobalization movements, are critical for understanding intercultural communication today. Yet, the conditions of globalization also require simultaneous attention to new and reconfigured sites of economic, political, and cultural power. The multifocal vision employed in the book, for example, in our discussions of globalization, world migration, and capitalism, connects the present with the past while recognizing the ways current conditions may also depart from and transform the past. While the legacy of colonization and U.S. hegemony are key to understanding intercultural communication today, non-Western centers of capital and cultural production are well established and positioned today to challenge Western domination in future decades (Shome & Hegde, 2002).

We noted the impact on intercultural relations of "free" trade policies in the global context and observed how neoliberal policies and practices rearticulate a 21st-century version of labor exploitation that built and consolidated the economic wealth and political power of Europe and the United States during the colonial period. Many of the intercultural challenges facing societies around the world today—racial and ethnic discrimination, tension and conflict, intensified economic inequity, as well as disputes over immigrant rights and immigration policies—are embedded in and structured by racist, classist, heteronormative, and ethnocentric ideologies forged and institutionalized through the past 500 years of colonization and Western imperialism. Underscoring the connections between the past and the present not only makes us aware of the deeply embedded inequities and highlights how asymmetrical relationships of power are reproduced over time, but it also reveals the pressure points for effective intervention for social justice as illustrated in the case study about the Community Coalition of South LA.

The third foundational principle is that intercultural communication today is always and inevitably situated within specific, local contexts as well as broader global contexts with interwoven cultural, social, economic, and political dimensions. Today, people, identities, cultural forms, practices, and ideas are located in particular places and simultaneously connected with places around the globe through phone, email, text messaging, advanced modes of transportation, social networks, and media. Case studies and examples presented throughout the book of cultural spaces, media circuits, interpersonal relationships, and intercultural alliances demonstrate the importance of understanding intercultural communication within interrelated contexts. Emphasizing linkages among various contexts—from the local to the global—makes visible the continuity and ties of cultural communities across geographic space as well as the disruptions and changes in cultural norms, values, and practices as people and cultural forms collide and coalesce in the global context.

The multilevel analysis used in the case studies on postcolonial migration and intercultural conflict highlights relationships of power, positionality, and privilege that inform intercultural communication in the global context. Attending to the local/global linkages and using a micro-/meso-/macro-analysis bring inequities and injustices on systemic and interpersonal levels into focus and illustrate how individuals and groups use their agency to create a more socially just world.

The fourth principle threaded throughout the book grounds the study and practice of intercultural communication in critical engagement, democratic participation, and social justice. The model of intercultural praxis introduced and developed along our journey joins the conceptual perspectives, affective capacities, and skill-based strategies needed to engage in intercultural communication for social justice. As we couple our theories and critical analysis with our individual engagement and collective action, we can create a more equitable, socially just world. As George (2004) noted, diversity of backgrounds, viewpoints, and skills are needed to address the challenges facing us—the 7 billion people who call this planet home. As a student and practitioner of intercultural communication, you are now positioned well to engage in critical, reflective action that includes multiple and diverse voices, builds alliances, and develops solidarity across various and shifting positionalities.

Consider these questions: Why are you learning about intercultural communication? How will you use what you have learned? We assume you are not learning about the topic so you can become more effective in taking advantage of others. We also assume you are not gaining skills and strategies so you can be more efficient in exploiting those who are positioned with less power than you. Having gained knowledge, capacities, and skills for intercultural communication, you have the potential to use your intercultural competence to join others as allies; connect across racial, gender, ethnic, cultural, and national boundaries in intercultural alliances; and engage in intercultural activism to create and struggle for a more equitable and just world. Imagine a world where equity and justice are the norm and not the exception. Using intercultural communication as a site of intervention, democratic participation, and transformation, you, in alliance with others, can create this world.

KEY TERMS

social justice
qualities of global citizens
empathy
capacities for global citizenship

intercultural competency
managing ambiguity
self-awareness
intercultural activism

DISCUSSION QUESTIONS AND ACTIVITIES

Discussion Questions

1. Based on the issues addressed in this chapter, how do you define "social justice"? What does it look like? How can we practice it?

2. What communication skills are needed to engage in intercultural praxis for social justice?

3. Have you engaged in intercultural activism? What are your experiences and insights? What kind of beliefs and values guided your activism?

4. Why do you think social justice is the exception rather than the norm in society?

5. What are the four principles that guided our journey throughout the book and how are they relevant to your everyday interactions?

6. What do you take away from this course, and how will you use it in future intercultural interactions?

Activities

1. Researching Local Community Organizations

    a. Research local community organizations that engage in social justice work. Study their websites and/or interview those who work at the organizations.

    b. Address the following questions:

        i. How does "culture" matter in their social justice work? Do they approach culture as resource, a system of shared meaning, and/or a site of power struggle?

        ii. How is intercultural praxis relevant in their activism? Do they exercise any of the elements of intercultural praxis?

        iii. Do the processes of globalization influence their activism? If so, how?

2. Qualities and Capacities of Global Citizenship

    a. Review qualities and capacities of global citizenship discussed in this chapter.

    b. In groups of 3 to 4 people, develop a concrete plan for developing global citizenship in your school, neighborhood, and/or community. Consider the following:

        i. Educational curriculum

        ii. Events and forums

        iii. Community organizing, intercultural activism

        iv. Creative expressions and activities

Glossary

Acculturation: Process by which migrants gain new information and insight about the norms and values of the culture and adapt their behaviors to the host culture

Action: Port of entry into intercultural praxis where you take actions based on critical reflection to create a more socially just, equitable, and peaceful world

Adjustment: Adjustment to a new environment as the sojourner learns to negotiate the verbal and nonverbal codes, values, norms, behaviors, and assumptions of the new culture

Alternative media or independent media: Media practices that fall outside of or are independent from the mainstream corporate-owned and controlled mass media

Americanization: Global cultural homogenization with U.S. culture, such as McDonald's and Disney

Anticipation: Excitement about the new culture characterizes the sojourner's experience

Antimiscegenation: Laws prohibiting marriage between people of different "racial" groups existed in over 40 states until 1967 when the laws were overturned in the landmark *Loving v. Virginia* Supreme Court case

Appropriation: Borrowing, mishandling, and/or stealing other people's culture to make it your own; raises questions about authenticity, ownership, and relations of power

Ascribed identity: The way others may view, name, and describe us and our group

Assimilation: Migrant values the host's culture more than his or her own culture

Authenticity: The notion that a "genuine," "pure," "untouched," and "sacred" culture exists or existed at some point. The "authentic" contrasts with and is distinct from modern or postmodern culture that is "affected," "contaminated," "profane"

Avowed identity: The way we see, label, and make meaning about ourselves

Body politics: Practices and policies through which power is marked, regulated, and negotiated on and through the body

Both/and approach: Approach to simultaneously hold contradictory, oppositional realities to guard us against essentializing, stereotyping, and closure

Bracero Program: Guest worker program started in the 1940s that allowed Mexican migrants to work legally in the United States

Brain drain: An aspect of high-skilled migration in which high-skilled workers migrate to another country, resulting in a huge loss in terms of knowledge, skills, investment, and capital for the sending countries

Capacities for global citizenship: Capacities of mind, heart, body, and soul that reimagine citizenship based on human needs rather than rights

Capitalism: A complex social logic that produces a set of relationships among capitalists, laborers, and consumers

Chain migration: Linkages that connect migrants from points of origin to destinations, leading to the segmentation of ethnic groups in the United States

Citizen media or participatory media: Media texts created by average citizens who are not affiliated with mainstream, corporate media outlets

Classism: The systemic subordination of class groups by the dominant, privileged class

Class prejudice: Personal attitudes that individuals of any class culture may hold about members of other classes

Commodification of culture: The practice in which cultural experiences are produced and consumed for the market

Confucian dynamism: Hofstede's cultural dimension that highlights the characteristics of East Asian countries, such as long-term orientation to time, hard work, frugality, and respect for hierarchy

Constructing the "Other": Process by which differences marked on or represented through the body are constructed as significant and are infused with meaning through a hierarchical racial system that justifies and promotes domination and exploitation

Contested cultural spaces: Geographic locations where conflicts engage people with unequal control and access to resources in oppositional and confrontational strategies of resistance

Context: The information that surrounds a communication event and shapes the meaning of the event

Contract workers: Contracted to work through labor agreements established between the governments of sending and receiving countries

Cooperative argument: A model of argument that manages the resolutions of disagreement within a set of rules that are responsive to intercultural differences

Coping stage: The second stage in racial/cultural awareness—couples develop proactive and reactive strategies to manage challenges

Cultural corruption: The perceived and experienced alteration of a culture in negative or detrimental ways through the influence of other cultures

Cultural forms: The products' format, structures, languages, and narrative styles that are produced when media technologies and institutions come together

Cultural globalization: Globalization characterized by migration, the formation of transnational cultural connectivities, cultural flows in the context of unequal power relations, and the emergence of hybrid cultural forms and identities

Cultural histories: Shared stories and interpretations of cultural groups that are passed along in written or oral form from generation to generation

Cultural homogenization: Convergence toward common cultural values and practices as a result of global integration

Cultural identity: Situated sense of self that is shaped by our cultural experiences and social locations

Cultural imperialism: Domination of one culture over others through cultural forms, such as pop culture, media, and cultural products; a dimension of cultural globalization in which unequal and uneven flow of culture and cultural forms negatively impacts local industry and culture

Cultural space: Communicative practices that construct meanings in, through, and about particular places

Cultural values: Ideas and beliefs about what is important to us, what we care about, what we think is right and wrong, and what we evaluate as fair and unfair, which are gained from our cultural group membership

Culture as a resource: Definition of culture as resource for political development, economic growth, and exploitation, as well as collective and individual empowerment, agency, and resistance

Culture as contested meaning: Cultural studies definition of culture that views culture as an apparatus of power within a larger system of domination where meanings are constantly negotiated

Culture as shared meanings: Anthropologic definition of culture that meanings are shared through symbols from generation to generation and allow us to make sense of, express, and give meaning to our lives

Culture industry: Industries that mass produce standardized cultural goods that normalize dominant capitalist ideologies and create social practices that are uniform and homogeneous among people

Culture jamming: The act of altering or transforming mass media and popular culture forms into messages or commentary about itself; a form of public activism that challenges, subverts, and redefines dominant, hegemonic meanings produced by multinational culture industries

Culture shock: Disorientation and discomfort sojourners experience from being in an unfamiliar environment

Decoding: Active interpretative and sense-making processes of audiences

Deculturation: Process by which migrants unlearn some aspects of their culture of origin

Deindustrialization: Process of economic globalization in which manufacturing jobs are lost to cheaper and less regulated labor conditions outside of the United States

Democratization: The transition toward a more democratic political system

Deterritorialized: Culture in the context of globalization where cultural subjects and cultural objects are uprooted from their situatedness in a particular physical, geographic location

Developing country/Developed country: Terms commonly used today based on a nation's wealth (gross national product [GNP]), political and economic stability, and other factors

Dialogue: Port of entry into intercultural praxis in which you engage in exchange of ideas, thoughts, and experiences that have both oppositional and transformative dimensions

Diasporic communities: Groups of people who have been forced to leave their homeland and who maintain a longing for—even if only in their imagination—a return to "home"

(Dis)placing culture and cultural space: Cultural space that emerges due to global circulation of people and products, constructed by displaced, intersecting, and colliding cultures that are geographically removed from the places of origin

Dominant reading: A way of reading/decoding in which the viewer or reader shares the meanings that are encoded in the text and accepts the preferred reading, which naturalizes and reinforces dominant ideologies

Dugri: A Jewish Israeli communication style characterized by direct, simple, aggressive, and fast-paced communication that values the preservation of the speaker's face and simultaneous participation by multiple speakers

Earth democracy: Democracy grounded in the needs of people and a sustainable, peaceful relationship with the planet, as opposed to free-market democracy, which relies on wars against the Earth, natural resources, and against people

Economic globalization: Globalization characterized by a growth in multinational corporations; an intensification of international trade and international flows of capital; and internationally interconnected webs of production, distribution, and consumption

Economic liberalization: Economic policies that increase the global movement of goods, labor, services, and capital with less restrictive tariffs (taxes) and trade barriers

Empathy: The ability to share the pain of others and the capacity to know the emotional experience of others from within their frame of reference

Encoding: Construction of mass mediated meaning by culture industries

Ethnicity: Shared heritage, place of origin, identity, and patterns of communication among a group

Ethnocentrism: Idea that one's own group's way of thinking, being, and acting in the world is superior to others

Exchange value: The value of a commodity determined by the profit it generates through exchange

Exoticization of the Other: A process by which "difference" from the dominant norm is exaggerated and constructed as mysterious, strange, and alluring—perpetuating stereotypical and limiting images of cultural Others

Exploratory interaction phase: A phase in intercultural friendship development process in which relationships move toward greater sharing of information, increased levels of support, and connection and growing intimacy

Face: Favorable social self-worth in relation to the assessment of other-worth in interpersonal relationships

Facework: The communication strategies used to negotiate face between the self and other

Feminization of the workforce: An increased demand for female migrant workers as domestic caretaker and low-skilled factory workers; women are often preferred for low-skilled work—can be paid less and are more easily exploited

Fetish: A spectacle that is represented as a commodity that is sought after, purchased, and consumed

Fetishization: The process of endowing commodities with symbolic and social power

First wave of world migration: Traced to the European colonial era from the 16th century through the 19th century; included thousands of migrants who sailed out of ports of Europe for colonies in the Americas, Africa, and Asia

First World: During the Cold War, First World nations were countries friendly to the United States and identified as capitalist and democratic; developed nations, more commonly used today, refer to former colonial powers with advanced capitalist economies, such as the United States, Europe, Australia, Canada, and Japan

Flaming: Abrasive, impulsive, or abusive behavior online

Folk culture: Localized cultural practices enacted for the sole purpose of people within a particular place

Fragmegration: Dual and simultaneous dynamic of integration and fragmentation that has emerged in the context of globalization

Framing: Port of entry into intercultural praxis in which you are aware of the frame of reference you use and are able to examine the situation both from micro- and macro-level perspectives

Free-trade agreements: Trade agreements that liberalize trade by reducing trade tariffs and barriers transnationally while maintaining protection for some industries

Fundamentalism: A term originally used to connote a return to basic irreducible tenets or beliefs within the Christian religion; yet, fundamentalism is used more broadly today, primarily in regard to religion, but not exclusively, to refer to literal interpretations of doctrines or texts

Globalization: Complex web of forces and factors that bring people, cultures, cultural products, and markets, as well as beliefs and practices, into increasingly greater proximity to and interrelationships with one another within inequitable relations of power

Global South/Global North: Terms in use today that highlight the socioeconomic and political division between wealthy, developed nations (former centers of colonial power) in the Northern Hemisphere and poorer, developing nations (formerly colonized countries) in the Southern Hemisphere

Glocalization: Dual and simultaneous forces of globalization and localization where globalizing forces always intersect with and operate in relationship to localizing forces

Guest workers programs: Brought workers from the periphery of Europe, Mexico, and so on, to fill the labor shortages in industrialized Western Europe and the United States due to the war and declining population after WWII through labor agreements established between the governments of the sending and receiving countries

Hegemony: Domination through consent where the goals, ideas, and interests of the ruling group or class are so thoroughly normalized, institutionalized, and accepted that people consent to their own domination, subordination, and exploitation

Heteronormativity: The institutionalization of heterosexuality in society and the assumption that heterosexuality is the only normal, natural, and universal form of sexuality

Heterosexism: An ideological system that denies and denigrates any nonheterosexual behavior, identity, or community

Hierarchy of difference: Hierarchical racial categorization developed in the late 18th century with Caucasians on the top, followed by the Malay, the Americans, the Mongolian, and the Ethiopian or the Black "race"

High- and low-skilled laborers: Educated, high-skilled workers migrate to developed countries to work in high-tech and medical professions; low-skilled laborers migrate to wealth-concentrated countries driven by poverty and seek work in places, such as factory, agriculture, food processing, sex industry, and domestic labor

High context communication: Communication where most of the information is implicitly communicated through indirect, nonverbal, and mutually shared knowledge

High culture: Culture of the elite class, or ruling class, who have power, including those who are educated at prestigious schools and are patrons of the arts, such as literature, opera, and ballet; associated with European culture

Historical legacy of colonization: Processes of globalization shaped by the historical legacy of colonialism and unequal power relations among nation-states, politically, economically, and culturally

Hofstede's cultural dimensions: Five dimensions of culture identified by Geert Hofstede, including individualism–collectivism, power distance, uncertainty avoidance, masculinity–femininity, and Confucian dynamism

Human trafficking: A form of involuntary migration in which people are transported for sex work and other types of labor against their will

Hybrid cultural forms: New and distinct cultural forms created by a mix of different cultures and appropriation of other cultural forms based on local knowledge and practice

Hybrid cultural space: The intersection of intercultural communication practices that construct meanings in, through, and about particular places within a context of relations of power

Hybrid cultural spaces as sites of intercultural negotiation: Hybrid cultural spaces as innovative and creative spaces where people constantly adapt to, negotiate with, and improvise between multiple cultural frameworks

Hybrid cultural spaces as sites of resistance: Hybrid cultural spaces where people challenge stable, territorial, and static definitions of culture, cultural spaces, and cultural identities

Hybrid cultural spaces as sites of transformation: Hybrid cultural spaces where hegemonic structures are negotiated and reconfigured through hybridization of culture, cultural space, and identity

Identity emergence: The third stage in interracial romantic relationship development—interracial or intercultural couples take charge of the images of themselves, challenge negative societal forces, and reframe their relationship

Ideology: Set of ideas and beliefs reflecting the needs and aspirations of individuals, groups, classes, or cultures that form the basis for political, economic, and other systems

Immigrants: Voluntary migrants who leave one country and settle permanently in another country

Immigration industrial complex: A systematic criminalization and exploitation of undocumented migrants from which public interests and private sectors mutually benefit

Independent orientation: A cultural orientation that views the self as an autonomous agent pursuing personal goals based on his or her individual beliefs

Individualism–collectivism: Hofstede's cultural dimension that highlights the differences between individualistic cultures and collectivistic cultures

In-groups: Groups of individuals that one belongs to culturally, socially, and emotionally

Initial encounter phase: A phase in intercultural friendship development process characterized by light conversation about general topics, beginning awareness of cultural differences and misunderstandings, and a process of questioning preconceived notions and stereotypes

Inquiry: Port of entry into intercultural praxis in which you have a desire and willingness to know, ask, find out, and learn without judgments and with willingness to take risks and be challenged/changed

Integration: Migrant values both her or his own culture and the host culture

Integrative theory of cultural adaptation: Theory of cultural adaptation that the individual and the environment co-define the adaptation process, including the attitudes and receptivity of the host environment, the ethnic communities within the majority culture, and the psychological characteristics of the individual

Intercultural activism: Engagement in actions that create a democratic world where power is shared; diversity is valued; and discrimination, domination, and oppression are challenged

Intercultural alliance: Relationships in which parties are interdependent, recognize their cultural differences, and work toward similar goals

Intercultural ally: A person, group, or community working across borders of nationality, culture, ethnicity, race, gender, class, religion, or sexual orientation in support of and in partnership with others

Intercultural bridgework: Developing sensitivity, understanding, and empathy and extending vulnerability to traverse multiple positions, creating points of contact, negotiation, and pathways of connection

Intercultural competency: The knowledge, attitudes, and skills needed to engage effectively in intercultural situations

Intercultural conflict: The real or perceived incompatibility of values, norms, expectations, goals, processes, or outcomes between two or more interdependent individuals or groups from different cultures

Intercultural praxis: Process of critical analysis, reflection, and action for effective intercultural communication in the context of globalization; six ports of entry: inquiry, framing, positioning, dialogue, reflection, and action

Intercultural relationships: Relationships between people from different racial, ethnic, linguistic, national, religious, class, and sexual orientation groups

Intercultural transformation: Occurs as a result of the stress–adaptation–growth process and includes three outcomes for migrants: (1) increased functional fitness, (2) improved psychological health, and (3) a shift toward an intercultural identity

Interdependent orientation: A cultural orientation that views the self as relational and values harmony and selflessness

Interethnic relationships: Relationships between people who identify differently in terms of ethnicity or ethnic background

Internally displaced persons: Refugees within one's own country of origin

International Monetary Fund (IMF): International organization established immediately following WWII to maintain global economic stability

International relationships: Relationships that develop across national cultures and citizenship lines

Interracial relationships: Relationships that cross socially constructed racial groups

Interreligious or interfaith relationships: Relationships between people from different religious orientations or faiths

Intersectionality: An approach to understanding how socially constructed categories of difference, such as race, gender, class, and sexuality operate in relationship to each other

Invitational rhetoric: A form of communication committed to equality, recognition, and self-determination through invitation, cooperation, and coordination

Involuntary migrants: Migrants who are forced to leave due to famine, war, and political or religious persecution

Locations of enunciation: Literal and figurative sites or positions from which to speak

Low context communication: Communication where a large amount of information is explicitly communicated through direct, specific, and literal expressions

Low culture: Culture of the working class, who enjoy activities, such as popular theater, folk art, "street" activities, movies, and TV

Managing ambiguity: The ability to handle the uncertainty, anxiety, and tension that arises from the unknown in intercultural situations

Maquiladoras: Foreign-owned assembly plants originally located in Mexico that allow companies to import materials duty free and export products around the world

Marginalization: Migrant places little value on either his or her own culture or the host culture

Masculinity–femininity: Hofstede's cultural dimension that distinguishes the societies with distinct gender roles and achievements (masculinity) and societies with flexible gender norms and balanced lifestyle (femininity)

Media: The modes, means, or channels through which messages are communicated

Melting pot: Metaphor of U.S. society that the migrants' adaptation to a new culture inevitably requires and allows newcomers to "melt" or "blend" into the mainstream to form a cohesive whole

Mercantilism: The implementation of protectionist policies that exclude foreign goods and subsidize cheap labor in certain industries

Migrant–host modes of relationship: The attitudes of migrants toward their host and own cultures

Migrants: People who move from their primary cultural context, changing their place of residence for an extended period of time

Migrant networks: Interpersonal connections among current and former migrants, as well as non-migrants in origin and destination areas through ties of kinship, friendship, and shared origin

Miscegenation: The term comes from Latin meaning "mixed" and "kind" and is used to refer to "mixed-race" relationships, specifically intermarriage, cohabitation, and sexual relationships between people of different races

Musayara: A communication style broadly shared by Arab cultures that promotes harmony and dialogue through the use of rhetorically complex language, repetition, careful listening, and high context communication

Nativist movements: Movements that call for the exclusion of foreign-born people

Negative identity: Group identity that is based on being the opposite of the Other or portraying a negative image of the Other

Negotiated reading: A way of reading/decoding in which the reader or viewer generally shares the codes and preferred meanings of the texts, but may also resist and modify the encoded meaning based on her or his positionality, interests, and experiences

Neoliberalism: The reassertion of liberal ideologies for reduced state intervention, deregulation, privatization, decreased social protection, and elimination of labor unions)

Network media: Media like the World Wide Web, which connects multiple points to multiple points, and serves interpersonal and mass media functions

North American Free Trade Agreement (NAFTA): Trade agreement established in 1994 among Mexico, the United States, and Canada that eliminates trade barriers and tariffs

Ongoing involvement phase: A phase in the intercultural friendship development process marked by greater connection, intimacy, involvement, shared rules of engagement, and norms that guide interaction with each other

Oppositional metaphors: Metaphors that use rigid and polarized dichotomies

Oppositional reading: A way of reading/decoding in which the social position of the viewer or reader of the text places them in opposition to the dominant code and preferred reading; the reader understands the dominant code yet brings an alternative frame of reference, which leads him or her to resist the encoded meaning

Out-groups: Groups of individuals that one sees as separate and different from him or her and as unequal to or potentially threatening

"Out-thereness": Characteristic of globalization where places around the world, out "there," are linked to particular locations "here" and how this linkage of places reveals colonial histories and postcolonial realities

Patriarchy: A form of social organization where men are dominant and women are subordinated

Pluralism: An ideology that emphasizes the maintenance of ethnic and cultural values, norms, and practices within a multicultural society

Political globalization: Globalization characterized by the interconnectedness of nation-state politics, the formation of bodies of global governance (i.e., WTO, IMF, WB), and global movements of resistance responding to inequities in political power

Polysemic cultural space: Condition in which multiple meanings are constructed about certain places, people, and phenomena

Popular culture: Culture that belongs to the "masses," much of which was previously considered low culture; artifacts that the general populous or broad masses within a society have some understanding of or share

Positionality: One's social location or position within an intersecting web of socially constructed hierarchical categories, such as race, class, gender, sexual orientation, religion, nationality, and physical abilities

Positioning: Port of entry into intercultural praxis where you consider how you are positioned within the geographical, sociopolitical, and historical relations of power and knowledge

Postcolonial migrants: Migrants who leave former colonies and relocate in colonizing countries

Power distance: Hofstede's cultural dimension that highlights how the less powerful members accept unequal distribution of power within organizations

The power of texts: Texts construct, maintain, and legitimize systems of inequity and domination by creating authorized and preferred versions of history and leaving out other perspectives, experiences, and stories

Push–pull theory: A theory of migration that circumstances in the country of origin "push" people toward migratory paths and conditions in the country of destination "pull" people toward particular locations

Qualities of global citizens: Three qualities defined by wisdom, courage, and compassion

Racework: Everyday actions and strategies through which close relationships that cross racial lines are maintained

Racial/cultural awareness: The first stage of intercultural romantic relationship in which partners develop awareness of similarities and differences as well as how they are viewed by others

Racial hierarchy: Socially constructed hierarchy of different racial groups in which Whites are placed at the top, and non-Whites are placed as inferior to Whites; legitimates conquest, colonization, and exploitation of labor in the rise of capitalism

Racial historicism: Belief that non-White people lack cultural development, but through education are capable of developing civilizing behaviors, democratic values, and self-determination

Racial naturalism: Belief that White people of European descent are naturally or biologically superior to non-White people

Reflection: Port of entry into intercultural praxis where you use the capacity to learn from introspection, to observe yourself in relation to others, and to alter your perspectives and actions based on reflection

Refugees: People who are forced for safety reasons to flee from their country of origin due to war, fear of persecution, or famine

Relational identity/culture: The system of understanding between relational partners as they coordinate attitudes, actions, and identities within the relationship and with the world outside the relationship

Relational maintenance: The fourth stage—couples negotiate racial, cultural, ethnic, class, and religious differences between themselves and with the society at large

Relative deprivation: A perceived sense of deprivation caused by the increased disparity in income levels and heightened exposure to images of material wealth that make people in the lower economic ranks desire to find ways to make money and accumulate wealth

Remittances: Financial support sent to a distant location

Reterritorialized: Culture in the context of globalization where cultural subjects and cultural objects are relocated in new, multiple, and varied geographic spaces

Second wave of migration: Took place from the mid-1800s to the early 1900s during the Industrial Revolution, when peasants from the rural parts of Europe, fleeing poverty and famine, migrated to urban areas in Europe and North and South America

Second World: During the Cold War, Second World nations were countries perceived as hostile and ideologically incompatible with the United States, such as the former Soviet bloc countries and China and their allies; identified as communist

Segregated cultural spaces: Segregated spaces based on socioeconomic, racial, ethnic, sexual, political, and religious differences, both voluntary and imposed

Self-awareness: An awareness or consciousness of oneself as a cultural being, whose beliefs, assumptions, attitudes, values, and behaviors are contoured by culture

Semiotics: Study of the use of signs in cultures

Separation: Migrant values her or his own or home culture more than the host culture

Signifiers: The physical form, such as the body, things, actions, images, or words of the sign

Signified: The idea, mental concept, or meaning of the sign

Signs: Consists of signifiers and signified; system of meaning (i.e., culture, language) produced through the process of assigning a signified to a signifier

Sign value: The symbolic value of a commodity that conveys social meaning and social positioning

Silenced histories: Histories hidden, unrecognized, and/or excluded from the historical record and awareness

Social capital: Sense of commitment and obligation people within a group or network have to look after the well-being and interests of one another

Social construct: Idea or phenomenon that has been "created," "invented," or "constructed" by people in a particular society or culture through communication

Social construction: Based on a sociological theory of knowledge, concepts, identities, social relations, practices, and so on that are created and maintained through collectively agreed on conventions, norms, and rules rather than inherent in the external world

Social construction of gender: The use of physical differences in human bodies to construct two mutually exclusive gender categories: women/men, femininity/masculinity

Social construction of race: Process of separating people into hierarchical categories using the physical characteristics of our bodies, such as skin color, facial features, hair texture, and body type

Social justice: A goal and process of enabling the equal participation of all groups and the equitable distribution of resources in society

Social networking sites: Online platforms to build social relations

Sojourners: Voluntary migrants who leave home for limited periods of time and for specific purposes, such as international students, business travelers, tourists, missionaries, and military personnel

Spectacle: The domination of media images and consumer society over individuals and their relationships with others

Standpoint theory: Feminist theory that claims that the social groups to which we belong shape what we know and how we communicate; one's position within social relations of power produces different standpoints from which to view, experience, act, and construct knowledge about the world

Surplus value: The profit made by reducing labor costs

Symbols: Words, images, people, ideas, actions, and so on, that stand for or represent other things

Telenovelas: TV soap operas made and popularized in Latin America

Third gender: People who live across, between, or outside of the socially constructed two-gender system of categorization

The third wave (of migration): Often labeled the postindustrial wave; more diverse and multidirectional than previous migrations and encompasses patterns of movement since WWII

Third World: During the Cold War, Third World nations were countries seen as neutral or nonaligned with either the First World (capitalism) or the Second World (communism); developing nations, more commonly used today, are formerly colonized countries and are economically less developed than First World nations

Time–space compression: Characteristic of globalization that brings seemingly disparate cultures into closer proximity, intersection, and juxtaposition with each other

Transgender: People whose gender identities differ from the social norms and expectations associated with their biological sex

Transmigrants: Migrants who move across national boundaries to new locations for work and family reunification and also maintain cultural, social, economic, and political ties with their country, region, or city of origin

Transnational communities: Communities constructed by transmigrants, characterized by intertwining familial relationships across locations, identification with "home" or sending locations, and the ability to mobilize collective resources

U-curve model: Model of cultural adaptation, consisting of three stages: (1) anticipation, (2) culture shock, and (3) adjustment

Uncertainty avoidance: Hofstede's cultural dimension that highlights the tendency to feel threatened by unknown and uncertain situations

Use value: The value of a commodity determined by its utility

Voluntary migrants: Migrants who voluntarily choose to leave home to travel or relocate

W-curve model: Extension of the U-curve model addressing the challenges of reentry or return to one's home culture

Whiteness: Location of structural advantage; a standpoint; and a set of core values, practices, and norms in which White ways of thinking, knowing, being, and doing are normalized as the standard

White supremacy: Historically based, institutionally perpetuated system of exploitation and oppression of continents, nations, and people of color by people and nations of European descent for the purpose of establishing and maintaining wealth, privilege, and power

World Bank (WB): International organization established after WWII to address poverty through development and education

World-systems theory: A theory of migration that international migration today is a result of the structure of global capitalism

World Trade Organization (WTO): International organization established in 1995 as a successor to the post–WWII General Agreement on Tariffs and Trade (GATT); deals with the global rules of trade between nations

Xenophobia: Fear of outsiders

References

Achbar, M., & Abbott, J. (Directors). (2005). *The corporation* [Motion picture]. New York, NY: Zeitgeist Films.

Ackerman, P., & Duvall, J. (2000). *A force more powerful: A century of nonviolent conflict*. New York, NY: Palgrave.

Adams, M., Bell, L. A., & Griffin, P. (2007). *Teaching for diversity and social justice*. New York, NY: Routledge.

Adbusters. (2011). *Adbusters spoof ads*. Retrieved from www.adbusters.org

Adler, P. (1987). Culture shock and the cross-cultural learning experience. In L. F. Luce & E. C. Smith (Eds.), *Toward internationalism: Readings in cross-cultural communication* (pp. 24–35). Cambridge, MA: Newbury.

Adorno, T. W., & Horkheimer, M. (1972). *Dialectic of enlightenment*. New York, NY: Herder and Herder.

Aidman, A. (1999). Disney's Pocahontas: Conversations with Native American and Euro-American girls. In S. R. Mazzareall & N. O. Pecora (Eds.), *Growing up girls: Popular culture and the construction of identity* (pp. 132–158). New York, NY: Peter Lang.

Aldama, F. L., & Rojas, T. N. (2013). Telenovelas. *Oxford Bibliographies*. Retrieved from http://www.oxfordbibliographies.com/view/document/obo-9780199913701/obo-9780199913701-0074.xml

Allen, B. (2004). Sapphire and Sappho: Allies in authenticity. In A. González, M. Houston, & C. Chen (Eds.), *Our voices: Essays in culture, ethnicity, and communication* (4th ed., pp. 198–202). Los Angeles, CA: Roxbury.

Allen, B. J., Broome, B. J., Jones, T. S., Chen, V., & Collier, M. J. (2002). Intercultural alliances: A cyberdialogue among scholar-practitioners. In M. J. Collier (Ed.), *Intercultural alliances: International and intercultural communication annual* (Vol. 25, pp. 279–319). Thousand Oaks, CA: SAGE.

Allen, T., & Seaton, J. (Eds.). (1999). *The media of conflict*. New York, NY: Zed Books.

American Association of University Women. (2014). *The simple truth about the gender pay gap*. Retrieved from http://www.aauw.org/resource/the-simple-truth-about-the-gender-pay-gap/

Anders Behring Breivik. (2012). *New York Times*. Retrieved from http://topics.nytimes.com/top/reference/timestopics/people/b/anders_behring_breivik/index.html

Anzaldúa, G. (1987). *Borderlands/La Frontera: The new mestiza*. San Francisco, CA: Aunt Lute Books.

Anzaldúa, G. (Ed.). (1991). *Making face, making soul: Haciendo caras*. San Francisco, CA: Aunt Lute Books.

Appadurai, A. (1988). Putting hierarchy in its place. *Cultural Anthropology, 3*, 36–49.

Appadurai, A. (1996). *Modernity at large: Cultural dimensions of globalization*. Minneapolis: University of Minnesota Press.

Archer, B. (2004). *The end of gay: And the death of heterosexuality*. New York, NY: Thunder's Mouth.

Armaline, W. T., Glasberg, D. S., & Purkayastha, B. (Eds.). (2011). *Human rights in our own backyard: Injustice and resistance in the United States*. Philadelphia: Pennsylvania Press.

Atton, C. (2002). *Alternative media*. Thousand Oaks, CA: SAGE.

Baig, N., Ting-Toomey, S., & Dorjee, T. (2014). Intergenerational narratives on face: A South Asian Indian American perspective. *Journal of International and Intercultural Communication, 7*(2), 127–147.

Bail, C. (2012). The fringe effect. Civil society organizations and the evolution of media discourse about Islam since the September 11th attacks. *American Sociological Review, 77*(6), 855–879.

Barthes, R. (1972). *Mythologies.* London, UK: Cape.

Basch, L. G., Blanc, C. S., & Schiller, N. G. (1994). *Nations unbound.* New York, NY: Routledge.

Bayoumi, M. (2008). *How does it feel to be a problem? Being young and Arab in America.* New York, NY: Penguin.

Beaud, M. (2001). *A history of capitalism: 1500-2000* (5th ed.). New York, NY: Monthly Review.

Bedford, K. (2014). To prevent homegrown Islamic radicalism, drop the media hysteria. *The Guardian.* Retrieved from http://www.theguardian.com/commentisfree/2014/sep/01/to-prevent-homegrown-islamist-radicalism-drop-the-media-hysteria

Beirich, H. (n.d.). *The anti-immigrant movement.* Southern Poverty Law Center. Retrieved from http://www.splcenter.org/get-informed/intelligence-files/ideology/anti-immigrant/the-anti-immigrant-movement

Bell, S., & Coleman, S. (1999). *The anthropology of friendship.* Oxford, UK: Berg.

Bennett, A. (2004). Hip hop am Main, Rappin' on the Tyne: Hip hop culture as a local construct in two European cities. In M. Forman & M. A. Neal (Eds.), *That's the joint! The hip hop studies reader* (pp. 177–200). New York, NY: Routledge.

Bennett, J. M. (1993). Cultural marginality: Identity issues in intercultural training. In R. M. Paige (Ed.), *Education for the intercultural experience* (pp. 109–135). Yarmouth, ME: Intercultural Press.

Berger, P. L., & Luckmann, T. (1966). *The social construction of reality: A treatise in the sociology of knowledge.* New York, NY: Doubleday.

Berry, J. (1992). Psychology of acculturation: Understanding individuals moving between two cultures. In R. W. Brislin (Ed.), *Applied cross-cultural psychology* (pp. 232–253). Newbury Park, CA: SAGE.

Biggs, C. (2008). *World savvy monitor: Democracy around the world in 2008.* Retrieved from http://worldsavvy.org/monitor/index.php?option = com_content&view = article&id = 164&Itemid = 356

Bird, S. E. (2014). Imagining Indians. In G. B. Rodman (Ed.), *The race and media reader* (pp.190–210). New York, NY: Routledge.

#BlackLivesMatter. (n.d.). Retrieved from http://blacklivesmatter.com/about/

Blake, M., & Brock, G. (2014). *Debating brain drain: May governments restrict emigration?* New York, NY: Oxford Press.

Blum, W. (1995). *Killing hope: U.S. military and CIA interventions since World War II.* Monroe, ME: Common Courage.

Blumenbach, J. F. (1969). *On the natural varieties of mankind.* New York, NY: Bergman. (Original work published 1775)

Boggs, G. L. (2011). The next American revolution. Sustainable activism for the 21st century (pp. 1–51). Berkeley: University of California Press.

Bohm, D. (1996). *On dialogue.* New York, NY: Routledge.

Borjas, G. J. (1990). *Friends or strangers: The impact of immigration on the U.S. economy.* New York, NY: Basic.

Bourdieu, P. (1984). *Distinction: A social critique of the judgment of taste.* Cambridge, MA: Harvard University Press.

Bournoutian, G. (2002). *A concise history of Armenian people.* Costa Mesa, CA: Mazda.

Bray, M. (2013). *Translating anarchy: The anarchism of Occupy Wall Street.* Hants, UK: Zero Books.

Brew, F. P., & Cairns, D. R. (2004). Do culture or situational constraints determine choice of direct or indirect styles in intercultural workplace conflicts? *International Journal of Intercultural Relations, 28*(5), 331–352.

British Broadcasting Corporation. (2014). China profile: China is the largest media market, and has the world's largest online population. Retrieved from http://www.bbc.com/news/world-asia-pacific-13017881

Broome, B., Carey, C., De La Garza, S. A., Martin, J., & Morris, R. (2005). "In the thick of things": A dialogue about the activist turn in intercultural communication. In W. J. Starosta & G. M. Chen (Eds.), *Taking stock in intercultural communication: Where to now? International and intercultural communication annual* (Vol. 26, pp. 145–175). Thousand Oaks, CA: SAGE.

Brummett, B. (1994). *Rhetoric in popular culture*. New York, NY: St. Martin's.

Buescher, D. T., & Ono, K. (1996). Civilized colonialism: Pocahontas as neocolonial rhetoric. *Women's Studies in Communication, 19,* 127–153.

Burawoy, M., Blum, J. A., George, S., Gille, Z., Gowan, T., Haney, L., . . . Thayer, M. (2000). *Global ethnography: Forces, connections, and imaginations in a postmodern world*. Berkeley: University of California Press.

Butler, J. (1990). *Gender trouble: Feminism and the subversion of identity*. New York, NY: Routledge.

Butler, J. (1993). *Bodies that matter*. New York, NY: Routledge.

Campus Antiwar Network. (n.d.). *Formation and growth of the U.S. independent, democratic and grassroots antiwar student movement*. Retrieved from http://www.grassrootspeace.org/campus_antiwar.html

Carrigan, A. (2011). *Postcolonial tourism: Literature, culture, and environment*. New York, NY: Routledge.

Carrillo Rowe, A., & Malhotra, S. (2006). (Un)hinging whiteness. In M. P. Orbe, B. J. Allen, & L. S. Flores (Eds.), *The same and different: Acknowledging the diversity within and between cultural groups* (pp. 166–192). Washington, DC: National Communication Association.

Carruthers, W. (2014). Charles Krauthammer: ISIS Is Global 'Ideological War.' *Newsmax*. Retrieved from http://www.newsmax.com/Newsfront/ISIS-War-airstrikes-worldwide/2014/09/23/id/596403/

Casey, E. S. (1996). How to get from space to place in a fairly short stretch of time: Phenomenology and prolegomena. In S. Feld & K. H. Basso (Eds.), *Senses of place* (pp. 13–52). Santa Fe, NM: School of American Research.

Castells, M. (1996). *The rise of the network society*. Oxford, UK: Blackwell.

Castles, S., de Haas, H., & Miller, M. J. (2014). *The age of migration: International population movements in the modern world* (5th ed.). New York, NY: Guilford Press.

Center for Media Literacy. (n.d.). *CML MediaLit Kit*. Retrieved from http://www.medialit.org/bp_mlk.html

Chang, J. (2005). *Can't stop, won't stop: A history of the hip hop generation*. Boston, MA: St. Martin's.

Chávez, K. R. (2013). Pushing boundaries: Queer intercultural communication. *Journal of International and Intercultural Communication, 6*(2), 83–95.

Chen, A. C., & Buenavista, T. L. (2012). Breaking the silence: Remembering Tam Tran the scholar. In K. Wong, J. Shadduck-Hernandez, F. Inzunza, J. Monroe, V. Narro, & A. Valenzuela (Eds.), *Undocumented and unafraid: Tam Tran, Cinthya Felix, and the immigrant youth movement* (pp. 47–50). Los Angeles, CA: UCLA Center for Labor Research and Education.

Chen, G. M., & Dai, X. (2012). New media and asymmetry in cultural identity negotiation. In P. H. Cheong, J. N. Martin, & L. P. Mcfadyen (Eds.), *New media and intercultural communication: Identity, community and politics* (pp. 123–137). New York, NY: Peter Lang.

Chen, Y., & Toriegoe, C. (2016). "We get bad looks, all the time": Ideologies and identities in the discourse of interracial romantic couples. In K. Sorrells & S. Sekimoto (Eds.), *Globalizing intercultural communication: A reader* (144–155). Los Angeles, CA: SAGE.

Chi-Ching, E. Y. (1998). Social-cultural context of perceptions and approaches to conflict: The case for Singapore. In K. Leung & D. Tjosvold (Eds.), *Conflict management in the Asia Pacific: Assumptions and approaches in diverse cultures* (pp. 123–145). Singapore, Asia: Wiley.

Childs, E. C. (2005). *Navigating interracial borders: Black-White couples and their social worlds*. New Brunswick, NJ: Rutgers University Press.

Chin, K. (2000). *Smuggled Chinese: Clandestine immigration to the U.S*. Philadelphia, PA: Temple University Press.

Cho, E. H., Puete, F. A., Louie, M. C. Y., & Khokha, S. (2004). Globalization, migration and worker's rights. *BRIDGE: A popular education resource for immigrant & refugee community organizers.* Oakland, CA: National Network for Immigrant and Refugee Rights.

Cho, M. (2005). *Harajuku Girls.* Retrieved from http://margaretcho.com/2005/10/31/harajuku-girls/

Cho, S. E. (2010). *Cross-cultural comparison of Korean and American social network sites.* Unpublished doctoral dissertation, Rutgers University, New Brunswick, N.J.

Chopra, S. (2012). 'Shahrukhism' is a global phenomenon! *Businessofcinema.com.* Retrieved from http://businessofcinema.com/news/shahrukhism-is-a-global-phenomenon/53472

Cohen, M. N. (1998). *Chauvinism, class, and racism in the United States.* New Haven, CT: Yale University.

Coleman, P. T. (2003). Characteristics of protracted, intractable conflicts: Toward a development of a metaframework—I. *Peace and Conflict: Journal of Peace Psychology, 9,* 1–37.

Collier, M. J. (1991). Conflict within African, Mexican and Anglo American friendship. In S. Ting-Toomey & F. Korzeny (Eds.), *Cross-cultural interpersonal communication* (pp. 132–154). Newbury Park, CA: SAGE.

Collier, M. J. (1996). Communication competence problematics in ethnic friendships. *Communication Monographs, 63*(4), 314–336.

Collier, M. J. (2002a). Intercultural friendships as interpersonal alliances. In J. N. Martin, T. K. Nakayama, & L. A. Flores (Eds.), *Readings in intercultural communication* (2nd ed., pp. 301–310). New York, NY: McGraw-Hill.

Collier, M. J. (2002b). Transforming communication about culture: An introduction. In M. J. Collier (Ed.), *Transforming communication about culture: Critical new directions. International and intercultural communication annual* (Vol. 24, pp. ix–xix). Thousand Oaks, CA: SAGE.

Collier, M. J. (2002c). Negotiating intercultural alliance relationships: Towards transformation. In M. J. Collier (Ed.), *Intercultural alliances: Critical transformations* (pp. 1–15). Thousand Oaks, CA: SAGE.

Collier, M. J. (2014). Community engagement and intercultural praxis: Dancing with difference in diverse contexts. New York, NY: Peter Lang.

Collins, P. H. (1986). Learning from the outsider within: The sociological significance of Black feminist thought. *Social Problems, 33*(6), S14–S32.

Collins, P. H. (1990). *Black feminist thought: Knowledge, consciousness and the politics of empowerment.* Boston, MA: Unwin Hyman.

Community Coalition. (2015a). About us. Retrieved from http://www.cocosouthla.org/about/ourmission

Community Coalition. (2015b). *CDF Freedom Schools transform lives.* Retrieved from http://www.cocosouthla.org/transforming_lives

Constable, N. (2003). *Romance on a global stage: Pen pals, virtual ethnography, and "mail order" marriage.* Berkeley: University of California Press.

Cooley, J. K. (2002). *Unholy wars: Afghanistan, America and international terrorism.* London, UK: Pluto.

Cordell, K., & Wolff, S. (Eds.). (2013). *Routledge handbook of ethnic conflict.* New York, NY: Routledge.

Crapanzano, V. (1990). On dialogue. In T. Maranhão (Ed.), *The interpretation of dialogue* (pp. 269–291). Chicago, IL: University of Chicago Press.

Crenshaw, K. (1989). Demarginalizing the intersection of race and sex: Black feminist critique of antidiscrimination doctrine, feminist theory and antiracist policy. *University of Chicago Legal Forum 1989,* 139–167.

Cross, B. (1993). *It's not about a salary: Rap, race, and resistance in Los Angeles.* London, UK: Verso Books.

Crothers, L. (2013). *Globalization & American popular culture* (3rd ed.). Lanham, MD: Rowman & Littlefield.

Daddy Yankee Interview. (n.d.). *1-Famous-Quotes.com.* Retrieved from http://www.1-famous-quotes.com/quote/1322231

Davies, J. B., Lluberas, R., and Shorrocks, A. (2014). *Credit Suisse Global Wealth Report 2014.* Retrieved from https://publications.credit-suisse.com/tasks/render/file/?fileID=60931FDE-A2D2-F568-B041B58C5EA591A4

Davis, F. J. (1991). *Who is black: One nation's definition*. University Park: Pennsylvania State University Press.

Debord, G. (1973). *The society of the spectacle*. New York, NY: Zone Books.

DePillis, L. (2013). Everything you need to know about the Trans Pacific Partnership. *Washington Post*. Retrieved from http://www.washingtonpost.com/blogs/wonkblog/wp/2013/12/11/everything-you-need-to-know-about-the-trans-pacific-partnership/

DeTurk, S. (2006). The power of dialogue: Consequences of inter-group dialogue and their implications for agency and alliance. *Communication Quarterly, 54*(1), 31–51.

Deutsch, L., & Lee, J. (2014). No filter: Social media show raw view of #Ferguson. *USA Today*. Retrieved from http://www.usatoday.com/story/news/nation-now/2014/08/14/social-media-ferguson-effect/14052495/

Dines, G., & Humez, J. M. (Eds.). (2015). *Gender, race, and class in media: A critical reader* (4th ed.). Thousand Oaks, CA: SAGE.

Durham, M. G., & Kellner, D. (2012). *Media and cultural studies*. Malden, MA: Blackwell.

During, S. (1999). Introduction. *The cultural studies reader*. London, UK: Routledge.

Dussel, E. (1995). Ethnocentrism and modernity. In J. Beverley, J. Oviedo, & M. Aronna (Eds.), *The postmodernism debate in Latin America* (pp. 65–76). Durham, NC: Duke University Press.

Dyson, M. E. (2006). *Come hell or high water: Hurricane Katrina and the color of disaster*. New York, NY: Basic Civitas.

Ellis, D. G. (2005). Intercultural communication in intractable ethnopolitical conflicts. In W. J. Starosta & G. Chen (Eds.), *Taking stock in intercultural communication: Where to now?* (pp. 45–69). Washington, DC: International and Intercultural Communication Annual XXVIII.

Fernando, M. (2014). *The republic unsettled: Muslim French and the contradictions of secularism*. Durham, N.C.: Duke University Press.

Fiske, J. (1992). *Introduction to communication studies: Studies in culture and communication*. London, UK: Methuen.

Floc'h, B. (2014, October 22). Ciel voile sur l'universite [Veiled at the University]. *Le Monde*, p. 14. Retrieved from http://www.lemonde.fr/education/article/2014/10/21/ciel-voile-sur-l-universite_4509726_1473685

Foeman, A. K., & Nance, T. (1999). From miscegenation to multiculturalism: Perceptions and stages of interracial relationship development. *Journal of Black Studies, 29*(4), 540–557.

Foreman, M. (2004). "Represent": Race, space and place in rap music. In M. Forman & M. A. Neal (Eds.), *That's the joint! The hip hop studies reader* (pp. 201–222). New York, NY: Routledge.

Foss, S. K., & Griffin, C. L. (1995). Beyond persuasion: A proposal for invitation rhetoric. *Communication Monograph, 62*, 15–28.

Foucault, M. (1975). *Discipline and punish: The birth of the prison*. London, UK: Penguin.

Foucault, M. (1978). *The history of sexuality: An introduction* (Vol. 1). New York, NY: Random House.

Fernandes, D. (2007). *Homeland security and the business of immigration*. St. Paul, MN: Seven Stories.

Frankenberg, R. (1993). *White women, race matters: The social construction of Whiteness*. Minneapolis: University of Minnesota Press.

Fredericks, J. (2007). Dialogue and solidarity in a time of globalization. *Buddhist-Christian Studies, 27*, 51–66.

Freire, P. (1998). *Pedagogy of freedom: Ethics, democracy, and civic courage*. Lanham, MD: Rowman & Littlefield.

Freire, P. (2000). *Pedagogy of the oppressed*. New York, NY: Continuum. (Original work published 1973)

Fukuyama, F. (1992). *The end of history and the last man*. New York, NY: Avon Books.

Gadamer, H. G. (1989). *Truth and method* (Rev. ed.). (J. Weinsheimer & D. G. Marshall, Trans.). New York, NY: Crossroad.

Garcia Saiz, M. C. (1989). *Las Castas Mexicanas: Un género pictórico Americano* (The Mexican castas: A genre of American paintings). Milan, Italy: Olivetti.

Geertz, C. (1996). Afterward. In S. Feld & K. H. Basso (Eds.), *Senses of place* (pp. 259–262). Santa Fe, NM: School of American Research.

Geertz, G. (1973). *The interpretation of culture: Selected essays.* New York, NY: Basic Books.

George, N. (1998). *Hip hop America.* New York, NY: Penguin.

George, S. (2004). *Another world is possible if . . .* London, UK: Verso.

Giddens, A. (1994). Living in a post-traditional society. In U. Beck, A. Giddens, & S. Lash (Eds.), *Reflexive modernization* (pp. 56–109). Cambridge, UK: Polity.

Gillum, R. M. (2013). There is no difference in religious fundamentalism between American Muslims and American Christians. *The Washington Post.* Retrieved from http://www.washingtonpost.com/blogs/monkey-cage/wp/2013/12/16/no-difference-in-religious-fundamentalism-between-american-muslims-and-christians/

Gilroy, P. (1993). *The Black Atlantic: Modernity and double consciousness.* Cambridge, MA: Harvard University.

Giroux, H. A. (2004). Cultural studies, public pedagogy, and the responsibility of intellectuals. *Communication and Critical/Cultural Studies, 1*(1), 59–79.

Global Issues. (2013). *Poverty facts and stats.* Retrieved from http://www.globalissues.org/article/26/poverty-facts-and-stats

Global Multidimensional Poverty Index. (2013). *Oxford Poverty & Human Development Imitative.* Retrieved from http://www.ophi.org.uk/multidimensional-poverty-index/mpi-2014-2015/

Globalization101.org. (n.d.). *Cultural impact #2: Popular culture.* Retrieved from http://www.globalization101.org/index.php?file = issue&pass1 = subs&id = 128

Global Poll. (2001, December 20). U.S. policies played "significant role" in terror attacks. *Agence France Presse.* Retrieved from http://www.commondreams.org/headlines01/1220-01.htm

Golash-Boza, T. (2009). The immigration industrial complex: Why we enforce immigration policy destined to fail. *Sociology Compass, 3*(2), 295–309.

Gold, S. J. (2005). A summary and critique of relational approaches to international migration. In M. Romero & E. Margolis (Eds.), *The Blackwell companion to social inequity* (pp. 257–285). Malden, MA: Blackwell.

Goldberg, D. T. (2006). The global reach of raceless states. In D. Macedo & P. Gounari (Eds.), *The globalization of racism* (pp. 45–67). Boulder, CO: Paradigm.

Goldring, L. (1996). Blurring borders: Constructing transnational community in the process of Mexican-U.S. migration. *Research in community sociology* (Vol. 6, pp. 69–104). New York, NY: Jai Press.

González, A., & Harris, T. M. (2013). *Mediating cultures: Parenting in intercultural contexts.* Lanham, MD: Lexington Books.

Gotham, K. (2002). Marketing Mardi Gras: Commodification, spectacle and the political economy of tourism in New Orleans. *Urban Studies, 29*(10), 1735–1756.

Gottdiener, M. (2000). Approaches to consumption: Classical and contemporary perspectives. In M. Gottdiener (Ed.), *New forms of consumption* (pp. 3–31). Lanham, MD: Rowman & Littlefield.

Grandmaster Flash and the Furious Five. (1982). *The message* [CD]. Englewood, NJ: Sugarhill Records.

Graves, J. L. (2005). *The myth of race: Why we pretend race exists in America.* New York, NY: Dutton.

Greenwald, R. (Producer/Director). (2005). *Wal-Mart: The high cost of low price* [Motion picture]. Culver City, CA: Brave New Films.

Greifat, Y., & Katriel, T. (1989). Life demands musayara: Communication and culture among Arabs in Israel. In S. Ting-Toomey & F. Korzenny (Eds.), *Language, communication and culture: Current directions.* London, UK: SAGE.

Grewal, I. (2005). *Transnational America: Feminisms, diasporas, neoliberalisms.* Durham, NC: Duke University Press Books.

Grey, M. A., & Woodrick, A. C. (2002). Unofficial sister cities: Meatpacking labor migration between Villachuato, Mexico, and Marshalltown, Iowa. *Human Organization, 61,* 364–376.

Grinde, D. A., & Johansen, B. E. (1991). *Exemplar of liberty: Native America and the evolution of democracy.* Los Angeles, CA: American Indian Studies Center.

Grossberg, L. (1986). History, politics and postmodernism: Stuart Hall and cultural studies. *Journal of Communication Inquiry, 10*(2), 61–77.

Grossberg, L., Nelson, C., & Treichler, P. (1992). *Cultural studies.* New York, NY: Routledge.

Grossberg, L., Wartella, E., Whitney, C. D., & Wise, J. M. (2006). *MediaMaking: Mass media in a popular culture* (2nd ed.). Thousand Oaks, CA: SAGE.

Gudykunst, W. B. (1995). Anxiety/Uncertainty management (AUM) theory. In R. L. Wiseman (Ed.), *Intercultural communication* (pp. 8–58). Thousand Oaks, CA: SAGE.

Gudykunst, W., & Kim, Y. Y. (1997). *Communicating with strangers: An approach to intercultural communication* (3rd ed.). New York, NY: McGraw-Hill.

Guerrero, L. (2009). Can the subaltern shop? The commodification of difference in the *Bratz* dolls. *Cultural Studies/Critical Methodologies, 9*(2), 189–196.

Gullahorn J., & Gullahorn, J. (1963). An extension of the U-curve hypothesis. *Journal of Social Issues, 19*(3), 33–47.

Hall, E. T. (1959). *The silent language.* New York, NY: Doubleday.

Hall, E. T. (1966). *The hidden dimension.* New York, NY: Doubleday.

Hall, E. T. (1976). *Beyond culture.* New York, NY: Anchor.

Hall, S. (1980). Encoding/decoding. In S. Hall, D. Hobson, A. Lowe, & P. Willis (Eds.), *Culture, media and language* (pp. 128–138). London, UK: Hutchinson.

Hall, S. (Ed.). (1997a). *Representation: Cultural representations and signifying practices.* Thousand Oaks, CA: SAGE.

Hall, S. (1997b). Introduction. In S. Hall (Ed.), *Representation: Cultural representations and signifying practices* (pp. 1–45). Thousand Oaks: SAGE.

Hall, S., Evans, J., & Nixon, S. (Eds.). (2013). *Representation: Cultural representations and signifying practices* (2nd ed.). Los Angeles, CA: SAGE.

Halualani, R. T., Chitgopekar, A., Morrison, J. H. T. A., & Dodge, P. S. (2004). Who's interacting? And what are they talking about?—intercultural contact and interaction among multicultural university students. *International Journal of Intercultural Relations, 28*(5), 353–372.

Hammer, T. (1985). *European immigration policy: A comparative study.* Cambridge, UK: Cambridge University Press.

Harding, S. (1991). *Whose science, whose knowledge: Thinking from women's lives.* Ithaca, NY: Cornell University Press.

Harris, R. (2010). Why France is banning the veil. *Prospect.* Retrieved from http://www.prospectmagazine.co.uk/magazine/why-france-is-banning-the-veil

Hartsock, N. (1983). The feminist standpoint: Developing the ground for a specifically feminist historical materialism. In S. Harding & M. B. Hintikka (Eds.), *Discovering reality: Feminist perspectives on epistemology, metaphysics, methodology, and the philosophy of science* (pp. 283–310). London, UK: D. Reidel.

Harvey, D. (1990). *The condition of postmodernity: An enquiry into the origins of cultural change.* Cambridge, MA: Blackwell.

Harvey, D. (2005). *A brief history of neoliberalism.* New York, NY: Oxford University.

Hasian, M. (2002). The siege and American media portrayals of Arabs and Moslems. In J. N. Martin, T. K. Nakayama, & L. A. Flores (Eds.), *Readings in intercultural communication* (pp. 227–243). New York, NY: McGraw-Hill.

Hatcher, E. P. (1967). *Visual metaphors: A methodological study in visual communication.* Albuquerque: University of New Mexico.

Hayes, J. (1995). *Religion, fundamentalism, and ethnicity: A global perspective.* United Nations Research Institute for Social Development. Retrieved from http://www.unrisd.org/80256B3C005BCCF9/%28httpPublications%29/265FAA83B0EA35EB80256B67005B67F6?OpenDocument

Hegde, R. (2002). Translated enactments: The relational configurations of the Asian Indian immigrant experience. In J. N. Martin, T. K. Nakayama, & L. A. Flores (Eds.), *Readings in intercultural communication: Experiences and contexts* (2nd ed., pp. 259–266). Boston, MA: McGraw-Hill.

Heidegger, M. (1962). *Being and time* (J. MacQuarrie & E. Robinson, Trans.). London, UK: SCM.

Held, D., McGrew, A. G., Goldblatt, D., & Perraton, J. (1999). *Global transformations: Politics, economics and culture.* Stanford, CA: Stanford University Press.

Hocker, J. L., & Wilmot, W. W. (1998). *Interpersonal conflict* (5th ed.). New York, NY: McGraw-Hill.

Hofstede, G. (1980). *Culture's consequences: International differences in work-related values.* Beverly Hills, CA: SAGE.

Hofstede, G. (2001). *Culture's consequences: Comparing values, behaviors, institutions, and organizations across nations* (2nd ed.). Thousand Oaks, CA: SAGE.

hooks, b. (1992). *Black looks: Race and representation.* Boston, MA: South End.

Howard, K. H., & Pardue, D. F. (1996). *Inventing the Southwest: The Fred Harvey Company and Native American art.* Flagstaff, AZ: Northland.

Huntington, S. P. (1993). *The third wave: Democratization in the late 20th century.* Norman: University of Oklahoma Press.

Ignatiev, N. (1995). *How the Irish became White.* New York, NY: Routledge.

Ikeda, D. (2005). Forward. In N. Nodding (Ed.), *Educating citizens for global awareness* (pp. ix–xi). New York, NY: Columbia Teachers College.

Inda, J. X., & Rosaldo, R. (2001). A world in motion. In J. X. Inda & R. Rosaldo (Eds.), *The anthropology of globalization: A reader* (pp. 1–36). Cambridge, UK: Blackwell.

Inda, J. X., & Rosaldo, R. (2008). Tracking global flows. In J. X. Inda & R. Rosaldo (Eds.), *The anthropology of globalization: A reader* (2nd ed., pp. 3–46). Cambridge, UK: Blackwell.

Institute of Inclusive Security. (2014). *Rose Kabuye.* Retrieved from http://www.inclusivesecurity.org/network-bio/rose-kabuye/

International Monetary Fund. (2009). *The implications of the global financial crisis for low-income countries.* Retrieved from http://imf.org/external/pubs/ft/books/2009/globalfin/globalfin.pdf

International Organization for Migration. (n.d.). *About migration.* Retrieved from http://www.iom.int/cms/en/sites/iom/home.html

Internet World Stats. (2014). *Internet usage statistics.* Retrieved from http://www.internetworldstats.com/stats.htm

Ito, M. (2010). *Hanging out, messing around, and geeking out: Kids living and learning with new media.* Cambridge: Massachusetts Institute of Technology.

ITU World Telecommunication. (2014). *ICT Facts and Figures.* Retrieved from http://www.itu.int/en/ITU-D/Statistics/Documents/facts/ICTFactsFigures2014-e.pdf

Jamet, C., & Ceilles, M. (2014). Port du voile: Ce que dit la loi [Headscarf: What the law says.]. *Le Figaro.* Retrieved November 8, 2014, from http://www.lefigaro.fr/actualite-france/2014/10/20/01016-20141020ARTFIG00055-port-du-voile-ce-que-dit-la-loi.php

Jenkins, H. (2010). Avatar activism: Pick your protest. *The Global and Mail.* Retrieved from http://www.theglobeandmail.com/globe-debate/avatar-activism-pick-your-protest/article4190179/

Jenkins, J. (2014). Why Obama is planning to use religion to fight ISIS. *Thinkprogress.* Retrieved from http://thinkprogress.org/world/2014/09/24/3571769/why-obama-is-planning-to-use-religion-to-fight-isis/

Johnson, T. D., & Kreider, R. M. (2010). Mapping interracial/interethnic married-couple households in the United States: 2010. Washington, DC: U.S. Census Bureau. Retrieved from http://www.census.gov/hhes/socdemo/marriage/data/census/InterracialMarriages_PAA2013_FINAL.pdf

Joseph, S. (2006). *In black and white: Representations of Arab and Muslim Americans and Islam in US print news media*. Retrieved from http://www.iue.it/RSCAS/Research/Mediterranean/mspr2006/pdf/joseph-bio-abstract.pdf

Kabute, R. (2005). Warriors for peace. In B. Medea & J. Evans (Eds.), *Stop the next war now* (pp. 39–40). Maui, HI: Inner Ocean.

Kakuchi, S. (2014). Japan seeks foreign workers, uneasily. *Inter Press Services News Agency*. Retrieved from http://www.ipsnews.net/2014/04/japan-seeks-foreign-workers-uneasily/

Kalmijn, M. (1993). Trends in Black/White in intermarriage. *Social Forces, 72,* 119–146.

Keefe, P. R. (2008). China's great migration. *Slate*. Retrieved from http://www.slate.com/articles/news_and_politics/dispatches/features/2008/chinas_great_migration/why_leave_changle.html

Keegan, R. (2013). USC study: Minorities still underrepresented in popular films. *Los Angeles Times*. Retrieved from http://articles.latimes.com/2013/oct/30/entertainment/la-et-mn-race-and-movies-20131030

Kidd, D. (2007). Harry Potter and the functions of popular culture. *The Journal of Popular Culture, 40*(1), 69–89.

Kim, S. (2014). The richest actors in the world are not who you expect. *Good Morning America*. Retrieved from https://gma.yahoo.com/richest-actors-world-not-expect-015943179--abc-news-celebrities.html

Kim, Y. Y. (2001). *Becoming intercultural: An integrative theory of communication and cross-cultural adaptation*. Thousand Oaks, CA: SAGE.

Kindly, K., & Horwitz, S. (2014). Evidence supports officer's account of shooting in Ferguson. *Washington Post*. Retrieved from http://www.washingtonpost.com/politics/new-evidence-supports-officers-account-of-shooting-in-ferguson/2014/10/22/cf38c7b4-5964-11e4-bd61-346aee66ba29_story.html

Kitae, K., & Staines, R. (2005). "Konglish" slogans hurt image. *Korea Times*. Retrieved from http://times.hankooki.com/lpage/nation/200506/kt2005062917203311990.htm

Kitwana, B. (2003). *The hip hop generation: Young blacks and the crisis in African American culture*. New York, NY: Basic Civitas Books.

Kitwana, B. (2005). *Why white kids love hip hop: Wankstas, wiggers, wannabes, and the new reality of race in America*. New York, NY: Basic Civitas Books.

Kivel, P. (1996). *Uprooting racism: How white people can work for racial justice*. Philadelphia, PA: New Society.

Klein, N. (2011). The most important thing in the world. In S. van Gelder (Ed.), *This changes everything: Occupy Wall Street and the 99% movement* (pp. 45–49). San Francisco, CA: Berrett-Koehler.

Kluckhohn, C., & Kroeber, A. (1952). *Culture: A critical review of concepts and definitions*. Cambridge, MA: Harvard University Peabody Museum of American Archeology and Ethnology Papers, 47.

Koffmar, L. (2014). Two out of five war fatalities occurred in Syria. *Uppsala Conflict Data Program*. Retrieved from http://www.uu.se/en/media/news/article/?id = 3514&area = 2,6,10,16&typ = artikel&na = &lang = en

Kosin, B. A., Mayer, A., & Keysar, A. (2001). American religious identification survey. *The Graduate Center of the City of New York*. Retrieved from http://www.gc.cuny.edu/faculty/research_briefs/aris.pdf

Koughan, F., & Rushkoff, D. (Producers). (2014). *Generation like* [Motion picture]. United States: PBS.

Krogstad, J. M., & Passel, J. S. (2014). 5 facts about illegal immigration in the U.S. *Pew Research Center*. Retrieved from http://www.pewresearch.org/fact-tank/2014/11/18/5-facts-about-illegal-immigration-in-the-u-s/

Krumrey-Fulks, K. S. (2001). *At the margins of culture: Intercultural friendship between Americans and Chinese in the academic setting*. Unpublished doctoral dissertation, University of Kentucky, Lexington.

Las Casas, B. D. (1992). *A short account of the destruction of the Indies*. London, UK: Penguin Books. (Original work published 1542)

Lasn, K. (2000). *Culture jam: How to reverse America's suicidal consumer binge—and why we must.* New York, NY: HarperCollins.

Laszloffy, T. A., & Rockquemore, K. A. (2013). What about the children? Exploring misconceptions and realities about mixed-race children. In E. Smith and A. J. Hattery (Eds.), *Interracial relationships in the 21st century* (pp. 45–65). Durham, NC: Carolina Academic Press.

Le, C. N. (2006). The first Asian Americans. *Asian-nation: The landscape of Asian America.* Retrieved from http://www.asian-nation.org/first.shtml

Leach, W. (1993). *Land of desire: Merchants, power, and the rise of a new American culture.* New York, NY: Pantheon.

Lee, P.-W. (2008). Stages and transitions of relational identity development in intercultural friendship: Implications for identity management theory [Electronic version]. *Journal of International and Intercultural Communication, 1*(1), 51–69.

Le Lam, L. (Director). (2014). *Not business as usual* [video]. Institute B. Retrieved from http://www.instituteb.com/changemakers/b-corporation/

Lerner, G. (1986). *The creation of patriarchy.* New York, NY: Oxford University Press.

Lewin, K. (1948). Social psychological differences between the United States and Germany. In G. Lewin (Ed.), *Resolving social conflicts.* New York, NY: Harper.

LGBT Republic of Iran: An online reality? (2012). *Small Media Report* [leaflets and audio cassettes] Retrieved from http://issuu.com/smallmedia/docs/lgbtrepublic

Lim, J. (2014). WeChat, one of the world's most powerful apps. *Forbes.* Retrieved from http://www.forbes.com/sites/jlim/2014/05/19/wechat-one-of-the-worlds-most-powerful-apps/

Litwack, L. F. (1998). *Trouble in mind: Black southerners in the age of Jim Crow.* New York, NY: Alfred A. Knopf.

Liu, I. J. (2007). Chinese immigrants chase opportunities in America. *NPR News.* Retrieved from http://www.npr.org/templates/story/story.php?storyId = 16356755

Loewen, J. W. (2006). *Sundown towns: A hidden dimension of American racism.* New York, NY: Touchstone.

Lopez, I. H. F. (1996). *White by law: The legal construction of race.* New York, NY: New York University Press.

Lorber, J., & Farrell, S. A. (Eds.). (1991). *The social construction of gender.* Thousand Oaks, CA: SAGE.

Low, S. M., & Lawrence-Zúñiga, D. (2003). Locating culture. In S. M. Low & D. Lawrence-Zúñiga (Eds.), *The anthropology of space and place: Locating culture* (pp. 1–47). Malden, MA: Blackwell.

Lui, M., Robles, B., Leondar-Wright, B., Brewer, R., & Adamson, R. (2006). *The color of wealth: The story behind the U.S. racial wealth divide.* New York, NY: The New Press.

Lysgaard, S. (1955). Adjustment in a foreign society: Norwegian Fulbright grantees visiting the United States. *International Social Science Bulletin, 7,* 45–51.

Macedo, D., & Gounari, P. (Eds.). (2006). *The globalization of racism.* Boulder, CO: Paradigm.

Markus, H. R., & Lin, L. R. (1999). Conflictways: Cultural diversity in the meanings and practices of conflict. In D. A. Prentice & D. T. Miller (Eds.), *Cultural divides: Understanding and overcoming group conflict* (pp. 302–333). New York, NY: Russell Sage.

Martin, J. (1984). The intercultural re-entry: Conceptualization and directions for future research. *International Journal of Intercultural Relations, 8,* 115–134.

Martin, J. N., & Nakayama, T. K. (2004). *Intercultural communication in contexts.* Boston, MA: McGraw-Hill.

Martinez, E. (1998). *What is white supremacy? Challenge white supremacy workshop presentation.* Retrieved from http://www.prisonactivist.org/archive/cws/betita.html

Massey, D., Arango, J., Hugo, G., Kouaouci, A., Pellegrino, A., & Taylor, J. E. (1993). Theories of international migration: A review and appraisal. *Population Development Review, 19* (3), 431–466.

McCannell, D. (1976). *A new theory of the leisure class.* New York, NY: Shocken Books.

McIntosh, P. (2005). Gender perspectives on educating for global citizenship. In N. Nodding (Ed.), *Educating citizens for global awareness* (pp. 22–39). New York, NY: Columbia Teachers College.

McKinney, C. (2006). McKinney warns of new underclass of "Katrina homeless." *The Final Call.* Retrieved from http://www.finalcall.com/artman/publish/article_2440

Meghelli, S. (2013). Hip-Hop à la Française. *New York Times.* Retrieved from http://www.nytimes.com/roomfordebate/2013/10/14/is-france-becoming-too-american/hip-hop-a-la-francaise-29

Melone, S. D., Terzis, G., & Beleli, O. (2002). Using the media for conflict transformation: The Common Ground experience. *Berghof handbook for conflict transformation.* Berlin, Germany: Berghof Research Center for Constructive Conflict Transformation. Retrieved from http://image.berghof-foundation.org/fileadmin/redaktion/Publications/Handbook/Articles/melone_hb.pdf

Mercado, A. (2016). Transnational practices of communication and social justice: Indigenous Mexican immigrants in the United States. In K. Sorrells & S. Sekimoto (Eds.), *Globalization Intercultural Communication: A Reader* (pp. 249–259). Los Angeles, CA: SAGE.

Metha, A. (2009, February). Consumerism in India. *Nazar: A South Asian perspective.* Retrieved from http://nazaronline.net/travel-living/2009/02/consumerism-in-india/

Mirrlees, T. (2013). *Global entertainment media: Between cultural imperialism and cultural globalization.* New York, NY: Routledge.

Mohn, T. (2013). Travel boom: Youth tourists spent $217 billion last year, more growth than any other group. *Forbes.* Retrieved from http://www.forbes.com/sites/tanyamohn/2013/10/07/the-new-young-traveler-boom/

Montagu, A. (1997). *Man's most dangerous myth: The fallacy of race* (6th ed.). Walnut Creek, CA: AltaMira.

Moon, M., & Rolison, G. (1998). Communication of classism. In M. L. Hecht (Ed.), *Communicating prejudice* (pp. 122–135). Thousand Oaks, CA: SAGE.

Moraga, C., & Anzaldúa, G. (Eds.). (1981). *This bridge called my back: Writings by radical women of color.* New York, NY: Kitchen Table.

Moraga, C., Anzaldúa, G., & Bambara, T. C. (1984). *This bridge called my back: Writings by radical women of color.* New York, NY: Kitchen Table.

Mullard, M., & Cole, B. A. (2007). *Globalisation, citizenship and the war on terror.* Cheltenham, UK: Edward Elgar.

Nakayama, T. K. (1998). Communication of heterosexism. In M. L. Hecht (Ed.), *Communication prejudice* (pp. 112–121). Thousand Oaks, CA: SAGE.

Nakayama, T. K., & Martin, J. N. (Eds.). (1999). *Whiteness: The communication of social identity.* Thousand Oaks, CA: SAGE.

Nandy, A. (2004). Consumerism: Its hidden beauties and politics. In F. Jandt (Ed.), *Intercultural communication: A global reader* (pp. 400–403). Thousand Oaks, CA: SAGE.

Naples, N. A., & Desai, M. (2002). *Women's activism and globalization.* New York, NY: Routledge.

Nederveen Pieterse, J. (2004). *Globalization and culture: Global mélange.* Lanham, MD: Rowman & Littlefield.

Neil, D. (2009, June 1). When cars were America's idols. *Los Angeles Times,* p. A1.

Noddings, N. (Ed.). (2005). *Educating citizens for global awareness.* New York, NY: Columbia Teachers College.

Nudd, T. (2013). It's 2013, and people are still getting worked up about interracial couples in ads: Cheerios spot gets cheers and jeers. *Adweek.* Retrieved from http://www.adweek.com/adfreak/its-2013-and-people-are-still-getting-worked-about-interracial-couples-ads-149889

Nurden, R. (1997, October 30). Teaching tailored for business people's every demand. *The European,* p. 39.

Oberg, K. (1960). Culture shock: Adjustment to new cultural environments. *Practice Anthropology, 7,* 170–179.

Occupy Wall Street. (2014). *About us.* Retrieved from http://occupywallst.org/about/

Olarn, K., & Bothlho, G. (2014). Lawyer: 5 Thai students detained after "Hunger Game" salute. *CNN*. Retrieved from http://www.cnn.com/2014/11/19/world/asia/thailand-hunger-games-salute/

Ong, A. (1999). *Flexible citizenship: The cultural logics of transnationality*. Durham, NC: Duke University Press.

Orbe, M. (1998). *Constructing co-cultural theory: An explication of culture, power and communication*. Thousand Oaks, CA: SAGE.

Orbe, M. (2011). *Communication realities in a "post-racial" society: What the U.S. public really thinks about Barack Obama*. Lanham, MD: Lexington Books.

Orbe, M. (2016). Diverse understandings of a "Post-Racial" society. In K. Sorrells & S.Sekimoto (Eds.), *Globalization Intercultural Communication: A Reader* (pp. 24–34). Los Angeles, CA: SAGE.

Orbe, M. P., & Harris, T. M. (2008). *Interracial communication: Theory into practice* (2nd ed.). Belmont, CA: Wadsworth.

Orfield, G., Frankenberg, E., Ee, J., & Kuscera, J. (2014). *Brown at 60: Great progress, a long retreat and an uncertain future*. The Civil Rights Project UCLA. Retrieved from http://civilrightsproject.ucla .edu/research/k-12-education/integration-and-diversity/brown-at-60-great-progress-a-long-retreat-and-an-uncertain-future

Osland, J. S., & Bird, A. (2000). Beyond sophisticated stereotypes: Cultural sense-making in context. *Academy of Management Executive, 14*, 65–79.

Osnos, E. (2014). "The Big Bang Theory" and our future with China. *New Yorker*. Retrieved from http:// www.newyorker.com/news/daily-comment/the-big-bang-theory-and-our-future-with-china

Oxfam. (2014). Working for the few. *Oxfam International*. Retrieved from http://www.oxfam.org/en/ policy/working-for-the-few-economic-inequality

Padilla, M. B., Hirsch, J. S., Muñoz-Laboy, M., Sember, R. E., & Parker, R. G. (Eds.). (2007). *Love and globalization: Transformations of intimacy in the contemporary world*. Nashville, TN: Vanderbilt University Press.

Payaslian, S. (2005). *United States policy toward the Armenian questions and the Armenian genocide*. New York, NY: Palgrave McMillan.

Perry, M. D. (2012). Global black self-fashioning: Hip hop as diasporic space. In M. Forman & M. A. Neal (Eds.), *That's the joint! The hip hop studies reader* (2nd ed., pp. 294–314). New York, NY: Routledge.

Pew Research Center. (2009). Mapping the global Muslim Population: A report on the size and distribution of the world's Muslim population. Retrieved from http://www.pewforum.org/files/2009/10/ Muslimpopulation.pdf

Pew Research Center. (2014). *Religious hostilities reach six-year high*. Retrieved from http://www.pewforum .org/2014/01/14/religious-hostilities-reach-six-year-high/

Pew Research Center for People and the Press. (2013). *Big racial divide over Zimmerman case: Whites say too much focus on race, Blacks disagree*. Retrieved from http://www.people-press.org/2013/07/22/ big-racial-divide-over-zimmerman-verdict/

Pew Research Internet Project. (2012). *Digital differences*. Retrieved from http://www.pewinternet.org/ files/old-media//Files/Reports/2012/PIP_Digital_differences_041312.pdf

Portes, A., Guarnizo, L., & Landolt, P. (Eds.). (1999). The study of transnationalism: Pitfalls and promises of an emerging research field. *Ethnic and racial studies, 2*(22), 217–237.

Postiglioni, G. (1983). *Ethnicity and American social theory: Toward critical pluralism*. Lanham, MD: University Press.

Potts, L. (1990). *The world labour market: A history of migration*. London, UK: Zed.

Ram, A. (2004). Memory, cinema, and the reconstitution of cultural identities in the Asian Indian diaspora. In M. Fong & R. Chuang (Eds.), *Communicating ethnic & cultural identity*. Lanham, MD: Rowman & Littlefield.

Reynolds, T. (2014). *The NBA has really gone global in the finals*. Retrieved from http://chronicle .augusta.com/sports/nba/2014-06-13/nba-has-really-gone-global-finals

Ridgeway, J. (2004). *It's all for sale: The control of global resources.* Durham, NC: Duke University Press.

Riding, A. (2006). Rap and film at the Louvre: What's up with that? *New York Times.* Retrieved from http://www.nytimes.com/2006/11/21/books/21morr.html

Rifkin, J. (2000, January, 17). The new capitalism is about turning culture into commerce. *Los Angeles Times.* Retrieved from http://www.uni-muenster.de/PeaCon/dgs-mills/mills-texte/Rifkin-Hyper capitalism.htm

Riley, N. S. (2010). *'Til faith do us part: How interfaith marriage is transforming America.* New York, NY: Oxford University Press.

Robbins, R. H. (2014). *Global problems and the culture of capitalism* (6th ed.). Boston, MA: Allyn & Bacon.

Roberts, R. E. (1994). Black-White inter-marriage in the United States. In W. R. Johnson & D. M. Warren (Eds.), *Inside the mixed marriage* (pp. 25–79). Lanham, MD: University Press of America.

Robertson, R. (1992). *Globalization: Social theory and global culture.* London, UK: SAGE.

Rodríguez, C. (2001). *Fissures in the mediascape: An international study of citizens' media.* Cresskill, NJ: Hampton Press.

Rogers, E. M., Hart, W. B., & Miike, Y. (2002). Edward T. Hall and the history of intercultural communication: The United States and Japan. *Keio Communication Review, 24,* 3–26.

Root, D. (1996). *Cannibal culture: Art, appropriation, and the commodification of difference.* Boulder, CO: Westview Press.

Root, M. P. P. (1996). A bill of rights for racially mixed people. In M. P. P. Root (Ed.), *Racially mixed people in the new millennium.* Newbury Park, CA: SAGE.

Rose, T. (1994). *Black noise: Rap music and Black culture in contemporary American society.* Hanover, NH: Wesleyan.

Rose, T. (2008). *The hip hop war.* New York, NY: Basic Books.

Rosenau, J. N. (2003). *Distant proximities: Dynamics beyond globalization.* Princeton, NJ: Princeton University Press.

Roubini, N. (2014). The great backlash. *Project syndicate.* Retrieved from https://www.project-syndicate.org/commentary/nouriel-roubini-likens-the-rise-of-nationalism-today-to-that-of-authoritarian-regimes-during-the-great-depression

Rumer, E., Weiss, A. S., Speck, U., Khatib, L., Perkovich, G., & Paal, D. H. (2014). What are the global implications of the Ukraine crisis? *Carnegie Endowment for International Peace.* Retrieved from http://carnegieendowment.org/2014/03/27/what-are-global-implications-of-ukraine-crisis#europe

Rushdie, S. (1991). *Imaginary homelands.* New York, NY: Penguin.

Rybas, N. (2012). Producing the self at the digital interface. In P. H. Cheong, J. N. Martin & L. P. Mcfadyen (Eds.), *New media and intercultural communication: Identity, community and politics* (pp. 93–107). New York, NY: Peter Lang.

Saenz, R., Morales, M. C., & Ayala, M. I. (2004). The United States: Immigration to the melting pot of the Americas. In M. I. Toro-Morn & M. Alicea (Eds.), *Migration and immigration: A global view* (pp. 211–232). Westwood, CT: Greenwood.

Said, E. W. (1978). *Orientalism.* New York, NY: Random House.

Sardar, Z., & Davies, M. W. (2002). *Why do people hate America?* New York, NY: The Disinformation Company.

Sassen, S. (1994). *Cities in a world economy.* London, UK: Pine Forge.

Sauerwein, K. (2000, January 13). Peer Pressure: Grant High students cross ethnic lines to foster peace on campus. *Los Angeles Times,* Valley Edition.

Saussure, F. de (1960). *Course in general linguistics.* London, UK: Peter Owen.

Schoen, R., & Wooldredge, K. (1989). Marriage choices in North Carolina and Virginia, 1969–1971 and 1979–1981. *Journal of Marriage and the Family, 51*(2), 465–481.

Searle, J. R. (1995). *The construction of social reality.* New York, NY: The Free Press.

Sentinel News Agency. (2014). *Community Coalition secures $3 million dollars from CDC for South LA residents.* Retrieved from http://www.lasentinel.net/index.php?option = com_content&view = art icle&id = 13884&catid = 80&Itemid = 170

Shapiro, S. F. (2000). The culture thief. *New Rules Project: Exploring community, mobility, scale and trade.* Retrieved from http://www.newrules.org/journal/nrfall00culture.html

Shapiro, T., Meschede, T., & Osoro, S. (2013). The roots of the widening racial wealth gap: Explaining the Black-White economic divide. *Institute on Assets and Social Policy.* Retrieved from http://iasp .brandeis.edu/pdfs/Author/shapiro-thomas-m/racialwealthgapbrief.pdf

Shepherd, R. (2002). Commodification, culture and tourism. *Tourism Studies, 2,* 193–201.

Shim, T. Y., Kim, M., & Martin, J. N. (2008). *Changing Korea: Understanding culture and communication.* New York, NY: Peter Lang.

Shiva, V. (2012). *Making peace with the earth.* London, UK: Pluto Press.

Shome, R., & Hegde, R. S. (2002). Culture, communication and the challenge of globalization. *Critical Studies in Media Communication, 19*(2), 172–189.

Short, J. E. (2013). How much media? *2013 Report on American consumers: Executive summary.* Retrieved from http://www.marshall.usc.edu/faculty/centers/ctm/research/how-much-media

Sias, P. M., Drzewiecka, J. A., Mears, M., Bent, R., Konomi, Y., Ortega, M., & White, C. (2008). Intercultural friendship development. *Communication Reports, 21*(1), 1–13.

Smith, A. (2005). *Conquest: Sexual violence and American Indian genocide.* Cambridge, MA: South End.

Smith, C. E. (1966). Negro-White intermarriage: Forbidden sexual union. *Journal of Sex Research, 2*(2), 169–177.

Smith, D. (2013). Images of black males in popular media. *Huffington Post.* Retrieved from http://www .huffingtonpost.com/darron-t-smith-phd/black-men-media_b_2844990.html

Smith, S. L., Choueiti, M., & Pieper, K. (2013). Race/ethnicity in 500 popular films: Is the key to diversifying cinematic content held in the hand of the Black director? *Media Diversity & Social Change Initiative.* Retrieved from http://annenberg.usc.edu/sitecore/shell/applications/ ~ /media/pdfs/race-ethnicity.ashx

Solnit, R. (2004). *Hope in the dark: Untold histories, wild possibilities.* New York, NY: Nation Books.

Sorrells, K. (2002). Embodied negotiation: Commodification and cultural representation in the U.S. southwest. In M. J. Collier (Ed.), *Intercultural alliances: International and intercultural communication annual* (Vol. 25, pp. 17–47). Thousand Oaks, CA: SAGE.

Sorrells, K. (2003). Communicating common ground: Integrating community service learning into the intercultural classroom. *Communication Teacher, 17*(4), 1–14.

Sorrells, K., & Nakagawa, G. (2008). Intercultural communication praxis and the struggle for social responsibility and social justice. In O. Swartz (Ed.), *Transformative communication studies: Culture, hierarchy, and the human condition* (pp. 23–61). Leicester, UK: Troubador.

Sorrells, K., & Sekimoto, S. (2016). Globalizing intercultural communication: Traces and trajectories. In K. Sorrells & S. Sekimoto (Eds.), *Globalizing intercultural communication: A reader* (pp. 2–13). Los Angeles, CA: SAGE.

Stannard, D. E. (1992). *American holocaust: Columbus and the conquest of the New World.* New York, NY: Oxford University Press.

Steinbugler, A. C. (2012). *Beyond Loving: Intimate racework in lesbian, gay, and straight interracial relationships.* Oxford, U.K.: Oxford University Press.

Stewart, L. P., Copper, P. J., & Stewart, A. D. (2003). *Communication and gender* (4th ed.). Boston, MA: Allyn & Bacon.

Stiglitz, J. (2002). *Globalization and its discontents.* New York, NY: W.W. Norton.

Stiglitz, J. (2012). *The price of inequality: How today's divided society endangers our future.* New York, NY: Norton.

Stone, O. (Director). (1987). *Wall street* [Motion picture]. United States: 20th Century Fox.

Strashin, J. (2014). Olivia Chow confronts racism, sexism in mayoral campaign: "Nasty stuff" accumulates online amid xenophobic remarks at debates. Retrieved from http://www.cbc.ca/news/canada/toronto/olivia-chow-confronts-racism-sexism-in-mayoral-campaign-1.2785984

Stryker, S., & Whittle, S. (2006). *The transgender studies reader.* New York, NY: Routledge.

Sullivan, T., Ali, M., de Alejo, C. P., Miller, B., & Beana, N. M. (2013). *The state of a dream 2013: A long way from home.* Retrieved from http://faireconomy.org

Sumner, W. (1906). *Folkways.* New York, NY: Ginn.

Swaine, J. (2014). Ferguson after Michael Brown's death. 'This a war and we are soldiers on the front line.' *The Guardian.* Retrieved from http://www.theguardian.com/world/2014/aug/13/michael-brown-ferguson-murder-race-relations-white-police

The roots of hip hop. (1986). *RM HIP HOP MAGAZINE.* Retrieved from http://globaldarkness.com/articles/roots_of_hiphop.htm

Thomas, P. (2009, February). The trouble with travel. *Geographic.* Retrieved from www.geographical.co.uk

Thompson, J., & Collier, M. J. (2006). Toward contingent understandings of intersecting identifications among selected U.S. interracial couples: Integrating interpretive and critical perspectives. *Communication Quarterly, 54*(4), 487–506.

Thussu, D. K. (20010). *International communication* (4th ed.). London, UK: Hodder Arnold.

Ting-Toomey, S., & Kurogi, A. (1998). Facework competence in intercultural conflict: An updated face-negotiation theory. *International Journal of Intercultural Relations, 22,* 187–296.

Ting-Toomey, S., & Oetzel, J. G. (2001). *Managing intercultural conflict effectively.* Thousand Oaks, CA: SAGE.

Ting-Toomey, S., & Oetzel, J. G. (2002). Cross-cultural face concern and conflict styles: Current status and future directions. In W. B. Gudykunst & B. Mody (Eds.), *Handbook of international and intercultural communication* (2nd ed., pp. 143–206). Thousand Oaks, CA: SAGE.

Todorov, T. (1984). *The conquest of the Americas: The question of the other.* New York, NY: Harper Row.

Tomlinson, J. (1999). *Globalization and culture.* Cambridge, UK: Blackwell.

Toro-Morn, M. I., & Alicea, M. (Eds.). (2004). *Migration and immigration: A global view.* Westwood, CT: Greenwood.

Triandis, H. C. (1995). *Individualism & collectivism.* Boulder, CO: Westview.

Tunstall, J. (2008). *The media were American: U.S. mass media in decline.* New York, NY: Oxford University.

UNESCO Institute for Statistics. (2013). *UIS fact sheet.* Retrieved from http://www.uis.unesco.org/literacy/Documents/fs26-2013-literacy-en.pdf

United Nations. (2013). *World migration in figures.* Retrieved from http://www.oecd.org/els/mig/World-Migration-in-Figures.pdf

United Nations, Department of Economic and Social Affairs, Population Division. (2013). *International Migration Report 2013.* New York, NY: Author.

United Nations High Commissioner for Refugees. (n.d.). *World refugee day: Global forced displacement tops 50 million for first time in post-WWII.* Retrieved from http://www.unhcr.org/pages/49c3646c11.html

United Nations High Commissioner for Refugees. (2012). *The state of the world's refugees: In search of solidarity.* New York, NY: Author.

United Nations Population Division. (2013). *International migration report.* Retrieved from http://esa.un.org/unmigration/documents/worldmigration/2013/Full_Document_final.pdf

United Nations Relief and Works Agency. (2007). *The United Nations and Palestinian refugees.* Retrieved from http://www.unrwa.org/userfiles/2010011791015.pdf

United Nations Relief and Works Agency for Palestine Refugees. (2014, July). *UNRW: In figures.* Retrieved from http://www.unrwa.org/sites/default/files/in_figures_july_2014_en_06jan2015_1.pdf

United Nations World Tourism Organization. (2014a). *International tourism on track to end 2014 with record numbers.* Retrieved from http://media.unwto.org/press-release/2014-12-18/international-tourism-track-end-2014-record-numbers

United Nations World Tourism Organization. (2014b). *Tourism highlights.* Retrieved from http://dtx-tq4w60xqpw.cloudfront.net/sites/all/files/pdf/unwto_highlights14_en_hr_0.pdf

United States Institute of Peace. (2011). *The impact of new media on peacebuilding and conflict management.* Retrieved from http://www.usip.org/sites/default/files/Adan/2011-2012_study%20guide_final_full.pdf

United We Dream. (n.d.). Retrieved from http://unitedwedream.org/about/history/

U.S. Census Bureau. (2012). *U.S. Census Bureau projections show a slower growing, older, more diverse nation a half century from now.* Retrieved from https://www.census.gov/newsroom/releases/archives/population/cb12-243.html

U.S. Census Bureau. (2014). *Poverty 2012 and 2013.* Retrieved from http://www.census.gov/content/dam/Census/library/publications/2014/acs/acsbr13-01.pdf

U.S. Department of Labor: Bureau of Labor Statistics. (2015). *Databases, tables, and calculators by subject.* Retrieved from http://data.bls.gov/timeseries/LNS14000000

Verán, C. (2012). Native tongues: A roundtable on hip hop's global indigenous movement. In M. Forman & M. A. Neal (Eds.), *That's the joint! The hip hop studies reader* (2nd ed., pp. 336–344). New York, NY: Routledge.

Villalobos-Romo, G., & Sekimoto, S. (2016). A view from the other side: Technology, media, and transnational families in Mexico-U.S. migration. In K. Sorrells & S. Sekimoto (Eds.), *Globalizing intercultural communication: A reader* (pp. 65–77). Los Angeles, CA: SAGE.

Wallerstein, I. (2000). *The essential Wallerstein.* New York, NY: New Press.

Wallerstein, I. (2011). *Historical capitalism with capitalist civilization.* New York, NY: Verso.

Waltz, M. (2005). *Alternative and activist media.* Edinburgh, Scotland: University of Edinburgh.

Walvin, J. (1986). *Questioning slavery.* New York, NY: Routledge.

Wang, W. (2012). The rise of intermarriage: Rates, characteristics vary by race and gender. *Pew Research Social & Demographic Trends.* Retrieved from http://www.pewsocialtrends.org/2012/02/16/the-rise-of-intermarriage/#executive-summary

Weeks, J., Holland, J., & Waites, M. (Eds.). (2003). *Sexuality and society: A reader.* Cambridge, UK: Polity.

Whoriskey, P. (2006, August 4). Latin American melodramas that are made in the U.S. *Washington Post.* Retrieved from http://hispanic7.com/latin_american_ melodramas_that_are_made_in_the_u_s_a_.htm

Wikimedia Commons. (2008a). *Colonisation 1800.* Retrieved from http://commons.wikimedia.org/wiki/File:Colonisation_1800.png

Wikimedia Commons. (2008b). *Colonisation 1914.* Retrieved from http://commons.wikimedia.org/wiki/File:Colonisation_1914.png

Williams, P. J. (2004). Of race and risk. In M. L. Andersen & P. H. Collins (Eds.), *Race class and gender: An anthology* (5th ed., pp. 108–110). Belmont, CA: Wadsworth/Thomson Learning.

Williams, T. T. (2005). The open space of democracy. In B. Medea & J. Evans (Eds.), *Stop the next war now* (pp. 36–39). Maui, HI: Inner Ocean.

Wilson, C. C., Gutiérrez, F., & Chao, L. M. (2013). *Racism, sexism and the media: The rise of class communication in multicultural America* (4th ed.). Thousand Oaks, CA: SAGE.

Wimmer, A. (2013). State of war: How the nation-state made modern conflict. *Foreign Affairs*. Retrieved from http://www.foreignaffairs.com/articles/140245/andreas-wimmer/states-of-war

Winant, H. (2001). *The world is a ghetto: Race and democracy since WWII*. New York, NY: Basic Books.

Wolf, E. R. (1982). *Europe and the people without history*. Berkeley: University of California Press.

Wong, K., & Ramos, M. (2012). Introduction: Tam Tran and Cinthya Felix undocumented and unafraid. In K. Wong, J. Shadduck-Hernadez, F. Inzunza, J. Monroe, V. Narro, & A. Valenzuela (Eds.), *Undocumented and unafraid: Tam Tran, Cinthya Felix, and the immigrant youth movement* (pp. 3–6). Los Angeles, CA: UCLA Center for Labor Research and Education.

Wood, J. T. (1982). *Human communication: A symbolic interactionist perspective*. McAllen, TX: Holt, Rinehart, and Winston.

Wood, J. T. (2005). *Gendered lives: Communication, gender, & culture* (6th ed.). Belmont, CA: Wadsworth.

Woodrick, A. C. (2010). Revitalizing a midwestern city: Immigrants in Marshalltown. *IIP Digital*. Retrieved from http://iipdigital.usembassy.gov/st/english/article/2010/10/20101019151854e nna0.6003992.html#axzz3NoTKB5L3

Woodson, J. (2006). Hip hop's black political activism. *Z Net*. Retrieved from http://www.zcommunications .org/znet/viewArticle/3784

World Employment Social Outlook. (2015). *International Labor Organization*. Retrieved from http://ilo .org/wcmsp5/groups/public/---dgreports/---dcomm/---publ/documents/publication/wcms_337070 .pdf

World Trade Organization. (2014). *The WTO*. Retrieved from http://www.wto.org/english/thewto_e/ whatis_e/whatis_e.htm

World Travel & Tourism Council. (2013). *Tourism employment—is more study needed?* Retrieved from http://www.wttc.org/global-news/articles/2014/dec/tourism-employment-is-more-study-needed/

Wright, B. W. (2001). *Comic book nation*. Baltimore, MD: Johns Hopkins University Press.

Xie, Y., & Zhou, X. (2014). Income inequity in today's China. *Proceedings of the National Academy of Sciences of the United States of America, 111*(19). Retrieved from http://www.pnas.org/con tent/111/19/6928.full

Yano, C. R. (2013). *Pink globalization: Hello Kitty's trek across the Pacific*. Durham, N.C.: Duke University Press.

Yep, G. A. (2008). The dialectics of intervention: Toward a reconceptualization of the theory/activism divide in communication scholarship and beyond. In O. Swartz (Ed.), *Transformative communication studies: Culture, hierarchy and the human condition* (pp. 191–207). Leicester, UK: Troubador.

Young, R. C. (2001). *Postcolonialism: An historical introduction*. Malden, MA: Blackwell.

Yúdice, G. (2003). *The expediency of culture: Uses of culture in the global era*. Durham, NC: Duke.

Zalan, K. (2014). The new separate and unequal: 60 years after *Brown v. Board of Education*, schools are still segregated. *U.S. News & World Report*. Retrieved from http://www.usnews.com/news/ articles/2014/05/16/brown-v-board-of-educations-60th-anniversary-stirs-history-reality

Zhou, M. (2009). *Contemporary Chinese America. Immigration, ethnicity, and community transformation*. Philadelphia, PA: Temple University.

Zhou, Y. (2004). Chinese immigrants in the global economy. In M. I. Toro-Morn & M. Alicea (Eds.), *Migration and immigration: A global view* (pp. 35–52). Westwood, CT: Greenwood Press.

Zupnik, Y. (2000). Conversational interruptions in Israel-Palestinian "Dialogue" events. *Discourse Studies, 2*(1), 85–110.

Index

Page references followed by (figure) indicate an illustrated figure; followed by (table) indicate a table; followed by (photograph) indicate a photograph.

Harvey, D., 83, 180, 184
Hasian, M., 169
Hatcher, E., 188
Hayes, J., 210
Hegde, R. S., 48–49, 96, 97, 250
Hegel, G.W.F., 13
Hegemony
    culture operating as a form of, 8
    how hybrid cultural spaces negotiate with
        structures of, 97
    injustice forged through colonization and
        U.S., 248–249
Heidegger, M., 234
Held, D., 29
"Here." *See* Place
Heteronormativity, 105
The Hidden Dimension (Hall), 90
Hierarchy of difference, 62–63
High context communication, 205
High culture, 4
High-skilled laborers, 132, 144–145
Hijab (headscarf) debate, 145 (photograph)–147
Hinduism, 104
Hip hop culture
    as alternative performances of
        difference, 52, 70–73
    appropriation of the, 89
    both/and approach to, 73
    as case study of cultural space, 85–90
    description and global spread of, 53–54
    global, 88–90
    going commercial, 87–88
    offering an alternative to existing racial order,
        70 (photograph)
    "tragic trinity" of, 89
    See also African Americans
"Hip hop wars," 89
Hirsch, J. S., 101
Historical legacy of colonization,
    29, 31 (figure)–32, 61–63
History
    legacy of colonization, 29, 31 (figure)–32,
        61–63
    silenced histories accounts of, 64
Hofstede, G., 108
Hofstede's cultural dimensions
    implications of, 109–110
    individualism–collectivism, 108
    masculinity–femininity, 109

power distance, 108
    time orientation–Confucian dynamism, 109
    uncertainty avoidance, 109
Hoggart, R., 8
Holland, J., 105
Homophobia, 105
Hope belief, 238–239
*Hope in the Dark: Untold Histories: Wild
    Possibilities* (Solnit), 237
Horkheimer, M., 155
Horowitz, S., 81
How Does It Feel to Be a Problem?
    (Bayoumi), 216
Howard, K. H., 189
Hudson's Bay Company, 181
Human needs paradigm, 234
Human rights paradigm, 234
Human trafficking, description of, 128
Humez, J. M., 157
Hunger Games series
    fandom of, 155
    protest using the salute from the, 152
Huntington, S., 41
Hurricane Katrina
    benefit concert for victims of, 157
    damage to New Orleans by, 92–93
Hussein, Saddam, 42
Hybrid cultural forms
    definition of, 48
    description and spread of, 48–49
    hybrid language as, 37
Hybrid cultural space
    "Borderlands/borderlands" of, 97
    description and social implications of, 95–97
    as sites of intercultural negotiation, 96
    as sites of resistance, 97
    as sites of transformation, 97
Hybrid languages, 37

"I can't breathe" (2014), 201
"I Have a Dream" speech (King, 1963), 66
Identity emergence (intercultural romance), 119
Identity. *See* Cultural identity
Ideological wars
    definition of, 43
    overview of the past and current, 42–43
Ideologies
    communication of capitalism, 185–186
    definition of, 43

Interreligious intercultural relationships, 104
Intersectionality
cultural identity through gender, race, and class, 59
of difference, 58–59
The Interview (film), 156
Invitational rhetoric, 225
Involuntary migrants, 128
Iranian popular culture, 159, 162
Iraq War, 42, 216
Irish immigrants, 129–130
IS (Islamic State), 42
ISIL (Islamic State in Iraq and the Levant), 42
ISIS (Islamic State in Iraq and Syria)
global ideological war being conducted by, 42–43
media representation of, 213
origins and description of, 42
Islam
hijab (headscarf) debate and, 145 (photograph)–147
PEGIDA (Patriotic Europeans Against the Islamization of the West) against, 203
See also Muslims
Israel
Boycott, Divest, and Sanctions (BDS) campaigning for compliance by, 203
Hagar School of, 229
Jewish fundamentalism and conflict in, 211
Zionist movement driving the establishment of, 207, 221
See also Middle East conflict
Italian immigrants, 129–130
Ito, M., 120
It's All for Sale: The Control of Global Resources (Ridgeway), 179
ITU World Telecommunication, 2
Izzat ("face"), 206

Jamet, C., 146
Japanese Americans internment camps, 91
Jenkins, H., 159
Jenkins, J., 43
Jewish fundamentalism, 211
Jim Crow segregation laws, 84, 91
Johansen, B., 63
Johnson, T. D., 102
Jones, T. S., 123, 245

Joseph, S., 170
Judaism, 104

Kabute, R., 242–243
Kakuchi, S., 137
Kalmijn, M., 102
Katriel, T., 223
Keefe, P. R., 144
Kellner, D., 157
Keysar, A., 104
Khaksar, S. (Venoosheh), 52, 70, 71, 72
Khan, S. R. ("King Khan"), 27, 33, 45
Khatib, L., 231
Khokha, S., 130, 212
Kidd, D., 155
Kim, M., 209
Kim, Y. Y., 14, 137, 138, 142
Kindly, K., 81
King, B. J., 166
King, M. L., Jr., 66, 238
Kitae, K., 36
Kitwana, B., 54, 72
Kivel, P., 209
Klein, N., 44
Kluckhohn, C., 4
Klume, C., 166
Koffmar, L., 215
"Konglish" slogans, 36
Kosin, B. A., 104
Krauthammer, C., 42–43
Kreider, R. M., 102
Kroeber, A., 4
Krumrey-Fulks, K. S., 112
Kurogi, A., 206
Kuscera, J., 92

Labor
Asian high- and low-skilled laborers, 132
Bracero Program (1940s) to bring migrants to U.S. from Mexico, 131
brain drain of high-skilled workers who migrate, 144–145
capitalism and creation of the working class, 181–182
capitalist culture and, 184–185
feminization of the workforce, 133
the 3D of, 196
See also Capitalism; Workplace

About the Author

Kathryn Sorrells is Professor of Communication Studies at California State University, Northridge (CSUN), and is currently serving as Department Chair. She teaches undergraduate and graduate courses in intercultural communication, critical pedagogy, performance, cultural studies, and feminist theory. She combines critical/cultural studies and postcolonial perspectives to explore issues of culture, race, gender, class, and sexuality. Kathryn grew up in Georgia; has lived in different regions of the United States; has studied and worked in Brazil, Japan, Turkey, and China; and has traveled extensively in Asia, Europe, and parts of Latin America. The critical, social justice approach she uses to study and practice intercultural communication is informed by her experiences growing up in the South during the tumultuous and transformative civil rights movement and her subsequent participation in the antiwar; women's; lesbian, gay, bisexual, and transgender (LGBT); and labor and immigrant rights movements. Kathryn has published a variety of articles related to intercultural communication, globalization, and social justice and is co-editor along with Sachi Sekimoto of *Globalizing Intercultural Communication: A Reader* (SAGE, 2015). She has been instrumental in organizing a campus-wide initiative on Civil Discourse & Social Change at CSUN aimed at developing students' capacities for civic engagement and social justice. Kathryn is a recipient of numerous national, state, and local community service awards for founding and directing Communicating Common Ground, an innovative service learning project that provided students opportunities to develop creative alternatives to intercultural conflict. Additionally, Kathryn has experience as a consultant and trainer for nonprofit, profit, and educational organizations in the areas of intercultural communication and multicultural learning.